Matthew Calbraith Perry

**Additional titles in the Library of Naval Biography Series,
edited by James C. Bradford**

LIBRARY OF NAVAL BIOGRAPHY

MATTHEW CALBRAITH PERRY

ANTEBELLUM SAILOR AND DIPLOMAT

John H. Schroeder

NAVAL INSTITUTE PRESS
Annapolis, Maryland

Naval Institute Press
291 Wood Road
Annapolis, MD 21402

Library of Congress Cataloging-in-Publication Data
Schroeder, John H., 1943-
    Matthew Calbraith Perry : antebellum sailor and diplomat / John H. Schroeder.
        p. cm. — (Library of naval biography)
    Includes bibliographical references and index.
    ISBN 1-55750-812-7 (acid-free paper)
    1. Perry, Matthew Calbraith, 1794-1858. 2. Sailors—United States—Biography.
3. Diplomats—United States—Biography. 4. United States—History, Naval—19th
century. 5. United States. Navy—Biography. I. Title. II. Series.
    E182 .P469 2001
    973.5'25'092—dc21
    [B]

                                                                    00-048203

Printed in the United States of America on acid-free paper ∞
08 07 06 05 04 03 02 01   9 8 7 6 5 4 3 2
First printing

Frontispiece courtesy of Library of Congress

For my sons, John and Andrew

ᴖ Contents ᴖ

ᵔᔆ Foreword ʑᵔ

Matthew Calbraith Perry was one of the preeminent officers of the antebellum navy. Every high-school student learns about "Perry and the Opening of Japan," and naval historians know that Perry was a leading reformer who advanced both the adoption of steam propulsion and professional education. Beyond these few facts, Perry's long career has slipped from public memory. He deserves better—not only for his achievements, but also for what his career can tell us about the U.S. Navy and the nation it served during the first half of the nineteenth century.

To a great extent Perry personified both the service and the nation. He came from one of America's greatest naval families and through service and the marriage of a daughter was linked to the Rodgers family, another naval dynasty. Calbraith, as his family called him, was the son of the Revolutionary War naval officer Christopher Raymond Perry. He was also a senior captain in the new U.S. Navy, the younger brother of War of 1812 hero Oliver Hazard Perry, and the father of Matthew C. Perry Jr., a navy captain during the Civil War, and Oliver H. Perry II, who served in the navy and later as U.S. consul to Hong Kong. Another of Calbraith's sons, William Frederick Perry, served in the Marine Corps during the Mexican War.

Matthew Calbraith Perry had the most varied career of them all. Like his brother Oliver Hazard, he fought the British during the War of 1812 and later fought pirates in the Caribbean. Like one of his sons, he led expeditions ashore against Mexican forces; and like another, he negotiated with leaders in the Far East. Beyond this, M. C. Perry backed ordnance reforms, promoted the idea of establishing a naval academy to train young officers, suppressed the trade in slaves, supported the republic of Liberia, and compiled the three-volume *Narrative of the Expedition of an American Squadron to the China Seas and Japan.*

As important as what Perry did was the way he did it. Perry entered the navy as a midshipman in 1809. While serving under John Rodgers during the War of 1812, the young midshipman learned the value of a taut ship and displayed courage in battle. As a junior lieutenant Perry visited Africa, Turkey, and Russia. Later, while touring England and France, he submitted reports on leaders such as King Louis Philippe of France that reflected the keen insight into character that would mark his negotiations with Japanese officials a decade and a half later.

As an officer Perry often found himself stationed ashore. Never idle, he established an experimental battery for testing ordnance, took the lead in organizing the Naval Lyceum, and published numerous essays advocating various naval reforms. When America went to war with Mexico, Perry led bluejackets and marines ashore to capture Frontera, Tabasco, Laguna, and Tuxpan. All these activities receive their due in this biography, as does the capstone of his career, command of the squadron that opened Japan to the West.

Perry's career of nearly fifty years provides an excellent vantage point from which to view the young U.S. Navy as it fought wars with Great Britain and Mexico, responded to technological innovations, and extended the reach of American power around the globe. It is not easy to capture the spirit of a man with such a multifaceted career, but John Schroeder has succeeded admirably in this interpretative biography.

James C. Bradford
Series Editor

~≫ Preface ≫~

Matthew Calbraith Perry is remembered primarily as the officer who led a naval and diplomatic mission to Japan in 1853–54. The successful Perry expedition established diplomatic contact with Japan, prepared the way for commercial relations with Japan, and hastened the subsequent political and economic transformation of Japan.

The expedition to Japan was indeed the outstanding achievement of Perry's career, and it placed him in the first rank of nineteenth-century American naval heroes. Often forgotten in the emphasis on Japan, however, is Perry's long and distinguished naval career preceding his departure for Japan in late 1852. Born in 1794, he entered the navy in 1809 and by 1850 stood as the preeminent officer of the naval generation that served between the War of 1812 and the Civil War. Part of a naval family that included Oliver Hazard Perry, the hero of the Battle of Lake Erie, and that was connected by marriage to naval legend Commo. John Rodgers, Matthew advanced steadily in the navy through his capable handling of challenging assignments and ever-increasing responsibilities. Unlike Oliver Hazard and other flamboyant officers of his time, Matthew was a serious and reserved person who earned the respect, but never the affection, of his fellow officers. Unlike many pre–Civil War naval heroes, he never won a major naval battle or engagement at sea. He commanded the Gulf Squadron during the Mexican War and demonstrated that he was an aggressive, resourceful, and courageous leader. Since Mexico had essentially no navy, however, Perry's victories all came in amphibious operations such as the capture of Tabasco and had little impact on the military outcome of the war. The Mexican War was primarily a land war that was fought and won by armies under the command of such generals as Zachary Taylor and Winfield Scott, and it was they who received the public's acclaim.

In the place of combat accomplishments, Matthew Perry built his career largely on a succession of peacetime naval assignments on both land and sea. He sailed to West Africa and assisted fledgling African American settlements there on several occasions. He fought pirates in the Caribbean. He helped to protect American commerce in the Mediterranean. And he served in the diplomatically sensitive position of commander of the African Squadron when it was first established in 1843. Back home in various shore assignments, he emerged as a leading naval reformer. Along with a small group of progressive young officers, Perry sought ways to make the U.S. Navy a more modern and efficient force. He advocated more efficient recruitment techniques, better training practices for enlisted men, and improved educational opportunities for officers. Perry was an early advocate of the establishment of a naval academy and a founder of the Naval Lyceum, which sought to enhance and extend the education of officers. Perry also worked to modernize the traditional navy of wooden sailing ships and solid-shot ordnance. His efforts to introduce steam power and improve its applications earned him the title "Father of the Steam Navy." He also supported the introduction of iron hulls, Paixhans guns, exploding-shot ordnance, and modern navigation aids.

By 1850, Matthew Perry stood as the most distinguished officer of his time. He would have been remembered as such even if he had not been selected to lead the naval expedition to Japan, but it was the subsequent success of the expedition that elevated Perry to his lofty place in American diplomatic and naval history. Perry was not the first to conceive of an expedition to establish diplomatic relations with Japan. Previous efforts had been made. Moreover, Perry benefited from the timing of the venture and from various developments in Japan. However, Perry rightfully received primary credit for the expedition because of his personal role in designing, executing, and documenting it. He understood and outlined the requirements for its success, including the size of the force and the tactics to be employed. He personally organized the myriad details of the expedition and insisted on exercising both naval and diplomatic authority. Once the mission was under way, Perry overcame various obstacles and almost flawlessly executed his plan. Although some of his fellow officers criticized his arrogance and inflexibility, Perry succeeded in establishing diplomatic, if not commercial, relations with Japan. For various reasons, Perry was not a genuinely popular national hero when he returned to the United States, but he was unquestionably the preeminent naval officer of his day.

In addition to being long and interesting in its own right, Perry's naval career is significant for a number of reasons. First, his career demonstrates the extent to which family ties and political connections as well as personal ability, determination, and character were requisites for an officer to rise to the top in the antebellum navy. Second, it reveals the extent to which antebellum American naval officers performed diplomatic duties for their government. The U.S. government routinely relied on naval officers to play diplomatic roles because of the absence of American diplomatic personnel in many areas of the globe. Third, Perry's advocacy of reforms to improve the efficiency of the navy reveals the extent to which the naval establishment and the federal government resisted change. In addition to resisting reformers' efforts to end flogging and eliminate the grog ration, the naval establishment routinely opposed the implementation of better recruiting and training methods as well as the introduction of technological innovations such as steam power and exploding-shell ordnance. In their efforts to prevent reform, government officials and politicians often became willing allies, both seeking to keep the peacetime military establishment as small and as inexpensive as possible. Finally, Perry's service in Africa demonstrates the extent to which the American public and the federal government were indifferent to Americans' participation in the African slave trade. Although the trade had been outlawed in 1807, Americans continued to participate until the Civil War without much threat of being apprehended by the U.S. Navy. The lack of commitment by a succession of administrations placed naval commanders in West Africa in a difficult position. Instructed to police the trade, they were not provided sufficient force or given enough political support to do the job effectively.

Before deciding to write a biography of Perry, I read Samuel Eliot Morison's classic biography, *"Old Bruin": Commodore Matthew C. Perry, 1794–1858,* which was originally published in 1967. Although Morison's work remains useful today and includes superb nautical and place descriptions, I concluded that a new biography of Perry was needed. More than three decades had passed since *"Old Bruin"* was published. In that time the historical context in which Morison wrote had changed and a substantial amount of new research had appeared on antebellum naval and maritime history as well as on U.S. relations with West Africa, Japan, and China. I have drawn on this research as well as on the extensive manuscript and primary sources that exist on Perry and the antebellum U.S. Navy.

~⅃ Acknowledgments ɜ~

In writing this book, I received assistance from a number of individuals and institutions. I want to acknowledge the support of University of Wisconsin System President Katharine C. Lyall, the University of Wisconsin–Milwaukee, and the UWM Foundation. I owe a considerable debt of gratitude to the professional staffs at the Golda Meir Library as well as to Director Christopher Baruth and the professional staff of the American Geographical Society housed at Golda Meir. Librarians and archivists at a number of repositories provided invaluable assistance, including the Manuscript Division of the Library of Congress, Houghton Library of Harvard University, the Beinecke and Sterling Libraries at Yale University, the Pennsylvania Historical Society, the State Historical Society of Wisconsin, the Milwaukee Public Library, and the library of the Naval Historical Center in Washington, D.C. I also received important assistance from individuals at the Chester Nimitz Library of the U.S. Naval Academy and from James Cheevers at the Naval Academy Museum. At the National Archives, I received invaluable assistance and suggestions on several occasions. Particularly important was the persistence of Rick Peuser, whose resourcefulness located six Perry letter books that had not been accurately cataloged.

The preparation of this book was also facilitated by the particular efforts of several individuals. I want to thank James Bradford and Paul Wilderson for encouraging me to undertake this project. Jane and Samuel Back hosted me at their Quonochontaug, Rhode Island, home and served as my enthusiastic guides as we searched for Matthew Perry's childhood Newport home and some of his childhood haunts. Susan Kerns is not much interested in nineteenth-century naval history, but she helped me solve the mysteries of my word-processing program on innumerable occasions. Somehow, she always managed to untangle mistaken commands and retrieve text that I had inadvertently deleted. Melinda Conner's copy editing eliminated numerous errors while considerably tightening the manuscript. At the Naval Institute, the exceptional talents of Kristin Wye-Rodney strengthened the manuscript and made the production process both smooth and pleasant. Harvey Sperling shared his extensive private collection of the Perry expedition with me. Todd Henry provided several pertinent Japanese sources. My son Andrew assisted me by finding a number of manuscript items while he was a graduate student at the University of Virginia. As with my previous two books, Reginald Horsman shared his comprehensive knowledge of early American history with me, read two drafts of the manuscript, and provided constructive criticisms that proved indispensable. Finally, my wife, Sandra, played an invaluable role by devoting the first month of her well-earned retirement to a careful reading of the manuscript. An able editor, she improved the manuscript immeasurably by excising grammatical mistakes, making stylistic suggestions, and clarifying the narrative.

~❧ *Chronology* ɞ~

Aug. 1846–Mar. 1847	Commanding officer of the *Mississippi* and vice commodore of the Gulf Squadron
Oct. 1846	First expedition to Tabasco
Mar. 1847– Nov. 1848	Commanding officer of the Gulf Squadron
27 Mar. 1847	Surrender of Vera Cruz
June 1847	Second expedition to Tabasco
Nov. 1848–Mar. 1852	General superintendent of ocean mail steamship construction
Jan. 1852	Assigned to command the naval expedition to Japan
1852–54	Commands U.S. Naval Expedition to Japan
Nov. 1852	Sails in *Mississippi* for Japan
Apr. 1853	Arrives Hong Kong
14 July 1853	First landing in Japan
July 1854–Jan. 1855	Returns to China
13 Feb. 1854	Arrives for return visit to Japan
Mar. 1854	Second landing in Japan
31 Mar. 1854	Signs Treaty of Kanagawa
Apr.–July 1854	Visits Shimoda, Hakodate, and Okinawa
Sept. 1854	Departs Hong Kong
Jan. 1855	Arrives in United States
June–Sept. 1855	Serves on Naval Retirement Board
Apr. 1856	Volume 1 of the *Narrative of an Expedition to the China Seas and Japan . . .* is published
4 Mar. 1858	Dies in New York City

Matthew Calbraith Perry

❧ I ☙

A RHODE ISLAND
NAVAL HERITAGE

*I often watched on the shore for the first glimpse of the gaily decorated
packet sloop that in those days brought the Governor from Providence
to this Town—and witnessed with childlike delight . . . the pomp,
parade and festivities of "Election Day."*

MATTHEW C. PERRY, 1855,
RECALLING HIS CHILDHOOD IN
NEWPORT, RHODE ISLAND

*M*atthew Calbraith Perry rose on 14 July 1853 and prepared for a momentous day. The early morning fog
had lifted to reveal bright sunshine. Onboard the
steam frigate *Susquehanna*, the fifty-nine-year-old commodore could
clearly see the Japanese shoreline, where no foreigner had ever before
been permitted to land. The American squadron, consisting of four
ships, was anchored in the Uraga Channel near the head of the Bay of
Yedo. A second steam frigate, the *Mississippi*, and two sloops-of-war, the
Plymouth and *Saratoga*, completed the group. The view from the anchorage presented an exotic and incomparable vista that morning for the
Americans. The hills rose sharply from the shore, "beautifully undulat-
ing in their outlines, and dotted with groves of pine trees." As the light
fell directly on Mount Fujiyama, sixty miles away, it revealed "the scars
of old eruptions, and the cold ravines of snow on its northern side."[1]

On this day, an American delegation was to land at Kurihama and
deliver a letter from the president of the United States to the imperial

emperor of Japan. Although they had been forewarned of the American expedition, the Japanese had not yet decided how to deal with it. Since the American ships had appeared five days earlier, Japanese officials had repeatedly attempted to turn them back, to divert them to the Dutch outpost at Nagasaki and thereby prevent a landing near Uraga, and to avoid any formal meetings between imperial officials and Commodore Perry. Their efforts had failed; the ceremony would occur at the small village of Kurihama two miles south of the town of Uraga.

On several previous occasions the Japanese had either rebuffed the overtures of American ship captains or convinced them to turn back. But Perry knew beforehand that he would meet resistance and had prepared accordingly, and he acted with a single-minded determination that baffled the Japanese. Polite and respectful, but insistent and unyielding, Perry demanded respect as a high-ranking representative of the United States and made it clear that he intended at all costs to complete his official mission.[2]

On the shore, hundreds of Japanese could be seen making final preparations to receive the Americans. Onboard the ships in the channel excitement prevailed. The Americans believed that Japanese deception and even violence were possible, but they still remained outwardly confident. After all, they had traveled thousands of miles over many months to reach this point. And so far all had gone well. Everyone believed that today would be a momentous occasion. In fact, since virtually everyone onboard wanted to participate in the landing, the crews had held a lottery to determine which junior officers and crewmen would go ashore and which would remain to tend the ships.[3]

Perry ordered the four American ships to move from the channel, around a point, and into a small bay close to the shoreline. Officers ordered the decks cleared for action as the men received their allotments of powder, balls, and muskets. By 10:00 A.M., fifteen American launches and cutters had set out for the shore. Led by Comdr. Franklin Buchanan, the Americans landed at a makeshift jetty. The landing party consisted of about three hundred sailors, one hundred marines, forty officers, and forty musicians. A thirteen-gun salute from the *Susquehanna* announced Commodore Perry's departure for shore. As the Japanese waited for their first glimpse of Perry, he rose and stepped ashore in his blue dress uniform to the roll of drums and the sounds of the American bands playing "Hail Columbia."[4]

The Japanese received the Americans with a military contingent announced officially at five thousand but probably larger. Surrounded by colorful banners and attired in traditional costumes, the soldiers carried military swords and other weapons. The Japanese had hastily constructed and decorated a special building for the occasion. When Perry arrived, his hosts greeted him formally and then led him with his official contingent inside, where he was met by two officials, Toda Izu no kami and Ido Iwami. Each man rose, bowed, and took a place, as did the Americans. After a silence of several minutes, the Japanese interpreter indicated that the emperor's representatives would now receive the papers Perry had come so far to bring to them.

Born by the sea into a navy family, Matthew Calbraith Perry took readily to the maritime world in which he was raised. His family heritage, childhood environment, and personal character all predestined for him a naval career. Matthew traced his American ancestry to 1639, when Edward Perry, an English Quaker, settled in Sandwich, Massachusetts. Eventually some family members tired of the persecution of their Quaker beliefs in Massachusetts and moved to Rhode Island, where the atmosphere was more tolerant and congenial. One of Edward's sons, Benjamin, settled in the Kingston area and fathered five children by his second wife, Susannah Barber. The third child, Matthew's grandfather Freeman, was born in 1733 and married Mercy Hazard from a prominent Narragansett family. Their son Christopher, who was born in 1760, broke the Quaker tradition of the family.[5]

Christopher Perry was a born adventurer and fighter who, at age fourteen or fifteen, joined the Kingston Reds, an elite local militia unit. At the outset of the Revolution, Christopher, acting as a militiaman, killed one of his neighbors when the man refused to join the fight against England. During the Revolution, Christopher Perry fought in various capacities, serving on several privateers, two colonial naval vessels, and briefly in the Continental army. He claimed to have been captured and imprisoned four times, and to have escaped each time. Whether or not all of his claims were true, he was a spirited and bellicose patriot. While a prisoner in Ireland during the war, he met fourteen- or fifteen-year-old Sarah Wallace Alexander, of Scots and Irish heritage. The meeting was brief, but Christopher supposedly announced to his compatriots after she left the room, "There goes my future wife!" Through a fortuitous series of events, Christopher and Sarah renewed their acquaintance the next year and courted on a subsequent transatlantic voyage from Ireland to Philadelphia in 1784. They married shortly after reaching the United States and then moved to Rhode Island. Finding that the life of a farmer did not suit him, Christopher returned to the sea as a master and a supercargo on merchant ships. More than a decade later, in 1799, Christopher Perry rejoined the navy and served as a captain of the frigate *General Greene* in the Quasi-War with France.[6]

Christopher Perry's service at sea did not prevent regular increases to his family. Oliver Hazard was born in 1785, Raymond Henry in 1789, Sarah Wallace in 1791, and Matthew Calbraith on 10 April 1794. Four more children followed: Anna Maria in 1797, Jane Tweedy in 1799, James Alexander in 1801, and Nathaniel Hazard in 1802. In all, Sarah Perry bore eight children, all of whom grew to adulthood.

The Perrys had deep roots in the western Narragansett Bay area in places such as Matunuck, Perryville, Tower Hill, and South Kingston. But in the early 1790s the family moved to the Point section of Newport, where they built a frame house with a gambrel roof at Second and Walnut. Here Matthew Calbraith was born in 1794. His parents named him Matthew James Calbraith after a friend from Ireland who became a successful merchant in Philadelphia. He never used the second name, and since the name Matthew was not popular in the family, he was known as Calbraith.

By all accounts, Matthew's mother was an extraordinary woman and mother. Her shining black hair, lively brown eyes, and radiant complexion made her a striking figure. Of strong character and an excellent constitution, Sarah was an intelligent, religious person who imbued her children with her own strong personal and religious values. She taught her children to be obedient but tempered her discipline with love. The Perry children learned to be resourceful, proud, and self-reliant. In the Perry household, duty and service to country were primary virtues. The force of Sarah's character also impressed her neighbors. In 1814, when word arrived that Oliver Hazard Perry had defeated the British in the Battle of Lake Erie, a local farmer reportedly insisted that it was actually Mrs. Perry who had "licked the British."

Christopher and Sarah Wallace Perry did not raise their sons to be farmers, entrepreneurs, or merchants, or to pursue an established civilian profession. Since theirs was a maritime world and the family placed a high value on military service, the U.S. Navy offered a logical and respected career. In fact, all five of the Perry sons pursued naval careers, and two of the three daughters married career naval officers. The other daughter never married.[7]

Other than periodic visits to the family's Tower Hill farm on the other side of Narragansett Bay, Matthew spent his childhood in the house at Second and Walnut, little more than a block from the shore of the bay. He played with his friends along its shores, swam in its waters, and watched ships of all sizes and shapes come and go across the sparkling waters.[8] When he visited downtown Newport, the sights, sounds, and excitement of a bustling seaport were all around him. The stories and tales he heard as a child from friends, parents, and other adults invariably centered on the sea, its adventures and dangers, and its connection to distant and exotic places. This environment made a lasting impression on young Matthew. More than fifty years later, he recalled the excitement of an election day in Newport. "I often watched on the shore for the first glimpse of the gaily decorated packet sloop that in those days annually brought the Governor from Providence to this Town—and witnessed with childlike delight . . . the pomp, parade and festivities of 'Election Day.'" In these years before the introduction of steamboats and railroads, young Matthew associated sailing ships with adventure and romance.[9]

Although they were neither wealthy nor socially prominent, the Perrys of Newport were a solid and respected middle-class family. Matthew admired his father, Christopher, whose appointment as captain of the U.S. Navy frigate *General Greene* in 1799 conveyed status and prominence in the community. Matthew also revered his mother and adored his older brother, Oliver Hazard. Oliver joined the navy at age thirteen as a midshipman and served in 1799 and 1800 on the *General Greene*, and soon established himself as one of the most capable young officers in the navy. Oliver was handsome, dashing, and outgoing. To his younger brother Matthew, Oliver seemed a most admirable and romantic figure when he returned home periodically to regale his younger brothers with real and embellished tales of the sea and life in the navy. His admiration for Oliver and his brother's stories reinforced Matthew's attraction to the maritime environment.[10]

Like most other boys his age, Matthew received a rudimentary education from local schoolmasters and seems to have been a serious student. Unlike the extroverted and self-confident Oliver, Matthew was reserved and thoughtful. Yet he pursued his childhood play with spirited enthusiasm and displayed an occasional streak of stubbornness. He had been christened on 18 January 1795 in Trinity Church, Newport, in a quadruple baptism with his older brothers, Oliver and Raymond, and Sarah, his older sister. Like his mother, young Matthew would take his religion seriously in time. He remained a lifelong Episcopalian who attended services regularly when he was onshore. Later, as a commanding officer at sea, Perry honored the Sabbath and personally organized services when a chaplain was not available. He claimed that he always read his Bible from cover to cover during each naval cruise of his career. Perry himself was never dogmatic or evangelical in his religious beliefs or activities. While he would later praise the spread of Christianity overseas, he never evinced a personal interest in converting souls to his faith. And while he set high standards of conduct and morality for himself, he did not attempt to impose his own particular religious views or morals on others.

In the 1790s and first decade of the 1800s, Newport and the other towns on Narragansett Bay were dominated by a maritime economy. Prior to the American Revolution, Newport had ranked with Boston, New York, Philadelphia, and Baltimore as one of the leading seaports in British North America. The city dominated Rhode Island politically and economically as a thriving, prosperous, and cosmopolitan town with a population of 9,208 in 1774. In the same year, 1,163 vessels entered and cleared the port. At any given moment Newport hosted a transient seagoing population from many places and backgrounds, a relatively large African American population of slaves and free blacks, and a small but thriving Jewish community. Each summer, a sizable number of southern families hoping to escape the heat augmented the city's population. With its elegant homes, fine craftsmanship, and imposing public buildings, Newport symbolized affluence and sophistication.[11]

The Revolution proved disastrous for Newport. In December 1776, eight thousand British troops took possession of the town without resistance, occupied it until 1779, and then blockaded it for the remainder of the war. Although many among Newport's large loyalist population remained during this time, many other residents left. The population dropped sharply to 5,530 in 1782, the Jewish community dispersed, and the local economy suffered badly. After the war, Newport and Rhode

Island recovered, but the physical destruction wrought by the war combined with the loss of trade impeded Newport's recovery. In addition, although many of the residents who left during the Revolution returned, many others, including key merchants and civic leaders, did not. A number of them were loyalists who were not allowed to return. The population totaled only 6,725 in 1790 and 6,999 in 1800, significantly smaller than the pre-Revolution total. Prosperity had returned by the mid-1790s, but Newport never again ranked with Boston, New York, Philadelphia, and Baltimore as a leading seaport. In Rhode Island, Providence had supplanted Newport as the political and economic center of the state.[12]

Although the city had lost much of its earlier importance, Newport continued to be a thriving seaport. And while Newport, like the rest of Rhode Island, was more than 90 percent white, it contained a relatively large slave and free black population for a New England state. Almost all of the white residents were of English derivation, with a small number of Scots, Irish, various Europeans, and a small but struggling Jewish community comprising the remainder. The population was still supplemented in the summertime by southern families seeking relief from the oppressive heat, and some left behind their sons to attend the local schools. The 1790 Rhode Island census counted 3,884 free African Americans, 5.6 percent of the total population, and 958 slaves, or 1.4 percent. The largest number of free blacks and slaves resided in Newport and the surrounding county. With the enactment of gradual emancipation in the 1780s, the number of slaves in Rhode Island declined by 60 percent during the 1790s, but the free black population remained stable after 1800.[13] Thus the immediate world in which young Matthew was raised brought him into contact with a reasonably wide range of people from different backgrounds, with different accents, and of different colors. By late eighteenth- and early nineteenth-century standards, Newport offered a cosmopolitan environment and represented a sharp contrast to the small, rural, inland farm towns and villages in which many Americans were raised at this time.[14]

The economy of Rhode Island at this time depended almost entirely on the sea. But Newport had two serious economic handicaps as it attempted to compete with the larger American seaports. It could not draw on a strong local financial community for capital investment funds, and it did not serve as a trading center for the cash crops of inland agricultural communities because the port was not tied to any extensive hinterland region. As a result, Newport merchant traders were typically not well financed by large investors. They did not carry local agricultural goods or natural commodities such as lumber. Nor did they have an extensive home market in Rhode Island for the goods they brought back from their voyages.[15]

Because Newport merchant traders tended to be less well financed than their Boston and New York counterparts, they operated in smaller ships closer to home and often engaged in more speculative ventures. They specialized in the domestic coastal trade and the Caribbean trade, not in commerce with the large ports of Europe or in the emerging East India trade. Known as opportunists and famous for privateering, Newport merchants developed a reputation for flexibility in the goods and products they carried and the ports they visited.

Given their economically precarious situation, it is not surprising that Rhode Island merchants and captains dominated the legal slave trade from the American side. According to one historian of Rhode Island, "Slavery, a highly speculative form of enterprise, met the classic Narragansett Bay requirements—low investments, high risk, rising demand, and speculative profits. Middling but ambitious merchants as well as the owners of small craft found the trade appealed especially." According to one estimate, throughout the eighteenth century "Rhode Island merchants controlled between 60 and 90 percent of the American trade in African slaves." To support their speculative enterprise, Rhode Island merchants imported large amounts of Cuban sugar and molasses, which they distilled into rum to be traded on the African coast for slaves, thus making Newport a leading distillery as well as a center of the slave trade. Newport slavers operated extensively between the Guinea coast of Africa and the West Indies, South America, and the southern United States, with Havana as their center. Slave trading was risky and entailed high costs for wages and insurance rates (15 to 30 percent of the ship's value per voyage), but the net profits were much higher than for other trading ventures.[16]

As a long-standing and lucrative enterprise, the slave trade created moral ambiguity in Newport. Both slavery and the legal traffic in slaves were known and accepted facts of life. Dr. Samuel Hopkins, an opponent of the slave trade, reported that a Newport printer had refused to print one of his anti–slave trade essays because "so large a number of his customers [are] either in the slave trade or in such connection with it, or so disposed with respect to it, to whom it will give the greatest offence that it is not prudent." In 1791, William Ellery lamented that an "Ethiopian could as soon change his skin as a Newport merchant be induced to change so lucrative a trade as that in slaves for the slow profit of any manufacturery." Tolerance for slavery and the slave trade was reinforced by the presence of the southern slaveholders who spent the summers in Newport and found not only the weather but also local attitudes on these issues congenial.[17]

In this environment, young Matthew Perry learned from what he saw and heard. At the Newport waterfront he saw the slave pens, and in town he watched slaves with their masters. When he attended Trinity Church, he and his parents had frequent contact with southern families and heard no antislavery sermons or moral attacks on the slave trade. As Matthew watched and listened to adults talking about slavery and the slave traffic, he observed a community that readily tolerated both. Whatever his nonslaveholding parents may have said to him about slavery or the slave trade, his environment taught him that both were acceptable and tolerable, if disagreeable, realities in the adult world.

The naval careers of his father and eldest brother were an important influence on young Matthew. In 1799 and again in 1800, during the undeclared naval war with France, Captain Christopher Perry and thirteen-year-old Oliver Hazard Perry sailed the Caribbean in the *General Greene* to protect American commerce and national rights. The cruises took Captain Perry and his eldest son into the world of pirates, enemy ships, and exotic places, where they met fascinating characters such as Toussaint-Louverture, the commander of black revolutionary forces in Santo Domingo.[18]

Captain Perry did not distinguish himself in this assignment. Both cruises were troubled, and the *General Greene* returned with problems that shortened Perry's naval career and left a lasting imprint on his sons. In July 1799, Perry cut his cruise short and returned directly to Newport after yellow fever erupted onboard his ship off the coast of Cuba. By the time the *General Greene* reached Newport, twenty men had died, and others had to be hospitalized. Although President John Adams suspected that too much shore leave in Cuba had caused the problem, Secretary of the Navy Benjamin Stoddert approved the premature return. After being fumigated and having the ballast changed, the *General Greene* sailed again the next year, but again returned to Newport with several cases of yellow fever. In late July and August 1800, the scourge spread from the ship's crew to local residents, who contracted the disease while working onboard. By 20 August, nine crew members and five civilians had died. The situation created panic in Newport, provoked action by the city council, and created a sharp split among local doctors about how best to prevent and treat the fever. Although neither Captain Perry nor his son contracted the fever, it was a topic of discussion and concern in the Perry household.[19]

Discipline was also a problem on the *General Greene*. The ship did not have its full complement of men, and the caliber of some of the midshipmen was particularly low. In 1799 in Newport, before the ship ever sailed, three midshipmen sexually assaulted and attempted to rape the pregnant wife of one of the ship's seamen while she was visiting the ship. The midshipmen used their authority to send seaman Joseph Paul on an errand, leaving his wife behind. Once the husband was out of the way, the three midshipmen dragged her into a storeroom, stripped her, and were about to rape her when a group of seamen forced their way into the room and stopped the assault. Although the three were arrested and publicly disgraced, they remained with the ship. As the cruise proceeded, their conduct and that of several other midshipmen worsened. They drank excessively, pilfered the ship's stores, slept on watch, fought with each other, cursed the officers, and damned the navy. One of the group, Midn. William Rhodes, actually tore up a copy of the Articles of War in the presence of Captain Perry. The captain imposed discipline and built a pillory chair to which offenders were sentenced. On one occasion, when one of the midshipmen missed his watch and was found drunk, Perry had three men urinate in his mouth to induce vomiting. The discipline imposed did not rectify the situation, however, or bring the midshipmen under control.[20]

When the *General Greene* returned to Newport in 1800, five of the midshipmen filed charges against Perry for cruelty and oppression. After a full hearing and trial, a naval court of inquiry forced the five midshipmen to resign but also censured Perry for having "been very much wanting in not having the proper discipline and good order kept aboard" the ship. The court also reviewed other, less serious charges against Perry.[21] After the court acquitted Perry on some charges and found him guilty of others, Secretary Benjamin Stoddert disciplined him with a three-month suspension from the navy without pay. He was subsequently relieved of command. When the navy was reduced in 1801 under new president Thomas Jefferson, Perry was not one of the nine captains selected to remain in the navy even though he was known as a good Jeffersonian Republican.[22]

These events had a lasting effect on Matthew Perry. Years later, he would become a stern disciplinarian who would take a keen interest in the conduct and health of his sailors. He maintained tight discipline and order on every ship he commanded and initiated extensive measures to prevent yellow fever and other tropical diseases on all of his ships.

In 1808, as a fourteen-year-old, Matthew made the entirely predictable decision to follow his father and two older brothers and join the U.S. Navy. President Thomas Jefferson signed his commission as a midshipman on 16 January 1809. Created in 1798 by President John Adams, the U.S. Navy had expanded rapidly during the Quasi-War with France from 1798 to 1800, but peace and the election of Thomas Jefferson reversed its fortunes. Jefferson saw little value in a strong navy and imposed a period of retrenchment, although the war with Tripoli and the resumption of war between England and France prevented him from completely dismantling the navy. The political misfortunes of the navy did not, however, prevent the development of a capable and dedicated group of young professional naval officers. When Perry entered the navy in 1809, he joined an officer core of almost 500 men, approximately 250 of them midshipmen in their late teens. Secretary of the Navy Robert Smith tried to balance the geographic composition of the new officers and to receive personal references attesting to their good character. Of the 185 midshipmen appointed in 1809, more than 62 percent came from the Atlantic seaboard states stretching from New York to Virginia, 18 percent were from the south Atlantic states, a mere 13 were from New England, and the remainder came from the new states of the trans-Appalachian West.

The military victories of the navy in the Quasi-War and in the Tripolitan War created new heroes for the young republic and set high standards for American naval officers. They were expected to be educated gentlemen of good character who were patriotic, brave, enterprising, and ambitious. Their superiors demanded exemplary professional conduct and ethics. In exchange for their patriotism, sacrifice, and service to country, young officers expected to win fame, which in the ethos of the time was a worthy and highly esteemed personal aspiration. For the officers of the young navy, it was a time of purpose, optimism, and high morale. Young men receiving appointments as midshipmen expected to serve their country with honor and make rapid career progress. Before 1815, a midshipman could expect to be promoted to lieutenant after six years and then to master commandant after another six years of service. On average, it took fewer than fifteen years for a newly appointed midshipman to reach the rank of captain; the average age of captains on promotion was thirty-three years old. The young navy, then, was an ideal place for an ambitious, patriotic, and capable young man.[23]

Perry trained for two brief months before joining the schooner *Revenge,* then under the command of Lt. Oliver Hazard Perry. Mounting twelve guns and carrying a crew of ninety men, the *Revenge* was assigned to the naval squadron commanded by Commo. John Rodgers, whose duty it was to guard the American coast from the Chesapeake to Passamaquoddy. Lieutenant Perry's assignment was to take soundings for nautical charts and to patrol between Montauk Point, Nantucket, Buzzard's Bay, and Newport. The work was boring and tedious. It was decidedly not the romantic and exciting duty that a fifteen-year-old midshipman envisioned. For a time, Matthew even thought about resigning and joining the East India trade, but while on furlough he received orders to the frigate *President* in October 1810. Early in 1811, the *Revenge* sank in a storm. Although Oliver survived, several other men died.

One of the early navy's legendary figures, Commo. John Rodgers, commanded the forty-four-gun *President.* Forty-eight years old in 1810, Rodgers was a forceful professional leader who, along with Thomas Truxtun and Edward Preble, shaped the training of the first generation of American naval officers. He insisted on strict obedience to orders and constant attention to duty and was famous for imposing unyielding discipline.[24] The *President,* a modern ship, had been the flagship of the Mediterranean squadron in the war with Tripoli. Reputed to be the fastest ship in the small American navy, the *President* carried a crew of four hundred officers and men, including both Matthew and his older brother Raymond as midshipmen. Assignment to the *President* represented an excellent but spartan billet. Life onboard was difficult for the midshipmen, or "reefers," as they were called. They received $228 per year and lived in the cramped steerage section below the frigate's normal waterline. Here they had only a little more than five feet of headroom and only minimal light and ventilation. The reefers kept their few personal belongings in lockers and slept in hammocks hung by hooks from the beams. They ate together at a long table separate from the other officers using their personal mess kits.[25]

Midshipmen stood watch like all officers and tried to learn the mysteries of operating a large warship—gunnery, rigging, splicing, sail making, and navigation. Many young officers found navigation difficult to learn because the science at that time relied on the traditional method of determining longitude from altitudes, logarithms, and the chronometer. The ship's chaplain had the duty of teaching the young men the fundamentals of trigonometry, logarithms, and celestial navigation. He also attempted to teach the reefers English composition, some international law, some languages such as French and Spanish, and various other subjects an officer supposedly needed to know.

The routine was difficult and the work hard, but Matthew, now age sixteen, took readily to it. He distinguished himself enough to be selected to serve as the commodore's personal aide—a position that required Perry to keep the ship's official sea journal and presented a distinct opportunity to impress one of the navy's leading senior officers. Matthew took full advantage of his chance. In April 1811, he received his first independent assignment. With the *President* anchored near the head of the Chesapeake Bay and the commodore visiting his nearby estate at Havre de Grace, news arrived that HMS *Guerrière* had been harassing American merchant ships and impressing American seamen off New York harbor. The Navy Department ordered the *President* to sail and respond immediately. Midshipman Perry was ordered to take a small detachment of men and travel the seventy-mile distance to reach and retrieve Rodgers. Persistent headwinds made the assignment difficult and forced the men to row all of one night and into the next day. Although the men were exhausted, Perry insisted that they continue rowing until they reached the Rodgers estate late that day. When the gig landed, Perry personally ran the remaining distance up a hill to the house. Rodgers was back onboard the following day, and the *President* sailed soon thereafter.[26]

By 1811 diplomatic relations with England were tense and deteriorating. The Jefferson administration and then the Madison administration tried using economic coercion to compel the British to respect Americans' neutrality on the seas. Most galling to Americans was the forcible impressment of seamen from U.S. merchant ships into the British navy, which required a constant supply of sailors to fight Napoleon's France.

The nature of impressment and the arrogance of British naval officers enraged sensitive Americans and made this an emotional as well as a diplomatic issue. The British had long used impressment as a "recruiting tool" and insisted that the sailors they took were either deserters or English citizens subject to military service; they refused to recognize naturalized American citizenship. They often boarded American merchant ships sailing close to the American coast, and their impressment parties were not scrupulous about whom they took. In fact, many seamen on U.S. merchant ships were British citizens who carried false identification papers. Furthermore, Americans and Englishmen at that time spoke in a similar accent, making it difficult for the British to determine on the spot exactly who was and who was not a British subject.

The atmosphere was tense as the *President* sought HMS *Guerrière*. On 16 May, about forty-five miles northeast of Cape Henry, lookouts raised a large ship to the east-southeast sailing toward the American frigate. The approaching ship proved to be the twenty-gun sloop-of-war HMS *Little Belt*. The British ship believed the American warship to be a French merchant ship and intended to make it a prize. Once the British captain realized his mistake, he reversed course and tried to escape to the south. Rodgers and the *President* pursued. Over several hours in a dying wind, the *President* gradually caught the *Little Belt*. At 7:30 P.M. the British sloop shortened its sails, hove to, and cleared for battle. In the twilight, the Americans could not identify the British ensign. Finally, at 8:30, Rodgers hailed the *Little Belt* and asked it to identify itself. In response, British captain Arthur Bingham asked Rodgers to do the same. Confusion followed as the British fired a cannon shot and an American cannon responded. When the British fired three guns with muskets, Rodgers gave the general order to fire. For fifteen minutes the two ships blasted away. The exchange silenced the *Little Belt*'s guns, destroyed one yardarm, and shredded the ship's colors. Although the British ship did not surrender, Rodgers ordered a cease-fire and the *President* sailed away. In addition to the damage to their ship, the British suffered thirteen dead and ten seriously wounded. The next day, the *President* approached the *Little Belt* to determine its name, offer assistance, and express Rodgers's regret at the damage.[27]

This naval skirmish created a diplomatic incident and subsequent investigations on both sides of the Atlantic. Some Americans happily claimed the action as retribution for the Chesapeake affair of 1807. But given the confusion of the moment and the size discrepancy between the American frigate and the British sloop, with less than half as many guns, this affair did not paint the U.S. Navy with honor or glory. Although the *Little Belt* affair did not become a significant diplomatic crisis, it did contribute to deteriorating Anglo-American relations and the coming of war in 1812. Both Matthew and his brother Raymond experienced their first taste of battle here, but it would be more than a year before actual war gave them further opportunity for action.

On 18 June 1812, Congress declared war on Great Britain. The crew of the *President* received the news two days later. Rodgers led his five-ship squadron to sea in the direction of Bermuda soon afterward, hoping to intercept and prey on a large convoy en route from Jamaica to England. Shortly after sunrise on 23 June, the *President* spotted a ship sailing toward the squadron about one hundred miles southwest of Nantucket Shoals. HMS *Belvidera*, a thirty-two-gun frigate commanded by Capt. Richard Byron, was headed for Halifax. Rodgers signaled his squadron to give chase as the *Belvidera* made its best speed in a north-easterly direction. Slowly the *President* closed the distance between them, but the other ships of the squadron lagged farther and farther behind. At 4:15 P.M., after a daylong chase, the *President* opened fire in the hope of slowing or stopping its prey. The *President*'s guns scored several hits, but after thirty minutes of firing one of its bow guns exploded. One man was killed in the explosion and thirteen others injured, including the commodore, Midn. Matthew Perry, and the gun captain. Perry's wound was negligible. When he recorded the event in the ship's journal, his entry noted cryptically that the wounded included "M.C. Perry, Mids."[28]

The explosion broke the commodore's leg, but he had himself propped up to continue the fight. His efforts to bring his ship's broadsides to bear failed while the enemy's guns did considerable damage to the *President*'s sails and rigging. As the wind died, the British ship lightened its weight by jettisoning anchors, casks of fresh water, and overboard boats. The tactic worked, and HMS *Belvidera* gradually increased its distance. At midnight, when the range had reached three miles, Rodgers reluctantly abandoned the chase. Throughout the entire chase and battle, the other, slower ships of the American squadron never came within gun range.[29]

This was a disappointing start to the naval war, and Rodgers was criticized for the squadron's conduct, particularly for his lack of patience. Some naval experts have argued that Rodgers, with the faster ship and more powerful guns, should have withheld his fire until he was close enough to fire a broadside into the enemy's sails and rigging. With the British ship disabled, the rest of his squadron could have closed and finished the job. Disappointment reigned onboard the *President* as well. An apparently perfect opportunity for a decisive victory over an enemy warship had been lost. The squadron resumed its search for the convoy from Jamaica but was frustrated once again as the convoy escaped detection. Finally, on 31 August, the *President* arrived in Boston after a seventy-day cruise with only seven small prizes to its credit. Adding to the crew's discouragement was the realization that they were not to be the first naval heroes of the war, for another American warship, the *Constitution,* commanded by Capt. Isaac Hull, had gloriously defeated and sunk HMS *Guerrière.*

Learning on their arrival that their father, Christopher, was now commandant of the Boston Navy Yard, Matthew and Raymond enjoyed shore leave and visited with their parents before the *President* sailed again in early October. Rodgers now headed a three-ship squadron consisting of the *President,* the frigate *Congress,* and the sloop *Wasp,* which was to join them at sea. Rodgers turned eastward into European waters and then back to an area north of Bermuda known to be a main convoy route between the West Indies and England. The Americans captured a British vessel with $175,000 in specie onboard, but this cruise turned out to be another disappointment. After sailing for eighty-five days and covering nearly eleven thousand miles, the *President* returned to Boston on 31 December 1812 with only two prizes. Meanwhile, other American warships had scored decisive and dramatic victories. The *Wasp* defeated HMS *Frolic* on 17 October. Capt. Stephen Decatur in the frigate *United States* defeated HMS *Macedonian* on 25 October and arrived in New London on 4 December with his prize in tow. The *Constitution,* under its new commander, William Bainbridge, destroyed the thirty-eight-gun British frigate *Java* on 29 December, and less than two months later the American sloop *Hornet* sank the British brig *Peacock* off the north coast of South America.

These victories had little strategic effect on the war and did not weaken the large and powerful British navy. Coming as they did, however, amid word of American military defeats along the Canadian border, the naval victories provided a heady elixir for American confidence and morale early in the war. They not only made legends of Isaac Hull, Stephen Decatur, and William Bainbridge but also demonstrated the importance of a strong navy with large ships.

During the unusually cold winter of 1812–13, Boston Harbor froze. The *President* remained in port for several months to be refit, repaired, and provisioned. The Perry boys used the time to visit with their parents at the Charlestown Navy Yard before the *President* finally put to sea on 30 April 1813. By this time the British had imposed a tight blockade on U.S. ports, making it difficult for single American warships to enter and leave their harbors. Even though the *President* sailed alone into the North Atlantic, this cruise was much more successful than previous ones. By the time the ship returned to Narragansett Bay on 26 September 1813, it had captured twelve prizes and taken 271 prisoners. The officers and men could at last be proud of their work, but Matthew and his shipmates still had not had an opportunity for glory in battle.

The months after he returned to Newport were an eventful period for Matthew Perry, who learned that he had been promoted to acting lieutenant. Now a full-fledged officer, he would be paid more than $660 per year. Then came word that Oliver Hazard Perry, in command of the American squadron on Lake Erie, had won a decisive victory over British naval forces there. Reports indicated that Oliver's courage, leadership, and decisiveness had carried the day. On Lake Erie with Oliver was the fourth Perry son, twelve-year-old James Alexander. Five Perrys now served in the navy, and one of them had been added to the growing pantheon of American naval heroes.

Although the future seemed likely to hold more glory for the Perry family, the remainder of the war offered only frustration and inaction for Matthew. During the fall of 1813 the navy transferred him to Commodore Decatur's flagship, the *United States.* But with Decatur bottled up by the British in New London, Matthew's duties were confined to the monotonous routine of a ship in port and to local recruiting trips. In April 1814, when it appeared that the *United States* would not be able to get out to sea, the navy transferred Matthew back to the *President,* which was stationed in New York harbor to guard against a possible British attack on the city. There he would remain for the duration of the war.

For the young American republic and its small navy, 1814 was a difficult year. The British had mounted a three-pronged offensive: they invaded from Canada, attacked the Chesapeake region, and prepared to invade New Orleans. In the Chesapeake, the British captured Washington, D.C., and burned many of its public buildings. The British had also reversed the initial American naval victories of 1812 and established a tight blockade of the American coastline. With their defeat of Napoleon in 1814, the British could now devote additional land and naval forces to North America. As a result, American warships had difficulty even getting to sea; and when they did, they proved ineffective against the superior Royal Navy.

With little to do in New York, Matthew Perry, now age twenty-two, spent much of his time ashore. He became acquainted with the family of John Slidell, a prominent merchant and banker, in particular with Slidell's seventeen-year-old daughter, Jane, whom Matthew met and courted during the summer and fall. They were married on Christmas Eve 1814 at Grace Church in New York City.[30] Perry's married life started the same day the United States and England signed a treaty of peace in Europe at Ghent.

Neither Jane nor Matthew was known for physical beauty, but the two were well suited. Intelligent, serious, and stable, they made a good marriage and over the next forty-one years remained a devoted and faithful couple. Years later, one of their granddaughters would remember that his wedding ring was "the thing [Matthew] always wore and had more sentiment about than anything else." No hint of scandal was ever associated with Jane. In the navy, Matthew was known as a "family man" who did not carouse or chase women in foreign ports. Unfortunately, very few of their letters to one another survive. Jane did not like to write letters, a habit that frustrated her husband and later led him to hope that their children would "not acquire that repugnance to writing that seems to grow on you." Jane bore ten children in the twenty-two years from 1816 to 1838; seven of them reached adulthood, three boys and four girls. Given her husband's frequent and extended absences, Jane necessarily assumed most of the responsibilities and duties of raising the family. By all accounts she was a loving and dedicated mother.[31]

His marriage into the Slidell family proved instrumental to Matthew's professional career. In the early nineteenth-century navy, family connections were an important asset to an officer. It was understood that those individuals who had connections would use them to their benefit. Christopher Perry had actively used his naval contacts to assist the careers of his sons.[32] Now Lieutenant Perry had married into a socially prominent New York family whose political influence would grow in the years ahead. In addition to Jane's father, her three brothers also figured in Matthew's destiny. The eldest Slidell son, John, moved to New Orleans, became a lawyer, and entered politics. He subsequently became an important Democrat, served in the U.S. Senate, and had a network of political friends and contacts around the country. John Slidell's political standing and influence in an era when the Democrats dominated the presidency would prove invaluable to Perry. The second son, Thomas, also migrated to New Orleans and pursued a legal career, and eventually became chief justice of the state supreme court in Louisiana. The youngest brother, Alexander, was eleven years old when he entered the navy in 1815. During his subsequent naval career he served under Matthew Perry on several occasions and became a close personal friend and associate. During the 1830s he added Mackenzie to his name and is known to posterity and in his writings—including a biography of Oliver Hazard Perry—as Alexander Slidell Mackenzie.

The marriages of Matthew Perry's brothers and sisters also contributed to his social stature and career. In 1811, Oliver Hazard had married Elizabeth Chapman Mason, a member of a very prominent Newport family. In 1814, Raymond married Mary Ann D'Wolf, whose father, James D'Wolf, was a wealthy merchant and ship owner active in the slave trade prior to 1808. The family remained involved in the trade after it became illegal, and James D'Wolf himself owned slaves and sugar plantations in Cuba. In 1815, Anna Maria Perry married Lt. George W. Rodgers, a younger brother of Commo. John Rodgers. In 1819, Jane Tweedy Perry, the sixth of the Perry children, married Dr. William Butler, a naval surgeon from South Carolina. Later, in 1828, the youngest Perry, Nathaniel, a purser in the navy, married Lucretia Thatcher, from a prominent New London family. Matthew's older sister, Sarah Wallace, never married, and his remaining brother, James Alexander, drowned in 1822 while serving as a lieutenant in the navy. Collectively, the Perry in-laws enhanced Matthew's social, political, and naval connections and gave him a significant advantage in the intensely political world of the postwar American navy.[33]

Shortly after his marriage, Matthew returned to active duty as the recruiting officer for the *Chippewa,* then being built near Bristol, Rhode Island. His brother Oliver was in charge of the construction, fitting, and arming of the new vessel, a sixteen-gun, four-hundred-ton brig-of-war. The project became a Perry family affair, with brothers Raymond and James Alexander acting as aides to Oliver and new brother-in-law Alexander Slidell serving as an acting midshipman onboard. For the Perrys these were pleasurable but hectic months. The parents had taken a house in Bristol, and Matthew and Jane shared another house with Oliver and his wife, Elizabeth. The Perry family made a strong impression on Alexander Slidell, who was struck by the warm and welcoming atmosphere and their great affection for one another. He particularly remembered mother Sarah Wallace Perry as a strong and loving person.[34]

By the time the *Chippewa* was launched in the spring, the war had ended. Commanded by Lt. George C. Read and assigned to a squadron under the command of Commo. William Bainbridge, the *Chippewa* had a crew of ninety men; Lt. Matthew Perry was second in command. Once the war with England had ended, Congress declared war on the dey of Algiers, who had been using his fleet to prey on American ships in the Mediterranean. To prosecute the conflict the United States dispatched two squadrons. The first, ten ships, including three frigates, commanded by Commo. Stephen Decatur, sailed in May. The second squadron, under Bainbridge, sailed in July from Boston. By the time the second squadron reached the Mediterranean, Decatur had already attacked, captured the Algerian flagship, forced the dey to release his American prisoners, and compelled him to sign a peace treaty. Decatur then sailed to Tunis and to Tripoli to demonstrate the naval power of the United States. The appearance of the second American naval squadron under Bainbridge dramatically emphasized the military strength of the United States and its determination to protect its commerce, merchant ships, and sailors in the Mediterranean.

The two squadrons rendezvoused at Gibraltar in September before returning to the United States in November. Perry had no chance to participate in any real naval action in the Mediterranean, but he made good use of his time there. And he now had additional duties to take up his time. As second in command, he was the executive officer in charge of the day-to-day operation of the ship. For the first time he was learning to sail a small warship in conjunction with a large squadron. He also taught himself Spanish and translated a book on hydrography and navigation from Spanish into English.

By the end of 1815, when Perry returned to his wife and family in Newport, a dramatic modification in all their lives seemed imminent. With the wars with England and the Barbary powers concluded, the navy's role was about to change. The headiness of war and military glory would now be replaced by the routine of peacetime service. Overseas naval activity might well decrease, as would assignments and opportunities for advancement and distinction. Although the events of the preceding decade had demonstrated the importance of a strong navy of large warships, long-term political support was unpredictable. As an eager, ambitious, and energetic midshipman and lieutenant, Matthew Perry had impressed his superiors and earned the respect of Commo. John Rodgers. However, the future for a young officer in the postwar navy was unclear. For Perry and the hundreds of other young officers who had risen quickly through the ranks before 1815, the prospects for a dynamic, challenging naval career suddenly appeared slim.

Matthew Perry clearly loved the navy and had excelled in each of his assignments. Now, however, it might be time for him to look for a career outside the U.S. Navy. When the *Chippewa* returned from the Mediterranean, he applied for a furlough, a practice then common among young naval officers.[35] In December 1815, the navy granted his request and later twice extended his furlough. He and Jane moved to New York and started a family. Their first child, John Slidell Perry, was born in leap year 1816 but died shortly after his first birthday. Sarah Slidell Perry was born on 8 January 1818.

As a child of the sea, Matthew Perry turned naturally to maritime activities during his furlough. On several occasions he commanded merchant vessels to Europe for his father-in-law, John Slidell. In spite of his good prospects and enviable connections, Perry decided after three years to end his furlough and return to active duty in the peacetime navy. His career prospects remained undefined, but it was clearly the career for which family traditions and his own early life had best prepared him.

～2～

LIEUTENANT IN WEST AFRICAN AND CARIBBEAN WATERS

I could not even hear of an American slaving vessel; and I am fully impressed with the belief that there is not one at present afloat.

LT. MATTHEW PERRY, 1822,
ON THE SLAVE TRADE IN WEST AFRICA

When Matthew Perry returned to active duty in 1819, he rejoined a navy that had entered a new era. The United States was at peace and would remain so for nearly three decades. Since the Barbary powers had been subdued and Europe was also at peace, the United States faced no major threats to its commerce or neutrality. In the flush of postwar nationalism in 1816, Congress had approved legislation that provided one million dollars annually for the next six years to build twelve 44-gun frigates and nine 74-gun ships of the line as well as three steam batteries. Advocates of naval expansion intended to build a navy comparable with those of England and France, but their hopes were dashed by the Panic of 1819, which forced the federal government to retrench and delay naval construction. By that time it had also become clear that the new challenges facing the navy could not be effectively met by large warships. In Latin America, a number of nationalist revolutions posed an immediate threat to U.S. commerce. In contrast to the pre-1812 era, however, the threat came not from the warships of opposing navies, but rather from scores of small privateers and pirate vessels operating in the shallow waters of the Caribbean. In response, Congress authorized immediate construction in 1819 of five small sloops-of-war and then, in 1822, authorized the acquisition of additional small schooners and vessels. In 1821, the Navy Department created the West India Squadron to patrol the Caribbean and the Pacific Squadron to police the west coast of North and South America, and then, in 1826, the Brazil Squadron to police the east coast of South America.[1]

In addition to combating the immediate threats to commerce in the Caribbean, the navy's role began to change in other significant and unforeseen ways; by the early 1820s the primary peacetime mission of the navy would be the protection of American commerce overseas. This responsibility meant that the navy would not only fight privateers and pirates but would also police smuggling, show the flag in various ports around the world, perform limited diplomatic duties, and maintain a continuous presence on various overseas stations. Regardless of their partisan affiliation, most politicians and government officials defined this mission in narrow terms. They assumed that the navy would confine its activities largely to the Caribbean, the Atlantic, and the Mediterranean. While the nation stockpiled building materials and supplies to meet future crises, the active navy would consist of a small force of several dozen warships supported by a stable budget of less than $4 million.

Between 1820 and the 1850s, the economy of the United States and its overseas commerce grew dramatically. Total U.S. foreign trade increased from $157 million in 1819 to $534 million in 1854. And although most of that commerce was conducted with Great Britain, Europe, Canada, and Cuba, trade with South America, the Pacific, and the East Indies grew steadily. Politicians, public officials, and newspaper editors all predicted a future bonanza for Americans in the vast reaches of the Pacific.

As American trade and commercial interests expanded geographically, so too did demands on the U.S. Navy. American merchants and investors expected protection and support for their interests. They needed better information about sea routes and distant ports, some formal naval presence in new markets, and protection from political upheaval and arbitrary acts by foreign rulers. Inevitably, the number of warships, officers, and sailors grew as the navy created new overseas stations in Africa, the

Pacific, and the East Indies. Expanding commercial interests and pressures functionally broadened the term *protection of commerce* to include more and more activities.[2]

By the 1850s, *protection of commerce* included expanding commerce as well as protecting it. The navy continued to defend and protect American lives, property, and trade overseas, but now its ships and men also engaged in many other commercial activities. The men of the navy helped to identify and open new markets. They explored and reported on the commercial potential of remote regions such as the Amazon River basin, the Dead Sea, Central America, the Antarctic, and the North Pacific. They collected valuable geographical and commercial information to be used by American merchants. They compiled nautical charts and surveys for American ship captains. They helped whalers identify likely locations of their prey in the Pacific. When necessary, they chastised natives or rulers who had attacked American ships or citizens overseas. And in remote places, naval officers acted as diplomats and concluded diplomatic agreements.[3]

Lt. Matthew Perry, then, entered a peacetime navy that was far different from the service he had known previously. Without formal naval battles between large warships or confrontations with the navies of England and France, most of his days would be unexciting. And in the coming decades, his own exploits and those of other naval officers would rarely capture the nation's imagination or create instant heroes. The new navy would create opportunities for a different type of naval officer with attributes and talents unlike those who had distinguished themselves so dramatically in the fighting navy of the War of 1812 and the Barbary Wars. Fortuitously for Perry, the era he and the navy were entering was ideally suited to his character, personality, and talents. His brother Oliver Hazard was an impetuous man who thrived in battle situations where quick, decisive action was needed. Even in peacetime Oliver instinctively acted in impulsive and heroic ways. For example, in January 1816 in Newport, he received word that the schooner *Eliza* had hit Seal Rock off Brenton's Neck in a storm and that the crew was in grave danger. It was customary for a senior officer to send a subordinate in such situations, but Oliver took control and personally commanded the successful rescue.

As a naval officer, Matthew was the reverse image of his eldest brother. Energetic and resourceful he was, but Matthew was also delib-

erate, careful, and thoughtful. His most impetuous act as a young officer was to injure himself in 1819 by jumping a fence in pursuit of a de-
serter. His anger could be aroused, but usually he kept his emotions
under control. Although he demonstrated his personal courage on
numerous occasions, Perry was not foolhardy and did not seek out situations for personal heroism.

The same qualities that had created military heroes in the War of 1812
later created trouble for some peacetime officers. Accustomed to settling
their differences violently, thirty-three officers were killed in duels, and
more than one hundred duels were fought between 1798 and 1843.[4]
Among the victims was the intrepid but rash naval hero Stephen
Decatur in 1820. The impulsive behavior of such officers as David Porter,
"Mad Jack" Percival, John Downes, and Thomas ap Catesby Jones created public incidents and professional problems in the antebellum
period. By nature, Matthew Perry was not vulnerable to such excess. He
opposed dueling and never participated as either a principal or a second.
Instead he thrived and excelled in peacetime assignments requiring him
to be deliberate, to plan carefully, and to adapt to different military and
quasi-diplomatic roles.

In the four years from 1819 to 1823, Perry began to mature and make
his mark as a career naval officer. He served first as second in command on the corvette *Cyane* on its cruise to West Africa in 1820 and
then as commander of the sloop *Shark* on cruises to the Caribbean and
West Africa in 1821 and 1822. These were excellent assignments for an
officer in his twenties because they offered important responsibilities
and considerable autonomy. Perry had the opportunity to combat
pirates, police the slave trade, and assist African American colonists in
Africa while also performing more routine duties. On these cruises
Lieutenant Perry demonstrated a particular interest in discipline and
established special measures to protect the health of his men. His performance impressed his superiors, and he began to establish a reputation as an energetic and capable man and one of the promising young
officers of his naval generation.

In August 1819, Perry requested and received appointment as first
lieutenant, the second in command, of the *Cyane*. Captured from the
British near the end of the war, the *Cyane* carried a crew of 180 men and
thirty-six guns. The corvette's commander, Capt. Edward Trenchard, had
been ordered to escort the first group of African American colonists to

the coast of West Africa. The American Colonization Society had chartered the merchant brig *Elizabeth* to carry thirty families comprising
some eighty free blacks to establish a new settlement there. The society
itself had been established in 1817, and some of the most prominent
Americans of the day were members, including President James Mon-
roe, Chief Justice John Marshall, Henry Clay, and Francis Scott Key. Its
purpose was to provide a homeland for free African Americans and
thereby to encourage slaveholders to emancipate their slaves voluntarily.
Presumably slaveholders would be more inclined to free their slaves if
they knew that these would be resettled in a free African colony rather
than remaining to contribute to the race problem in the United States.
Supporters of colonization also hoped that the founding and development of a republican colony in West Africa would bring both civilization
and Christianity to the continent. Although the experiment was doomed
to eventual failure, in 1819 its future held promise. The African American leaders of the venture seemed capable. In the United States the
society enjoyed enthusiastic and influential political and religious support, and the federal government provided both diplomatic and naval
assistance.[5]

Initially scheduled to depart during the fall of 1819, the *Elizabeth* did
not sail until 6 February 1820. Several days later the *Cyane* followed.
While he was waiting for his ship to sail, Matthew Perry received word
of a terrible personal tragedy. His beloved brother Oliver Hazard had
died of yellow fever on 23 August 1819 in the Gulf of Paria. Tragic news
for the nation, it was a shocking blow for Matthew and his family. Oliver
had been not only the eldest child but also the most popular and famous
Perry. He had been barely thirty-four years old at his untimely death. In
tribute, Matthew and Jane named their next child, a daughter born on 31
October 1819, Jane Oliver Hazard Perry. Oliver's death from yellow fever
was also a painful reminder to Matthew of the dangers that disease held
for men serving in tropical climates.

In addition to escorting and helping the settlers of the colonization
society in West Africa, Captain Trenchard was to police the coast in
search of slave traders and to return any Africans taken from them to
Africa. The United States had banned the importation of slaves in 1808
and subsequently passed legislation in 1820 declaring the African slave
trade to be piracy; Americans involved in the trade were labeled pirates
and could be punished by death.

The *Elizabeth* reached the planned rendezvous at Cape Mesurado before the *Cyane* and proceeded westward to the British colony of Sierra Leone. Here local authorities denied the colonists asylum and forced them to settle on nearby Sherbro Island, a swampy and disease-infested place. They set about building their settlement, but it was now the rainy season; moreover, the settlers had not prepared well for their task. In sum, they found conditions harsh, the climate unhealthy, and the local natives hostile.[6]

The *Cyane* reached Cape Mesurado on 27 March 1820 and then followed the *Elizabeth* to Sherbro Island to offer assistance to the colonists. In response to a request from Rev. Samuel Bacon, Captain Trenchard sailed his warship back toward Cape Mesurado to try to find a better place for the settlement. En route, the *Cyane* located a group of seven brigs and schooners that were suspected slave traders and gave chase. All seven of them were captured on 10 April off the mouth of the Gallinas River, a known center of the slave trade. Captain Trenchard then captured two additional slavers. Of the nine captured slavers, he released two, after removing their captives, and dispatched four of the others to the United States under the command of officers from the *Cyane*. The slaves they carried were taken to Sierra Leone.[7]

Three days later, the *Cyane* arrived at Cape Mesurado, which Lieutenant Perry quickly identified as the best available site for the African American settlement. "This appears to me to be the most elligible [*sic*] situation for a settlement I have yet seen," he wrote in his journal.

> The natives are pacific in their disposition, engage but little in the Slave Trade and . . . express a willingness to admit our Countrymen among them. The land is extremely rich and is capable of producing Rice, Coffee, Sugar Cane, Indigo, Cotton, and the common fruits and vegetables of Tropical climates.

Cape Mesurado's advantages included a good harbor and the healthiest location on the coast because "its projection into the sea affords it the advantage of the sea breeze, the strongest preventative of sickness." Perry's recommendation led eventually to the acquisition of land at Cape Mesurado. The African American community resettled there from Sherbro Island in 1822 and named their new home Monrovia.[8]

The *Cyane* cruised in search of more slavers and then proceeded north and west several hundred miles to Port Praia in the Cape Verde

Islands. Since the U.S. Navy did not yet have a formal naval station or depot in the area, Trenchard needed to find a source for supplies, provisions, and fresh water as well as a place to repair his ship and refresh his crew. Mainland West Africa offered no ports with these amenities, and offshore islands such as the Cape Verdes seemed the best alternative even though they were hundreds of miles from the ship's cruising station.

As the executive officer, Perry devoted significant effort to locating a port suitable for navy ships to repair and refit, and filled his journal with detailed descriptions of the various ports the *Cyane* visited. As the closest offshore port to the waters of West Africa, Port Praia seemed an obvious choice, but Perry was not impressed. Although it offered a good harbor as well as readily available provisions and fresh water, Port Praia could not provide important items such as salt, bread, and flour. Moreover, Perry judged it to be a rather miserable place. The town of two thousand inhabitants contained "but a few houses, most of them miserable hovels inhabited by a motley race of Whites, Mulattoes, and Negroes." While the whole island had a total population of about seventeen thousand and an ample amount of rich soil, much of the land went uncultivated. "Unfortunately the inhabitants like all of the Portuguese do not feel disposed to labor more than absolute necessity compels them." The town contained a fort, but the troops were poorly equipped, miserably paid, and frequently seen "without shirt, shoes, or Coat" on guard at the governor's house. As his description makes clear, Perry believed this was no place for an American naval establishment. Nevertheless, Port Praia was the closest and the least objectionable site on the Africa station for U.S. warships to refit, find provisions, and escape from the unhealthy climate of the West African coast, and American naval vessels would touch there often in the years ahead.[9]

From the Cape Verdes, Trenchard sailed north to Tenerife on Santa Cruz in the Canary Islands. After receiving a cold reception from Portuguese officials, he proceeded to Funchal in the Madeiras. At each place, Perry carefully collected information and noted the port's special characteristics in his journal. By September the *Cyane* had returned to the West African coast, where, in company with the *Hornet* and *Adams*, the corvette captured four more slavers before heading for home in early October.

Although the *Cyane* had been on station only since April and had spent weeks of that time away from the coast, West Africa had taken its toll on the officers and men. Navigation was often unpredictable and difficult, the climate was oppressive, and the work was tedious and debilitating. On station, officers and men had no way to escape the heat or the monotony of the duty. Perry's journal contains not only daily recordings of air temperature, wind, and water temperature but also regular descriptions of the climate's effects on the men. On 19 March, Perry noted that the "heat is becoming extremely oppressive and already debilitating and unnerving . . . our crew." The captain of a passing ship confirmed that "white men could not withstand the oppressive heat of this climate if exposed to the Sun or any hard duty."[10] The absence of any nearby port of respite made the duty even worse.

The constant threat of disease made the West Africa station dangerous as well as oppressive. Unable to maintain an adequate diet, the crew suffered first from scurvy and then from African fever (or malaria); fifty men were stricken by the fever and two died. An "excellent young officer," Midshipman Townsend, and a small detachment of men died after they contracted the fever while ashore assisting the settlers at Sherbro Island. African fever also devastated the new colony as every one of the new settlers contracted the disease in 1820.[11]

The men of the *Cyane* contracted the fever in spite of the precautions taken onboard. Perry already knew of the danger when the ship sailed for Africa. His father's experience in 1799 and 1800 on the *General Greene* and his brother's recent death had underscored the perils of yellow fever. He was familiar with the work of British naval surgeons who had studied the health problems experienced by the British navy on the African coast. As a result, Perry convinced Trenchard to institute various health precautions. En route to Africa in March 1820, Perry had noted in his journal that the "coast of Africa is generally considered an unhealthy station" and it would therefore be "necessary for us to adopt every precaution to guard against the disease incident to that climate[. E]xposure to the night air, the meridian Sun, intemperance, and fatigue are considered the principal causes of disease." As one of his precautions, Perry ordered the men to wear flannel clothing. The crew were never to be allowed "to sleep on deck, or to remain in wet clothes for a moment it can possibly be avoided." Officers were "to pay the strictest attention to their cleanliness, and never to turn them out into the night unless absolutely necessary, to have fires burning upon the Berth deck a part of the day" to disperse foul air and to introduce fresh air. Perry also insisted that the berth deck be whitewashed every day and tried to do what was possible to raise the crew's spirits.[12]

At every settlement along the coast of Africa that the *Cyane* visited, Perry hired local natives, known as krumen, to perform hard labor and to haul goods between ship and shore. Perry paid the krumen $1.25 per week to navigate their surfboats through the troublesome West African surf carrying passengers, provisions, and equipment back and forth between ship and shore, saving American seamen from heavy manual labor in the oppressive sun and heat. The krumen proved to be helpful, good-natured, and indispensable.[13]

Trenchard readily accepted Perry's health measures, but they achieved only partial success both because the officers did not enforce them rigorously and because some men, such as Midshipman Townsend and his working party, remained for extended periods onshore where they were particularly vulnerable to disease-carrying mosquitoes. At the time, prevailing opinion held that damp, noxious air, such as that found in swamps and on poorly ventilated ships, caused the disease. The prescribed precautions of the day were to keep the air on the decks of warships clean, dry, and circulating and to keep the men themselves onboard unless it was absolutely necessary for them to go ashore. Then they were to go only in daylight and return by dark. The connection between mosquitoes and African fever would not be scientifically verified for decades. At times, Perry and some of his contemporaries seemed very close to identifying and taking action against the real culprit, but they never reached the correct conclusion. So their rather crude and imprecise regimen had to suffice. In fact, cleansing the air had no effect, but protecting the men from the mosquitoes was helpful. The most useful antifever measure, however, was hiring local krumen to perform the work onshore. In any event, when officers applied these rather primitive precautions rigorously, they served the navy well and probably saved hundreds of lives.

On Christmas Day 1820, the *Cyane* reached New York harbor after a long and difficult passage. Trenchard and his crew had done their job well under difficult conditions. In capturing a number of slavers, they had policed and temporarily suppressed the slave trade. They had also helped launch the new African American colony and identified an excellent future site for the settlement. The settlers were not so successful. All eighty-eight of them contracted the fever; twenty-three had died by year's end. Thirty-five others left the colony for Sierra Leone or the United States. Although the fever did not strike him, Perry complained that the cruise had injured his health permanently. Trenchard also suffered lasting effects from the voyage. He never fully recovered from the damage to his health and died of pneumonia in 1824.[14]

The first six months of 1821 offered a pleasant respite in New York for Perry as he spent extended leaves with Jane and the family. He was back at sea, however, thousands of miles away from home, when Jane gave birth to Matthew Calbraith Perry Jr. on 6 October 1821. The previous spring Perry had requested and received command of one of the navy's newest ships, the schooner *Shark*. The two-hundred-ton, eighty-six-foot-long *Shark* carried seventy officers and men, mounted twelve guns, and proved to be an superb sailer.[15]

The Navy Department had treated the twenty-seven-year-old Perry very well in promoting him to lieutenant commander and giving him his first command—to convey the U.S. commissioner, Rev. Eli Ayers, to Monrovia. Once in Africa Perry would enjoy considerable autonomy because the *Shark* would sail alone and he would carry only general sailing instructions. In addition to being his first command, this assignment was attractive to Perry because of his genuine interest in Africa and the African American settlement there. He believed in the work and goals of the American Colonization Society and cared about the well-being of the African American settlers.

The passage went well. The *Shark* sailed in late July and reached the Azores on 1 September en route to Tenerife. Unlike the previous experience, the Americans received a warm reception because a new government in Portugal and a new colonial governor were in place. From the Canary Islands the *Shark* sailed to Porto Grande in the Cape Verdes, touching at Maia and Port Praia, and finally sailed on to Sierra Leone, arriving there by the end of October.

Perry was determined to run an efficient and tightly disciplined ship in his first command. As a young midshipman and then a new lieutenant, he had learned directly from Commo. John Rodgers, a well-known disciplinarian, how to command a warship. The "Rodgers system," widely used in the navy, sought to keep the crews healthy, disciplined, and hard at work. Rules and regulations were to be strictly enforced, crews were to be engaged in constant work duties, corporal punishment or flogging was to be used judiciously, and shore leave was to be kept to an absolute minimum. Matthew Perry admired his mentor and instituted the Rodgers system on the *Shark*. Midn. William Lynch sailed on the ship and recorded an account of the cruise that depicts a tightly disciplined but not very contented crew. Lynch noted that Perry "strictly enforced" the Rodgers system, "the ruling feature of which is, to render every one as uncomfortable as possible." Rigorously enforcing shipboard rules and regulations, Perry punished all violators and used the lash whenever necessary. Like Rodgers, Perry kept shore leave to a minimum, although this policy was not a pressing issue on the West African coast, where there was no place to enjoy shore leave anyway. Perry also insisted on constant activity for both officers and men. He constantly drilled the crew and kept the ship, its guns, and its boats in superb condition, believing that such activity would raise the morale and maintain the health of everyone onboard.[16]

Perry's regimen produced a well-disciplined and efficient ship, but it also created a climate of fear and intimidation. Nor was blind obedience to orders necessarily a good thing. As a dramatic example, during the chase of a slave ship, Perry sent a young midshipman to the head of the bowsprit to direct the helmsman and to give word when to fire. The young man obeyed his orders precisely. Unfortunately, it did not occur to anyone onboard that he would be directly in the line of fire. The first shot passed so close to his head that it nearly knocked him overboard, but he said nothing from "fear of misconstruction." The firing continued until he nearly collapsed from the intensity of the repeated concussions. Finally, when his danger became apparent to Perry, the midshipman was "immediately ordered in, but instead of an expression of regret for the great and unnecessary peril to which he had been exposed, he received a severe reprimand for not having made it known immediately after the first discharge."[17]

While the *Shark* was not a happy ship, Perry's health regulations made it a healthy one. He had learned from his earlier cruise to Africa and now instituted additional measures. Stressing the importance of diet to maintain a healthy crew, he regularly tried to replenish the ship's supplies of fresh fruits, vegetables, and meats as well as fresh water. He also demanded strict adherence to his health precautions. According to Midshipman Lynch,

no one was permitted, on any pretext, to sleep on shore, and all were required to wear flannel next to the skin. Nor was he [Perry] content with merely issuing the order, but to his credit, saw it carried into rigid execution, and morning and evening the crew were mustered at quarters for inspection.

Although Lynch chafed under the discipline on the *Shark,* he gratefully acknowledged that to "the enforcement of this judicious regulation, the comparative preservation of our health is mainly attributable."[18]

En route to Sierra Leone from the Canaries the *Shark* bespoke and overtook numerous vessels but captured no slavers. Near Freetown, Sierra Leone, where the American colony had temporarily relocated, Perry delivered Reverend Ayers as instructed. Ayers found the colonists to be in a demoralized state. Another boatload of colonists had arrived, but the settlers continued to be devastated by disease and had not yet acquired a permanent site for their colony. After landing Ayers, the *Shark* cruised south along the coast, through miserable weather, in search of slavers. "The squalls, which were preceded by a gathering murkiness of the atmosphere, were absolutely terrific," wrote Lynch, "and the clouds hung so low, that the vivid lightning seemed to shoot in horizontal lines about us. I have read of 'the wreck of matter and the crush of worlds,' but had no conception what it sounded like, until I heard African thunder." The *Shark* identified, stopped, and released a small Dutch schooner and then stopped another schooner flying French colors. Although it had no slaves onboard, it did carry a revealing cargo consisting of thousands of gallons of rum, thousands of pounds of tobacco, and a large quantity of umbrellas, all items frequently carried by slavers trading along the coast. Unable to find any evidence that this was an American ship or proof that the vessel had broken any American laws, Perry was forced to release it in spite of the schooner's unmistakable intent.[19]

The next encounter was far less ambiguous. On 10 November, the *Shark* raised an unidentified ship, gave chase, and after several hours finally boarded it. The slaver *Caroline* was a French schooner then flying French colors. Carrying a crew of mixed nationalities with an American mate, it was bound for Martinique with a cargo of 153 slaves. A four-foot-high deck about fifteen feet wide and forty feet long confined the slaves and forced them to sleep in dovetail fashion with the children on top of the adults. All were naked, their bodies fully shaved to protect them from vermin. They subsisted on a daily ration of one pint of water and one-half pint of rice. Emaciated with severely shrunken skin, "they resembled so many Egyptian mummies half-awakened into life." Most of the *Shark*'s crew had never seen the horror of a slaver fully loaded with human cargo. The sight moved them as they provided water and a meal of bread and beef to the captives. Meanwhile Perry interviewed Capt. Victor Ruinet and examined his papers carefully, reluctantly concluding that the slaver's papers were in order. Since it was not an American ship, Perry had no authority to seize the *Caroline*. He could only remove the American mate and send him to the United States for trial.

The decision to release the *Caroline* was painful for Perry, for he fully appreciated the inhumane spectacle before him and the fate of the slaves onboard. But he also understood his instructions and the limits of his authority. Perry's decision upset his officers, who, according to Midshipman Lynch, blamed Perry for "timidity and want of human feeling." They even offered to reimburse Perry financially for any monetary damages he might suffer as a result of the seizure. But Perry refused, and the *Caroline* sailed away. "With feelings which I cannot undertake to express," Lynch watched the slaver disappear "bearing into life-long captivity the unhappy wretches who we had inspired with a hope of freedom."[20]

Before he released the slaver, however, Perry took the remarkable step of forcing the French captain to sign an oath in which he and his crew "most solemnly" promised, "never to be directly or indirectly engaged in transporting slaves in any manner whatever from the coast of Africa." Captain Ruinet and his crew also abjured "the slave trade for ever hereafter" and promised "to treat with humanity and kindness the slaves now on board during the passage to Martinique." This action was atypical for Perry and went well beyond naval regulations. Perry dispatched the signed pledge to the Navy Department, but its impact was entirely symbolic. And while the pledge soothed the consciences of Perry and his men, it did not alter the fate of the captives or change Captain Ruinet's ways. He would be involved in at least two subsequent slave voyages.[21]

This emotional incident, combined with the *Shark*'s inability to identify and apprehend any American slavers, heightened Perry's personal frustration at his inability to police the slave trade. Nevertheless, he concluded that Europeans, not Americans, were at fault. In January 1822, after he returned to the United States, Perry reported that the slave trade remained very active in the Cape Verdes as well as along the coast he had patrolled. He claimed that the Portuguese captured Africans, brought them to the Cape Verdes, baptized them into the "Roman faith," detained them one year, and then shipped them to Brazil as Portuguese subjects. In West Africa, Perry noted, "this species of commerce is pursued along the whole coast with increased activity, success and profit by vessels wearing the French, Portuguese, Spanish and the Dutch flags but more openly by vessels of the French and Portuguese nations." The demand for slaves was so intense that small African villages frequently attacked one another "mainly for the purpose of making prisoners to be disposed of to the captains of the slave vessels." In such "predatory warfare," Perry noted, "the most flagitious acts of cruelty are committed and it is not unfrequent that parents dispose of their own children."[22]

In his report to the Navy Department, Perry carefully detailed his own efforts to police the trade. He listed not only the fifteen ships he had stopped but also the ships boarded by the British. According to Perry, this offered "conclusive evidence that no Americans are at present engaged in the Trade" because an American slaver had "no inducement" to hide its true identity from the British.

> It gives me great pleasure to inform the Department that it is the opinion of all the British officers on the African Station and indeed of everyone whom I have consulted with that the late severe laws of Congress prohibiting the slave trade, enforced as they have been by the prompt and vigorous measures of the Dept., have had the desired effect of preventing American citizens from employing their time and capital in this iniquitous traffic.[23]

Soon after its encounter with the *Caroline*, the *Shark* headed for the West Indies, arriving by early December. Here Perry was supposed to search for pirates, but he lacked the information necessary to pursue them effectively. Since he did not have adequate time to gather intelligence, he turned north to reach his home port by the end of the year. Unfortunately, soon after passing through the Florida Straits, the *Shark* sailed into the teeth of a severe northeastern snowstorm, converting the voyage from a tropical to an arctic one. "The driving spray, freezing as it fell, coated everything with an incrustation of ice," wrote Lynch.

> The running rigging soon became of the size of shrouds, and the shrouds as thick as cables. Coming from the hot and relaxing climate of Africa, we could ill endure the keen north wind which cuts, and burns as it cuts, like a red hot razor. Some of the officers and many of

the men were frost-bitten; a few of the latter so severely, that they subsequently lost the use of their feet for life.[24]

Frostbite aside, once the *Shark* had finally reached home Perry took particular pride in reporting that because of the health precautions he had instituted and the skillful work of his naval surgeon, Dr. John Wiley, not a single life had been lost to disease. In Perry's mind, this fact vindicated both his methods and his zeal in enforcing them.

After a relatively brief winter break, Perry sailed the *Shark* in February 1822 to join the newly created West Indies Squadron under Commo. James Biddle. The Navy Department had created the new squadron in 1821 to combat the escalating problem of piracy in the West Indies and the Gulf of Mexico. After 1815, the nationalistic revolutions in Latin America had created an unstable diplomatic and commercial situation. As the new countries fought Spain for their independence, U.S. merchant ships found themselves caught in the middle, subject to attack and seizure by privateers and Spanish ships alike. Outfitted with letters of marque from the rebel nations, the privateers seized foreign ships engaged in trade with Spain and its colonies. The problem was exacerbated by the estimated fifteen to twenty thousand American seamen who had become privateers after the War of 1812, when the United States no longer needed their services. Spanish officials duly responded and began to seize U.S. merchant ships trading with the revolutionaries. Some colonial merchants loyal to Spain outfitted their own privateers and preyed on U.S. ships. The United States reacted by dispatching warships whose actions soon made it difficult for privateers of any stripe to operate, and by 1820 had greatly reduced the privateering threat to U.S. commerce in the Caribbean.[25]

As the privateers disappeared, however, pirate ships took their place. In fact, many privateers simply shed any vestige of legitimacy and began acting blatantly as pirates. By one estimate, some three thousand piratical acts were committed in the Caribbean between 1815 and 1822. Intensifying the problem was the brutality of many pirates. Commo. David Porter later wrote that "piracy of the worst kind" filled the annals of the West Indies with

accounts of horrors that seem almost incredible in these days. The coast of Cuba, Porto [*sic*] Rico, St. Domingo, and the Spanish main were the resorts of merciless freebooters who plundered and burned vessels with impunity, and frequently murdered their passengers and crews, after inflicting upon them the most shocking brutalities. Families bound for the West Indies, in merchant vessels, disappeared from the face of the earth, and often the only clue to the fate of the passengers and crew, would be the charred hulk of their vessels drifting about the Gulf of Mexico.[26]

Congress first passed legislation to protect U.S. commerce and punish pirates and then strengthened its laws to give U.S. naval officers the authority to seize any ship suspected of piracy. But the pirates were not easy to eliminate. When the navy destroyed or captured the larger pirate vessels, smaller ones took their place. These smaller vessels appeared and disappeared quickly, operating effectively from the innumerable shallow inlets, bays, and streams adjacent to shipping routes in the Caribbean. The pirates would spring from a coastal hiding place along the trade routes and attack a slow, unsuspecting or becalmed merchant ship. After looting their prey, the pirates would return to shore with their booty, conceal their small craft, and disperse into the countryside. Furthermore, these small ships, once lost, were easily replaced. Although in retrospect chasing pirates may seem a glamorous business, for the men of the U.S. Navy the work was hot, unhealthy, tedious, and discouraging.[27]

Pirates presented an elusive and troublesome challenge for the U.S. Navy for several reasons. First, most warships, even small sloops-of-war, were too large and of too deep draft to operate efficiently in shallow water, near shore, or close to treacherous keys. Second, reliable information on the pirates' movements was difficult to obtain. Finally, the navy needed the assistance of local authorities to combat pirates in foreign waters, but this was not always forthcoming. Spanish officials, for example, were not only hostile to the ever-aggressive United States but in some cases also benefited from piracy. Commodore Porter complained that Spanish authorities "connived at the depredation of American commerce" because it was "more lucrative to protect the freebooters than to give them up to justice." Once on station in 1822, however, Commodore Biddle did get the very reluctant governor general of Cuba, Don Nicholas Mahy, to agree informally that he would not object if American troops landed on uninhabited Cuban keys in pursuit of their suspects.[28]

When he sailed in February 1822, Perry carried instructions from Secretary of the Navy Smith Thompson to proceed first to the Florida Keys, where he was to examine Key West and take formal possession of the strategically placed island. Thomas explained that as "one of the most commanding places on the whole coast of Florida," a naval establishment on the island "would be of great importance to the Government as well as the Merchants of the United States." When he reached his destination, Perry ordered Midn. Joseph Moorhead and one other man to take and retain possession of Key West, then known as Thompson's Island.[29] Reporting to the secretary that his instructions had been executed, Perry concurred that Key West was indeed a valuable possession. "Capacious and sheltered" from prevailing northerly and easterly winds, the harbor offered water three to five and one-half fathoms deep. Wood, fresh water, fish, and game as well as fresh fruit and vegetables were readily available. Although local navigation could be difficult, Perry believed that Key West's location between the Florida mainland and Cuba, the south Atlantic states, and Louisiana guaranteed that it would become a "place of considerable commerce." More important was its strategic value. There will come a time, predicted Perry, "when our country shall be enjoined in a War with some giant Maritime State and the Florida Keys will be critical to the commerce and security of Florida, the Gulf of Mexico, and access to Cuba." Accordingly, he suggested that the navy take steps to improve local navigation, for the treacherous waters of south Florida were then strewn with shipwrecks that provided an active local salvage business. Perry proposed that four lighthouses be erected and maintained as "an act of Justice" and safety for "the lives and fortunes of our Citizens." Although the strategic value of Key West's location was obvious, Perry greatly overestimated its value as a naval base. More realistic was Commo. David Porter's recommendation that the island not be made a permanent military base because the pestilent climate made it impossible to "keep one's self free from Musquitoes [sic] and Sand Flies." Instead, Pensacola eventually became the navy's main base in the Southeast.[30]

From Key West, Perry commenced his search for pirates. Off Tampico, Mexico, on 5 May 1822, the *Shark* chased a suspicious schooner ashore. A shore party gave chase, but the schooner's crew fled. From there the *Shark* sailed to the north coast of Cuba, where Perry's initial efforts were energetic but unsuccessful. He pursued but lost three suspected pirate schooners. Then, operating in conjunction with the *Grampus,* commanded by Lt. Francis H. Gregory, the *Shark* attacked and captured a pirate schooner near Sagua la Grande. Shortly thereafter the two ships captured another pirate schooner. In the first case, they killed most of the pirates; in the second, most of the bandits escaped ashore. Perry himself left the *Shark* and spent six days in one of the armed boats, scouring "the coast from Sugar Key to Matanzas." Perry later sighted and boarded a suspected pirate schooner with eight Americans onboard. Since the ship carried no passports or registration documents, he seized it and sent it to port.[31]

Perry and his men had labored hard but had little to show for their efforts. By the end of June, the heat and oppressive conditions had taken their toll. On 29 June, a discouraged Perry reported to Biddle: "Sir, we have searched the coast of Cuba, from Sugar Key to Matanzas, and . . . have become acquainted with a system of abominable fraud, rapine, and Murder, openly permitted by the Spanish authorities, and encouraged by the most wealthy men in the Island." Perry charged that there was "not a fisherman who is not a Pirate, nor a Canoe that is not a pirate Vessel in miniature. The plundered Goods are publicly sold, at the large Commercial Towns, and the first merchants become the purchasers."[32]

Short of supplies by early August, the *Shark* sailed to Key West, dispatched two more pirate prizes, took on provisions at Nassau, and then sailed for the West African coast on 14 August 1822. He arrived there on 23 September and departed twenty-four days later on 17 October. During his stay, Perry visited the American settlement at Monrovia and reported it to be in good condition. The settlers were working hard, "appeared much pleased with their situation," and experienced no hostility from the local natives. By the end of the next dry season, Perry predicted naively, they would be "in a state comparatively prosperous." Perry did not apprehend any American slave traders during this cruise, but near the mouth of the Gallinas River he did board two French slavers that had not yet been loaded but had an estimated capacity of 550 slaves. On one of the ships, the *Eugene,* the Americans discovered a fifteen-year-old slave hidden under a large pile of firewood. The frightened and exhausted boy could barely stand when he was pulled from his hiding place. He belonged to one of the crewmen, who had purchased him for "an old coat." Perry recorded this sordid incident but said and did nothing further.[33]

As he had the year before, Perry discovered a thriving slave trade on the windward coast of West Africa but again concluded that American slavers were not involved in it. In November 1822, he recorded that the trade "is still carried on with great activity under French and Portuguese Flags and it is supposed that not less than 50,000 Negroes have been taken from the Coast during the last twelve months." Perry leveled primary blame for the trade on France. "The French still process undisturbed the profits as well as the iniquity of the Trade—the whole Windward Coast swarms with Vessels wearing the French Flag and manned by French subjects." Ironically, the Royal Navy's effectiveness in patrolling the coast and suppressing the traffic had given the French a monopoly in the trade. Thus Perry condemned France for depressing the native civilization in West Africa and encouraging native chiefs to depend solely on profits of the slave trade for their livelihood. In December, Perry reported that during his stay on the coast, "I could not *even hear* of an American slaving vessel; and I am fully impressed with the belief that there is not one at present afloat."[34]

Although the recent U.S. naval presence had temporarily suppressed American participation in the slave trade between Cape Verde and Cape Palmas on the windward coast of Africa, Perry's assessment was overly optimistic and inaccurate; it was also misleading. Unfortunately, his report, coming from an officer who had viewed the situation firsthand, carried weight and would influence his government's future responses to the issue. In fact, in the early 1820s the African slave trade not only flourished along the Gold and Slave Coasts farther to the east and south but also remained active along the windward coast. Americans participated actively in the traffic, although their ships might carry false papers and fly the colors of France or Portugal. By continuing to allow the slave trade, France and Portugal encouraged slavers of all nations to fly their colors.[35]

In fact, Perry's underassessment of American participation in the slave trade and his activities during his cruise accurately reflected both his own personal background and the attitude of his government. Perry had been raised in a community that both tolerated and profited from the slave trade. Slaves were a common sight in and around Newport when he was growing up. His older brother Raymond had married into the D'Wolfe family, which had long been involved in the slave trade and continued to own Cuban sugar plantations run on slave labor. During the 1820s, Raymond's father-in-law, James D'Wolf, served in the U.S.

Senate, where he voted against an unsuccessful proposal that would have permitted the British to board suspected American slavers.[36] As a young naval officer after the War of 1812, Lieutenant Perry enthusiastically supported the efforts of the American Colonization Society, sharing its belief that colonization would benefit free African Americans while helping to spread civilization and Christianity to Africa. When he sailed to Africa in 1820, 1821, and 1822, his respective ships carrying instructions to assist the society's settlers, Perry performed his duties enthusiastically. Unlike some of his fellow officers who avoided assignment to West Africa, Perry requested a second and then a third cruise. Nevertheless, his personal interest in Africa and the African American settlement there did not make Matthew Perry either an antislavery advocate or a social reformer. When the colonization movement was discredited and replaced by more direct antislavery initiatives, Perry did not participate. He remained a strong supporter of African colonization more than two decades later. Believing that slavery was a problem that could be solved only by southerners, not by outside politicians and reformers, he condemned slavery only in private.

Perry's actions in Africa in the early 1820s also mirrored the position of the U.S. government, which did not view the illegal slave trade as a pressing issue. The State Department refused to sign any agreement that would have permitted the English navy to board, search, and seize American merchant ships whether or not they were slavers operating in African waters. Less than a decade after the War of 1812, British interference with American merchant ships remained a sensitive and emotional issue for many Americans. In June 1822, several months before Perry returned to West Africa, Secretary of State John Quincy Adams met with the British minister to the United States, Stratford Canning, and insisted, based on evidence presented by Canning himself, that "there was not a single vessel under American colors" involved in the illegal trade. Undeterred, Canning pressed for a joint search agreement and asked if Adams "could conceive of a greater and more atrocious evil than this slave-trade." To which Adams replied, "Yes: admitting the right of search by foreign officers of our vessels upon the seas in time of peace; for that would be making slaves of ourselves." The response of Adams, a native of Massachusetts and an opponent of slavery, captures the relatively low diplomatic priority the federal government had assigned to policing Americans' participation in the international slave trade.[37]

Instructions to American naval officers sailing for Africa also reflected the views of the U.S. government. Preventing British interference with American shipping and assisting the African American settlement in Africa were clearly higher priorities than policing the slave trade. Like his fellow officers, Perry knew his orders and acted accordingly. Once in African waters, American naval officers operated under severe constraints. The United States had outlawed the trade and declared participation in it by Americans to be piracy punishable by death but was not party to any international treaty that would have allowed U.S. warships to search and seize slavers from other nations. U.S. naval vessels could seize only American slave ships—and only if they were loaded with slaves. Astute American slaving captains adapted readily, sailing under the registration and flying the colors of other nations, particularly the French and Portuguese.

By December the *Shark* had returned from West Africa to New York. Perry had acquitted himself well in his first command. An energetic commander and a skilled seaman, he had executed his orders effectively and had not exceeded his authority. Onboard his tight and well-disciplined ship, his manner was always serious, his movements purposeful, and his presence intimidating. By this time his crew had given him the apt nickname "Old Bruin" for his gruff bearing and powerful voice in roaring out his commands.

Once again Perry had delivered a healthy crew, with not a man lost to disease. Perry took considerable personal pride in the health of his men. Other ships in the West Indies squadron had been devastated by disease, but the men of *Shark* had not. Perry also praised his surgeon, Dr. John Wiley, to whom he confided that three years of active service in "an African and West Indies Climate" had made "consequent inroads upon my naturally strong constitution."[38] In 1823, despite his weakened state, Perry and the *Shark* returned to the West Indies Squadron for a brief cruise in the Caribbean, where he found American commerce to be in a "perfect state of tranquility." He returned to New York in July with his entire crew in good health.[39] In August, Perry was reassigned to the Brooklyn Navy Yard. After three cruises on the *Shark*, the twenty-nine-year-old Perry welcomed the temporary respite of shore duty and reunion with his family.

⚛ 3 ⚛

FIRST LIEUTENANT AND COMMANDER IN THE MEDITERRANEAN

He was a fine looking officer in uniform, somewhat resembling the portraits of his brother . . . but not so handsome, and had a sterner expression and was generally stern in his manner.

REAR ADMIRAL ALMY
DESCRIBING MATTHEW PERRY, 1828

"*I* saw her coming before a gentle levanter, with sky sails and studdingsails—a perfect cloud of snow-white canvas," observed a thrilled Lt. Alexander Slidell as he described the arrival of the massive seventy-four-gun *North Carolina* at Gibraltar on 29 April 1825. The "gallant ship stood boldly into the harbor, with yards a little braced, sails all filled and asleep, and hull careening enough to improve the beauty of the broadside . . . nothing could exceed the beauty of the spectacle."[1]

Onboard was thirty-one-year-old Matthew Calbraith Perry. After a year of shore duty at the Brooklyn Navy Yard, Perry had been ordered to join the *North Carolina*. Shore duty had allowed Perry to rejuvenate his health, attend to personal matters, and spend time with his growing family. The Perrys lived in New York City on Mercer Street, about two miles from the ferry that took him back and forth to the navy yard. Matthew and Jane took advantage of their social connections and the resources of the city. In 1824, for example, Perry helped organize a formal dinner with his fellow officers for James Fenimore Cooper.[2]

By the summer of 1824 Perry was ready to return to active sea duty, and the assignment to the *North Carolina* was a superb billet. The ship was slated for the Mediterranean, the most preferred overseas station in the navy, and, for Perry, a far more pleasant assignment than his previous cruises to Africa and the West Indies. More important, Perry would be the first, or senior, lieutenant and second in command of the navy's newest and largest battleship. And perhaps best of all, the Mediterranean Squadron was commanded by Commo. John Rodgers, who had resigned his position as president of the Board of Navy Commissioners to assume this command.[3] Since Perry's sister Anna Maria had married Rodgers's younger brother, Lt. George Washington Rodgers, in 1815, the commodore was now Perry's relative and friend, not merely his mentor and former commander. On this assignment, then, Perry had the opportunity to gain the further confidence of the navy's most influential senior officer.

Although no major diplomatic or naval crisis brewed in the Mediterranean, this cruise was not viewed as a routine one. By the mid-1820s, while American trade with Turkey, the Levant, and Egypt had increased sharply, the Mediterranean Squadron had declined in size and stature. In addition, the Greek revolution endangered American commerce as pirates and privateers preyed on American shipping in the Aegean Sea and the Greek archipelago. The Adams administration wanted to strengthen the squadron and protect American commercial interests in the eastern Mediterranean. Adams also hoped to conclude a commercial treaty with Turkey. Although the navy did not authorize Rodgers to negotiate such a treaty, it did instruct him to contact Turkish naval officials as a means of conveying American goodwill to the sultan. Up until this time, diplomatic efforts with the Turks had been unsuccessful, allegedly stalled by European intrigue in Constantinople.[4]

John Rodgers, although an obvious choice for the mission, was also selected for the purpose of restoring discipline to the Mediterranean Squadron, whose officers and sailors had earned a reputation for dissipated and rowdy behavior onshore. Brawls between Americans and the sailors of other navies occurred frequently. Among officers, dueling increased as oversensitive Americans defended their personal "honor" against "insults" from officers of other nations. In Port Mahon, dozens of prostitutes reportedly were permitted on the warships in port. Such behavior both undermined the discipline of American warships and lost the respect of other nations for the U.S. Navy. Known as the author of the Rodgers system for shipboard discipline, Rodgers was the clear choice to remedy the situation.[5]

To accomplish these multiple purposes, the Navy Department increased the size and the strength of the squadron. The 24-gun corvette *Cyane,* the 18-gun sloops *Erie* and *Ontario,* and the 12-gun schooner *Nonsuch* were already on station. Joining them would be a 44-gun frigate, the *Constitution,* and the commodore's huge flagship, the *North Carolina.* Rated at 74 guns, the *North Carolina* actually carried 94 and could mount 102 guns if necessary. One of the last sailing ships of the line to be built by the United States, it became obsolete within a generation. In 1824, however, it was a formidable and impressive vessel. With a length of 380 feet and a height of 280 from the top mainmast to the bottom of the keel, the *North Carolina* was an awe-inspiring sight. It carried 960 men, including the commodore, the captain of the fleet, the captain of the ship, ten lieutenants, thirty-four midshipmen, and a full complement of noncommissioned officers and seamen. Joining Rodgers as senior officers were Daniel Patterson as captain of the fleet and C. W. Morgan as captain of the ship.

After a shakedown cruise in the Chesapeake in January 1825, the *North Carolina* sailed from Hampton Roads on 27 March 1825 and arrived at Gibraltar thirty-three days later. Rodgers was annoyed to discover that the rest of the squadron was not already at Gibraltar when he arrived. As a result, he was forced to postpone his actual cruising activities until the following spring. For the next two years, Rodgers and the *North Carolina* would sail during the months when the weather permitted and would spend the winter months refitting, taking on provisions, and resting the crew. The winter of 1825–26 was spent at Port Mahon and the winter of 1826–27 at Malta and Port Mahon.

In 1825, Rodgers had requested and received permission to establish a naval depot at Port Mahon with the right to deposit duty-free food and other supplies for the squadron. Located on the island of Minorca, Port Mahon offered a strategic location and a magnificent harbor. A narrow entrance and long channel opened into a deep, sheltered harbor in which even warships could anchor safely. "Nothing can surpass the sentiment of quietude and security, which one feels riding here at anchor while the raging ocean is beating against the rocky barrier without," wrote Walter Colton. "It is like a snug seat by the side of a cheerful fire, in a cold winter's night, while the storm and sleet are driving against your secure casement." Another American wrote that Port Mahon "is one of the most beautiful and boldest harbors in the world, where the largest ships can lie in perfect safety, in the most severe gale, without danger of any description." The harbor contained a quarantine island and a hospital island. Onshore was a large lazaretto, with the navy yard close to a town of approximately fifteen thousand inhabitants.[6]

Minorca was known for its extreme poverty, but amusements were plentiful in Port Mahon, where opera, theater, music, and dancing as well as gambling and drinking could be enjoyed. The residents were accommodating and friendly. Possibly because of their poverty, the women were known for their easy virtue. In fact, one chaplain ascribed their frequent "aberrations from rectitude . . . less to want of virtue than the yearning instigations of want. Poverty . . . is a prolific source, not only of wretchedness, but of moral turpitude." In any event, American naval officers liked Port Mahon, which served as the U.S. Navy's main supply base and winter port in the Mediterranean for the next twenty years.[7]

In 1825, the squadron touched at Gibraltar, Málaga, Algeciras, and Tangiers before sailing to the Levant by way of Tunis to show the American flag there. Rodgers arrived in Smyrna on 20 July but was unable to determine the location of the Turkish fleet, the Turkish minister of marine, or the Turkish grand admiral. Rodgers then proceeded to Napoli de Romania, the capital of the Greek revolution, where he greeted Greek officials before sailing west to Gibraltar via Algiers. Joined by the frigate *Brandywine* in November, the squadron had settled in for the winter at Port Mahon by the end of the month.

In the spring of 1826, Rodgers sailed the squadron to Gibraltar and then turned east, touching at Algiers, Tunis, Milos, and Paros before arriving at Smyrna on 19 June. There, with the assistance of U.S. consul David Offley and American agent George English, Rodgers completed his diplomatic assignment. He contacted and established an amicable relationship with Capudan Pasha Husrev, the high admiral of the Turkish navy. Following their productive meeting on 6 July, the capudan visited the *North Carolina* and Rodgers returned the courtesy by visiting the Turkish flagship. The Turks and the Americans demonstrated mutual admiration for each other. The capudan expressed his appreciation for

American friendship, announced that he would convey the best regards of the commodore to the sultan, and promised that the sultan would respond with a letter. Although the sultan's response had not arrived by the time the *North Carolina* departed, the U.S. Navy's first meeting with the Grand Fleet of the Ottoman Empire was termed a success. Friendly relations had been established, gifts had been exchanged, and salutes had been fired. When Rodgers departed from the Turkish flagship, his hosts flew at the main the sultan's personal flag, an honor never before conferred on a naval officer of any other nation. Although a formal treaty would be delayed until 1830, Rodgers had made a significant contribution to the eventual agreement.[8]

In August, the *North Carolina* again turned west, arriving at Port Mahon on 10 September. In early December the flagship sailed to Toulon, Marseilles, back to Toulon, and then to Tunis. Bad weather on the return route prevented the *North Carolina* from reaching Port Mahon and eventually forced it to Malta, where it arrived with a very sick crew on 20 January 1827. Ninety smallpox cases were transferred to the hospital, where four men died. After the crew recovered, the ship returned to Port Mahon and departed for the United States two months later. As they left the Mediterranean, Rodgers and the entire squadron could take satisfaction in their efforts. The cruise had been a substantive, if unspectacular, success. Relations with Turkey had been advanced and discipline restored to the squadron. And by showing the American flag far and wide, U.S. warships had bolstered America's reputation and commerce even though piracy in the Aegean Sea remained a problem.[9]

Commodore Rodgers received and deserved primary credit for the squadron's success. Nonetheless, he had received considerable assistance from his subordinate officers. As first lieutenant on the *North Carolina*, Perry was in charge of the day-to-day operations and readiness of the flagship and its enormous crew. The duties of the "first luff," as he was called, were demanding and complicated, and required energy, knowledge, and vigilance. When William C. Nicholson asked for Perry's advice as he prepared to assume the role of first lieutenant on the *North Carolina* a decade later, Perry responded with a wealth of information: "The duties of a 1st Lieut. involve great responsibility and demand a reflecting and circumspect course of conduct." Because the Navy Department had not precisely defined the duties of a first lieutenant, they had evolved "through customs and usage" as well as being determined by the disposition and inclinations of the captain. On some ships, captains were content with the name and privileges of their station; on others, captains were "constantly meddling with the minor details, which are generally better executed without their interference." According to Perry, the navy had too many of both types. The effectiveness of the first lieutenant depended, then, on his relationship with the captain. His authority derived from the captain and was "entrusted" to him by "that confidence" which needed to exist between the commander and his executive officer. The first lieutenant must never "misuse" that confidence or permit "trifles to mar this good understanding."[10]

As the executive officer, Perry continued, the first lieutenant "is the second in command and the business officer of the Ship." He must know the ship's every detail and "every event that transpired" onboard whether it was reported to him officially or not. Accordingly, he should make himself familiar with the placement and weight of the stowage, tanks, casks, and water provisions; the armament, powder, shot, munitions, and gun equipment; and the tackles, stores, and storage of other items. Because he must maintain the ship in full readiness at all times, the first lieutenant must directly supervise all officers and midshipmen as well as take primary responsibility for the ship's paperwork.

In describing these duties, Perry devoted particular attention to two matters, rigging and discipline. Reflecting his own traditional attitudes, Perry criticized the "mistaken idea" and current fad of "neatness, lightness, and dandyism" in using as little rigging as possible to improve the visual appearance of a ship under sail. Reduced rigging stripped the masts of support and made them vulnerable to "the first good 'smart squall.'" Sufficient rigging, whatever its appearance, was critical. "The more stays you apply to lower masts, whether as shrouds or fore and aft stays, to any reasonable extent, the better are masks supported, and the slacker . . . the rigging, thereby giving the masts more play, and thus improving the sailing of a ship."[11]

On the subject of discipline, Perry echoed his mentor, John Rodgers. All regulations should be enforced in a strict and uniform manner. "No circumstance should permit the slightest deviation from [a regulation] whether to suit the convenience of one, or the indolence of another." By strict adherence, the first lieutenant would "secure the confidence and the respect of the Officers and men." He should also keep all crew members active and involved in the operation of the ship: "every individual

even to the smallest boy, should have some daily and hourly employment, involving a responsibility, however trifling, the mind thus occupied, and an interest excited with every one in the good order of the
Ship." To maintain "perfect order and discipline," Perry advised that
punishment should be neither "severe" nor "frequent." Instead, "a dignified dispassionate course of conduct and an uncompromising determination never to permit the slightest fault to pass unnoticed, will ultimately induce every one to fall into a regular routine of duty and
subordination."

Perry concluded by listing the cardinal principles to be followed by an
effective first lieutenant:

> A prompt, cheerful and unconditional obedience to all lawful orders.
> An equal determination to enforce obedience from Juniors.
> A perfect command of temper and a kind respectful deportment to all
> whether senior or junior.
> A parental interest and regard for the improvement and welfare of the
> Midshipmen; and an equal regard for the health, comfort, and
> cheerfulness of the crew.
> A patient and unevinced industry and last of all a *disinclination to
> leave the ship.*[12]

There is every indication that Perry labored to put these precepts into
action onboard the *North Carolina,* where a picture emerges of him as a
capable, energetic, and even zealous officer who won the respect, but
not the admiration or affection, of the crew. Commissioned in 1815,
Samuel Francis Du Pont was already a relatively experienced midshipman when he joined the *North Carolina* in 1824, but both Commodore
Rodgers and Lieutenant Perry left an indelible impression on him. "Our
commodore says that there has been an unjustifiable relaxation of discipline in the Navy and he is determined to revive it," wrote Du Pont in a
letter. "To do [so] he intends punishing every offender to the fullest
extent of the laws. The fact is that half the officers . . . are half frightened to death. . . . At all events, we will see discipline, order, & style carried to its highest pitch." Young Du Pont worked directly under taskmas-
ter Perry. "I have charge of one of the decks as a master's mate," wrote
Du Pont to his father, "which keeps me employed from daylight to 8 ock
[*sic*] without the least interruption. I can scarcely get my meals, and,
indeed, I am never seated at the table more than two minutes, without

hearing myself repeatedly called by the first lieutenant with some new order to execute." From this inauspicious beginning grew respect and later close friendship between Perry and Du Pont.[13]

A more critical review came from crewman James Garrison. More than a decade after the cruise, Garrison, the older brother of abolitionist William Lloyd Garrison, wrote his "confessions." One chapter, "Hell Afloat," offers a harsh description of life onboard the *North Carolina* in general and of Lieutenant Perry in particular. Garrison charged Perry with brutality, uncontrolled anger, abuse of authority, excessive profanity, and even theft from crewmen. On one occasion, Perry allegedly asked seaman David Seeley for his name. When Seeley replied, "I am a man," Perry asked, "Did you come out in this ship?" "Yes, sir," responded Seeley. Perry called him a liar, accused him of being "too ugly to be seen about decks!" and sentenced him to thirteen lashes. On another occasion, as men stood by their hammocks in silence, Garrison whispered for the man next to him to remove his foot from Garrison's toe. For this act, Perry allegedly cursed Garrison and sentenced him to thirteen lashes.[14]

While in the Aegean at Paros, Garrison was ordered to take a boat and pick up a work detachment from shore. When he arrived, however, Garrison refused to allow the men onboard because they carried anvils and bellows and were filthy, and his boat was to be kept clean at all times. For his refusal to pick up the workers, Garrison claimed, Perry attacked him verbally and used "the most obscene and blasphemous language that I ever heard flow from man's mouth." He again sentenced Garrison to thirteen lashes, stopped his grog ration for one month, and ordered him to ride the bow gun for a week. On yet another occasion, Perry allegedly punished Garrison for singing with his messmates after hammocks were down but before lights were out. That time he received thirteen lashes, lost his grog ration for a fortnight, and had permission for shore leave temporarily suspended. For urinating from a part of the ship where the fore rigging was attached to the hull, two sailors received thirteen lashes and lost their grog ration. They were also taken to the head, where the master at arms filled "their face and eyes with the execrescene [*sic*] of man, and rub[bed] it well in."[15]

Garrison also charged that before the *North Carolina* sailed from Hampton Roads for the Mediterranean, Matthew Perry and his brother Nathaniel, the ship's purser, conspired to enrich themselves at the crew's expense. First Lieutenant Perry allegedly required all hands without a pea jacket to purchase one from the purser. Since navy pursers at this time were paid less than five hundred dollars per year, they were permitted and expected to sell clothing and gear to the sailors at a personal profit. Later, when some of the men went aloft to mend sails and left their jackets below, Perry ordered the master at arms to collect all of the jackets, put them in bags, and remove them from the ship. "And that," wrote Garrison, "was the last we ever heard of our monkey jackets. Thus was poor Jack robbed of his jacket which cost him 8 dollars from the Purser."[16]

How are Garrison's allegations to be judged? Overall, he seems to be an unreliable source. A ne'er-do-well and an alcoholic, Garrison was an unhappy sailor and a troubled man. He disliked authority in general and focused on Perry as one object of his discontent. When he wrote his memoirs more than a decade after the cruise, he was a sick man with a questionable memory; he would die in 1842 in his early forties. Even William Lloyd Garrison, a strong opponent of flogging, chose not to publish his brother's account. In fact, the Garrison memoir got certain basic facts wrong. For example, Nathaniel Perry did not join the ship until January 1826, more than a year after the alleged pea jacket incident. Moreover, Garrison's most dramatic charges are not corroborated by the official record or by any contemporaries. Although Garrison described frequent floggings, the North Carolina's log recorded only thirteen floggings during its more than two-year cruise, a very small number for such a large ship. Finally, some of Garrison's charges conflict with well-documented aspects of Perry's personality. Although he became angry and no doubt used profanity from time to time, Matthew Perry was not a profane man of unrestrained temper. In fact, his trademark was composure and controlled emotions.[17]

These inconsistencies notwithstanding, there is some substance to Garrison's recollections. The North Carolina was a new ship with a new crew, which had to be forcibly molded into a disciplined state by a demanding commodore and his unyielding first lieutenant. For Garrison and for other unruly seamen, this ship must indeed have seemed to be "hell afloat." Whatever the feelings of the crew, Perry retained the full confidence of Rodgers. In October 1825, when Captain of the Fleet Daniel Patterson left to take command of the Constitution, Perry became acting commander, a position he held until the North Carolina returned to the United States. While in the Mediterranean, Perry also received his official promotion to master commandant, effective 21 March 1826, although he did not receive news of this action until later that year in Smyrna.

In addition to Perry's shipboard duties, Rodgers relied on his first lieutenant to execute other matters. In 1825 on the island of Paros, Greek slave traders offered to sell Rodgers, at forty dollars apiece, eight Turkish women they had captured. Rodgers refused and the traders left, but Rodgers dispatched Perry after them to make one final offer. After the slave traders failed to make a deal with the captain of a British ship, Perry purchased all eight women for fifty dollars. The women wanted to remain onboard and be taken to the United States, but Rodgers put them ashore at Smyrna to an uncertain fate.[18] While the *North Carolina* was at Smyrna in 1825, a large waterfront fire erupted and threatened to damage the city. Rodgers responded by providing American fire-fighting assistance in the form of a crew commanded by Perry. The U.S. naval detachment helped to extinguish the fire and returned to the ship exhausted and drenched. From his own exertion, Perry developed a rheumatism that plagued him the rest of his life.[19]

Rodgers also relied on Perry to perform routine but nevertheless important duties. When one of the Turkish ships hit a rock and suffered damage off the island of Tenedos, Rodgers dispatched Perry and an interpreter in the schooner *Porpoise* to offer assistance. Two days after the initial interview between Rodgers and Capudan Pasha Husrev, the commodore extended an additional courtesy by having Perry in the *Porpoise* convey the pasha ashore. The *Porpoise* actually towed the pasha in "his magnificent barge" to the mainland. On his arrival, he expressed to Perry "the great delight his meeting us had afforded him." Several days later, the pasha and the commodore exchanged visits. On 14 July, when the pasha visited the *North Carolina,* Rodgers sent Perry to greet him and inform him that he was about to be honored with a twenty-one-gun salute. Two days later, Rodgers included Perry in the party that visited the Turkish flagship. These activities were important experiences for Perry. In each instance he carried himself with an innate sense of solemn dignity that proved useful in dealing with Turkish officials. He also learned firsthand about the different, and to him sometimes strange, customs and behavior of the Turks. Equally important to his professional education was the opportunity for Perry to observe the conduct and actions of Commodore Rodgers. And he was very impressed by what he saw. Rodgers's delicate diplomacy with warring Turks and Greeks had protected American commerce and maintained the neutrality of the American flag while convincing the Turks of his impartiality and the Greeks of his sympathy for their cause.[20] While dealing with the sensitive Turks, Rodgers treated the pasha with the utmost respect. When the pasha visited the American warship, Rodgers made every effort "to render the compliments shewn him novel and imposing. . . . Accordingly the yards were manned, the men dressed in white, and a salute of 21 guns fired." Rodgers also allowed Turkish officials to inspect the massive American ship. After their tour, two Turkish naval officers commented that they had seen some of the finest ships of England, France, and other nations "but that they had seen none that would bear any comparison" to the *North Carolina*. Finally, after the discussions and visits had been concluded, Rodgers made sure that his squadron left an unforgettable picture in the minds of their hosts: "Each ship bore up in succession and ran down through the Turkish fleet, and, on coming abreast of the Flag of the capudan pasha, manned her rigging, the crew dressed in white, and gave him three cheers, the band at the same time playing 'Hail Columbia.'" Rodgers, who understood that the Turks would grant their goodwill only if they respected the power and peaceful intentions of the United States, was satisfied that the exhibition had left "a lasting impression not only on the mind of the capudan pasha, but on that of every other Turk who happened to witness the scene." Perry rightly admired the commodore's diplomatic balancing act, which preserved the "dignity and neutrality of the American flag" and protected American commerce in the region while antagonizing neither the Turks nor their Greek enemies, and he remembered and learned from what he had witnessed.[21]

The *North Carolina* completed its twenty-eight-month cruise when it returned to the United States in July 1827. Perry was then detached and assigned to the Boston Navy Yard. Once again, the long cruise in foreign waters had affected Perry's health. When he reported in mid-October, he complained of an "extremely severe and long protracted sickness" and said that his "health was still feeble."[22] He recovered his health during the two and one-half years he commanded the yard under Commo. Charles Morris. His multifaceted duties included recruiting new sailors, building new shore facilities, and repairing warships that came to Boston. The Perry family moved to the new officers' quarters and continued to grow. William Frederick Perry was born on 20 May 1828 and Caroline Slidell Mackenzie Perry on 23 August 1829. There were now six Perry children, not including two others who had died as infants.

By 1828, thirty-four-year-old Matthew Perry was one of the outstanding young officers in the U.S. Navy. His network of family and professional connections had helped him secure several plum assignments. He had commanded a new sloop-of-war in the West Indies Squadron and on two cruises to Africa. And he had also served under a distinguished senior officer as first lieutenant on a new ship of the line heading the prestigious Mediterranean Squadron. Perry handled each of these challenging and very different assignments impressively. He also looked the part. An acquaintance at the time noted that "he was a fine looking officer in uniform, somewhat resembling the portraits of his brother . . . but not so handsome, and had a sterner expression and was generally stern in his manner." It was this manner that created his commanding presence. "His military bearing and his countenance betokened his iron will and commanded attention, respect, and when necessary prompt obedience. Strict obedience was invariably required."[23] To his duties Perry brought his characteristic zeal, demonstrating an absolute commitment to his objective, whatever it was—instituting health precautions in tropical climates, imposing strict discipline, fighting a fire in Smyrna, transporting a Turkish capudan, or swiftly executing the order of a superior. Although he had no dramatic personal exploits to his credit, Perry had compiled impressive credentials.

Perry commanded respect from those around him, but not necessarily affection or popularity. To some he seemed overzealous and too anxious to please his superiors. Some of his fellow officers resented his naval connections. Personal rivalries and petty jealousies were quite common among naval officers at this time and produced backbiting, enduring quarrels, and even duels. Sometime after returning from the Mediterranean in 1827, Perry received word from marine Lt. L. N. Carter that Capt. C. W. Morgan, under whom Perry had served on the *North Carolina,* had called him "a damned rascal." When confronted, Morgan categorically denied the report as being "without the least foundation." When Perry demanded that Lieutenant Carter name his source, Carter refused. Perry then wrote to Secretary of the Navy Samuel Southard asking for justice from rumor and unfounded personal allegations. The secretary wrote to Carter, who again refused to divulge the source. The secretary then lectured the lieutenant on the evils of idle gossip. Perry himself asked for a court-martial to clear his name and his reputation, but it was refused. Eventually, the matter passed without staining Perry's reputation.[24]

It is indicative of Perry's stubborn nature that he pursued the matter through channels and insisted that his name be cleared. He knew, of course, that his friend, mentor, and relative Commodore Rodgers had begun another term as president of the Board of Navy Commissioners following the Mediterranean cruise. Rather than take the matter into his own hands and challenge Carter to a duel, Perry persisted in a typically direct manner through proper channels. Though personally aggrieved, his reputation under attack, Perry ruled out dueling, which solved nothing and weakened the navy in the process. When confronted with his own crisis of honor, he sought redress quietly and methodically.[25]

In the late 1820s, Perry was a rising naval figure with strong views about the future of the service. Based on personal experience, his reading, and the influence of distinguished senior officers such as Commodore Rodgers, Perry had developed firm opinions about the future of the navy. From December 1827 to February 1828, he expressed his views in a series of articles that were addressed to Senator Robert Y. Hayne, the chairman of the Senate Committee on Naval Affairs, and published in the *National Gazette* of Philadelphia. Signed "Perry," the articles reflected views he shared with Commodore Rodgers. As a navy commissioner, Rodgers wanted to strengthen the navy and counter the antinaval sentiments of many politicians in Washington, D.C. He supported the creation of a naval academy on Chesapeake Bay at Annapolis and sought the creation of additional senior ranks such as admiral. Had that rank been created during the 1820s or 1830s, Rodgers would have assuredly been one of the first American admirals.[26] Although Rodgers realized the importance of publicly defending the navy's interests, he also recognized that the president of the Board of Navy Commissioners could not be writing opinion pieces in newspapers. It is likely that he encouraged Perry to write articles embodying many of his own views and used his influence to get them published in Philadelphia. The fact that the Rodgers family had an estate at Havre de Grace, Maryland, near the head of Chesapeake Bay, made the Philadelphia newspaper a logical choice.

Perry's articles addressed a number of issues and advocated an array of improvements. "Viewing the navy as the right arm of our national defense," Perry praised recent legislation strengthening the navy but warned that a great deal remained to be done. "The plant has its roots in congenial soil," observed Perry, but "let us now turn our attention to the best means of improving and rearing it to perfection." In an era when the British and the French were strengthening their own navies, common sense dictated that the United States "at least advance step by step with them."[27]

First, Perry urged that the navy be authorized to increase the number of its officers. Estimating a deficiency of 210 commissioned and 585 warrant officers, Perry advocated the immediate promotion of one hundred existing midshipmen and the appointment of four hundred new midshipmen. This step would admittedly be expensive, but it was much preferable to recruiting foreigners or men from the merchant service. "Parsimonious patriotism may be as dangerous to the state as treason itself," warned Perry. Once appointed, the new midshipmen needed to learn by performing numerous duties, but they also needed to study "their profession, and all the sciences connected with it." For that purpose "Congress ought to establish one or more naval academies." The academy should strive to reach "that high degree of excellence" already achieved by West Point. Since both shore facilities and training vessels would be required to "combine practice with theory," the "most desirable" location was Annapolis, Maryland, situated on Chesapeake Bay, which "for width, length and safety of navigation, is unknown, it is believed, in any part of the world."

Perry also argued that an expanded system of rank was essential to provide a "better organization" for the navy. Perry, Rodgers, and other American naval officers believed that the navy lacked a sufficient number of officer ranks. Unlike European navies and the U.S. Army, the U.S. Navy had only the ranks of lieutenant, master commandant, and captain. A fourth title, commodore, applied to those who commanded a multiship station or squadron, was only an honorary designation. This disparity rankled American naval officers.[28]

The size of the navy—fifty-six commissioned ships, four hundred commissioned officers, and five hundred warrant officers—the range of its responsibilities, and the different sizes of its warships argued for the creation of more ranks, Perry said. "Experience has taught and science demonstrated [the] good effects of these classifications, in the development of skill and power; and, in regard to the naval service, both declare the necessity of the additional grades of rank." He continued, "If our ships were all of one size and equipment, and the nature of the naval service" had them always employed independently, then only the specific rank required to command a single ship would be sufficient. But even in this case, the present system still made no distinction between an officer who commanded a sloop-of-war and one who commanded a ship of the line, six times larger. The situation was tantamount to the "extensive, important, multifarious functions of Nelson at Trafalgar . . . classed in the same grade—with the command of a single sloop of war!!"[29]

Perry proposed equating the four existing titles of lieutenant, master commandant, captain, and commodore to command of the corresponding ship classes of brig, sloop, frigate, and battleships, respectively. The title commodore would be established as a formal rank with attendant power and prerogatives. In addition, the ranks of rear admiral and vice admiral would be created. The navy would have one vice admiral, two rear admirals, and six commodores, with the number of officers in the remaining ranks equal to the number of ships at the corresponding grade. Although this proposal did make sound organizational sense to naval officers, it had little hope of gaining political support beyond the navy. Many Americans believed that the navy was already too aristocratic. Additional ranks would only make it less republican in character than it already was.

In his final essay, Perry stressed the need for an apprentice system to provide an adequate supply of new recruits for the navy. The current haphazard system of providing bounties and pay advances was seriously flawed. An apprentice system would enlist and train hundreds of teenage boys while saving the navy thousands of dollars in the cost of manning its ships. More important, however, were the nonfinancial benefits. "The obvious tendency of the system to increase the number of our seamen—to supply our ships with American petty officers—and the means of speedily manning them . . . to raise a body of men peculiarly attached to the public service and eager to embrace every opportunity of manifesting their devotion" were "powerful" arguments in favor of his proposal.[30]

Perry's articles on the organization and day-to-day operations of the navy focused primarily on the recruiting and training of seamen, increasing the number of officers and improving their education, and expanding the number of senior officer ranks. Referring to the navy as the "right arm of our national defense" only in passing, the articles did not address the peacetime role of the navy; dwell on commercial, diplomatic, or strategic matters; or recommend ways to improve the condition of the common seaman. Instead, they proposed ways to strengthen and improve operational efficiency. In this sense, the articles reflected the preoccupations of both Perry and Rodgers. As an officer, Perry had to recruit and train his crews, educate younger officers, and manage the ships he commanded. As the president of the Board of Navy Commissioners, Rodgers focused on the complex but mundane details of peacetime naval administration. Whatever the merits of their arguments, the articles had no immediate political influence, and Congress did not address the changes they advocated.

After more than two and one-half years at the Boston Navy Yard, Perry happily accepted command of the sloop *Concord* in April 1830. The time with his family had been enjoyable, but his shore duties were monotonous and, at times, irksome. Recruiting new sailors, building and maintaining shore facilities, and repairing ships were mundane tasks and details. On a daily basis, Perry had to deal with new recruits, navy workmen, and civilians whose work often did not meet his own standards. The *Concord*, one of the new sloops-of-war authorized by Congress in 1825, was 127 feet long, mounted eighteen to twenty-four guns, and carried 190 officers and men. Built in Portsmouth, New Hampshire, and named after that state's capital, the *Concord* was a powerful, handsome, and fast ship.[31]

The Navy Department instructed Perry to join the Mediterranean Squadron after first conveying the new U.S. minister to Russia to his post in Kronstadt.[32] Transporting diplomats had long been one of the duties of the navy. The practice supposedly saved money and enhanced the stature of the diplomat, who arrived impressively on an American warship. Although these journeys were usually routine, naval officers disliked them because their diplomatic guests often had inflated egos and pressed their authority onboard, treating the commander of the ship as a sailing master subordinate to their diplomatic authority.

In this instance, Perry's passenger had a reputation that almost guaranteed a troublesome passage. Fifty-seven-year-old John Randolph of Roanoke was already a legend. As an old Republican, the Virginia congressman and senator found little to praise and much to condemn in contemporary politics and politicians. He was a formidable political gadfly, brilliant, irascible, and erratic. Although Randolph's high-pitched voice made him an object of some derision, he was generally respected for his sharp mind, feared for his unvarnished verbal attacks, and privately loathed for his devastating and sarcastic wit. In sum, Randolph was self-important, impulsive, nasty, and eccentric, and a very poor choice for a diplomatic post. Andrew Jackson's reasons for choosing him were a mystery. In 1826, he had fought a duel with Henry Clay, an act that some suggested had endeared Randolph to Jackson. Possibly President Jackson made the appointment to reward Randolph for his help in the 1828 election, or perhaps he merely wanted to get him far away from Washington, D.C. Randolph himself knew little of Russia and, as events would prove, had no genuine interest in furthering diplomatic relations with that nation.[33]

Perry experienced difficulty in recruiting a full crew, but the *Concord* finally sailed to Norfolk in June to pick up Randolph. Perry was delighted with his new ship in spite of a persistent leak that soaked the vessel's gunpowder. "I am happy to say that I consider her a fast sailer and an uncommonly fine vessel," he reported to Secretary of the Navy John Branch. In late June, Randolph, his entourage, and his baggage boarded. With Randolph were John Randolph Clay, secretary of the legation; three personal slaves; and a huge amount of baggage including "a lot of wine and books, and some firearms . . . bags of hams, a barrel of bread, and a coffee-pot and mill, even a caged mockingbird."[34]

The *Concord* sailed on 28 June 1830 after honoring Randolph with a thirteen-gun salute. That same day, Randolph sent a letter to President Jackson praising the *Concord* as "a fine ship" and acknowledging Perry's "politeness" in giving up "his own state Room and dressing Room to me. . . . Nothing can surpass Captain Perry's polite and kind attentions to myself and Mr. Clay." This letter, had he seen it, would have pleased Perry, who four days earlier had assured Secretary Branch that "every attention and exertion of mine shall be used to render the passage of Mr. Randolph agreeable and comfortable."[35]

The voyage itself went well, and Perry sent an enthusiastic report to Branch on the seaworthiness of the *Concord*.[36] After a smooth twenty-two-day passage, the *Concord* was nearing Portsmouth, England. At that point the problems commenced. Perry's sailing orders instructed him to touch at any port Randolph wished to visit en route to Russia. It was understood that Randolph wanted to visit London and would travel there by way of Portsmouth, so Perry sailed to the Isle of Wight and anchored off Ryde in the Solent. Although Spithead would have been a better place to anchor and disembark Randolph, the presence of a British admiral there would have required an exchange of gun salutes which the British would not exchange gun for gun. Thus, to avoid embarrassment to the flag and to his diplomatic passenger, Perry avoided Spithead. On 20 July, the American consul came out to meet Randolph and the two departed immediately in the consul's boat rather than waiting for the *Concord* to be cleared so that he could use Perry's larger gig. The trip to the shore was rough, uncomfortable, and wet. Randolph immediately complained that the site Perry had chosen for the anchorage had caused him discomfort, inconvenience, and delay. Randolph maintained that if Perry had anchored earlier at Cowes, as Randolph claimed he had preferred, rather than at Ryde, his subsequent trip ashore would have been shorter and more comfortable. Randolph's charges shocked Perry, who responded immediately with a letter of apology. "I have to express my extreme regret," wrote Perry, that "any misconception of mine of your wishes in regard to the place of anchorage . . . should have put you to the least delay or inconvenience. . . . [I]t has been my sincere wish to contribute all in my power to your comfort, expedition and convenience."[37]

This exchange was the first of several incidents that tried Perry's patience to the limit. Randolph proceeded to London and then informed Perry that he would travel on to Dover, where the *Concord* should wait for him. After a short trip to London, Perry returned to his ship, received two sheep onboard for Randolph, and sailed on 24 July for Dover. He arrived the next day and anchored in the traditional roadstead between Goodwin Sands and the coastline because the port of Dover was too shallow for the seventeen-foot draft of the *Concord*. Perry then sent Lt. William Nicholson ashore to contact Randolph at Dover, ask him when he wished to depart, and respectfully suggest that he embark at Deal, not Dover. Randolph replied that he now wanted to visit Ramsgate and would rejoin the ship there. To this change in plans Perry replied that the *Concord* would have to anchor four to six miles off Ramsgate, thus requiring a long, rough boat trip for Randolph. Instead, Perry suggested Margate, but Randolph embarked at Ramsgate anyway and reached the ship the evening of 27 July. He next ordered Perry to Yarmouth. Neither Perry nor the pilot believed it advisable for the ship to risk the narrow and difficult approach to the harbor of this fishing port. Perry so advised Randolph in writing, and the Virginian agreed. On 29 July, with the *Concord* anchored in Yarmouth Roads, Randolph again went ashore and returned later that day. Perry then sailed for Elsinore en route to Copenhagen.

After reaching Copenhagen on 4 August, Perry continued to Kronstadt, arriving on 9 August. To the enormous relief of Perry and his officers, Randolph disembarked with his entourage, his baggage, his caged mockingbird, and his sheep. On 11 August, Randolph received a thirteen-gun salute, boarded a steamboat, and headed for St. Petersburg. During the next week, Perry repaired the damaged mainmast, waited for dispatches from Randolph, and visited St. Petersburg, where he had a formal interview with Czar Nicholas. As he was preparing to sail, he received word that Randolph had decided to leave Russia and return to England on the *Concord*. By 22 August, Randolph, his entourage, and all of his baggage were back onboard. The *Concord* sailed the next day, but because of adverse winds did not reach Copenhagen until 6 September. Perry then proceeded to England, touched at Margate Roads, and sailed to Cowes where, blessedly, Randolph left the ship for the last time.

Randolph spent the winter in London and returned to the United States on another ship in 1831. In the meantime, the Jackson administration sent another envoy, James Buchanan, to St. Petersburg, where in December 1832 he concluded the treaty that Randolph had been sent to Russia to negotiate. This ridiculous and costly episode undoubtedly provided the grist for jokes among Randolph's contemporaries. But for Master Commandant Perry it was a traumatic experience. When he was assigned to transport the irascible and eccentric Virginian, Perry foresaw trouble and took great pains to make the voyage as comfortable and expeditious as possible. When difficulties erupted and Randolph became unreasonable, Perry reacted with great patience and forbearance though he must have been seething privately. Indeed, although Randolph complained of mistreatment, he never charged or even implied that Perry had treated him disrespectfully.[38]

Since Randolph had the reputation of an outspoken and vindictive politician, Perry feared retribution for the alleged mistreatment. Negative newspaper stories were a distinct possibility, and surely Randolph would complain in writing to the president, the secretary of state, the secretary of the navy, and possibly other officials as well. Thus, while Randolph was still his passenger, Perry had taken steps to protect himself. First, Perry collected his officers' accounts of the voyage. Not surprisingly, their recollections corroborated his own. Perry dispatched his own long account of the facts to Secretary Branch while the *Concord* was still en route to Russia with Randolph.[39]

"Notwithstanding my strong desire and great exertions to gratify all the wishes of the Hon. Mr. Randolph," wrote Perry, "I have unfortunately failed to do so." Explaining to Branch that Randolph had already complained to the president, Perry denied that he had disobeyed the envoy's instructions, caused Randolph any inconvenience, or delayed his voyage. Perry also wrote a candid "private" letter to his friend Commo. John Rodgers. Fortunately for Perry, Rodgers, as president of the Board of Navy Commissioners, would occupy a critical position if any controversy developed. "Mr. R. notwithstanding his well known character for strangeness and eccentricity, has actually outdone himself since he came on bd. this ship," confided Perry. "His conduct and deportment has been that of a man out of his wits and he has shown a degree of malevolence against me & others truly astounding." Perry promised to send Rodgers "all the particulars" from Elsinore, but "in the mean time, I beg you not to permit the Prest. or Mr. Branch to support that I have in any way committed myself with Mr. R. tho' I have been surrounded with snares & vexations."[40]

As it well should have, this incident came to nothing back in the United States. Randolph's bizarre behavior embellished his legend as a disagreeable eccentric but did nothing to tarnish Perry's reputation. For Perry this distressing episode underscored the value of forbearance and self-control while it highlighted the importance of shipboard authority. Although Perry commanded the ship, the minister was authorized to instruct him to stop at any port Randolph saw fit to visit en route to Russia. Randolph interpreted this limited authority to mean control of the *Concord*. In a letter to Secretary of State Martin Van Buren on 2 August 1830, Randolph complained that Perry was trying to force him "to give up the control which the Govt. had given me over the ship." Perry did not contest the issue of authority directly with Randolph, but in his 1 August letter to Branch he noted the right of a naval commander to sail and anchor his ship where he deems "most convenient, safe, and eligible."[41] Perry never forgot this incident and the potential for conflict between diplomats and commanding naval officers over shipboard authority. More than twenty years later, this painful lesson would inform his planning for a naval and diplomatic mission to Japan.

When he finally left Randolph in England for the last time in September, Perry thought he was done with the prickly Virginian, but more than a year later, Randolph complained to President Jackson about "naval discipline" and brutality aboard the *Concord*. Although he did not refer to Perry by name, Randolph objected strongly to the excessive use of flogging onboard. As the cruise began, wrote Randolph, "the men were raw; some of them landsmen; most of them fishermen (not whalemen—*they* are the best of seamen) utterly ignorant of the rigging or management of the rigging of a square rigged vessel." The frequent punishment by irons and by the lash was "so revolting" that Randolph claimed he would never again take passage on a new warship. "I always retreated to my stateroom to avoid the odious spectacle which surprised and shocked my negroe [*sic*] slaves." He claimed that in seven years he had not given out as much punishment on his own plantation among the same number of slaves as was meted out on the three-week cruise to England.[42]

When Perry learned that a newspaper article had made these allegations public, he wrote from the Mediterranean to the new secretary of the navy, Levi Woodbury, on 16 February 1832 "to contradict in the most positive manner" the charges. "So far from there having been an excess of punishment in the ship," explained Perry, "the infliction of corporal punishment has been unusually infrequent." Of the nine men confined on the cruise, five were forgiven and only four were flogged. The four men flogged were guilty of theft, sleeping on duty, drunkenness, and assault, respectively.[43]

Although the matter ended there, Randolph's complaint addressed a continuing issue of public concern. Long a staple of naval discipline, flogging was considered by many to be a brutal and inhumane practice and had attracted a growing number of public critics by 1830. In Congress, John Randolph was of like mind and drew on his experience on the *Concord* to support his position, not to attack Perry personally. However, like most naval officers, Perry employed the lash, although judiciously, he claimed. The navy's recruiting practices at that time consistently supplied raw and undisciplined crews for new ships, and the recruits needed to be quickly trained, disciplined, and molded into an efficient crew. Indeed, Perry had personally confronted this problem three times in the past decade with the *Shark, North Carolina,* and *Concord.* Fear and intimidation, the threat of physical punishment, and the specter of the "cat" or the "colt" were basic disciplinary tools. The cat-o'-nine tails consisted of nine small, hard, eighteen-inch cords of cotton or flax fastened to a wooden handle with a knot or lead pellet at the end of each cord. The colt was a single, small, hard cord about three feet long.[44] Using either a cat or a colt, the boatswain administered the prescribed lashes to the culprit in an open deck area with the entire crew assembled, thus simultaneously inflicting the prescribed punishment and setting an example for everyone onboard. Perry insisted that corporal punishment should never be administered in anger or on the spot. He emphasized this principle in his instructions to others and prided himself on his own restraint throughout his career.[45]

The *Concord* finally reached the Mediterranean from England in the fall and spent the winter of 1830–31 at Port Mahon. In April, it sailed to Cartagena, Málaga, Marseilles, Genoa, Leghorn, and Naples, and then back to Port Mahon. After spending the winter of 1831–32 at Syracuse on Sicily, the *Concord* sailed in March to Malta and then headed east to Alexandria, Egypt. Perry intended "to show the flag as a measure of intimidation" in as many ports as possible to anyone inclined "to renew their depredations on our American Commerce." At Alexandria, Perry put his *North Carolina* experience to good use as he received a formal visit and gifts from the khedive of Egypt. For that occasion, Perry had the crew dressed in white, the guns manned, and the band playing. From Alexandria, the *Concord* sailed to Nauplia in the Greek islands with a well-known passenger, the wife of Sir John Franklin, who was then assisting the Greeks in their battle for independence. After an official visit from Admiral Kanaris of the Greek navy, Perry proceeded to Smyrna, arriving on 1 May. American trade was increasing steadily in this part of the Mediterranean, as were pirate attacks on American merchant ships. After learning of one such attack on the brig *Bruce*, Perry attempted without success to apprehend the attackers. "Although we have not caught any of these scoundrels, I am convinced that our close pursuit of them will have the effect of intimidating them," he wrote to U.S. consul David Offley at Smyrna.[46]

By the end of June 1832, the *Concord* had returned to Port Mahon after visiting ten ports in eighty days. The Mediterranean station allowed Perry to combine diplomatic, scientific, and educational activities with his naval duties. He enjoyed the formal state visits from the Egyptian khedive and the Greek admiral. He also pursued his longtime interest in botany. While stationed at the Boston Navy Yard, Perry had developed a close friendship with H. S. Dearborn, president of the Massachusetts Horticultural Society. The two men subsequently corresponded, and Perry, who was elected a corresponding member of the society in 1829, collected and sent specimens of grape vines, roses, currant roots, and jasmine to Dearborn.[47]

Perry also took the education of his midshipmen seriously, maintaining a school onboard and keeping them "constantly at their studies." He had two instructors: a schoolmaster who taught English and mathematics, and a clerk who taught French, Spanish, and Italian. "My forward Cabin is appropriated as a school room," wrote Perry to a friend, and "we have regulations which require a most rigid attendance at school between the hours of 9 and ½ past 11 A.M. . . . and between 3 and 4 in the afternoon." Perry also maintained a library, which he encouraged the midshipmen to use; it contained books on the ancient classics in translation and the history of places in the Mediterranean. At every port where interesting historical monuments or ruins existed, Perry organized tours for his midshipmen and officers.[48]

When he returned to Port Mahon on 25 June, Perry learned that a diplomatic dispute was brewing. Long-standing claims against the Kingdom of the Two Sicilies (Naples) for spoliation against American commerce during the Napoleonic Wars remained unresolved. In Naples, American chargé d'affaires John Nelson reported that because Sicilian officials had repeatedly refused to negotiate seriously, the new commodore of the Mediterranean Squadron, David Patterson, was now expected to deal with the matter.[49] After serving with him on the *North Carolina*, Patterson had confidence in Perry's ability and judgment. Thus, when Patterson decided to remain at Port Mahon for health and personal reasons in July 1832, he made Perry acting commodore and commander of the frigate *Brandywine*. On 23 July, Perry sailed the *Brandywine* in company with the frigate *Constellation* into the harbor of Naples. The royal palace, overlooking the inner harbor, was within easy gun range. The presence of the two American warships caused "great uneasiness" in the city, but they sailed in August without incident and returned to Port Mahon. Perry then conveyed outgoing commodore James Biddle on the *Concord* to Marseilles.[50]

Once Biddle and his baggage were ashore, Perry returned to Naples. In the meantime, the frigate *United States* had arrived with new instructions from Washington for Nelson. He was to reopen negotiations, remain for a period of twenty days, and then request his passports and leave Naples, severing formal diplomatic relations. Perry arrived on 17 September and within days became part of a naval force that included the *Brandywine* and the sloop *John Adams,* as well as the *Concord* and *United States.* Even with this show of force, Nelson did not make immediate progress. When Nelson requested his passports on 1 October, Patterson instructed Perry to prepare to transport Nelson back to the United States on the *Concord.* But a final effort by Nelson succeeded, and the minister of foreign affairs signed a treaty for King Ferdinand II on 14 October. The agreement specified that Naples would pay the United States 2.1 million ducats (about $1.7 million) within nine years. In return, the United States promised to sign a formal commercial agreement once this treaty had been ratified.[51]

Perry learned another important lesson in diplomacy from this incident. Clearly the appearance of various warships in Naples and the incremental increase in their number in September had made a dramatic statement about the power and determination of the United States on the matter at issue. This naval display strengthened Nelson's hand and facilitated negotiations. In a dispatch to Washington, Patterson reported that it was "admitted by Mr. Nelson that the appearance of the Squadron in this bay had great effect in producing so favorable a result." Further, the naval tactic had succeeded without one shot being fired. Perry never forgot the importance of an intimidating naval presence in facilitating difficult negotiations.[52]

Once the treaty was signed, it became Perry's duty to transport Nelson and the treaty back to the United States as quickly as possible. Nelson hoped to get word of the agreement to President Jackson before his annual message to Congress in the first week of December. Unlike Perry's previous negative experience in conveying a diplomat, this one went well, although weather conditions slowed the journey home. The *Concord* did not reach Cape Cod until 4 December 1832, almost two and one-half years after it had first set sail from home. On 21 December, Perry relinquished command of the *Concord* with great pride, reporting that the ship "has visited the Dominions of nine European monarchs besides Greece & Egypt, she has anchored in and communicated with, 40 different Ports, many of them several times. She has been 345 days at sea, and sailed 2,800 miles." Moreover, discipline had been good, the health of the men had been excellent, and the crew had discontinued the use of "ardent spirits." Perry's personal financial condition, however, had suffered. In the Mediterranean, his official duties had required him to entertain and incur expenses for which he paid personally. Such expenditures were a constant problem for Perry and other officers at this time. In this instance, he was fairly reimbursed fifteen hundred dollars by Congress more than two years later.[53] In the meantime, however, Perry needed to secure a profitable assignment to remedy his financial position.

4

CAPTAIN AND
NAVAL REFORMER

*The destinies of Nations are henceforth to be in a great measure con-
trolled by a power of which steam will be the great governing element.*

CAPT. MATTHEW PERRY, 1838

he day after he relinquished command of the *Concord,*
Matthew Perry wrote to Secretary of the Navy Levi Woodbury
and asked to be considered for an open position in the New York
Navy Yard. It would be "particularly acceptable" to him, he said, "as my
family resides in New York, and as the unavoidable expense of my late
cruise render the additional emoluments appertaining to a shore station
extremely desirable & necessary." His request was granted. On 7 January
1833, he received orders to report to Commo. Charles Ridgely, the commandant of the New York Navy Yard. Perry would serve under Ridgely as
commander of the naval rendezvous, or captain of the yard, with his primary responsibility being to direct the recruiting service there.[1]

The next decade kept Perry close to home. Based in New York beginning in 1833, Perry performed routine shore duties but also became
deeply involved in efforts to reform and modernize the navy. He found
ways to improve the education of naval officers and to make the recruiting and training of crews more efficient. Envisioning an expanded peace-

time role, he urged that the navy be strengthened and pressed a reluctant naval establishment to embrace new technologies. He demonstrated the potential of steam power in warships, experimented with different propulsion techniques, proved the superiority of new explosive-shell ordnance, and lobbied for modern lighthouses. Appropriately named the "Father of the Steam Navy," Perry sought ways to organize and integrate the new specialties required by steam power into the regular navy. Neither a utopian visionary nor a social reformer, he focused simply on modernizing the navy and improving its operating efficiency and effectiveness as a fighting force. In so doing, by the early 1840s he had emerged as one of the navy's most progressive officers.

The decade after 1832 proved to be personally fulfilling as well as professionally productive for Perry. It was the longest period that he was able to live at home during his entire career. When Jane's father, John Slidell, died, he left enough money for Jane and Matthew to buy a home in a better neighborhood in New York City. They moved to 95 Spring Street in lower Manhattan west of the Bowery, a location close to the ferry to Brooklyn where the navy yard was located. These were important years for Matthew to be with his family. In January 1833, when his assignment began, the Perry family's six children ranged in age from three-year-old Caroline Slidell Perry to fifteen-year-old Sarah. The eldest son, Matthew Jr., was eleven and destined to begin a naval career in 1835 as a midshipman. Jane gave birth to yet another child, Isabella Bolton Perry, on 1 September 1834. The family enjoyed living in the city, where Jane was close to family and lifelong friends and Matthew could participate in the social and intellectual life.

Perry's primary responsibility at the navy yard was to supervise recruiting activities, but he also assisted the commandant with other duties while instituting his own initiatives to improve the education of his fellow officers. Although his own formal education was limited, Perry was eager to learn and master a wide range of subjects. He studied foreign languages and read about the classical civilizations whose ruins he had toured during his cruises in the Mediterranean. He pursued his amateur interests in shells and botany as well as other aspects of natural history. And he researched and embraced new inventions and innovations in naval engineering and technology. On all the ships he had commanded, Perry had provided both formal classes and informal learning opportunities for his junior officers and midshipmen. Along with other young officers such as Samuel Du Pont and Alexander Slidell, Perry recognized the importance of ongoing education for naval officers. He continued to support the creation of a naval academy, but he also sought ways to better inform and educate naval officers throughout their careers.[2]

The establishment of a lyceum for naval officers served this need. The Naval Lyceum was part of the American Lyceum movement, which began in 1826. Local lyceums promoted individual education and self-improvement through the study of worthwhile subjects and public issues. The lyceums offered lectures and debates, small libraries of books and pamphlets, and museum-like collections and exhibits. Unfortunately, the national movement was short-lived. After an initial burst of new lyceums centered in New England, the movement declined after the 1830s, although some chapters remained active for many years.[3]

One such organization was the U.S. Naval Lyceum. Founded in 1833, its initial purpose was to "incite the officers of the naval service to increased diligence in the pursuit of professional and general knowledge."[4] Perry's superior at the New York Navy Yard, Commo. Charles Ridgely, was the lyceum's first president even though Perry was the driving force behind its organization and activities. In the lyceum's early years, Perry served as first vice president and later as president and as a member of the executive committee, the board of curators, and the editorial board of the magazine. In 1835, two years after its founding, the Naval Lyceum was formally incorporated in order "to promote the diffusion of useful knowledge, to foster a spirit of harmony . . . and to cement the links which united us as professional brethren." The organization provided four categories of membership: two for naval officers and two for other individuals. Regular members were required to be naval officers. They paid a five-dollar initiation fee and annual dues of three dollars. The lyceum met each Tuesday morning. Members had free access to the various collections housed in the lyceum cabinet and could borrow books from the library. Any member who did not return a book after the customary two-week loan period received a rather stiff fifty-cent fine. By the end of 1835 the naval lyceum listed 166 naval officers as members as well as fifty-two corresponding and twenty-nine honorary members. The honorary members included President Andrew Jackson, the navy commissioners, various cabinet officers, and diplomatic officials as well as literary figures such as James Fenimore Cooper and Washington Irving. The corresponding members included Prince Charles Bonaparte of Italy and British naval officers Sir John Ross, Sir John Franklin, and Sir William Edward Parry.[5]

Physically housed at the Brooklyn yard in a new building to which Perry had persuaded the Navy Department to add an extra story, the lyceum's quarters included a library and reading room, a lecture hall, and a cabinet housing various collections and items. The cabinet included a bust of George Washington by Horatio Greenough; naval paintings; and exhibits of shells, minerals, and other items from nature. In 1836, the lyceum recognized numerous contributions, including, from Commo. Daniel T. Patterson, a large shell collection from the Mediterranean and, from J. L. Payson, U.S. consul at Messina, "two splendid collections of lavas, one from Mount Vesuvius, the other from Mount Etna."[6]

The society did not have a regular lecture series, but it did establish a journal, the *Naval Magazine*. Dependent on "general patronage," the magazine tried to maintain a balance between general interest and "scientific and instructive purposes," so that "while an occasional yarn may be spun for the amusement of general readers, the more important object of soliciting, and imparting useful information may still be kept strictly in view." Accordingly, the bimonthly publication carried articles on scientific matters such as astronomy, geology, and ocean currents as well as essays on naval and travel subjects. It also printed some fiction and a miscellany of intelligence on navy marriages, deaths, promotions, and command assignments. Rev. C. S. Stewart served as editor, assisted by an advisory board that included Perry and Alexander Slidell. Perry himself contributed information and wrote for the magazine on occasion, although he did not identify himself as the author of these articles. Among the other contributors were prominent civilians such as James Fenimore Cooper, writing on the navy; William C. Redfield, on ocean currents and the Gulf Stream; and Dr. Usher Parsons, on disease.[7]

Lacking adequate financial support, the *Naval Magazine* circulated for only two years in spite of the quality of its content and the enthusiasm of its backers. In that brief time, however, it served as a catalyst for a budding movement seeking to institute a number of reforms and technological advances in the navy. In addition to Perry and Slidell, such officers as Robert F. Stockton, Samuel Du Pont, and Franklin Buchanan were part of this movement. The *Naval Magazine* provided a mechanism to disseminate their views. In January 1837, Perry and Slidell summarized the ideas of these reformers in their article "Thoughts on the Navy," which argued that only an expanded navy could defend the nation and protect its commercial interests overseas. "All our misfortunes as a nation," claimed the authors, "from the day we became one, have proceeded from the want of a sufficient navy." Most recently in the claims dispute with France, the strength of the French navy and the weakness of the American navy had combined to increase the vulnerability of the United States. The country needed to learn from this example.

> With the errors and disasters of the past so glaringly before us, let us henceforth establish the safe, the economical, the honorable principle, that attacks on our commerce and assaults on our nation honor shall be prevented at the time by a prompt display of power. . . . Instead of repeating the ludicrous spectacle of the tortoise seeking refuge in its shell, let us hereafter present ourselves to contending nations in the noble and imposing attitude of some antique statue of Achilles, armed and defended at all points . . . threatening nothing, dreading nothing, yet equal to either fortune.[8]

Recognizing that the U.S. Navy had neither ships nor resources "sufficient to extend effectual protection to our commerce in every sea," the article proposed that the navy's size should be determined by the extent and value of American commerce, by the relative size of the other navies of the world, and by the necessity of being able to expand to full wartime strength within one to two years. Currently, the American navy ranked eighth in size behind Britain, France, Russia, Turkey, Holland, Sweden, and Egypt. Given the ever-increasing extent of American trade overseas, which had already exceeded that of France, this "enormous disparity" was dangerous. The goal for the United States in a time of prosperity and budget surplus should be to "follow the adventurous trader, in his path of peril, to every sea with cruisers ready to spread over him the protecting flag of the republic."[9]

For the navy to be truly efficient, the article continued, internal reforms must also be instituted. The present promotion system should be revamped and additional officer ranks created so that promotion could be earned on a systematic and meritorious basis. A class of able seamen should be created by instituting an apprentice system that required each merchant ship to carry at least one apprentice for every one hundred tons it displaced, and by maintaining one school ship for training. Moreover, better discipline and order should be established and maintained. Finally, American naval architecture, once the best in the world, had "rather retrograded" in recent years "during which we have launched some ships that would be a disgrace to the Chinese Navy." To rejuvenate it, the best models and designs for ships should be emulated so that various classes of ships would be built with uniform dimensions.[10]

Although this particular article did not address the issue of naval technology, the *Naval Magazine* carried articles on steam power, new ordnance, propellers, and other innovations. In July 1836, the article "On Steamers of War" noted the use of steam power in the British and French navies and detailed the multiple uses of steam warships: they could effectively protect a coastline or harbor, patrol in shallow water, and maneuver in formal battles. The authors also discussed the special potential for steam warships in the Caribbean and the Gulf of Mexico, where protection of America's "rich, fertile, and productive commerce" could "only be effectually rendered by a fleet of well-constructed, well-appointed, and formidable steamers."[11]

During its short life, the *Naval Magazine* espoused a traditional navalist point of view while advocating change. Its many recommendations all fit into a very conventional perspective. The editors and writers accepted the importance of large warships and wanted America's navy to be comparable in size and character with the navies of Great Britain and France. Moreover, they believed in the navy's historical roles of deterring European military attacks on the United States and defending the nation's coastline when war did occur.

The recommendations of the *Naval Magazine* were, alas, poorly timed. By the spring of 1837, America's dispute with France had been settled peacefully and a serious financial panic had erupted. The Panic of 1837 and the ensuing depression destroyed the federal government's surplus and its capacity to undertake a major naval expansion program. Moreover, naval expansion, reform, and modernization did not interest new president Martin Van Buren or his secretaries of the navy, Mahlon Dickerson and James K. Paulding, although both Dickerson and Paulding made a few reluctant concessions to steam power and new technology.

One proposed reform that did survive was an apprentice system. Recruiting seamen had long been a serious problem to which the U.S. Navy had responded in a haphazard manner. Service on a naval crew was not attractive because the pay was poor, the work backbreaking, and the conditions harsh. Training, advancement, and reward were unpredictable. Drunkenness was rife. Only the threat of flogging inculcated a tolerable level of discipline. The harsh reality of the sailor's life bore little resemblance to the romance and adventure of literature and legend. Many young men enlisted for one cruise and then left the navy as soon as their time was up.

For years the navy had used various bounties and bonuses as well as the services of waterfront landlords and "crimps" to man its warships. Crimps played the same role for recruits as pimps did for prostitutes, typically identifying, befriending, and persuading an unsuspecting or intoxicated young man to enlist. For outfitting and delivering his victim to a warship, the crimp received a four-dollar fee and all or most of the new recruit's three-month signing bonus of thirty-six dollars, which was meant to cover the recruit's debts and the cost of his outfit.[12] Not surprisingly, such practices did not supply nearly enough capable seamen, particularly native-born Americans of good character. Instead, drunks, derelicts, and ex-convicts proliferated. On some ships, foreigners outnumbered Americans. And many of the American recruits from farming communities were totally ignorant of even the rudiments of sailing an oceangoing vessel. In 1826, a British naval officer visiting New York noted "the extreme difficulty which the American[s] experience in manning their navy." Several years later, an American sailor claimed that many of the crewmen on the frigate *Brandywine* were actually convicts taken from the New York penitentiary.[13]

Perry had experienced these problems firsthand. He had served as a recruiting officer during the War of 1812 and had recruiting experience in his tours of duty at the Boston and New York navy yards. In 1821, as commander of the new schooner *Shark*, Perry had run into such difficulty recruiting the crew that he complained to the Navy Department. In 1824, he had a similar experience as first lieutenant in the *North Carolina*. Complaining of the scarcity of "good boatswains," he wrote to his commanding officer, Commo. John Rodgers, "I have not seen a man who would be considered by you competent to the *efficient* discharge of the duties of that station." When he was appointed to command the new sloop *Concord* in 1830, the recruiting problems remained unresolved.[14]

Perry had proposed a practical solution to the problem more than a decade earlier. On 5 January 1824, the twenty-nine-year-old Lieutenant

Perry took the presumptuous step of proposing an apprentice system to Secretary of the Navy Southard. In his letter, Perry noted the navy's failure to recruit able-bodied American seamen at a time when the service was growing steadily. "The remedy for all these evils is simple," wrote Perry. An apprentice system would enlist annually a certain number of boys about fourteen years old. They would not be paid a regular wage but would be clothed, fed, and trained, and might earn promotion to the level of master's mate by the time their seven-year apprenticeship ended. Moreover, by enlisting between several hundred and one thousand boys per year, the navy would simultaneously be removing a "useless class of population" from local communities. Many of these boys lacked either "honest employment or parental instruction," were susceptible "to every species of crime," and would "ultimately become a burden to society and a disgrace to themselves." As apprentices, such boys would "in a few years" become "excellent seamen" whose "habits, attachments, and inclinations" would lead them to embrace naval life with all of its "advantages and gratifications" as well as its "attendant hardships and privations."[15]

Native-born apprentices would also provide in time a ready source of naval petty and warrant officers such as boatswains and gunners, most of whom were currently foreigners. Their patriotic feelings as American citizens "would be identified with the honor and fortunes of the service." The navy would also enjoy a substantial cost savings. The cost of training and clothing, but not paying, one thousand apprentices over seven years, Perry estimated, would be $462,000. Since the navy was then spending $792,000 to pay the wages of one thousand enlisted boys, the cost reduction would be $330,000. If the spirit ration was withheld from the boys in their first two years as apprentices, an additional $43,800 would be saved, for a potential total savings of $373,800 over seven years at a time (1824) when the navy's annual budget was only $2.9 million.[16]

Although Southard took an interest in the recruiting issue and recommended the creation of an apprentice program, nothing happened at the time. Almost ten years later, from his position in the New York Navy Yard, Perry renewed his efforts with new secretary Mahlon Dickerson. Sixty-four years old and in poor health, Dickerson had received the appointment for political reasons and had no experience in naval matters. A dilatory administrator without strong convictions on naval issues, he was persuaded to support various recommendations by committed men such as Commodore Rodgers and Senator Samuel Southard, ex–secretary of the navy and now chairman of the Senate Naval Affairs Committee. Both advocated the apprentice system.[17]

In October 1834, Perry renewed his arguments for a naval apprentice system in a letter to Secretary Dickerson. The current bounty practices worked poorly, stole men from the merchant marine, would be deficient in wartime, and provided no way to train new recruits. In contrast, an apprentice system, argued Perry, would offer multiple benefits by supplying recruits for the merchant marine as well as the navy while simultaneously relieving urban communities from the burden of supporting these boys. "The Alms house, the House of Refuge, and the Orphan Asylum" in addition to the "many parents" who "would be glad to dispose of their troublesome sons in this way" would afford a ready source of apprentices. Dismissing the claim that "juvenile delinquents" would be unfit for naval service, Perry assured the secretary that these boys "generally [become] excellent seamen, the very spirit which prompted them to youthful indiscretions gives them a zest for the daring & adventurous life to which they are called in our Ships of War."[18]

Almost three months later, Perry wrote again and this time stressed the cost savings of an apprentice system. Unlike the "great expense, delay, and trouble" as well as the 25 percent failure rate of the existing system, an apprentice program would easily produce one thousand apprentices per year, five hundred of them from New York alone. Perry repeated his earlier estimate that in a seven-year period the navy would save $373,800 for every one thousand apprentices. The proposed system, then, would "mutually benefit the Navy and the Community at large."[19]

With support from President Jackson, Secretary Dickerson, Senator Southard, and others, legislation to create an apprentice system passed the Senate on three different occasions before it was finally approved by the House on 2 March 1837. President Jackson signed the bill the same day. The legislation authorized the enlistment, with parental consent, of boys between ages thirteen and eighteen to serve as apprentices until they reached age twenty-one. By this time Perry had moved on to other issues and was about to receive a new command, but his interest in and commitment to the apprentice system did not waiver. In fact, he used his new assignment as an opportunity to demonstrate its efficiency.[20]

On 9 February 1837, the navy promoted Perry to captain, the highest rank in the service. Forty-three-year-old Perry now ranked forty-third in seniority on the navy's list of fifty captains according to the Naval Register for 1837.[21] Like almost everyone else in the navy at that time, Perry was following developments in the planned U.S. Exploring Expedition that had been approved by Congress in May 1836. The project was to send a multiship naval expedition to the Pacific, where it would attempt to sail to the South Pole, visit major island groups in the South Seas, chart ocean currents and winds, and collect biological and botanical information. In 1836, Perry wrote a long letter to Lt. William L. Hudson, one of the expedition's officers, offering advice on the organization and activities of the expedition. Perry believed the primary purpose of the expedition should be to gather information and improve the navigation of the South Seas by charting their uncharted "islands, reefs and dangers" and thereby to provide "new channels of trade and new fields for the exercise of the extraordinary enterprise of our adventurous countrymen. . . . To watch over the American interests in that quarter whether by land or by sea, and to assist and protect the Whalemen." Perry also wrote a detailed letter on behalf of the Naval Lyceum in response to a request from Secretary Dickerson for recommendations on the activities of the expedition.[22]

Preparations for the expedition dragged on, however, hampered by individual jealousy, bureaucratic delay, and mismanagement by Secretary Dickerson. In November 1837, eighteen months after the project had been approved, Comdr. Thomas ap Catesby Jones resigned his command of the expedition and the search for a replacement began. Given his connections, scientific interests, and command experience, Perry was a logical choice. In December 1837, Perry wrote an "unofficial and confidential" statement on his interest in the command. He did not want to be seen as attempting to dislodge Jones, but he stood "ready to engage in that Service should the Department think proper." Yet, when the command was offered, Perry refused it for "reasons of an imperative character." The main issue was his authority as commander with regard to the civilian scientists on the expedition. When he had written to Lieutenant Hudson more than a year earlier, Perry had stressed the need for the commander to have unquestioned authority over everyone on the expedition. Perry understood that civilian scientists would be needed, but it was a matter of "first importance" that everyone onboard have a service appointment and rank of some kind to guarantee the commander complete authority "to control so many persons of different habits and pursuits and to direct their talents and energies. . . . Upon this point," Perry had advised Hudson, "will depend in a great measure the success or fail-ure of the expedition." When the department refused to guarantee such authority, Perry refused the command. In fact, the eventual commander, Lt. Charles Wilkes, would sail without supreme authority, and it would be a cause of controversy and contention on the successful but troubled expedition.[23]

A secondary factor in Perry's decision to refuse command of the U.S. Exploring Expedition was his pleasure with his new duties on the steamer *Fulton II,* which he had been ordered to command in August 1837. At this time, both England and France were building steam war-ships, but the United States lagged behind. The construction of the first steam naval vessel, the *Fulton* or *Demologos,* had started during the War of 1812 but was not completed until after the war had ended and Robert Fulton had died. Although test runs in 1815 were successful, the *Fulton* was not fitted out and ended up being used as a receiving ship until an explosion destroyed it in 1829. In the early 1820s, the navy had used a small steam galliot, the *Sea Gull,* effectively in Commo. David Porter's "mosquito fleet" in battling pirates in the shallow coastal waters of the Caribbean, but it was a small ship used for a special purpose. By the 1830s, many domestic vessels were using steam power; an estimated seven hundred steamers operated on the rivers, lakes, and harbors of the United States. In the Atlantic, steamers such as the *Great Western* made regular runs between England and the United States. Within the U.S. Navy, however, only a few naval officers such as Perry, Slidell, Franklin Buchanan, and Robert F. Stockton enthusiastically supported steam power.[24]

Resistance to the use of steam power in warships was strong among naval traditionalists everywhere but especially so in the United States. Many naval officers totally opposed it, but even those who supported the application of steam viewed it only as an auxiliary power, not as a substi-tute for sail power. Steam might be used for coastal defense batteries, to tow warships from one point to another, or to power small warships operating in shallow coastal waters close to a home base, but steam war-ships would never replace the large sailing frigates and battleships.[25]

The opposition sprang from several sources. First, the new steam machinery was crude and unreliable. Second, steam technology came with inherent drawbacks even when it did work well. The boilers burned coal rapidly and required a large supply of coal, which occupied valuable space onboard and made the ship less seaworthy. In addition, the large, cumbersome paddle wheels of early steam vessels offered an easy target for enemy guns, as did the steam boilers and machinery located on deck above the waterline. Enemy fire could easily disable the steam machinery and paddle wheels and paralyze the warship. Believing that the disadvantages of steam power simply outweighed the advantages, many naval officers saw steam-powered ships as awkward, vulnerable liabilities, not formidable war machines. The inefficiency of early steam engines also greatly reduced the effective range of steamers. While they might be useful along a coast or in a harbor, on a lake or a river, steam vessels seemed incapable of making long ocean cruises.

Third, even when the technology improved and innovations such as the screw propeller began to replace the paddle wheel, many naval officers still resisted because they found the new technology offensive, an insult to naval tradition. The new steamers were ugly, noisy, and dirty. They offered little challenge because, once under way, they could be steered against wind, currents, or tides. In contrast, sailing conventional wooden ships of the line powered only by the wind required great skill, considerable experience, and expert seamanship. The commanding officer had to understand and utilize prevailing winds and currents to the ship's advantage. Although a great amount of technical information had to be mastered, sailing a large nineteenth-century warship remained as much an art as a science. A bad tactical decision, a misjudged wind, or a mistake with the complicated sails and rigging could easily spell disaster. Dating back centuries, the traditions and heritage of the sailing warships were revered by officers in all navies. Adding to this mystique was the recent advent of large warships of majestic and formidable dimensions. Their tall masts with unfurled sails and intricate rigging made an awe-inspiring and unforgettable sight. Unless they were engaged in an actual battle, the ships were elegant and quiet. They only creaked and groaned, enabling voices onboard to be easily heard.

The first steam warships were indeed ungainly, inelegant, and noisy. The stacks and paddle wheels were strange looking and asymmetrical. They belched clouds of black smoke until anthracite coal was introduced in the mid-1840s. They demanded less skill to operate. And the skilled sailors who had climbed masts and handled rigging and sails seemed certain to be supplanted by deck-bound coal heavers, mechanics, and firemen. Anyone with a reverence for naval tradition or the romance of the sailing ship could not help but ridicule, criticize, and resist these new steam vessels.

The navy's initial response to steam power was not much different, of course, from the military's initial response to the mechanized tank, the airplane, or the submarine. Eventually steam power proved itself a superior technology that could not be arrested, no matter how much the traditionalists might long for the past. The transformation in the U.S. Navy did not occur quickly, however. In 1850, the navy listed only seven ocean-going steamers, and four of those were still under construction. During the 1840s and 1850s, the navy even continued to build some ships without auxiliary steam power and had not yet completed its first ironclad warship.[26]

In selecting Matthew Perry to command the *Fulton II*, the navy made a superb appointment. A new captain with impeccable credentials, he was part of a distinguished naval family, held traditional views about the service, and evinced a passion to excel in any assignment given him. At the same time, he was also one of the handful of American officers prepared to embrace the new technology. He believed that a steam battery could be an effective coastal defense weapon, having observed how the steam-powered *Sea Gull* had operated against pirates in ways that were impossible for a sailing vessel to imitate in the shallow waters of the Caribbean. Perry was also an individual innately fascinated by new technologies. Perry could have used his rank, his seniority, and his family connections to secure more desirable commands and lead the good life of a senior naval officer during an era of peace. He chose, instead, a challenging, less predictable path in accepting command of the new *Fulton*.

Although he had no formal training as an engineer or a scientist, Perry's intrinsic interest in technology served him well. His letters from these years are filled with information, opinions, and details about steam power and machinery, new weapons and ammunition, steam paddle wheels and screw propellers, and other mechanical innovations. His language was not that of the professional engineer, but Perry clearly studied these subjects closely and developed considerable expertise. He exchanged views with scientists and engineers. The typical energy, enterprise, and persistence he applied to his new assignment were critical to his success because at every step he encountered entrenched resistance from fellow naval officers, the Board of Navy Commissioners, and two civilian secretaries of the navy. At one point, the tenacity of Perry and other steam advocates drove Secretary Paulding to exclaim, "I am *steamed* to death," though he admitted grudgingly that he would have to yield on the steam issue. "I am willing therefore to go with the wind . . . and keep the steam enthusiasts quiet by warily administering to the humour of the times; but I will never consent to let our old ships perish, and transform our Navy into a fleet of sea monsters."[27]

Perry had carefully watched construction of the second *Fulton* for three years at the Brooklyn Navy Yard. Launched on 18 May and commissioned on 13 December 1837, the *Fulton* was an odd-looking ship. A side-wheel steamer 180 feet long, displacing 698 tons, and with a beam of almost 35 feet, the *Fulton* carried four 32-pound guns, was powered by two steam engines, generated 625 horsepower, used two side wheels, and had three masts. Perry recognized the special requirements and demands of building a steam warship. Later, when he learned that recommendations were being made to reorganize the Navy Department and shift its reliance on the Board of Navy Commissioners to a department with different administrative bureaus, Perry urged that a separate bureau be created to supervise the construction and management of steamers and their machinery.[28]

Perry's assignment was to make the *Fulton* as efficient a vessel as possible, to test its capabilities, and to demonstrate its military potential. The ship's machinery was not reliable at first, and it quickly exhausted its supply of coal. On the *Fulton*'s first cruise, on 27 December 1837, the condensing apparatus failed to work properly, compelling a return to port after the ship had gone only thirty-five miles out and back. In addition, one of the wheels was broken by the "enormous power of these engines." Nevertheless, Perry believed the trial "confirmed the favorable opinion of her power and speed. . . . [A]gainst a strong wind and tide, with no great pressure of steam, [the ship made] 18 miles in two hours and four minutes." The *Fulton* later covered twenty-eight miles in two hours on Long Island Sound. Perry realized that the *Fulton* would never be a seagoing vessel, but it could be very useful in coastal defense moving from port to port. In February 1838, Perry took the *Fulton* on a cruise along the coast. In May, he sailed the *Fulton* to Washington, D.C., and invited President Martin Van Buren, members of his cabinet, and other dignitaries aboard for an inspection. This firsthand demonstration of a ship moving against wind and current advanced the cause of steam power in the capital. In March 1839, Congress approved legislation authorizing construction of three steam warships. The high point of the *Fulton*'s early service occurred on 23 November 1838, when it bested the British steamer *Great Western* in a brief race near New York.[29]

The *Fulton* also demonstrated the potential for reintroducing an ancient naval tactic when, on 23 August, it accidentally rammed and destroyed the merchant brig *Montevideo* near Sandy Hook. Although Perry was not onboard at the time, he immediately identified the significance of the event: steam vessels with specially designed and reinforced prows might be used effectively as ramming vessels in naval combat. Perry wrote to the department suggesting that the ship be modified and a test conducted, but his proposal was ignored.[30]

In addition to testing the new steamer, Perry sought to create a new steam corps in the navy. Unlike sailing ships, steam warships required crews with engineering and mechanical skills. Since steam engineering was a new and technical area, sailors, noncommissioned officers, and commissioned officers from sailing ships could not be reassigned to steam vessels without special training. Perry was fortunate to have Charles H. Haswell as his chief engineer, but he needed to organize a whole new corps. Once granted the authority, Perry proceeded to organize the new unit. He defined the duties of the assistant engineers, firemen, and coal heavers along with their qualifications, wages, and status. He designed the uniforms of engineering officers to be identical with those of line officers except for an olive branch and paddle wheel insignia on the collars. In September 1837, the Board of Navy Commissioners concurred with Perry's detailed recommendations with only minor modifications. The department also approved Perry's recommendation for a training program for engineers and firemen and authorized him to appoint apprentice engineers.[31]

In order for service in the steam corps to be admired and sought after by young officers, engineering officers needed to enjoy equal status with regular line officers. On the *Fulton,* Perry insisted that his own line officers accept their engineering peers as equals, and he exercised great forbearance in dealing with firemen and engineers with little or no previous naval experience. He hoped thereby to make the steam service so popular and respectable that it would be attractive to those who wanted to serve in a new and interesting professional field.[32]

Perry also used this command to demonstrate the benefits of a naval apprentice system. He appointed the first apprentices in 1838 and reported to Secretary Paulding a year later that they had demonstrated "the great value of their service. Already they perform nearly all the Duties of so many men, give less trouble, and are more to be depended on." The apprentices received daily instruction in English, seamanship, "cannon, musket, sabre, and in rowing." Divided into the categories of engineer, gunnery, carpentry, and boatswain, they improved "astonishingly fast," and Perry recommended that each boy receive partial pay based on his duties. Five months later, Perry requested twenty "more boys, selected from the most intelligent of those aboard the *North Carolina*." He was so pleased that he now believed the *Fulton* crew could be composed almost exclusively of apprentices. He even protected his boys from public criticism, vehemently denying in April 1840 that his apprentices had been allowed to roam the streets of New York unsupervised.[33]

In June 1838, Secretary Paulding ordered Perry to visit England and France to gather information "in reference to Armed Steamers and other matters connected with Naval Affairs" in those countries. Perry was to collect models of steamers and information on the internal organization and discipline in the naval steamer services and to report on issues of fuel, engine operation, boiler safety, armament, protection of steam machinery from artillery shells, and the relative size of the steam naval forces of Great Britain and France.[34]

Traveling on the British steamer *Great Western*, Perry reached Bristol, England, in July. He reported to the secretary that his voyage had confirmed not only that it was "practical to navigate the ocean for limited periods with Steamers of War," but also that steam forces "will soon become a necessary arm of our naval strength, to enable the country to sustain with suitable dignity, its maritime rights." After only three weeks in England, Perry could report that dramatic naval changes were under way there. "Steam Navigation is a subject of universal interest" in England, he wrote. "[A]ll now seem to be satisfied . . . [of] the acknowledged practicality of the application of Steam to vessels of all descriptions. . . . [Permanent] change in the art of Naval War and of Navigating the High Seas must be the result." Perry further noted the practicality of arming privately owned steamships in wartime to provide a "preponderating Steamer force, and by consequence an overwhelming advantage." He had also observed the increasing popularity of steamships made entirely of iron. These were

preferable for peacetime use because they were "less costly, more buoyant
. . . [q]uite as safe," and lasted longer. It remained a matter of conjecture,
however, whether iron ships would serve well as warships.[35]

In August, Perry took an eight-day trip to France and returned to
London even more convinced of the importance of building a steam-
powered navy. On 28 August, he wrote that "the destinies of Nations are
henceforth to be in a great measure controlled by a power which steam
will be the great governing element." Four days earlier he had expressed
the same sentiment, almost to a word, to Commo. Charles Morris in
describing an England that seemed "to be touched by a steam mania."
Noting the current French naval buildup, Perry warned that it "behooves
England and America to look with jealous eyes upon the rapid aggrandizement of the French Marine."[36]

Perry's trip was not confined to investigating European steam technology. He had long acknowledged the need to improve the number and
quality of lighthouses along the Atlantic and Gulf coasts of the United
States. Back in 1822, from Key West, he had recommended the erection
of a series of lighthouses to improve safety for naval and merchant ships
alike. By the 1830s, the civilian lighthouse service of the United States
did not befit a rising maritime power; it lagged behind those of Great
Britain and France, and it was under political attack. In November 1837,
the publishers of Blunt's *Coast Pilot* accused the service of being "badly
managed." On the recommendation of the Board of Navy Commissioners, Congress in 1838 deferred construction of the 31 additional lighthouses it had already authorized.[37]

According to the board, the problem was not the number, which had
increased from 55 lighthouses and a few other navigational aids in 1820
to 210 lighthouses and twenty navigational aids in 1838. Instead, the
lighthouse system was plagued by administrative, political, and equipment problems. First, the lighthouse service resided in the unlikely
administrative location of the Treasury Department and was under the
supervision of the fifth auditor of the Treasury. Known as the general
superintendent of lights, Fifth Auditor Stephen Pleasanton managed the
service from 1820 to 1852 as an honest, competent, but unimaginative
bureaucrat. The lighthouse service had no formal connections to either
the naval or merchant sea captains who depended on it most. Various
customs collectors oversaw the individual lighthouses, and private subcontractors performed necessary maintenance. Second, the position of

lighthouse keeper tended to be a political sinecure, and many of those who held it were unqualified and undedicated. Finally, the service used antiquated and inferior equipment. American lighthouses used direct reflectors powered by weak lights that burned whale oil. In contrast, the English used a much better system of reflecting lenses, and the French, still further advanced, were installing the lenticular lenses invented by Augustin-Jean Fresnel.[38]

In 1837, Secretary Dickerson had assigned Perry, under the supervision of the Board of Navy Commissioners, to investigate and provide information in response to a congressional act on "lighthouses, buoys, beams, etc." In 1838, largely as a result of pressure from Senator John Davis, a Massachusetts Whig, Congress appropriated funds to purchase two sets of French lenticular lenses. Perry was ordered to collect information on lighthouses in Great Britain and France and to purchase the new lenses. After he arrived in England, Perry reported that both governments seemed eager to cooperate. In France, Perry met with Frederic Fresnel, the late inventor's brother, to order the lenses. Later, when he returned to the United States, Perry nominated Fresnel as a corresponding member of the Naval Lyceum, a nomination that was approved unanimously.[39]

Perry had not anticipated, however, the resistance of Fifth Auditor Pleasanton, who resented criticism from congressmen and naval officers and opposed both organizational change and technological innovation. After Perry had ordered the French lenses, and in spite of Congress's appropriation of funds for the purchase, Pleasanton refused to authorize payment. In June 1839, Perry wrote to his American friend Eugene Vail, who was then living in France, to explain why Fresnel had not been paid for the lenses.

> The truth is . . . Mr. Pleasanton has purposely thrown these difficulties in the way. He always strenuously opposed any innovation upon the existing Light House system of our country shamefully defective as it is. . . . Now he will persevere in thwarting the advocates by continuing to interpose delays and objections until the appropriations are exhausted.[40]

Nearly eighteen months later, Perry was still complaining about his bureaucratic opponent. "The truth is the old egotist has pronounced his America light house system the best in the world, and was excessively annoyed at the exposure of its utter worthlessness which I had a principal hand in doing, so he acted in such a manner . . . as to cause us to denounce him and all his plans." Perry's annoyance with the bureaucracy was well placed. Although the size of the lighthouse service budget and the number of lighthouses continued to grow in the 1840s, Fresnel lenses were not substituted for the inferior reflectors until the early 1850s, when finally, under the Fillmore administration, an independent lighthouse board was appointed and reforms began to be implemented.[41]

After Perry returned to New York in January 1839, he continued to press his superiors to adopt innovations. He wrote a stream of letters filled with information on steam boilers and machinery, blowers and smokestacks, propellers and paddle wheels, as well as with ideas on guns and ordnance. Perry served as president of the Board upon Models and Machinery, which recommended specifications for the new steamers *Mississippi* and *Missouri*. He then personally supervised construction of the *Mississippi*, which was launched in 1841. The *Mississippi* and other early oceangoing steam warships were, in fact, steam-assisted vessels that also relied on sail power. These ships could not carry enough coal to rely solely on steam power because of the inefficiency of the early steam engines. For example, the *Mississippi* burned 20 to 30 tons of coal per day at sea, but its coal bunkers could carry only 450 tons, thus limiting the range of its engines on long cruises.[42]

In 1839, Perry was appointed to supervise gunnery tests off Sandy Hook, his job being to test new guns and new shells. Warships had traditionally used smooth-bore cannon to fire solid shot, but by the late 1830s the British and French had added shell guns to their warships. The weapon of choice was the Paixhans gun. The technology for the weapon had been invented in the United States but was developed in France by Henri-Joseph Paixhans. Although exploding shells had been used previously, they had been fired by mortars or howitzers at high angles. The Paixhans gun could fire a shell at high velocity on a flat trajectory. The traditional naval long gun and carronade, which fired solid shot in a curved or pitched trajectory, had a longer range than the new gun but were less accurate and their solid shot less destructive than the new ordnance. An early advocate of the shell gun, Perry worked hard and effectively to demonstrate its value and improve its performance; he even installed the new guns on the *Fulton* to test them. He also created the first "school of practice" to improve "the science of naval gunnery."[43] At Sandy Hook, he extensively tested Paixhans guns and ordinary cannon and fired different kinds of explosive shells—solid shot, grape, and canister. The results demonstrated the superiority of the new guns; they were much more accurate than solid-shot cannons and their shells more devastating than the traditional cannon-fired solid shot. They also penetrated and did greater damage to the hull of an enemy ship than solid shot. Perry had Paixhans-type guns installed on the new steamers *Mississippi* and *Missouri*. Skeptics complained about the danger of carrying explosive shells onboard, but the new shells proved their superiority. Although an explosion killed two men on the *Fulton* in October 1841, the guns and their shells were generally safe.[44]

A far-reaching naval revolution was under way in the 1840s. Unlike many of his peers, Perry welcomed it regardless of his nostalgia for the era that was ending. Clearly, the new vessels of war were "ultimately destined to drive from the Ocean the heavy ships of the present and former times." Nevertheless, Perry lamented that the

> vocation of the sailor will be sadly changed, he will become a sort of amphibious animal, partaking in part of the salamander, & when killed in battle, instead of being genteelly knocked over by an old fashioned Cannon Ball or Splinter, he will be scalded to death or blown to atoms by the appalling effects of a hundred pound shell.[45]

While Perry was stationed in New York, he lived at home with his family. In 1839, the Perrys decided to leave the city and move up the Hudson River to Tarrytown, where they purchased 120 acres of land and built a cottage that they named "The Moorings." Here Perry improved the land by planting trees and a garden. Among his neighbors were Alexander Slidell Mackenzie, Washington Irving, James Watson Webb, and Capt. Jacob Sloop, owner of the *William A. Hart*, which often ferried Perry back and forth to the city. In March 1839, the Perry's youngest child, Anna Rodgers Perry, died shortly before her first birthday. Of Matthew and Jane's ten children, four girls and three boys still lived. Sarah was the eldest at age twenty-one, and Isabella, the youngest, was four. The eldest boy, Matthew C. Perry Jr., had joined the navy in 1835.

On 12 June 1841, Perry was appointed to command the New York Navy Station. Since he now commanded the navy yard as well as the ships assigned there, Perry also received the title of commodore. At age forty-seven, thirty-two years after joining the navy, Matthew Perry had reached the top of his profession. His first two years as commodore would be marked by professional accomplishment mixed with personal joy and disappointment. On 20 October 1841, in the commandant's quarters at the Brooklyn Navy Yard, Jane Oliver Hazard Perry, just shy of her twenty-first birthday, married John Hone, from one of the most socially prominent families in New York. His mother was a de Peyster, and he was the great-nephew of the diarist and social leader Philip Hone. The latter attended the marriage service and recorded that "the wedding was handsomely conducted, everything genteel and in good taste and the company most respectable."[46] Two months later, in December, the Perrys' eldest daughter, twenty-three-year-old Sarah Perry, wed Robert S. Rodgers at the commandant's quarters. The groom was the son of Commo. John Rodgers. Both marriages pleased the parents for personal and other reasons. The first marriage had enhanced the Perry family's social status in New York; the second had strengthened its ties to the Rodgers family.

These weddings at the commandant's quarters were memorable family celebrations for Matthew and Jane, but more commonly the commodore and his wife entertained for professional reasons at their official quarters. Visiting dignitaries in New York often toured the navy yard, where they would be entertained by the Perrys, an unanticipated burden on the family's finances. In November 1841, Perry complained to fellow officer David Conner that "this is a confounded expensive station I have, which with Princes, Lords, Governors, etc., I have my hands full, with *empty* pockets." Because the navy did not provide the commodore with a cook or a steward, Perry was forced to pay the additional expenses from his own thirty-five-hundred-dollar annual salary.[47]

Unexpectedly, 1841 was as good a year for the proponents of naval reform as it was for Perry personally. He was surprised by the "political revolution" wrought by the Whig victory in 1840. As a Democrat, Perry had been pessimistic about the political future of the nation. "I fear that such is the corruption of party tactics," wrote Perry on January 2, "[that we shall have] very few purely patriotic politicians, until the Presidential term is restricted to one period of service."[48] Only three months later, on 4 April 1841, new president William Henry Harrison died only weeks after taking office. He was replaced by Vice President John Tyler, a conservative Virginian whose administration became an unlikely friend of the U.S. Navy. Tyler's agrarian values and strong states' rights principles soon put him at odds with Whig leader Henry Clay and the majority in Congress. After he vetoed several pieces of Whig legislation, Tyler was read out of the Whig Party, and almost his entire cabinet resigned. Only Secretary of State Daniel Webster remained for the purpose of conducting diplomatic negotiations with Great Britain. Ironically, the navy fared well in this upheaval. When Harrison had taken office in 1841, Anglo-American relations were extremely tense, and war seemed possible. In response, following Harrison's death, Tyler took steps to strengthen the nation's defenses. Harrison's secretary of the navy, George Badger of North Carolina, served only six months before resigning, but he supported naval expansion as well as the adoption of steam power, modern ordnance, and other technological innovations. When Badger resigned, Tyler selected his personal friend and fellow Virginian Abel P. Upshur to be secretary after Capt. Robert F. Stockton declined the post. Like Tyler, Upshur held conservative states' rights views. He was a lawyer, a member of the Virginia Supreme Court, and a slave owner. Although without naval experience, Upshur was a capable and hardworking individual with administrative skills. He relied on his connections to reform-minded naval officers like Virginian Lt. Matthew Fontaine Maury and accepted many of their ideas to reform and modernize the navy.[49]

In the meantime, Perry had begun to press his initiatives with the new administration. In March, he wrote to Secretary Badger about the "defenseless condition of our Seaports." He thought it "equally apparent that a few hostile steamers might with almost certain impunity commit immense depredations" on the United States before it could respond. Genuinely alarmed by the prospect of war with Great Britain, Perry warned that the British navy already had a large number of war steamers and urged an immediate emergency stopgap measure. The United States should protect its seaports by purchasing four domestic steamers, arming each with Paixhans guns, and shielding each steamer by chaining two small hulls to each side of the vessel and placing bales of cotton or hay around the paddle wheel. Capable of speeds of nine or ten knots, each of these vessels could cover and protect more than fifty miles of coastline. Each steam vessel "alone would certainly be able to cope with the largest ships in smooth water." To illustrate his recommendation, Perry attached a careful drawing of the strange-looking vessel he proposed.[50]

Perry worked with men such as William Redfield to build support for stronger coastal defenses. Between March and July 1841, as war loomed, they corresponded on the issue, with Redfield publishing his letters to Perry as articles in the *New York Journal of Commerce* in July and August and then in the *Journal of the Franklin Institute* in Philadelphia. Concentrating on coastal defense, not deep-water naval tactics, Redfield stressed the importance of steam power.[51] He argued that heavily fortified steam batteries, battleships, and frigates were relatively useless for coastal defense. Instead, the navy should build a large number of "light and firmly built steam vessels of good length and the least possible draft." Placed under the command of "young and enterprising officers," these speedy steamers could defend the coastline and harbors of the United States while attacking enemy commerce. "These capacious steamers, armed with the most formidable guns and borne through the water with a speed which has never been equaled," Redfield predicted, would have "an important influence upon the events of war." In fact, some of Redfield's views conflicted with those of Perry, who believed that light steamers did not have nearly the potential that Redfield ascribed to them. However, Perry very much agreed with Redfield's basic arguments that steam power and modern ordnance were essential elements of national defense. In fact, a decade later, in 1851, Perry would write a paper on coastal defense that incorporated some of Redfield's ideas.[52] The Navy Department did not put any emergency defense measures into place, however, because the war scare with England had passed. With a change of government in Great Britain, Anglo-American tension began to diminish during the fall of 1841. In August 1842, negotiations between Secretary of State Daniel Webster and English special minister Alexander Baring, Lord Ashburton, produced a treaty that resolved outstanding issues and removed the threat of war.

In the meantime, Secretary Upshur had moved aggressively to reform and reshape the navy. One of Upshur's initial steps was to order an investigation of abuses at the New York Navy Yard resulting from political patronage practices there. For many years, two local congressmen had selected the yard's master craftsmen, who in turn controlled the appointment of mechanics and laborers. At Upshur's instigation, Perry investigated these abuses and instituted changes that reduced idleness and insubordination and thereby reduced construction costs by almost one-half. These actions proved only a temporary solution, however, and within several years the patronage practices reemerged.[53]

At the same time that he attacked operational abuses, Upshur rapidly absorbed the ideas of reform-minded officers such as Maury, Stockton, Perry, Du Pont, and Mackenzie. In December 1841, less than two months after becoming secretary, Upshur in his first annual report to Congress proposed sweeping changes. One year later, his second annual report outlined additional reforms. Upshur was the first navy secretary to recommend that the navy's peacetime role be redefined to correspond to the nation's dramatic overseas commercial growth. Accordingly, the navy needed to be converted from a small, defensive force of sailing ships into a large, modern steam navy that could actively protect the nation's far-flung commercial interests. Upshur recommended that the size of the navy be enlarged significantly, that more of its existing ships be placed on active duty overseas, and that its budget be increased. He also supported the construction of steam warships and experimentation with shell guns, screw propellers, and iron hulls. During his term, construction of a new steam battery, the *Stevens Battery*, was started; a screw-driven steam warship, the *Princeton*, was launched; and the first iron-hulled warship, the *Michigan*, was constructed.

Upshur's proposals included major organizational changes as well. He won approval from Congress to replace the outmoded Board of Navy Commissioners with a system of separate naval bureaus. He improved the organization of the officer ranks, fought for better naval training, supported creation of a naval academy, and assisted the apprentice system. Given the political upheaval of the time and the fact that he served a president who was without a party, Upshur was surprisingly effective. Fortunate to have friend and fellow Virginian Henry A. Wise to work with as chairman of the House Ways and Means Committee and the Naval Affairs Committee, Upshur capitalized on his advantage. Although Congress modified some of his proposals, reduced his budget requests, and rejected his proposals to create a naval academy and the rank of admiral, Upshur had reshaped the navy by the time he resigned in July 1843 to become Tyler's secretary of state. Tragically, he was killed in an explosion on the *Princeton* during a demonstration near Washington on 28 February 1844.

After years of political and bureaucratic opposition, Perry was gratified to see the navy embrace and implement many of the initiatives and ideas he had championed. But an ugly scandal with personal overtones soon diminished his sense of accomplishment. During the summer of 1842, Perry supervised the construction and outfitting of the brig *Somers,* the sister ship of the *Bainbridge.* Both of the 103-foot-long ships were built primarily for speed, being sleek in appearance and heavily sparred. The *Somers* carried more than one hundred officers and men and mounted ten guns. Once the *Somers* was completed, Perry had it assigned as an experimental school ship under his direct supervision. This was an ideal chance, Perry thought, to demonstrate the success of the apprentice system. Perry organized the cruise and selected the officers carefully. To command, he chose his close friend and brother-in-law, Master Commandant Alexander Slidell Mackenzie, with whom Perry had collaborated on naval reform issues for the past decade. Perry respected and trusted Mackenzie. Also onboard were twenty-one-year-old Lt. Matthew C. Perry Jr.; seventeen-year-old Oliver H. Perry as captain's clerk; Acting Midn. Henry Rodgers, the youngest son of Commo. John Rodgers; and Adrien Deslonde of Louisiana, a brother of Mrs. John Slidell who had actually lived in the Perry household for a time as a youngster.[54]

The *Somers* carried a very young crew of twenty-two enlisted men and seventy-four apprentices; 70 percent were under age nineteen, and only four individuals were over thirty. With 121 men onboard, the ship was badly overcrowded. Although Perry had selected the officers with care, the crew included troublesome individuals in key positions. Both Samuel Cromwell, the senior petty officer, and Elisha Small, the captain of the main top, had checkered histories and had served previously on slave ships. Also aboard was nineteen-year-old Midn. Philip Spencer, the son of New York lawyer John Spencer, who was then the secretary of war in Tyler's cabinet. By the time he came onboard the *Somers,* Philip Spencer had compiled a tarnished naval record. On previous assignments he had struck another midshipman, become obnoxiously drunk, and even plotted mutiny. Secretary Upshur reluctantly forgave Spencer and assigned him to the *Somers,* but Mackenzie refused to accept the appointment. Commodore Perry overruled his brother-in-law and forced him to accept Spencer. It turned out to be a major mistake. Possibly Perry believed that a training cruise might correct Spencer's bad habits, but it is more likely that Perry wanted to avoid offending the secretary of war and the secretary of the navy. In any event, everyone on the ship would come to regret Perry's decision.

After a shakedown cruise, the *Somers* departed in gala fashion from New York on 13 September 1842 bound for the west coast of Africa, where it was to deliver dispatches to the *Vandalia* and then return directly to the United States. The outward cruise went smoothly, and the *Somers* reached Monrovia on 10 November. Learning there that the *Vandalia* had already departed for home, Mackenzie made the logical decision to follow. On the return trip, the mood and circumstances onboard changed dramatically. On 26 November, the purser's steward reported that he had been approached the day before by Midshipman Spencer about joining a planned mutiny that was being masterminded by Spencer, Cromwell, and Small. When the plot was reported to him, Commander Mackenzie confronted and questioned Spencer and then had him arrested, handcuffed, and chained to the bulwarks near the wheel. A search of Spencer's sea chest revealed written evidence for the plot. Based on an incident that occurred the following day, Mackenzie also ordered the arrests of Cromwell, Small, and several other suspects.[55]

On 30 November, Mackenzie ordered his four wardroom officers and three senior midshipmen to investigate further, deliberate, and make appropriate recommendations. Both Matthew C. Perry Jr. and Henry Rodgers were members of the investigating group. On 1 December, they reported that Spencer, Cromwell, and Small were guilty of the intention to commit mutiny and should be sentenced to death in the interest of the safety of the ship and the men onboard. Mackenzie agreed and proceeded at once with the three executions. Although he was acting without a formal trial or court-martial, Mackenzie felt compelled to move immediately to discourage others onboard the small ship from trying to free the three men and renew the mutiny. Mackenzie did not even wait until the *Somers* reached St. Thomas on 5 December to carry out the sentences. After touching there, the ship proceeded without incident to New York, anchoring on 14 December.

When word of the events on the *Somers* became known, controversy erupted. Secretary of War Spencer pressed to have Mackenzie charged with murder and tried by a civilian jury. Instead, over the next three and one-half months the navy held a court of inquiry at the navy yard in Brooklyn conducted by three commodores with Charles Stewart presiding. After interviewing each of the *Somers*'s officers, twenty-two enlisted men, and sixty-eight of the seventy-four apprentices, the court exonerated Mackenzie on 20 January 1843 and declared the executions to be fully justified.

At Mackenzie's own request, Secretary Upshur then ordered a formal court-martial. Mackenzie was to be tried on five counts: murder, oppression, illegal punishment, cruelty, and conduct unbecoming an officer. The court-martial convened on 2 February 1843 and met for two months. Composed of thirteen senior officers, the court rendered its verdict on 1 April: the first three charges were "not proven" and the other two were dismissed. Upshur subsequently confirmed the decision to acquit Mackenzie.

The inquiry and court-martial created sensational publicity and national controversy as newspapers covered the proceedings. Mackenzie had defenders and detractors. Capt. Robert F. Stockton refused to serve on the court because he claimed to have already made up his mind on Mackenzie's guilt. Boston merchant captain William Sturgis, a veteran of the China trade, criticized Mackenzie's handling of the affair. At the same time, other merchants in Boston and New York signed petitions of support. Charles Sumner wrote a laudatory account in the *North American Review*. Richard Henry Dana, the author of *Two Years before the Mast*, wrote a series of letters defending Mackenzie.[56]

In Brooklyn, Matthew Perry lived painfully through every day of the proceedings. He attended regularly, offered advice, and discussed the proceedings frequently with Mackenzie and other friends. This was a trying time for Perry. His insistence on appointing Spencer to the ship's crew was to some extent responsible for the events that followed. And not only was his brother-in-law the central figure in the controversy but also two of his own sons and two other relatives were directly involved. And not least, the episode dealt a serious blow to the apprentice system, a reform Perry had long championed. Whether one concluded that Mackenzie was guilty or innocent, the experimental apprentice cruise had been an undeniable failure. As a result, it would be two decades before another such experiment was attempted. As he watched the legal proceedings in early 1843, a dejected Perry contemplated taking a command that would remove him from the sensationalism of the *Somers* affair.

~⭒5⭒~

COMMODORE OF THE
AFRICAN SQUADRON

While the United States sincerely desire the suppression of the slave
trade, and design to exert their power in good faith for the accomplish-
ment of that object, they do not regard the success of their efforts as
their paramount interest nor as their paramount duty.

INSTRUCTIONS OF SECRETARY OF THE NAVY
ABEL UPSHUR TO COMMO. MATTHEW PERRY, 1843

On 5 June 1843, Commo. Matthew C. Perry unfurled his broad blue pendant on the *Saratoga*, received an eleven-gun salute, and set sail from Sandy Hook for the coast of West Africa. As the newly appointed commander of the African Squadron, Perry would command a force of four ships: the twenty-two-gun sloop *Saratoga*, the razeed thirty-six-gun sloop *Macedonian*, the sixteen-gun *Decatur*, and the brig *Porpoise*. Perry's senior officers—Capt. Josiah Tattnall, Capt. Isaac Mayo, and Comdr. Joel Abbot—were capable and seasoned naval commanders. This would be Perry's fourth cruise to the coast of West Africa and his first as the commander of a multiship squadron on a foreign station. Although the Africa station was not an easy billet, Perry was looking forward to visiting the African American colonial settlements in Liberia that he had helped to establish. And it was a good time for Perry personally to be out of the United States.

The previous five months had been wrenching for him. In New York, he had witnessed firsthand the highly publicized dispute and proceedings wrought by the *Somers* affair. The negative publicity, personal pain, and public attacks on his relatives had wounded him deeply. Then, there was the question of his own professional future. The *Somers* affair had tainted Perry by association and produced unneeded controversy for the Tyler administration, already in severe disarray. Fortunately, Perry retained the confidence of Secretary Upshur, who continued in his position until July 1843. In the midst of the proceedings on the *Somers* affair, Perry was ordered on 20 February 1843 to prepare to assume command of the African Squadron. Perry readily accepted but then quickly became suspicious that "bad persons" in Washington were conspiring to deprive him of his new command. Perry held firm to his course, however, and determined to proceed as he had been ordered to do. "Although the path before me is one filled with difficulties, it is not my nature to fly from them," he wrote angrily to his friend Capt. Beverly Kennon, the new chief of the Bureau of Construction, Equipment, and Repair. A "Captain in this Navy has rights as well as others." Perry's suspicions and fears did not materialize, and he received his formal sailing instructions shortly thereafter in a letter dated 30 March 1843.[1]

With the acquittal of Mackenzie on 1 April, Perry was free to devote his full energies to his new duties. Knowing that the hazards of naval operations in African waters required particularly careful preparation, he devoted great attention not only to cleansing, fitting out, and provisioning his ships but also to such unusual details as the fabric and specifications of the crew's uniforms.[2] To C. W. Goldsborough, chief of the Bureau of Supplies and Accounts, Perry provided an itemized list of the food, clothes, and many other provisions he would need as well as specific details on the fabric, length, and even the color of the jackets and trousers. The correct uniform, he believed, would help protect his men from disease in the African climate. To shield men in rain and at night, the jackets needed to be "made longer than the ordinary mustering jacket," and the jackets and trousers should be made of "blue boiled flannel." When he learned that only red flannel was available, Perry reluctantly acquiesced, even though the appearance "on wash days of so many colors on the clothes line must be disagreeable to the eye of an officer who may be at all particular. Blue and white should in my opinion be the only colors allowed."[3]

No detail was too small; Perry even surveyed his sailors regarding the coffee and cocoa served on his warships. He discovered that both beverages were tainted by being brewed in the same boilers used to cook other items, that the water used to brew the coffee was not sufficiently hot, and that the cocoa was not heated long enough. In response, Perry issued specific cooking instructions and installed new boilers dedicated exclusively to brewing coffee and cocoa. In filling out his crews, Perry sought to "ship a few black seamen" for the *Saratoga* because he believed this "class of men" could better endure the hot climate. Perry also requested approval to hire native krumen once he had reached Africa. Based on his previous experience there, Perry knew that krumen were invaluable "as messengers, interpreters, boatmen, and in communicating with the shore, in bringing off provisions, wood, water, etc. and in all these services of exposure to the climate, which the constitution of the white man is incapable of bearing."[4]

Perry's thoroughness and careful attention to detail were founded on his recognition that the comfort, health, and success of his squadron depended on meticulous planning; service on the Africa station was arduous, uncomfortable, and unhealthy. Assuredly, the climate had not improved in the intervening two decades since his last stay. The entire cruising area was within 15 degrees of the equator, an environment of unrelenting and oppressive tropical heat. The rainy season, which lasted from May to November, produced torrential downpours and violent squalls that exacerbated the general misery of the tropical conditions. Moreover, disease, particularly African fever, posed an ever-present threat. "There is no fun I can assure you in being on this Africa station," wrote Comdr. Joel Abbot to a friend. "[S]corching sun & drenching rains with numerous privations & disagreeable circumstances is one's common lot to say nothing of a good chance of dying."[5]

Under these harsh conditions Perry confronted a sensitive and challenging assignment with potentially serious diplomatic ramifications. The creation of the African Squadron had resulted directly from the 1842 Webster-Ashburton Treaty, which resolved a number of troublesome issues between the United States and Great Britain, such as the long-standing northeastern border dispute. The treaty also provided for American naval assistance to suppress the African slave trade. After banning the importation of slaves in 1808, the United States in 1820 had declared Americans' involvement in the international slave trade to be piracy punishable by death. But the U.S. government seldom enforced the legislation. American warships infrequently visited the west coast of Africa, and

American slavers were rarely apprehended. American courts failed to deal effectively with the few cases they did receive. In contrast, Great Britain policed the illegal trade assiduously. British naval vessels patrolled African waters, and the British government pressed other European governments either to send their own police ships or to permit British naval vessels to search ships flying their colors. The Quintuple Treaty of 1839 permitted the British navy to stop suspected slave vessels from Spain, Portugal, Russia, Prussia, and Austria. The French did not sign the treaty, but by the early 1840s their warships patrolled the coast as well.

These developments placed the United States in an increasingly untenable position as slavers flying the American flag increased their trade with impunity in the early 1840s. In addition to its own failure to patrol West African waters, the United States still refused to permit British naval officers to board merchant vessels flying the American flag even though they might be suspected slavers. Memories of the War of 1812 and British violations of American neutral rights remained fresh and sensitive. As an alternative to British searches of American vessels, article 8 of the Webster-Ashburton Treaty stipulated that the United States would maintain a squadron of at least eighty guns on the coast and that its warships would engage in joint cruising activities with British warships there. Presumably, American and British warships acting in concert could stop and board virtually any ship along the coast while ensuring that American ships would be searched only by American naval vessels. As later events would prove, this agreement solved an outstanding diplomatic issue but did not suppress the slave trade.[6]

Secretary Upshur's instructions to Perry outlined the way in which the United States intended to implement article 8 of the treaty. The instructions were carefully drafted and reviewed, and were even scrutinized by Congressman John Quincy Adams, one of the administration's sharpest critics in Congress. Now a vocal antislavery activist, the Massachusetts Whig was no friend of Upshur, but Adams read and approved the secretary of the navy's instructions in 1843. In fact, Upshur's language provided a model that would be used almost verbatim in the instructions to commanders of the African Squadron for the next fifteen years.

Dated 30 March 1843, Upshur's instructions defined the squadron's mission as "the protection of American commerce in that quarter, and the suppression of the slave trade, so far as the same may be carried on by American citizens, or under the American flag." The protection of

America's "rapidly increasing" and "more and more valuable" commerce was the squadron's primary mission; the suppression of the slave trade was a secondary and limited one. "The rights of our citizens engaged in lawful commerce are under the protection of our flag," wrote Upshur, "and it is the chief purpose, as well as the chief duty of our naval power, to see that these rights are not improperly abridged or invaded."[7]

With respect to the slave trade, Upshur explained to Perry that the United States was "sincerely desirous wholly to suppress this iniquitous traffic." In light of the recent treaty, Upshur observed that "I need not, I am sure, impress upon you the importance of strictly observing this stipulation, and of preserving inviolate the pledged faith of your country upon this point." Nevertheless, Upshur reminded Perry that the United States did not acknowledge "a right in any other nation to visit and detain the vessels of American citizens engaged in commerce." Even for suspected slavers, "there is no right of visitation or search so far as American vessels are concerned, except by our own vessels-of-war." Any vessel flying the American flag "claims to be American, and therefore may be rightfully boarded and examined by an American cruiser. . . . But this privilege does not extend to cruisers of any other nation."[8]

At the same time, Upshur emphasized the desirability of cooperation with British warships. British and American vessels acting in concert would allow each "to assert the rights and prevent the abuse of the flag of its own country. In this way all just grounds of difference of collision will be removed, while this harmonious co-operation . . . will go far to insure . . . the suppression of the slave trade." Upshur concluded by repeating that while Americans sincerely desired to suppress the slave trade and would "exert their power in good faith" to accomplish that objective, they did not regard such efforts "as their paramount interest nor as their paramount duty. They are not prepared to sacrifice to it any of their rights as an independent nation." Therefore, Perry was simultaneously to exercise "the utmost vigilance" to detect slave traders and to take "great care" not to interrupt "the lawful pursuits" of citizens of the United States or any other country. These instructions sent the unmistakable message to Perry that protecting the rights of U.S. "citizens engaged in lawful commerce" was the "chief purpose, as well as the chief duty of [U.S.] naval power."[9]

The secretary defined the "cruising ground" of the squadron as extending from the Canary Islands to the Bight of Biafra and from the coast of West Africa to 30 degrees west longitude. Perry was to keep his vessels as active as possible by having them cruise down the coast, return to Port Praia for rest and supplies, and then run down the coast again. In this way, the squadron could cover the entire cruising ground and thereby most effectively protect American commerce.[10]

The administration's instructions and its decision to maintain only a small squadron in Africa demonstrated the secondary importance it attached to the slave trade. Both President John Tyler and Secretary Upshur were slaveholding Virginians with strong proslavery attitudes. The election of 1844 would replace Tyler with another southern slaveholder, Democrat James K. Polk of Tennessee. The administrative turnover in Washington would also affect the navy's performance in Africa. During Perry's twenty-three-month cruise, five different men, three of them southerners, served as secretary of the navy. The requisite political pressure to eliminate the illegal participation of Americans in the international slave trade, however, was not forthcoming from any of them.

By the early 1840s, relatively few slaves from the illegal trade reached the United States; most ended up in Brazil, Cuba, or elsewhere in the West Indies. Southerners were not concerned about eradicating the trade, and even abolitionists and antislavery activists found more important issues to address as they pushed slowly ahead with their cause. In Congress, for example, the "gag rule," which prevented any discussion of slavery by automatically tabling all antislavery petitions, was not rescinded until December 1844. In the slave states, and even in the nation's capital, slaves could be legally bought, sold, and traded.[11]

The example of John Quincy Adams is particularly instructive. By 1843, the seventy-six-year-old former president and secretary of state was a veteran congressman. "Old Man Eloquent," as Adams's admirers called him, was also a determined antislavery activist who advocated his cause in Congress along with a small band of other antislavery representatives. Adams despised President Tyler and criticized his proslavery administration. Several years earlier, he had also criticized Perry's association with Virginia Democrat Andrew Stevenson, who at the time was the U.S. minister to Great Britain. Nevertheless, Adams read and approved the administration's instructions to Perry for the African Squadron. Given the administration's equivocation on the slave trade, Adams might well have excoriated the instructions as another example of Tyler's treachery. But his suspicion of British intentions outweighed his determination to end the African slave trade. Before the War of 1812, Adams had defended American neutral rights against British impressment and other violations. After the war, as secretary of state, he continued to maintain that any visitation of an American merchant vessel by British naval officers represented a serious threat to American sovereignty and freedom. Now, Adams suspected that the British were using their antislavery policies merely to advance their own selfish, anti-American purposes. For example, he believed that the British sought to undermine American influence in Texas by promoting abolition in the Lone Star Republic. "I distrust the sincerity of the present British Administration in the anti-slavery cause," Adams confided to his diary on 31 May 1843, just days before Perry departed for Africa.[12]

The cruise to Africa was uneventful. The *Saratoga* anchored at Cape Mesurado on 1 August 1843 after touching at Tenerife and the Cape Verde Islands. To preserve the health of his men, Perry had ordered that comprehensive health regulations be enforced on each ship. In a report written in 1839, Perry had made recommendations that the Navy Department now used as standard advice to commanders bound for West Africa. Perry believed that the "deleterious effects of the climate" could be mitigated by the "strict and somewhat painful observance of numerous precautionary measures." Although the climate was completely "unsuitable to the constitution of the White Man," there was "comparatively little risk" of disease if the precautions were enforced rigorously. The decks of each ship must be cleaned and washed daily. The lower decks must be fumigated regularly by burning "fuge balls" consisting of gunpowder, camphor, niter (potassium nitrate), and chopped rope mixed with vinegar. Officers and crewmen must never be allowed to sleep onshore. They must "wear flannel constantly next to their bodies," shower or bathe twice each week, eat a "wholesome" diet of "fresh and ripe fruits" and vegetables, and practice temperance in their consumption of alcohol. Moreover, constant vigilance by officers was necessary because "sailors are like children who require to be constantly watched." On 21 June, Perry had issued the health regulations in the form of a general order and emphasized to Capt. Josiah Tattnall of the *Saratoga* that "too much care and vigilance cannot be devoted to the preservation of the health of the Officers and men."[13]

Not everyone took the regulations seriously. Shortly after the *Saratoga* left Port Praia in July for the coast, Purser Horatio Bridge reported that the health regulations had caused "considerable mirth and some growling" as old hands scoffed at the absurdity of some of Perry's rules. For example, every man had to wear a jacket and trousers at night and "flannel next to his person" while stoves burned on the berth deck to dry the air. "It is a curious fact," Bridge noted, "that, in March last, at Portsmouth N.H., with the thermometer at zero, we were deprived of stoves the moment the powder came on board; while now in the month of July, on the coast of Africa, sweltering at eighty degrees of Fahrenheit, the fires are lighted throughout the ship."[14]

When Perry arrived in West Africa in 1843, African American settlements stretched along the Grain, or Pepper, Coast of West Africa from the mouth of the Saint Paul River in a southeasterly direction for 250 miles to Cape Palmas. The relatively straight coastline, which lacked natural harbors, was intersected by a number of rivers and streams, none of which was navigable for more than a few miles. The coastal waters were treacherous and characterized by strong undertows, beach ridges, and heavy, sweeping surfs that built sandbars in the river estuaries and lagoons along the shore. The weather along the coast was oppressively hot and humid with frequent and violent storms. The average annual rainfall exceeded one hundred inches.[15]

The political situation Perry confronted was far more complicated than it had been two decades earlier. New colonies had been established to the south of the Monrovia. Marshall was founded by the Virginia Colonization Society in 1827 at the junction of the Junk and Farmington Rivers. Bassa Cove was established by colonization groups from New York and Pennsylvania in 1835 at the mouth of the Saint John River, and Greenville by the Mississippi Colonization Society in 1838 at the mouth of the Sinoe River. By 1843, these settlements had merged into the colony of Liberia, which then had a total population of 2,390 settlers, not including native Africans or Africans recaptured from the slave trade. Monrovia, population 912, was the largest settlement. The various settlements boasted sixteen schools, twenty-three churches, dozens of buildings, and 3,482 acres under cultivation. In the two-year period ending 30 September 1843, the settlements had imported $157,829 in goods while exporting $80,148 in African goods. The governor of Liberia, Joseph H. Roberts, was a free black from Virginia who proved to be a strong and capable leader. The colony of Maryland in Africa, located at Cape Palmas, remained separate from Liberia. Founded in

1827 by the Maryland Colonization Society, by the early 1840s Maryland had a population of 424 at its main settlement of Harper and several smaller communities nearby. John Russwurm, a former editor from New York, served as its governor.[16]

Various tribal African groups, including the Bassa, Dru, and Grebo, inhabited the coast from Cape Mesurado to Cape Palmas. Constant tension and sporadic conflict had characterized relations between the American settlements and the tribal Africans from the very beginning. The founders of the settlements had expected the colonies to develop primarily as farming communities, but most of the settlers preferred commerce to agriculture. Tensions flared when the tribal Africans along the coast objected to the newcomers' interference in their trading activities. First the colonists attempted to stop slave trading, and then they sought to prevent tribal Africans from trading legitimate goods with foreigners with whom they had conducted commerce long before the arrival of the settlers. In addition, the concept of private property was foreign to the Africans, who did not understand how they could be permanently excluded from their communal lands after these had been purchased by the African American settlers. Most likely, the African chiefs, who did not have the authority to dispose of communal land, did not realize the permanent consequences of agreeing to sell land to agents of the colonization societies.[17] During the 1820s and 1830s, wars had periodically erupted and the tribal Africans had refused to trade with the new settlements or to provide them with food. When the new African Squadron arrived in 1843, the level of tension and distrust remained high.

A strong and sympathetic supporter of the African American settlements, Perry took pride in the small role he had played in identifying the site for Monrovia in 1821. Now, two decades later, the progress of the settlements pleased him. Like "Ancient Israel," Liberia possessed the "germs of a powerful empire to be populated by a class of people hitherto unknown at least to modern times, *a community of religious and educated Blacks destined to enjoy all the advantages of civilization and to exercise its full share of political influence in the family of nations.*"[18] Perry saw the African settlements as a model for repatriating slaves. If only private or government funds had been available to compensate slave owners, many slaves "now groveling in the United States" would have achieved "competency and . . . the independent exercise of their own thoughts, opinions and movements" in Liberia. Nevertheless, Perry did not personally subscribe to antislavery political opinions or believe in abolition. "I am not one of those who cry out against the institution of domestic slavery because I myself have no property in slaves," wrote Perry. It was no more just, he felt, to call on a slaveholder to relinquish his slaves without adequate compensation than it was to ask someone who owned a cargo of sugar or coffee "to throw it into the Sea . . . for reason only that it might have been grown or prepared for market by the labor of slaves." The worldwide abolition of slavery in his lifetime seemed "altogether chimerical," but Perry believed that a "gradual design of universal disenthalment" was under way. The process would take generations, but colonization societies in the United States and their African American communities in Africa could accelerate the process. Perry also believed that the African American communities played a critical role in eradicating the slave trade. As the colonies grew, they would bring republican government, Christianity, and civilization to the region, and their American-style commerce and agriculture would supplant the slave trade.[19]

Although he reported on his arrival that all was quiet, Perry soon heard about the colonists' various grievances. He wanted to help them, but first he asked for instructions from Washington. His overt support of the colonies would strengthen their position in Africa, but he intended to "hold out merely the *appearance* of a recognition of these settlements" and to "be careful not" to deviate in any way "from the settled policy of the nation, not to hold colonies abroad." Although Perry did not receive a response until the following year, his actions in the meantime were based on personal views closely approximating those of the administration.[20]

While he was awaiting instructions, Perry decided that initially he would "proceed by strategem and with great caution." He also elected to keep his squadron together because "an imposing force before the Towns and along the neighboring Coast" would create a "greater awe of the American flag." Since his top priority was to protect American commerce, Perry gathered information on the condition of American trade and investigated several recent attacks on American merchant ships. At Sino, near Cape Palmas, Kru people had murdered the cook and mate of the schooner *Edward Burley.* At Setta Kru, natives had assaulted Capt. J. R. Brown of the brig *Atalanta.* And east of Cape Palmas at Little Berebee, natives had plundered the schooner *Mary Carver* and murdered the captain and crew. Before leaving the United States, Perry had dispatched a confidential letter to the governor of the colony at Cape Palmas asking for information on the *Mary Carver* massacre, including the "names of the ring leaders in the massacre," their places of residence, and details about their movements.[21]

Once the rainy season ended in November, he planned to hold conferences, or "palavers," as they were known locally, at a number of tribal African settlements along the coast. Perry wanted to teach "a lesson to these and other natives on the Coast" responsible for the outrages on American trade by punishing the culprits who had destroyed the *Mary Carver*, but he did not want to compromise "the safety of the missionaries in the neighborhood." Counseling caution to his officers, he reminded them that "nothing will be lost by delay, and . . . an unsuccessful attempt to punish these people would make matters worse." The reality of the situation validated Perry's judiciousness, for he soon realized that most disputes between American merchant captains and natives were not one-sided. He reported to Washington that "in most cases, the natives have been as much sinned against as sinning . . . if accompanied by a recital of the facts . . . some apology might be allowed to the natives. The Government at home hears but one side of the story." Typically, foreign masters of trading vessels mistreated the natives, sometimes even attacking them or delivering them to their enemies. The "exasperated" natives then wreaked "their vengeance on the first vessel, or boat, or white man, whether innocent or guilty that may chance to fall in their way."[22]

In late November, Perry moved his squadron from one village to another along the southeastern coast from Sino above Cape Palmas to Grand Berebee beyond the cape. The four American warships created the dramatic impression of formidable American military power that Perry sought. On 29 November, for a palaver at the village of Sino with a contingent of local African chiefs and notables, Perry loaded dozens of armed sailors and marines into thirteen boats, formed them into a battle line, and moved toward shore with "flags flying and muskets glittering." On the beach, the officers and men formed a line as a band played. After Commodore Perry and Governor Roberts stepped ashore, the whole contingent marched to the Methodist church, which served as the palaver house. In full dress, with his blue coat, gold epaulets, and sword, Perry underscored his rank and authority with his serious, formal manner.[23]

The immediate issue at Sino was the killing of two crew members of the *Edward Burley*. After listening patiently to different versions of the incident, Perry and his senior officers accepted the African version and determined that the natives had acted in self-defense. Perry also signed treaties with chieftains from the villages of Sino and Blue Barra that pledged the inhabitants to assist the local American settlers at Cape Palmas and to deal peacefully with all American merchant vessels. At this palaver, Perry tacitly permitted his presence and that of his naval force to be used cleverly by Governor Roberts to advance the interests of his colony. Giving the natives the distinct impression that "everything was done at the instance and under the authority" of the American navy, the governor enlisted some local Africans to convince their African neighbors to forfeit a territorial claim on the coast. One of the observers, Purser Horatio Bridge, admired the governor's shrewdness but observed that "in some points, the affair had remarkably the aspect of a forcible acquisition of territory by the colonists."[24]

Farther down the coast at Setta Kru, the American squadron repeated its landing and held another palaver on 4 December. The issue here was the assault on Captain Brown of the *Atalanta*. The conciliatory local leaders claimed that the individual responsible for the assault had fled the area. Since this was the first offense, Perry and his officers agreed to accept a formal apology from the local chief and to receive reparations consisting of ten bullocks, four sheep, and five goats. The chief also agreed that Captain Brown would be allowed to trade at Setta Kru in the future without paying the mandatory local duty known as the "chief's dash."

The squadron next sailed on to Cape Palmas, where Governor John Russwurm had requested Perry's assistance in resolving difficulties with the Grebo tribe, which refused to trade with the American settlement. As a precaution, Perry sent a detachment of troops ashore to guard against an attack that seemed imminent.[25] A large and impressive group of twenty-four chiefs and potentates led by King Freeman met the commodore and the governor. Among the Africans was a chief who bore a striking resemblance to Henry Clay "both in face and figure." When "not speaking, [he] moved constantly about the palaver house, as is Mr. Clay's habit in the senate-chamber." The interpreter, Yellow Will, was elaborately dressed for the occasion "in a crimson mantle of silk damask, poncho-shaped, and trimmed with broad gold lace." The assembly discussed the trade boycott that the Grebo had imposed on the African American colonists. The boycott had been decreed after the chiefs had doubled the price of rice and other products and the colonists had refused to pay. The chiefs had retaliated by imposing the boycott and refusing to permit merchant vessels to trade with the colonists. At the palaver, the chiefs agreed to restore trade, but they would not agree to Governor Russwurm's proposal that King Freeman cede land on Cape Palmas in return for an equivalent parcel elsewhere. On this issue, Perry took no position and remained silent.[26]

Perry assumed an unusual role at Cape Palmas by intervening personally to save a native from execution. The man was being forced to drink a poisonous concoction from sassy-wood to determine his guilt or innocence in an unspecified crime. If he died, he would be presumed guilty, but if he lived through the ordeal, he would probably be beaten to death. Perry intervened, took the man from his executioners, had medical treatment administered, and saved his life.

The squadron next proceeded from Cape Palmas to the village of Little Berebee to deal with the *Mary Carver* massacre. Perry's investigation had confirmed that the attack was unprovoked and had not resulted from a legitimate dispute between the traders and the villagers or from any previous injury or assault on Little Berebee. The question, then, was not whether or not to retaliate, but how to do so, especially because it was not clear who had been involved, where they resided, or even whether they were still in the vicinity. At a council on 9 December that included Governors Roberts and Russwurm, Perry, Captains Mayo and Tattnall, and Commanders Abbot and Stellwagen, the group decided to hold accountable the four towns located nearest the outrage. Each village would be expected to arrest, try, and execute the guilty perpetrators and provide an indemnity. Since the estimated value of the *Mary Carver* and its cargo was twelve thousand dollars, each village would be assessed a fine of three thousand dollars and presented with a mortgage that could be paid off in six years by providing free labor to the settlement at Cape Palmas. However, the initial plan was modified so that no action would be taken against a village unless its guilt could be proven. In effect, this meant that only one village would be targeted because of "the guilt of Little Berebee there could be no doubt."[27]

Before reaching Little Berebee, the squadron stopped at nearby Rock Boukir, where Perry held a palaver on the morning of 11 December. The king, who was described as "an old man of sinister aspect," strenuously denied any involvement with the *Mary Carver* but agreed to assist in a "grand palaver" at Little Berebee and to take passage on the *Macedonian*. The meeting at Rock Boukir was tense and formal, but its aftermath awarded a few moments of comic relief. Rough surf forced the Americans into canoes so they could be taken two at a time to the squadron's boats, which were waiting beyond the pounding surf. To the delight of hundreds of onlookers, some of the canoes capsized, throwing the Americans in their dress uniforms into the surf. Some Americans were even forced to swim to the boats. Everyone "reached the vessels in safety, but few with dry jackets."[28]

Once the officers and crews had reassembled, the squadron set sail for Little Berebee. On the morning of 13 December, thirteen boats loaded with sailors, marines, officers, and dignitaries landed. The Americans disembarked and marched to the palaver house, a temporary shed that Perry had had erected fifty yards outside the town gate for the occasion. King Ben Krako, an immense, powerful man whose presence seemed to intimidate those around him, approached with several chiefs. Once the meeting began, Perry confronted Krako directly and insisted that he provide an explanation for the *Mary Carver* incident. His interpreter explained that the American captain, John Farwell, had killed two natives and had been executed by the late elder King Krako as a legitimate punishment for the crime. Perry, who thought this explanation preposterous, reacted angrily. He stepped forward and demanded the truth from Krako. At this moment, a shot was fired. In the brawl that ensued, the interpreter ran and was shot by Captain Tattnall. Krako himself attempted to flee, but Perry grabbed his robe. When it pulled free, Perry grabbed Krako's loincloth and was dragged fifteen or twenty yards through the sand. A sailor knocked Krako down with a musket stock, but the king grabbed another musket and fought with Captain Mayo before the American officer finally stabbed the chief with his pistol bayonet. Gunfire and general chaos prevailed. The villagers were driven away and then fled from their village. Once the melee had ended, Perry ordered the burning of Little Berebee and then commanded the Americans onshore to return to their ships. An estimated eight Africans had been killed, and the gravely wounded Krako, who was treated on the *Macedonian,* died the next morning.[29]

Although no Americans had been killed in the brawl, Perry was furious. After meeting with his senior officers, he ordered further retribution on several nearby villages. On 15 December, an American contingent landed and marched along the beach for ten to twelve miles. In response to sporadic gunfire, the Americans blasted back with their muskets and set fire to four more villages. The native dwellings, built of highly combustible wickerwork and topped by thatched roofs, burned quickly to the ground, leaving several hundred people homeless. The landing party, with only three men wounded, spent the day in high spirits. "Man is perhaps never happier than when his native destructiveness can be freely exercised, and with the benevolent complacency of performing a good action," observed Purser Bridge, a member of the shore party. "It unites the charms of sin and virtue. Thus, in all probability, few of us had ever spent a day of higher enjoyment than this, with a musket in one hand and a torch in the other, devastating what had hitherto been the homes of a people."[30]

The squadron then sailed on to the villages of Grand Berebee, Rock Boukir, Grand Tabou, and Bassa, where Perry signed agreements with local chieftains before sailing back toward Monrovia. En route, Perry landed again at Sino, where he informed the local chiefs that he had learned that they were not observing their agreements and warned them to honor their compacts. This coastal odyssey ended the first phase of the squadron's work. By the end of December 1843, Perry was on his way to the Cape Verde Islands and then on to Madeira.[31]

In accordance with his instructions, Perry had acted to protect American commerce in Africa by investigating and avenging unjustified attacks on it. By keeping his squadron together and touching at numerous spots, he maximized American visibility and forced respect for the American flag and the power of the United States. Although he wanted to befriend local African chiefs and create goodwill, he intended to awe and intimidate them rather than negotiate with them as respected equals. Friendship would come only if the African chiefs honored American naval power. At the same time, Perry believed that he treated the Africans fairly. "In all my intercourse with the Kings and Chiefs, I have endeavored to convince them that the American Government will be as ready to recognize wrongs by American traders as it will be to chastise the Africans." Accordingly, Perry urged Captain Brown of the *Atalanta*, who had been assaulted at Setta Kru, to be just and kind in all of his dealings with the Africans because while the American government was "determined to protect the rights of its citizens in the pursuit of their lawful business . . . [it would] be equally mindful on the other hand to notice and redress any and every aggression committed by Americans on the Natives."[32]

Perry's agreements with local chiefs were intended to create a peaceful atmosphere for legitimate American traders. In that spirit, he sought only an apology for the assault on Brown and determined that the murder of two crew members on the *Edward Burley* was justified as self-defense. Perry retaliated aggressively for the *Mary Carver* massacre, but only after he had determined the facts. In his palavers before he reached Little Berebee, Perry learned that other local chiefs considered King Krako and his followers violent and malicious. This knowledge strengthened Perry's hand because attacking Krako would not automatically condemn the Americans in the region. Perry no doubt hoped to force Krako to admit his crime and to punish him accordingly, but once shots were fired and chaos ruled, Perry believed that his hand had been forced.

At that point, however, Perry overreacted. He could defend the destruction of the village where the fight had taken place, but there was no strong justification for the burning of four additional villages along a ten-mile stretch of coast three days later. In ordering this action, Perry had demonstrated his contempt for the local Africans and destroyed the homes of many innocent people. Perry's quarrel was with King Krako, not the local people. By putting Krako's followers to flight and killing Krako himself, Perry had made his point more than adequately. Nevertheless, Perry decided that additional action was necessary to send an unmistakable message to the people of Little Berebee. Other Americans concurred. "The degree of retribution meted out by no means exceeded what the original outrage demanded; and the mode of it was sanctioned by the customs of the African people," observed Purser Bridge. "An example was of preemptory necessity; and the American vessels trading on this coast will long experience a good effect from this day's battle and destruction. The story will be remembered in the black man's traditions, and will have its due weight in many a palaver."[33]

Perry reported to the secretary of the navy that the actual bloodshed was "unpremeditated and accidental," and emphasized that the natives had fired the first shot. But he acknowledged that the killing of King Krako seemed "providential," as he was the chief culprit. Perry also emphasized that the "known firmness and treachery of most of the African tribes made it a measure of necessary prudence to land with a considerable armed force." Most important, Perry said, "this act of retributive justice upon the Little Bereby Tribe" would "furnish an impressive lesson to the people of other towns suspected of piratical acts." At the same time, Perry believed that his "friendly demonstrations" to the tribes not implicated in the massacre would "go far to show them that the American Government greatly prefers a pacific interchange with all nations."[34]

In his dealings with the African American colonists, Perry was friendly but restrained. He entertained the leaders, praised them, and encouraged them. Perry invited Governors Roberts and Russwurm onboard his ships and included them in his councils. In turn, these leaders offered advice and thereby influenced the specific issues to be addressed at Perry's palavers. The participation of Roberts and Russwurm at the palavers implied strongly that the American settlers enjoyed the full support of the U.S. Navy. Although Perry did not endorse or press their issues, his presence made it easier for Roberts and Russwurm to do so. Perry also provided direct military assistance on occasion. In November 1843, he dispatched muskets and ammunition requested by Governor Roberts. Perry also dispatched the *Decatur* to protect missionaries at Caraway and at Cape Palmas. On another occasion, Perry refused a request for his forces to join an assault on the Grebo tribe. In a later interview with Governor Russwurm, Perry explained that he was not authorized to interfere in the affairs of the settlements unless "the lives and property of American citizens were endangered." Perry "would cheerfully render any assistance to the settlers in the *defence* against the natives, but could not take any *offensive* measures."[35]

At the beginning of 1844, Perry was pleased with the African Squadron's performance thus far. "The Squadron has been actively employed for the last three months," he reported on 15 January, "holding Palavers (conferences) with several of the Native Tribes, chastising some and conciliating others. . . . [E]verything has transpired in a satisfactory manner, and with much less loss of life than I had anticipated from the nature of the service." Moreover, his ships had been very active along the coast and within four months would visit "every known Trade or Slave Mart from Cape Verde to the Equator. . . . Indeed, I have never known vessels of War kept in more constant motion." In the previous seventy-three days, the *Macedonian* had been anchored fifty times.[36]

Perry's positive evaluation was confirmed by Governors Roberts and Russwurm, who expressed their appreciation, as did two local missionaries,

Revs. James Kelly and J. Hazelhurst. Privately, Comdr. Joel Abbot spoke of Perry in glowing terms. "Our Noble Commodore has so far done what I consider just and right," wrote Abbot to a friend.

> I think the admirable manner in which Commo. Perry has punished past crime & aggression on this coast, and caused a settlement of difficulties between the Colonists & Natives, in a way calculated to extend & protect our trade & at the same time foster a friendly feeling on the part of the Natives to our Country, is worthy of all praise.[37]

Its first five months in African waters was the African Squadron's most rewarding period. The next year would be markedly different in several ways. By January, for example, the crews' health had begun to deteriorate and would continue to degenerate throughout 1844. With declining health would come increasing tension, shorter tempers, and eroding discipline. And unlike 1843, 1844 would offer no incidents like Little Berebee to raise the squadron's spirits.

While Perry's own health suffered as well, other problems distressed him more: meeting the supply needs of the squadron; suppressing the slave trade; and watching the squadron's health, discipline, and morale decline despite his best efforts. Obtaining supplies proved to be a constant problem because the geography and climate of West Africa prevented the creation of a permanent naval supply depot. The coast did not offer a deep, protected harbor, and southerly winds produced huge swells and crashing surf that made it difficult to move men and supplies between the ships and settlements along the shore. The tropical climate made it impossible to store and preserve most foods. And the constant danger of African fever precluded American naval officers and men from residing onshore to manage and garrison a depot. Nor was there a healthy place along the coast for the officers and men to relax and recuperate.

The closest reasonable liberty port was Port Praia in the Cape Verde Islands, but it was more than a thousand miles northwest of Liberia. And although it had a good harbor, fresh water, and some available fresh foods, Port Praia presented problems as both a naval depot and a port of refuge. Supplies had to be carried through the prevailing high surf at shoulder height "at great expense and risk of damage." To American naval officers, the population seemed "intemperate, dissolute, and vile," and their Portuguese rulers "but little better." Moreover, Port Praia lacked the amusements and attractions that appealed to naval personnel.[38]

In fact, Perry had little choice but to use Port Praia, as other American naval commanders would after him, as the main supply depot for his ships, but he would have much preferred the Canary Islands or Madeira. Both had delightful climates and a civilized atmosphere. To his friend and neighbor from Tarrytown, Washington Irving, who was then the U.S. envoy to Madrid, Perry extolled the benefits of Grand Canary and urged Irving to visit this Spanish possession personally. The women, he said, "though without much education," were "remarkable for beauty and grace and affability," and the wine was superb. In fact, Perry had twelve bottles of the finest Madeira reserved for Irving. Unfortunately, the Canary Islands and Madeira lay a thousand miles or more beyond Port Praia.[39]

In the absence of a reasonable naval depot close to the squadron's cruising waters, Perry believed the only feasible alternative was supply ships. He requested that at least one and preferably two be assigned to the squadron. Ever penurious, the Navy Department preferred a permanent supply depot on the Liberian coast. Perry agreed to "experiment" with a depot at Monrovia, but he remained skeptical, noting that "nothing of any importance can be obtained on the coast" at a reasonable cost. In addition, the struggling African American colonies could not begin to provide the nine hundred pounds of fresh meat required each day by the squadron.[40]

As the supply situation worsened in 1844, Perry sent repeated pleas and then, in May, attempted to bring the issue to a head. The assignment of a "permanent Store and Hospital vessel capable of being moved from one place to another," he wrote the department, "can alone obviate these difficulties." In contrast, a permanent shore depot on the African coast would "paralyze" the squadron.

> My long acquaintance with the coast allows me to reply without hesitation that there is no part of the West Coast of Africa from the Gambia to the Equator where the annual mortality of unacclimated white persons living on shore would not be . . . from 30 to 50 percent. . . . Hence there is no place for a Naval Depot.[41]

Persist as he might, however, the supply problem remained unresolved for the duration of the cruise.

In early 1844, Perry turned seriously to his secondary mission: controlling the involvement of Americans in the African slave trade.

Unfortunately, his own information and the reports he had received since arriving in Africa led him to underestimate such involvement. When he first arrived in Monrovia in August 1843, he had reported that "so far as I can learn through diligent inquiry, the American flag has not been used, within two years, on this part of the coast, by any vessel engaged in the slave trade." From Cape Palmas, Governor Russwurm had written to Perry to confirm this appraisal. Perry's palavers along the coast further corroborated his own assessment. At the end of December 1843, Perry had reported to Secretary David Henshaw: "With all my observation and inquiry, I have not seen or heard of a single instance of an American citizen being engaged in the slave trade." In fact, these statements were correct as they pertained to the Liberian coast, which had never been a center of the slave trade, but they certainly did not describe the extent of Americans' involvement in the illegal slave trade north of Monrovia or east of Cape Palmas. American ships, American sailors, American masters, and American money were all very much implicated there.[42]

Despite his sanguine view at the beginning of 1844, Perry expanded his efforts by dividing his four-ship squadron in accordance with his instructions from the Navy Department. While two ships sailed to Port Praia or Madeira or Tenerife for supplies and rest, the other two would cruise south from Cape Verde to Cape Palmas and then east along the Gold and Slave Coasts to the Bight of Biafra. In deploying his small squadron, Perry sought "constant motion" to patrol an extensive coastline and show the flag, a practice traditionally employed by the navy on other stations to protect American commerce. He instructed Captain Tattnall of the *Saratoga,* for example, to touch at as many "Slave and Trading marts as time and circumstance will authorize" and to collect as much information as possible about the "trade of the coast, legal and otherwise . . . [with] a special eye to the protection and advancement of American trade." Constant cruising not only extended U.S. influence, Perry argued, but also helped maintain morale and prevent disease among the officers and men. Over the next year, the four ships of the African Squadron collectively covered thousands of miles of African coastline.[43]

Although impressive when described on paper, these efforts failed in execution. At the time Perry was in Africa in the 1840s, the international slave trade was thriving. Some nations had outlawed the trade, but others had not; and some nations aggressively policed the trade while others ignored it altogether. Slavers were a tough, savvy, and clever lot who took advantage of the patchwork of laws and enforcement and frequently outsmarted and eluded their pursuers. In the Middle East, Brazil, Cuba, and some of the West Indies, the trade continued to be legal. Demand for new slaves remained high there, and prices for slaves rose. In spite of its many uncertainties and risks, the slave trade produced impressive profits. One experienced slaver estimated that he could make a 100 percent profit on a successful voyage. Perry estimated that speculators made a handsome profit even if only one of three ships succeeded.

By the 1840s, most slave ships were sleek, fast vessels that could both outrun many warships on the high seas and operate in the shallow inlets and rivers where they loaded their human cargoes. Legal restrictions hampered efforts to stop them. U.S. Navy vessels could not board and seize American ships involved in "legitimate" trade even if these ships were carrying irons, handcuffs, casks of water, bags of rice, and other telltale tools of the slave trade. Moreover, U.S. warships were authorized to stop and board only ships flying American colors. Unscrupulous slavers took advantage of the situation in various ways. For example, an American slaver would carry a legitimate cargo to Africa, clear the American patrol en route, and reach the coast, then "sell" or transfer the ship's papers to a ship master from another nation. The slaver would then take on a slave cargo and run the patrol flying a Spanish, Portuguese, French, or Brazilian flag. If the ship was stopped by Americans, it carried evidence that it had been sold and now carried the papers of another nation.[44]

Once identified, suspected slavers on the inward voyage to Africa had to be shadowed and watched until they had actually taken on human cargo at one or more of the barracoons along the coast. Often a cat-and-mouse game commenced as the slave captains monitored their pursuers, waited as long as necessary for the right moment to board their cargo, and then eluded the patrols with a run to open water. To combat these tactics, Perry realized that he needed small, shallow-draft steam vessels that could disguise themselves and operate close to the river and slave marts where slavers loaded their human cargoes. He had requested such vessels before he left for Africa, but the Navy Department never assigned them to his squadron.[45]

The African Squadron's failure to stop the participation of Americans in the slave trade is not surprising. In addition to underestimating the extent of American involvement, Perry had only four sailing ships to patrol twenty-five hundred miles of African coastline. Local conditions also required that he frequently send his ships for supplies and recuperation at far-flung Port Praia, Madeira, and Tenerife, reducing significantly the time each ship spent actually on patrol. For example, Perry's flagship, the *Macedonian,* was absent from the African coast from January to May in 1844.

Moreover, the tactic of "constant cruising" prescribed by the Navy Department might protect legitimate American trade, but it did not work well in suppressing the slave trade. Slavers simply bided their time, waited for the warships to cruise on, and then went about their illegal business. Perry would have apprehended more slavers had he stationed his ships close to the mouth of the Gallinas River between Liberia and Sierra Leone and at other sites between Cape Palmas and the Equator known to be slave marts. In spite of its constant activity, the squadron apprehended only one slave ship, the *Uncas,* and the outcome of that capture was disappointing. The slaves were freed, but a court in the United States acquitted the captain of any crime. The increased American naval visibility may have discouraged other American slavers, but there is no hard evidence to support such a claim; indeed, American involvement seems to have increased throughout the 1840s.

Complicating Perry's policing of the slave trade was the Webster-Ashburton Treaty, which required the cooperation of American and British naval forces on the west coast of Africa. In his instructions to Perry, Secretary Upshur emphasized that he considered "it highly desirable" for American and British ships to cruise together but left the operational details to Perry's judgment.[46] Perry's personal antipathy for Great Britain made it difficult for him to follow the secretary's orders at all. His father had fought and been imprisoned by the British in the American Revolution, and Matthew and three of his brothers had fought the British in the War of 1812. Quite naturally, he thought of the British as enemies in war and adversaries in peace.

Perry also blamed the British for the weakness of legitimate American commerce in West Africa. The British monopolized at least two-thirds of the trade there, while Americans, "contrary to the results of their usual enterprise, enjoy but a share of what is left." British traders enjoyed the protection of the Royal Navy; American traders did not and suffered not only from the hostility of tribal Africans but also from the "not infrequent insolence of the British naval officer." But Perry was confident that the American navy could "put an effectual stop to interference with the rights of the American flag" by British naval officers. And once placed on an equal footing with the commerce of other nations, American trade would expand the African market for American goods and help check the illegal traffic in slaves.[47]

Given his attitude, close cooperation between Perry and his British counterparts was unlikely. Instead, Perry pursued a dual approach that technically followed Upshur's instructions: he extended every courtesy to the British while insisting that they not infringe on any American rights. On 21 July 1843, before he had even reached Africa, Perry issued a general order emphasizing such courtesy. He also wrote to Adm. John Foote, the senior British naval officer on the African coast, assuring him that the American naval force would join in "mutual acts of courtesy and friendship" with the British squadron. He accepted Foote's suggestion that ships of the two squadrons adopt private signals to communicate with one another.[48] At the same time, Perry reminded his commanders:

> Under no circumstances are you to permit, without resistance, *to the extent of your means*, any foreign vessel of war of whatever force or *nation*, in the exercise of any assumed *right* of *search* or *visitation*, to board in your presence (you having first forbidden it) any vessel having the American flag displayed.

In unequivocal language, Perry instructed his commanders to use force, if necessary, to prevent such a violation.[49]

The changing political situation in the United States further troubled Perry's relations with his British counterparts in 1844. Upshur had left the Navy Department the previous July, and Perry suspected that the Tyler administration included individuals who would use any mistake or misstep to embarrass him now that Upshur was no longer there to protect him. For example, he wrote to his brother-in-law John Slidell in March that he had not yet received additional instructions to deal with the latest assertion of the British that they could visit, if not search, any suspect vessel flying American colors on the West African coast. "Now it seems to me that I have taken the true American stand, and so far have fairly carried it out, but, as I am no favorite with the Present administration. . . . I do not much expect any approbationary communications from the Department on the subject." His suspicions notwithstanding, Perry need not have worried about criticism of his conduct. In June, new secretary of the navy John Mason assured the commodore that his actions had afforded the president the "highest gratifications" and that he fully approved of Perry's actions as commander of the squadron.[50]

Perry met British complaints of previous American inactivity in African waters by keeping his ships in "constant motion," but he retained his misgivings about joint cruising operations. In May 1844, when Admiral Foote formally recommended a joint cruising plan, Perry thanked him but emphasized that the small size of his squadron limited any joint operations with the much larger British force. Perry also wrote immediately to the secretary of the navy for instructions. Foote had suggested that American and British vessels not only cruise together but also assist each other "in bringing to and visiting vessels of whatever flag suspected of being engaged in the slave trade." Instinctively suspicious, Perry feared that the British would expect him to abjure his strict policy that only U.S. Navy ships could stop and board American vessels. To his own commanders, Perry counseled vigilance, and he warned Comdr. Thomas Craven of the *Porpoise* to be "careful not to waive any right of the American flag."[51]

In his dealings with Foote, Perry was aggressive but amicable. In March 1844, when he learned that a British naval officer had boarded and acted insolently toward the master of the American barque *Roderick Dhu,* Perry requested an immediate explanation from Foote. Receiving a response that exonerated the British officer, Perry reasserted the American position that ships flying the American flag were not to be boarded by foreign warships for any reason. In the same exchange, Foote alleged that the United States was permitting its merchant vessels to trade legitimate cargoes with slavers who then traded their cargo items for slaves. Foote also asserted that since Perry's arrival, several American ships had been sold along the coast, had taken on cargoes of slaves, and then had escaped. Avoiding a direct response, Perry charged that British citizens were more guilty than Americans of trading legitimate items to slavers who then exchanged them for slaves; but he refused to let these exchanges escalate into open controversy. Both the American and British governments, he wrote, sought earnestly "to suppress a traffic obnoxious to religion and humanity" and hoped that both navies would emulate each other in carrying out their respective instructions and not interfering "with the duties of each other." He then transmitted his report to

Washington and let the matter stand. Perry also asked the Navy Department to pursue legally the cases of two alleged American slavers. He acknowledged that American vessels and their cargoes had been sold to slavers. Nevertheless, Perry claimed that not "a single American has for some years been engaged directly in the purchase and exportation of slaves from Africa."[52]

Ironically, Perry achieved greater success in dealing with British naval officials than in suppressing the slave trade. He developed cordial relations with the British while still protecting American merchant vessels from British naval harassment. In November 1844, only ten months after complaining of the "indiscretions" and "insolence" of British naval officers, Perry now praised them. With only one exception, reported Perry, there had not been a "solitary instance of an improper interference with the American flag. On the contrary, there appears to be a mutual disposition . . . to cultivate a friendly understanding."[53]

As the cruise entered its second year, the "wasting effects" of the Africa station had begun to enervate Perry and his men. In March, Perry asked Secretary Henshaw to recall him after eighteen months on station. "I have been on the coast more than eight months engaged without interruption in the most active duties and I find my health is very seriously affected," wrote Perry. Although he had escaped the African fever, he felt the "debiliating [sic] effects of the climate. . . . [I]t is my opinion that few constitutions can hold out beyond eighteen months on a station remarkable for its privations and unhealthiness." In April, Perry again asked for relief at a period "not exceeding eighteen months or two years."[54]

Perry's deteriorating health in the last months of 1844 made more vexing the supply problems, discipline cases, and serious disease in the squadron. Duty remained monotonous, the weather oppressive, and moments of genuine relaxation for the men were few. A rare high point for Perry and the men of the *Macedonian* occurred on 4 July 1844, when the ship reached the Equator and fired a twenty-six-gun salute in honor of the nation's twenty-six states. Perry then sailed west along the Equator until he reached o degrees longitude in the early evening and fired a thirteen-gun salute to honor the original thirteen colonies. Perry also reported that almost two months earlier, he had crossed the precise spot where, almost thirty years before, Capt. Stephen Decatur, in the frigate *United States*, had defeated and made a prize of HMS *Macedonian*, Perry's current flagship.[55]

As the months passed, the squadron's morale sank ever lower. In August, Perry allowed himself to be drawn into a very uncharacteristic argument with his friend Isaac Mayo, flag captain of the *Macedonian*, who irritated Perry by quoting publicly a casual remark Perry had made during their "usual evening game of Backgammon." Discipline also continued to erode. Perry's correspondence for late 1844 and early 1845 contained frequent references to courts-martial as he wrote to his officers on specific aspects of their disciplinary regulations and punishments. A final exasperating episode occurred when Midn. J. B. Creighton wounded Lt. William Hurst in a duel. Although both men were on the newly arrived *Truxtun,* Perry was "much grieved" by the incident and the example it set. "If disputed points of duty are to be referred to the arbitrament of single combat," he wrote to Secretary Mason, "it will be necessary to supply each vessel with a double complement of officers."[56]

The last months of Perry's African assignment were marked by serious illness and death. There were no cases of fever on the *Macedonian,* but both officers and men suffered from "cutaneous eruptions" that resisted treatment. On the *Saratoga,* where Captain Tattnall had applied the health precautions less rigorously after Perry shifted his flag to the *Macedonian* in September 1843, conditions were much worse. By December, the ship's surgeon, H. N. Glentworth, reported widespread general debilitation, African fever, and other maladies onboard. Within another three months, fourteen men had contracted the fever, and the number continued to increase. Although many of the stricken men had slept onshore or been "exposed to the peculiar malaria of rivers," the "enervating influences of the increasing heat, and the frequent penetrating rains" of the African coast had also taken their toll.[57]

During the rainy season in October 1844, the squadron's medical problems intensified when Perry sent the recently arrived sloop *Preble* to assist the Portuguese town of Bissau in defending itself against an impending attack by native Africans. Perry's intent was to protect American interests, which amounted to forty thousand dollars in debts owed by Portuguese traders there to Americans. In the process of protecting Bissau, more than one-half of the officers and crew contracted the fever; within three months, sixteen had died. In response, Perry sent the *Preble* north because it had "been placed completely *hors de combat* by the prostration by fever" of its men. An angry Perry identified the cause to be the "imprudent relaxation of the rigid Sanatary [*sic*] regulations established by me." Subsequent investigation confirmed Perry's initial allegations that "careful observations on board that ship of the rigid sanatary [sic] regulations . . . which had hitherto protected the vessels of the original Squadron from serious sickness" had been lacking. In fact, the squadron had suffered a range of maladies, but it had not been stricken with a devastating attack of African fever until the *Preble* incident. Considerable credit must be given to Perry's health precautions, particularly those that kept men on the ships and away from the deadly mosquitoes onshore. In January 1845, Perry noted that he had not yet lost one life on the *Macedonian* during the cruise.[58]

Perry eagerly awaited his replacement, but before he returned to the United States, he had to deal with one final vexation. In early 1845, the Roman Catholic church in Porto Grande refused to allow Protestant sailors to be buried in its cemetery. Perry's solution was to create a separate cemetery. "With us the same spirit of intolerance will not prevail," Perry reported, "and the remains of the Protestant and the Catholic, the Jew and Gentile will be laid in place together."[59]

In December 1844, the Navy Department informed Perry that he was free to return as soon as Commo. Charles Skinner arrived in the sloop-of-war *Jamestown*. When the *Jamestown* came into the Cape Verdes in February 1845 flying the broad pendant of the new commodore, a dispute erupted between the new commander and the old one. Although Skinner was an old friend, Perry, clearly a tense and tired man, objected to his flying the commodore's pendant prior to a formal exchange of command lest it suggest that Perry was being involuntarily relieved. A compromise resolved the matter. Perry would continue to fly his blue pendant "until the entire and complete termination" of his cruise while Skinner would fly a red one. Perry sailed in the *Macedonian* before the end of February and reached New York on 28 April 1845. He had been gone for almost twenty-three months on an exceedingly demanding assignment.[60]

On his most challenging assignment to date, Perry had acquitted himself well. He had vigorously defended American commerce and assisted the African American settlements. He had also handled his diplomatic assignments adroitly by dealing skillfully with the British, cooperating with them, and avoiding increased enmity. No aspect of Perry's conduct provided a ready target for potential political critics in the United States.

In retrospect, Perry can be criticized for overreacting at Little Berebee. Perry can also be criticized for his shortcomings in policing American slave traders. The fact that his squadron captured only one slaver in more than a year and a half of effort speaks for itself. But his superiors in Washington did not criticize him for either lapse. The outgoing Tyler administration and the incoming Polk administration had other priorities and concerns. Dominated by southerners, both administrations had little sympathy for tribal Africans on the West African coast and paid little attention to suppressing the African slave trade; both were more concerned with the form rather than the substance of Perry's efforts. As a result, Perry found himself in good favor with the Polk administration on his return to New York.

Portrait of Matthew Calbraith Perry in 1835, by William Sidney Mount.
Courtesy of Naval Academy Museum

Daguerreotype print of Matthew Calbraith Perry in 1852. *Courtesy of Naval Academy Museum*

Portrait of Vice Commodore Perry in 1846, by J. Beaufort Irving. *Courtesy of Naval Academy Museum*

Woodblock print portrait of Perry by an anonymous Japanese artist in 1854. *Courtesy of Smithsonian Institution*

U.S. steam frigate *Mississippi* en route to Hong Kong, 1853. Reprinted from Francis L. Hawks, *Narrative of the Expedition of an American Squadron to the China Seas and Japan* (Washington, D.C.: Beverley Tucker, Senate Printer, 1856–57)

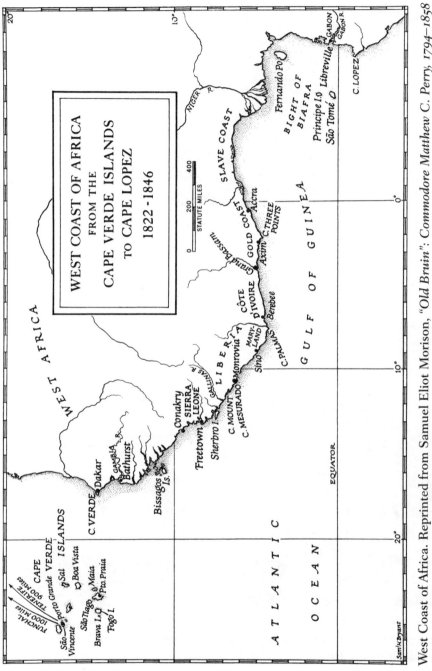

West Coast of Africa. Reprinted from Samuel Eliot Morison, "Old Bruin": Commodore Matthew C. Perry, 1794–1858
Copyright (c) 1967 by Samuel Eliot Morison. By permission of Little, Brown and Company.

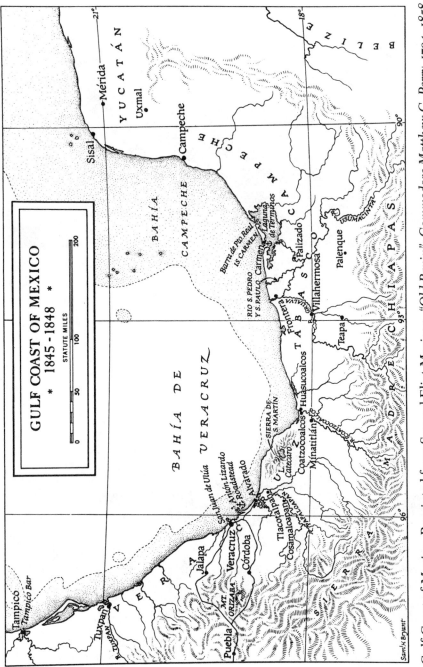

Gulf Coast of Mexico. Reprinted from Samuel Eliot Morison, "Old Bruin": Commodore Matthew C. Perry, 1794–1858
Copyright (c) 1967 by Samuel Eliot Morison. By permission of Little, Brown and Company.

Okinawan reception for Commodore Perry at the Shuri Castle, June 1853. Reprinted from Francis L. Hawks, *Narrative of the Expedition of an American Squadron to the China Seas and Japan* (Washington, D.C.: Beverley Tucker, Senate Printer, 1856–57)

American landing at Kurihama, July 1853. Reprinted from Francis L. Hawks, *Narrative of the Expedition of an American Squadron to the China Seas and Japan* (Washington, D.C.: Beverley Tucker, Senate Printer, 1856–57)

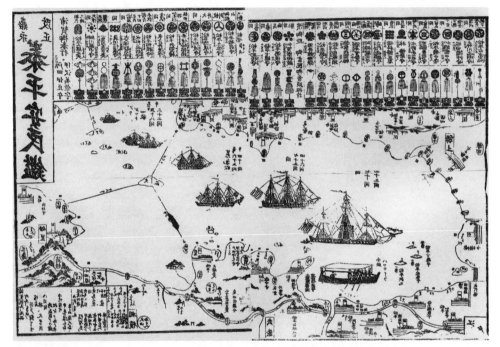
Japanese woodblock print map of Tokyo Bay depicting the arrival of the American squadron in July 1853. *Courtesy of Smithsonian Institution.*

Commodore Perry's delivery of the president's letter at Kurihama, July 1853. Reprinted from Francis L. Hawks, *Narrative of the Expedition of an American Squadron to the China Seas and Japan* (Washington, D.C.: Beverley Tucker, Senate Printer, 1856–57)

Commodore Perry meets the Japanese commissioners at Yokohama, March 1854. Reprinted from Francis L. Hawks, *Narrative of the Expedition of an American Squadron to the China Seas and Japan* (Washington, D.C.: Beverley Tucker, Senate Printer, 1856–57)

Dinner for the Japanese commissioners on USS *Powhatan*, March 1854. Reprinted from Francis L. Hawks, *Narrative of the Expedition of an American Squadron to the China Seas and Japan* (Washington, D.C.: Beverley Tucker, Senate Printer, 1856–57)

Farewell visit of Commodore Perry to Japanese commissioners at Shimoda, June 1854. Reprinted from Francis L. Hawks, *Narrative of the Expedition of an American Squadron to the China Seas and Japan* (Washington, D.C.: Beverley Tucker, Senate Printer, 1856–57)

Commodore Perry's East India Squadron operations area, 1853–54. Reprinted from Chang-su Houchins, "Artifacts of Diplomacy: Smithsonian Collections from Commodore Matthew Perry's Japan Expedition (1853–54)." *Courtesy of Smithsonian Institution*

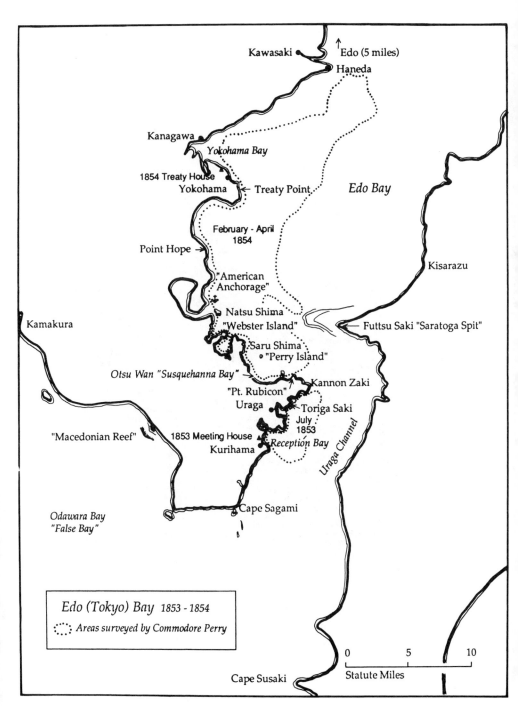

Edo (Tokyo) Bay, 1853–54. Reprinted from Chang-su Houchins, "Artifacts of Diplomacy: Smithsonian Collections from Commodore Matthew Perry's Japan Expedition (1853–54)." *Courtesy of Smithsonian Institution*

Japanese interpreters Maryamo Yenoski and Tako Juro, 1854. Reprinted from Francis L. Hawks, *Narrative of the Expedition of an American Squadron to the China Seas and Japan* (Washington, D.C.: Beverley Tucker, Senate Printer, 1856–57)

~⟩ 6 ⟨~

COMMODORE OF
THE GULF SQUADRON

*He is at present certainly the man for the navy; in many respects he is
an astonishing man, the most industrious, hard working, energetic,
zealous, persevering, and enterprising officer of his rank in our navy.
He does not spare himself or anyone under him.*

DESCRIPTION OF COMMO.
MATTHEW PERRY AT TABASCO, MEXICO, 1847

*M*atthew Perry returned to the United States in the
spring of 1845. In the following year, diplomatic relations between the United States and Mexico deterio-
rated steadily. Serious issues divided the two republics. Mexico's leaders were infuriated when the United States fomented revolution in
Texas and then annexed the territory in early 1845. Mexico demanded
an apology and reparations from the United States, but the new president, James K. Polk, took a hard line. Rejecting the idea of an apology
or reparations, he instead pressed Mexico for payment of the two million dollars in outstanding claims it owed to American citizens. The
Polk administration also insisted that Mexico discuss the sale of Upper
California and New Mexico to the United States. Both sides grew
intransigent, and hostilities became likely, if not yet inevitable. When
news reached the White House on Saturday, 9 May 1846, that Mexican
soldiers had attacked American troops along the Rio Grande, President Polk moved quickly. In the next thirty-six hours, he met with his

cabinet, consulted with congressional leaders, and drafted a war message that he sent to Congress on Monday. Democratic majorities in both houses quickly passed legislation that declared that "by the act of the Republic of Mexico, a state of war exists between that government and the United States."[1]

Political controversy and criticism surrounded the president's role in starting the war and his subsequent conduct of the war effort, not to mention the justice of the conflict. The Whig opposition and some Democrats condemned the war and the president, but the war itself proved popular in most communities. In the heyday of Manifest Destiny, exuberant patriotism and aggressive nationalism created strong support as thousands of American volunteers and professional soldiers and sailors rushed to join the action. Since the United States had not been in a formal war for more than three decades, an entire generation of military officers eagerly awaited their chance for glory.

When the war erupted, Matthew Perry was well positioned to take full advantage of the opportunities it would present. Since the Democrats had returned to power and controlled Congress, the Slidell and Perry families were back in favor. The president selected John Slidell as the U.S. envoy to Mexico and sent him on an important mission in 1845. Although Slidell's mission failed, he remained in good graces with the administration and close to Secretary of State James Buchanan.

The war with Mexico would be very different from the war in which Oliver Hazard Perry had won glory. In the War of 1812, the U.S. Navy had played a key role in fighting Great Britain's formidable Royal Navy. The war with Mexico was to be an army war. The army would win the major battles and produce most of the individual heroes. The War of 1812 had involved major naval engagements on the Great Lakes as well as dramatic victories for individual American warships. Now, in 1846, the enemy was a beleaguered nation without a navy worthy of the name. There would be no opportunities for American warships to destroy or capture their Mexican counterparts because Mexico had none for them to attack. Nor would there be much opportunity for American warships or privateers to prey on Mexican merchant ships because Mexico did not have a large overseas commerce. Although American naval forces played an important role in California, the navy was relegated to a secondary, and largely frustrating, role in the main theater of war. In the Gulf of Mexico and along its coast, the navy would support American ground forces by protecting supply routes, capturing various small ports, collecting revenue duties, and assisting with large amphibious landings such as that at Vera Cruz. But the navy's primary role in the Gulf would be to blockade the thousand miles of coastline from the Rio Grande to Campeche in Yucatán to prevent Mexican privateers from preying on American shipping and Mexican blockade-runners from reaching the coast. The main port, Vera Cruz, had the only harbor along the coast that oceangoing ships could enter without crossing a shallow bar. There were, however, a number of small coastal trading towns, including Tampico, Tuxpan, Alvarado, Coatzacoalcos, Frontera, and Carmen, that had to be patrolled for Mexican privateers and blockade-runners. Given the overwhelming numerical superiority of the American navy, the result was never in doubt, but the duty itself was personally unrewarding in that it involved little combat action.

After his return from Africa in April 1845, Perry remained on leave in New York but performed various naval duties. In June 1845, Secretary of the Navy George Bancroft asked the Board of Examiners—comprised of Perry, Commos. Thomas ap Catesby Jones and George C. Read, and Capts. Isaac Mayo and E. A. F. Lavallette—to advise him on the establishment of a naval academy at Fort Severn, Maryland. Specifically, he asked the board if it was advisable to have a permanent system of instruction onshore for midshipmen. If so, what plan of studies should be adopted, and who should be the officers of the school's board?[2]

The board submitted its report less than two weeks later on 25 June 1845. Since Bancroft already intended to create a naval academy, he had actually asked a rhetorical question to which the board responded with enthusiasm. It strongly endorsed the idea, recommended the creation of the new grade of naval cadet, proposed the composition of the officers and faculty, and outlined a curriculum and plan of study. The suggested program of study combined periods of academic study onshore at the new academy with periods of practical training at sea. The curriculum was to include conventional academic subjects such as English, French, mathematics, natural philosophy, and chemistry as well as practical subjects such as drawing, mapping, gunnery tactics, and steam engineering. Perry was undoubtedly instrumental in ensuring that instruction in steam engines and steam power was included as a basic part of the first curriculum. The board recommended a six-year program comprised of two initial years of instruction at the academy, three years at sea as warranted midshipmen, and one final year on a practice frigate and a small steamship. Secretary Bancroft modified the recommendations but relied on the board's report when he created the new academy in August 1845. Although Perry did not seek the position of superintendent, he was very pleased when his friend and associate Franklin Buchanan received the appointment. The U.S. Naval Academy opened formally on 10 October 1845, thus giving reality to an idea that Perry and other officers had advocated for two decades.[3]

During 1845 and 1846, Perry also continued his campaign to get the navy to build more steam vessels. He complained to Bancroft in January 1846 that the construction of war steamers in the United States still lagged such that in "case of hostility with any great maritime power our naval operations will be seriously thwarted for want of vessels of their description." Perry found the two steamers whose construction he had supervised, the *Mississippi* and *Missouri,* to be excellent vessels and strongly recommended that future war steamers be built by the navy in its own yards. Although more expensive, vessels constructed by the navy would be superior to those built by subcontractors because of their higher-quality hulls, steam boilers, and ordnance. Perry also criticized the new plan to build domestic steamships that could be readily converted into warships when needed. Although converted steamers might be useful for coastal defense, he believed that they could never serve effectively as oceangoing warships.[4]

While Perry continued to press for naval reform, he realized that little had changed in the past decade despite all the efforts of naval reformers and the work of former secretary of the navy Abel Upshur. A naval academy had at last been created, but other proposals to better recruit, train, and promote officers languished. Most senior officers and civilian naval officials still subscribed to antiquated strategic views and refused to envision a peacetime navy commensurate with the commercial and diplomatic interests of the expanding American republic. In Congress, few politicians were prepared to push for a larger modern navy. In 1837, when Perry's article "Thoughts on the Navy" was published, the United States had the eighth largest navy in the world. In 1845, the U.S. Navy was still eighth and had fallen far behind the leading navies of England and France in technological innovation. While the English and French had embraced steam power, built ironclad warships, and adapted the revolutionary exploding-shell ordnance, the United States had only seven steam warships; only one ironclad steamer, the *Michigan;* and only one propeller-driven steamer, the *Princeton.* The American navy did not adopt exploding shells until 1845, and while some officers such as Perry insisted that the new Paixhans guns with their revolutionary exploding shells be mounted on their ships, many others did not. Moreover, the situation was not about to improve. By the early 1850s the United States still ranked eighth in naval power.[5]

This sad state of affairs reflected a combination of public indifference and strong antinavy political sentiment in Congress. Most American politicians and public officials strongly opposed the creation of a large peacetime naval establishment. Even in times of emergency, such as the Anglo-American crisis of 1840–41 or the Oregon crisis of 1846, they refused to appropriate funds to modernize or increase the size of the navy significantly. James K. Polk, the most bellicose president of the time, challenged the British over Oregon and fought a war against Mexico, but the Tennessee Democrat staunchly refused to provide more money than absolutely necessary to the navy.

In September 1845, Secretary Bancroft approached Perry about a new assignment as commander of the Home Squadron, or the Gulf Squadron, as it was generally known. According to Bancroft, the current commander, Commo. David Conner, was in poor health and would have to be replaced when his two-year term as commander expired. Conner, who had commanded the squadron since 1 January 1844, was suffering from tic douloureux, a painful and debilitating neuralgia. Perry immediately accepted but indicated that he was in no hurry to assume command since he had just returned from Africa in April and wished to have more time with his family to recuperate.[6] Furthermore, in spite of his poor health, Conner was not prepared to relinquish his command in the midst of rising tensions between the United States and Mexico. When Perry wrote to him about the matter, Conner was noncommittal about a specific replacement date, and even Secretary Bancroft seemed in no hurry to make the change.[7] In December, Bancroft informed Conner that he could retain his command as long as it was "agreeable" to him and suggested that he wait until the Mexican-American dispute was resolved. Conner replied that he would do just that. At this time, both Bancroft and Conner expected the dispute to be settled amicably and war avoided. But five months later, when war erupted and Conner still gave no indication that he was prepared to relinquish his command, Bancroft took no action to replace him.

When the war began, Perry had been recuperating from his African cruise for more than a year and was impatient to get into the action. In August, he accepted command of the *Mississippi* in the Gulf until he could succeed Conner. The secretary also authorized Perry to fly the red pendant of a vice commodore who was second in command. Although Perry's pay remained the same, Bancroft reiterated that Perry would succeed Conner when the commodore was ready to return home. Since the *Mississippi* was already on station, Perry departed in the new steamer *Vixen,* which arrived at the main naval roadstead at Anton Lizard, eleven miles south of Vera Cruz, on 23 September.[8]

Although the war was only four months old, Perry found morale in the Gulf Squadron low when he arrived. The war had already produced victories in northern Mexico at Palo Alto and Resaca de la Palma for the army of Gen. Zachary Taylor. "Old Rough and Ready" had then marched his army south and laid siege to Monterrey, which finally surrendered on 25 September. These victories quickly made Taylor the first popular hero of the war; but the navy in the Gulf could boast of no comparable victories. While Taylor and his army were invading Mexico, winning battles, and creating excitement at home, the Gulf Squadron had protected the army's coastal flank and imposed a blockade as ordered. Conner's squadron of twelve ships went unchallenged, and the blockade duty was monotonous and unexciting. Adding to the navy's woes were logistics problems. The nearest naval supply base, at Pensacola, was poorly equipped and was nearly nine hundred miles from Vera Cruz. When the war erupted, the base was not prepared; coal was not available there and fresh water was difficult to obtain in sufficient quantities. It took nearly thirty days to bake enough bread to supply the needs of the squadron for three months.[9] Local conditions along the Mexican coast did not raise the crews' comfort levels. From April to October, the rainy season brought mosquitoes, malaria, and yellow fever, or the *vómito negro.* The dry season from October into April brought healthier weather, but with it, fierce and unpredictable "northers." These winter gales, "the most furious periodical winds known anywhere in America," were often accompanied by driving rain.[10]

Since the squadron operated without a base on the Mexican coast, its ships were either cruising, anchored at Anton Lizard, or en route to or from Pensacola. The nature of the blockade duty often required ships to operate in shallow waters near the coast or trading towns, which greatly reduced the usefulness of frigates and oceangoing warships. As a result, most of the active blockade cruising was done by small sailing or steam vessels. Here, in close quarters under hot, oppressive, and unhealthy conditions, the men went about their thankless task for weeks at a time without relief.

Envy ran high among navy officers and crewmen when they learned about the exploits of their army counterparts onshore, noted Lt. Raphael Semmes.

> We looked forth from our ships as from a prison. . . . Day after day, without other variation than the occasional arrival of one of the blockading squadron to fill up with water and provisions and depart again . . . a war, for the navy, of toils and vigils, without the prospect of either excitement or glory,

Young officers longed to attack the heavily fortified Castle of San Juan de Ulua, which stood offshore and guarded the entrance to Vera Cruz. But no such assault was planned. "We juniors chafed somewhat under the curb which was thus placed on our ambition of emulating the army in its glorious achievements."[11]

Several initial setbacks magnified the squadron's disenchantment. In early August, Conner decided to capture the coastal town of Alvarado, south of Anton Lizard. Because the town was located several miles up the Papaloapau River, American forces had to cross a shallow bar, overcome any gunfire from the shore, and ascend the river. Conner planned to have the war steamers *Princeton* and *Mississippi* cross the bar and bombard the fort protecting the river. He launched the attack on 7 August, but the two steamers were unable to overcome the strong current and get within close firing range. That evening Conner ordered a cease-fire and postponed another assault because a storm was predicted. When the storm did not materialize, the Americans withdrew, to the anger of the mortified officers. "Nothing was easier than the capture of the whole place, but after making great preparations we were foolishly frightened away," wrote Lt. John Winslow of the *Cumberland*. "All the officers and men in the other ships are indignant. I am no fighting man myself, but I never felt more contempt."[12]

Shortly thereafter, Mexican general Antonio López de Santa Anna embarrassed the navy by slipping through the American blockade into Vera Cruz. More bad news followed when the squadron learned that the brig *Truxtun* had run aground, been attacked, and surrendered to the enemy. By the time American help arrived two days later, it was too late. The ship had been severely damaged, and the enemy had removed everything of value including the guns. After determining that the ship could not be salvaged, an American boarding party burned it.[13]

As tempers rose and morale sank, discipline in the squadron suffered. The low point came in August when a popular young seaman, Samuel Jackson, struck an officer in a minor dispute on the St. Mary's after the officer had thrown Jackson's shoes from their resting place on deck. Jackson was executed for his offense. "There was a gloom that hung over our ship for days after the execution," remembered one seaman. Grumbling about Commodore Conner increased. Some midshipmen joked that the commodore had been elected an honorary member of the peace society. One lieutenant wrote that Conner seemed more interested in butchering cattle, "catching a pail of water and such things than injuring the enemy."[14]

This was the atmosphere Perry encountered when he arrived in late September. It did not take him long to identify the source of the general malaise. To his son-in-law John Hone he wrote privately that he did not intend to remain with the squadron as second in command very long because Conner showed "no disposition to vacate" and held on to his "command with a pertinacity very extraordinary." Perry did not want "to share the odium of a mismanagement which every one talks about . . . when I have not the power to prevent or avert it. . . . I am not disposed to submit patiently to an arrangement which favours him at my expense, his period of command should have expired a year ago." Nevertheless, Perry put his impatience and petty private thoughts aside and concentrated on the immediate task at hand.[15]

By this time the Navy Department was putting pressure on Conner to move against the main coastal towns. In October, Conner decided to lead another attack on Alvarado. The Mississippi was to bombard the outer fort to provide cover for several small boats as they crossed the bar and ascended the river toward the town. The assault began on 15 October and proceeded even though the Mississippi could not get within firing range of the outer fort. Conner was on the small steamer Vixen, which towed two gunboats in one line while another steamer, the McLane, towed three gunboats in a second line. The Vixen successfully crossed the bar, but the McLane grounded, forcing Conner to decide whether to continue with his reduced force or withdraw. He chose to withdraw, a decision that observers at the time and historians since have generally praised as sensible and prudent. After all, there was little danger in withdrawing and preparing for another assault later, when he could bring his full force to bear. Lieutenant Semmes agreed: "It would have been madness to proceed to the assault."[16]

Sensible as the decision was, this second failed attack further harmed both Conner's reputation as a fighting man and the squadron's morale. To offset the failure, Perry sought immediate action and suggested an expedition to Tabasco. American forces would enter the Grijalva River, take the town of Frontera six miles upstream, and then continue another seventy miles up the river to capture the town of La Villahermosa de San Juan Bautista, known to the Americans as Tabasco. Although it contained only a few thousand residents, Tabasco was an active trading center that had been visited by seventy vessels from twelve nations in 1845. Conner authorized Perry to lead the mission with an independent force consisting of the *Mississippi,* the two small steamers *Vixen* and *McLane,* four schooner gunboats, and a landing party of 253 men led by Capt. French Forrest.

Perry moved quickly. At the mouth of the Grijalva he shifted his pendant to the *Vixen,* a three-gun, 118-foot-long side-wheeler commanded by Comdr. Joshua Sands, because the bar was too shallow for the *Mississippi* to cross. On 23 October at noon, with Perry onboard and two gunboats in tow, the *Vixen* led the way up the Grijalva. The *McLane* also had two gunboats in tow and formed a second column, but again it grounded on a bar. Unlike Conner at Alvarado, however, Perry did not hesitate. The *Vixen* moved upriver and by 3:00 P.M. had Frontera in sight. After casting off the boats it towed, the *Vixen* approached the town at full speed and captured two steamers as well as three schooners without a fight. Perry secured Frontera, left a small marine detachment there, and the next morning set off for Tabasco. The *Vixen* had two schooners in tow, and the *Petrita,* one of the captured steamers, carried most of Captain Forrest's landing force. The Americans sailed all day and all night, moving cautiously between riverbanks densely covered by hardwood jungle. At one point, a detachment landed to examine an enemy breastwork. They found it deserted and spiked the guns. Along the way up the river, the squadron took six more prizes: two sloops, two brigs, and two schooners. Finally, shortly after noon on 25 October, the American force sighted Tabasco. Perry formed his ships into a battle line off the town and sent Captain Forrest to demand an immediate surrender. When the Mexicans refused, Perry opened fire from the river and ordered the marines to land. They fought their way into the town plaza and occupied that part of the town before Perry ordered them to withdraw to spend the night onboard the ships.[17]

Although local merchants and most residents wanted to surrender, the provincial governor and captain general, Don Juan Bautista Traconis, preferred to fight. Since he had no authority to take the town unless local authorities surrendered it, Perry decided to return to Frontera and avoid further fighting. But when the Mexicans fired on them early the next morning, the Americans returned fire and hit the customhouse and other public buildings with cannon shots. When a white flag appeared, Perry ceased firing and dispatched Captain Forrest to town, where local merchants and foreign consuls gave him a message asking that Perry stop firing in order to spare civilian lives and property. Perry agreed. As his forces withdrew, however, one of the American prizes grounded, drew Mexican gunfire, and required the assistance of a small armed boat. In the rescue effort, Lt. Charles Morris and one seaman were mortally wounded by the enemy. Attributing the unnecessary deaths to Traconis's treachery, the enraged Perry resumed firing on the town. By one estimate, his squadron fired 170 cannon shots in thirty minutes and killed four civilians before departing and moving downriver without further incident.

Although it had been only a minor skirmish with few casualties on either side, General Traconis claimed victory, boasting that his forces had forced the Americans to retreat. This was an insult that Perry did not forget. In fact, even though Tabasco had not surrendered, Perry had reason to hold his head high. On 1 November, he returned to Anton Lizard with nine prize vessels including two steamers and a Mexican sloop-of-war. His losses were two men killed, two drowned, and two wounded. Commerce into Mexico through Tabasco had been disrupted and the town of Frontera secured. Equally important, the expedition had broken the drudgery of blockade duty, ended the string of naval setbacks, allowed some officers and men to get into action, and lifted spirits in the squadron. This action helped break the "monotony of the blockade," wrote Raphael Semmes. "The war, by this means, became more endurable, though we still pined for something to do, that should give us more *eclat*, and better satisfy our countrymen at home." Lieutenant

Winslow, whose individual bravery at Tabasco was praised by Perry, noted that this was "the only successful" mission "which the Navy accomplished. For this, we are indebted to Commodore Perry."[18]

Conner's next objective was the town of Tampico, more than two hundred miles north of Vera Cruz. Conner prepared a full task force, not knowing that General Santa Anna had already evacuated his garrison and left the town undefended. On 14 November, the U.S. task force crossed the bar and began a virtually unopposed attack. Conner led the first division on the *Spitfire* while Perry led the second on the *Vixen.* Both vessels towed two schooners and several boatloads of men. A white flag appeared as the vessels approached Tampico, and surrender followed without any American casualties. The American forces captured and added three gunboats and one schooner to the U.S. Navy. Conner occupied Tampico and organized a provisional government there. Lacking sufficient troops to garrison the town, Conner then sent Perry north to Brazos Santiago and New Orleans for additional men. Perry made both stops and returned in the amazingly short time of one week with additional troops, provisions, and artillery pieces.

On 16 December, Conner ordered Perry to lead a mission to Yucatán, a province with a checkered political history. After seceding in January 1846, Yucatán had rejoined the Mexican republic in November and was currently serving as an important link in Mexico's chain of supply. With the Americans blockading in force to the north, supplies could be shipped into Yucatán and then carted overland into the interior of Mexico. Perry's job was to blockade the province and occupy the town of Carmen, or Laguna, as it was known locally. The town was located on the island of Carmen, which stretched for twenty miles along the coast and provided a protected trade route for small vessels. During the war, supplies from Europe, the Caribbean, and even the United States were sent to the Yucatán coastal town of Campeche, then transferred to small ships that sheltered in the lagoon created by the island of Carmen. Ships then left the lagoon, sailed along the Mexican coast, and transferred their goods at one of the small towns or made their way up the Grijalva River to Tabasco, where supplies were transferred to wagons and sent to Mexican forces in the interior.[19]

Conner intended to stop the illegal trade by occupying the town of Carmen. Perry was to take possession of the town, destroy the public buildings, order neutral vessels to leave, and station two naval vessels there to patrol. The mission turned out to be an easy one. Perry's force consisted of the *Mississippi, Vixen, Boneta,* and *Petrel.* Perry again transferred his flag to the *Vixen* because of the shallow water and, on the evening of 20 December, entered the harbor with three small warships and four barges. The next morning local officials agreed to surrender. Perry occupied the town's two forts, spiked the guns, and unfurled the American flag. On 22 December, Perry departed, leaving Comdr. Joshua Sands in command, and the *Vixen* and *Petrel* behind to enforce the blockade. Unfortunately for the American task force, Conner ordered the blockade lifted when he learned that, in early December, Yucatán had officially declared its neutrality in the war. Perry returned in the *Mississippi* to Anton Lizard on 27 December after visiting Frontera and capturing two blockade-runners along the coast. Conner next ordered Perry to return to Norfolk for long overdue repairs to the *Mississippi,* whose pipes and joints were leaking and boilers were in disrepair.[20]

Perry had completed his first phase of service in the Mexican War with some successes—most notably his expeditions to Tabasco and Yucatán. In each case, Perry was aggressive but not impetuous. At a time when his officers and men sought combat, Perry provided action but made sure that they did not overreact or become trigger-happy. Rather than launch an all-out attack on Tabasco, which his men would have welcomed, Perry withdrew in accordance with his instructions. Unquestionably, Perry's assertive presence and energy had helped to restore the morale of the squadron. Once Perry arrived, things began to happen. After months of numbing blockade duty, the squadron engaged in four landing operations within two months. The improved morale proved Perry's philosophy that constant activity benefited the morale and health of his men. Unfortunately for the navy, these assaults created no dramatic battles, major victories, or gallant heroes even though they gave the navy nearly complete control of the Mexican Gulf coast.

When the *Mississippi* reached Norfolk in mid-January, Perry immediately attended to various duties. Most pressing was the repair of the *Mississippi,* for which he convinced the navy's chief engineer, Charles Haswell, to come to Norfolk and work his crews day and night to finish the job quickly. In Washington, Perry met with Secretary of the Navy John Y. Mason, with other department officials, and on two occasions with President Polk. Perry reported on the conditions in the Gulf, pressed for better logistical support, and presented his own comprehensive plan to prosecute the war. According to Perry, the United States should annex Upper California, establish a "military cordon" along Mexico's northern frontier, and occupy the principal Mexican ports on both the Pacific and Gulf coasts. The navy should garrison these ports, open them to non-contraband trade, and collect duties on various items. In this way, revenue could be raised for the war effort and American goods imported into Mexico.[21]

Harboring his own doubts about the justice and morality of the war, Perry reasoned that his plan would convert the conflict from an invasion to a war of "occupation and necessary expedience . . . more congenial to the institutions and professions of the American people." Perry argued that his plan would save lives, reduce the cost of the war by three-fourths, counteract the "baleful influences" of the Catholic clergy in Mexico, remove false prejudices of the Mexicans about their American neighbors to the north, and encourage Mexican commerce. "As an argument in favor of humanity, the Mexican people would be led to agriculture and mining, so that it would be hard to rouse sufficient military spirit in them to dislodge forces holding their ports."[22]

Although Perry's plan was intriguing, the Polk administration wanted decisive military victories. And while it would have elevated the role of the navy, the plan would have prolonged the war by abandoning the military offensive, reducing military pressure on Mexico, and substituting a passive approach. Perry badly underestimated the hatred of the Mexicans for their Yankee neighbors, an animosity that would not have been diminished by foreign military occupation of Upper California and all of Mexico's primary ports. Perry's recommendations were strangely atypical of his normally direct, aggressive approach to dealing with military situations. In any event, there is no evidence that Secretary Mason ever considered Perry's plan seriously, much less discussed it with the president or the cabinet.

Perry was determined to resolve the ambiguity of the Gulf Squadron command while he was in the United States. It had now been sixteen months since Perry had been offered the command. Yet, despite his deteriorating health and the declining confidence of his men, Conner still held tight to the position. The sorry state of squadron morale was known in the administration and in the press. Conner's failures at Alvarado had been well publicized. From New Orleans, John Slidell made sure that

Secretary of State James Buchanan and President Polk appreciated the severity of the matter. On 6 January 1847, Slidell wrote that Conner

> has not the qualities of energy and decision which are imperatively required for an emergency like the present. Commodore Conner is a brave man, an accomplished officer, and a good seamen, but his health is, and has been for some time, so much impaired . . . [as] to neutralize these qualities.

Observing that Conner's tic douloureux had affected the "clearness of his perception and the vigor of his action," Slidell cited the failures at Alvarado as an example. "Alvarado might have been taken without difficulty on either occasion. He does not command the confidence of those who serve under him, and confidence is the vital principle of success."[23]

By January 1847, Polk's hope that decisive military victories would win a quick peace had been dashed; the prospect of a long war now loomed. The administration needed a vigorous, healthy squadron commander who enjoyed the full confidence of his men and could stay the course in a protracted war. Mason decided that Perry should replace Conner as soon as he returned to the Gulf. Although Perry was later accused of plotting shamelessly behind Conner's back to push his superior aside, Mason's decision was overdue; given the situation, it was also entirely logical and justifiable. Significantly, when Conner's son wrote a brief account of his father's command of the Gulf Squadron, he did not repeat these allegations or charge Perry with bad faith. When he met with President Polk on 26 February, Perry had already been informed of Mason's decision, and Polk noted in his diary that Perry "has been ordered to relieve Commodore Conner in the command of the Gulf Squadron."[24] Secretary Mason added eight additional small warships to the squadron, making it the largest ever collected under an American flag.[25]

Although Mason had made a sound decision, its timing proved to be extremely unfortunate. A major offensive was imminent, and Conner had already begun the operation. Several months earlier, the administration had decided to invade central Mexico and capture Mexico City with an army commanded by Gen. Winfield Scott. The plan required the capture of Vera Cruz, which was connected by road to Mexico City. The full participation of the Gulf Squadron would be required to land the ten to twelve thousand soldiers involved. Scott and Conner made final plans in early 1847 for the landing to occur in February or early March before the rainy season began in April.[26]

Vera Cruz presented a beautiful but formidable objective. From the sea, the bold outline of the coast was visible for many miles. The lofty Cordilleras mountain range appeared to Raphael Semmes clearly "robed in 'azure hue.'" Orizaba, the tallest of the peaks, rose "with the regularity of a faultless cone" more than seventeen thousand feet above sea level, its "hoary summit covered, for the distance of five thousand feet, with perpetual snow." From a distance the many cupolas and church spires of Vera Cruz presented "a beautiful and picturesque appearance," but as one drew closer, the city assumed a more somber picture of dark buildings and massive stone houses dominated by heavy churches and convents. The city was heavily walled, well fortified, and protected by the heavily armed castle fortress, San Juan de Ulua. With its sixty-foot walls, the fort commanded the harbor and all seaward approaches from its position one-half mile offshore.[27] Although it was reputed to be impregnable, the castle had been captured by a French naval assault in 1838, a feat observed personally by Comdr. David F. Farragut. When the United States went to war with Mexico in 1846, Farragut, David D. Porter, John Rodgers, and other glory-hungry young naval officers wanted to repeat the French feat by scaling the castle's high walls in a daring naval raid. Both Farragut and Porter submitted proposals and badgered the department for approval, but the navy had other plans. As it turned out, naval planners overestimated the strength of the fortress, as did Scott, who assumed that a direct naval assault would prove too costly. Instead he decided to land his army on the coast to the south out of range of the castle's guns. Once onshore, American troops would attack Vera Cruz from the rear and deal with the castle after the city itself fell.

The landing point selected was Collado Beach, opposite Sacrificios Island and two and one-half miles south of Vera Cruz. The beach offered a good landing place; the tide was not severe, the water was sufficiently deep, and the area beyond the beach was unfortified. To land ten to twelve thousand men, a huge enterprise for its day, more than sixty special surfboats with a capacity of thirty-five to forty-five men each would be required. Transports embarked troops at Brazos Santiago and Tampico while others brought soldiers directly from New Orleans and Mobile. By 4 March, nearly one hundred transports had arrived at Anton Lizard.

Although Scott held overall command, full responsibility for organizing the actual landing fell to Conner. This duty playing to his strengths
as a commander, Conner did a superb job of planning the exercise
despite his ill health. On 2 March, he wrote to his wife that he had
just "got over the longest and most severe fit of the *tic* that I have ever
had . . . the anxiety and vexation I suffer here is intolerable." According
to Lieutenant Semmes, who was present, Conner "had become almost a
confirmed invalid" by March.[28]

After one postponement, the mission took place in perfect weather
on 9 March 1847. Complicated and potentially troublesome, the landing plan required that all troops be transferred from their transport
ships to the small surfboats and taken through a narrow anchorage to
the beach. The operation was completed without mishap or confusion
among the landing vessels. The Mexicans offering no resistance,
eighty-six hundred men had been landed in a four-hour period. Scott
landed with more troops the next day, and for the next two weeks the
Americans secured their position as equipment and supplies poured
ashore. Scott praised the work of Conner and his squadron. Even Conner's critics acknowledged that his plans were "simply perfect." The
Vera Cruz landing was the largest amphibious operation by the U.S.
Navy prior to the invasion of North Africa in 1942. Conner's carefully
planned and flawlessly executed landing was indeed an "impressive
achievement."[29]

It was at this point, on 20 March, after the landings but before the
siege, that Perry arrived and delivered Secretary Mason's letter to Conner. The brief letter explained only that given the "uncertain duration of
the War," the president had decided not to suspend any longer the rule
limiting the term of a squadron commander to two years. Since Conner
had commanded the squadron for more than three years since 1 January
1844, he was to step down immediately. The change of command was
announced the next day. Disappointed but not surprised, Conner
accepted the news graciously. Two weeks before, he had informed his
wife that although he had requested relief, his replacement had not yet
arrived. On 21 March, Scott, Perry, and Conner met to make final plans
for the siege. Scott needed artillery, particularly heavy artillery. Conner
had earlier offered some of his squadron's heavy guns. Scott now
accepted the offer, and acquiesced when Perry insisted that "wherever
the guns went, their officers and men must go with them."[30]

After the meeting, Perry personally announced to each ship in the squadron that naval guns and naval gun crews would participate in the attack. For men who had expected to be merely spectators of the anticipated army victory, the announcement brought immediate jubilation. "I shall never forget the thrill which pervaded the squadron, when . . . he announced from his barge . . . that we were to land guns and crews to participate in the investment of the city of Vera Cruz," wrote junior officer John Upshur.

> Cheer after cheer was sent up in evidence of the enthusiasm this promise of a release from a life of inaction . . . inspired in every breast. In a moment everything was stir and bustle. . . . Under the energetic chief who succeeded to the command of a squadron dying of supineness . . . the navy of the United States sustained its old prestige.[31]

To bolster spirits yet further, Perry ensured wide participation. He selected guns from five different warships, assigned two crews to each gun, and rotated each crew every twenty-four hours. It took the next three days to land the heavy guns, drag them through the sand, and site them properly. Enthusiastic volunteers for this laborious task were plentiful and without complaint. In the meantime, on 22 March, Scott had begun to bombard the city. The steamers *Vixen* and *Spitfire* and five other gunboats joined in the attack. Despite heavy enemy fire, they suffered no casualties. The naval battery opened fire on 24 March and continued through the next day. In those two days the battery fired one thousand shells and eight hundred rounds of shot, more than a quarter of the total fired by American artillery at Vera Cruz. On 25 March, Scott decided to launch a frontal assault if his surrender demands were not accepted by the next day. While they were planning the assault, Perry convinced Scott that one of the three assault columns should be composed of sailors and marines. Perry planned to lead this force personally, but his plans evaporated when Mexican officials raised a truce flag and began to negotiate their surrender. The timing of the truce was fortuitous, for a fierce norther hit the evening of the twenty-fifth and continued through the next day and night. Finally, on 27 March, the capitulation agreement—including Castle San Juan de Ulua, which had not yet been assaulted—was signed.[32]

The surrender ceremony took place on 29 March. From the castle, Perry reported to Secretary Mason that at the exact time he was writing, batteries in the city were saluting the American flag. To his squadron Perry proclaimed, "Never at any period of our naval history has the true spirit of professional gallantry been more strongly exhibited than at the present time." Scott also formally thanked Conner, Perry, and the squadron for their "prompt, cheerful, and able assistance." Back in Washington, Secretary Mason immediately commended Conner, Perry, and their men for their role in the victory.[33]

Commendations notwithstanding, primary credit and public praise for the capture of Vera Cruz went to Scott and his army, not to Conner, Perry, or the Gulf Squadron. Conner and Perry had done their best to magnify the navy's role, and it was a central one. Yet the capture of Vera Cruz remained an army victory. Moreover, the unfortunate and abrupt timing of the command change left bad feelings and created the impression, correct or not, that Conner's unsatisfactory performance had been the cause. Accusations that Perry had engaged in unscrupulous political treachery during his trip to Washington the previous January tarnished his reputation. After the war, Perry gathered evidence that he had not connived to have Conner removed. He called on his friend and colleague Franklin Buchanan for a firsthand account of Bancroft's initial offer of the command to Perry in September 1845; he also asked Lt. Raphael Semmes to add an addendum to his memoir of the war, *Service Afloat and Ashore*, which was published in 1851.[34]

After occupying Vera Cruz, Winfield Scott turned his attention southward to Alvarado. There a joint army and naval expedition commanded by Gen. John A. Quitman and Commodore Perry was to capture the town to secure livestock and food for Scott's march to Mexico City. Because the capture of Vera Cruz had rendered Alvarado militarily indefensible for Mexico, significant resistance was not anticipated. But the plans went awry when navy lieutenant Charles Hunter exceeded his orders: in command of the steamer *Scourge*, Hunter was ordered simply to blockade the town. Instead, on 31 March, Hunter fired some shells, accepted the town's unexpected surrender, and then proceeded upriver. What Commodore Conner had not been able to do with a task force on two occasions, Lieutenant Hunter had done virtually single-handed. When Perry's squadron and Quitman's army arrived at Alvarado the next day, they were surprised to see an American flag flying. The Mexicans had abandoned their garrison and scattered the local livestock, thus defeating the main purpose of the mission. Quitman took the situation graciously, but Perry was furious and had Hunter court-martialed, repri-manded, and dismissed from the squadron for exceeding his orders and acting in a vainglorious manner. Most observers thought Perry had over-reacted. And, indeed, his intense focus on the purpose of the mission had caused Perry to act in haste. A reprimand and discipline were in order, but not Hunter's banishment from the squadron. In this case, Perry's zeal backfired. He was criticized in the squadron and ridiculed by some newspapers at home. Hunter meanwhile returned to the United States, where he was nicknamed "Alvarado Hunter." The matter eventu-ally reached the president, who overruled Perry's discipline. Hunter eventually received another command.[35]

Secretary Mason expected Perry to be much more aggressive than his predecessor had been. In his orders to Perry, Mason emphasized the need for "vigorous and effective measures to harrass the enemy." Perry and his forces were to maintain the Gulf coast blockade and to "attack and capture any places" that would promote the military effort and allow the collection of customs revenue on neutral commerce. The squadron was also to put into place and administer the customs regula-tions.[36] By this time the squadron comprised more than thirty assorted ships, including one ship of the line, three frigates, six sloops-of-war, as well as various brigs, schooners, gunboats, and bomb brigs. The large warships had been built for the navy, but most of the smaller ships were converted vessels that had been either purchased in the United States or captured as prizes during the war. The supply problem had improved by April 1847; indeed, so much coal was now available that Perry had a shipload returned to Pensacola. Mason's instructions gave Perry consid-erable discretion in capturing the remaining small port towns along the coast. With Vera Cruz, Alvarado, and Tampico under U.S. control, only four others remained: Tuxpan, 150 miles north of Vera Cruz, and Coatzacoalcos, Tabasco, and Carmen to the south and east of Vera Cruz. Each of these objectives would require some ground forces, but Perry had few marines and expected to lose most of those to Scott's army. In response, Perry organized the navy's first infantry brigade. Since most of the men in the squadron were bored and eager for com-bat, hundreds volunteered. These men served under their own officers, slept on their ships, and drilled each day onshore or on the decks of the ships. At one time Perry had more than two thousand men organized and drilling daily.[37]

Perry first moved against Tuxpan, located six miles inland from the mouth of the Tuxpan River. The town seemed well protected and promised resistance. The battery called La Peña was perched on a forty-foot promontory that jutted into the river and commanded the river approach two miles below the town. Two additional batteries stood farther upstream, one on each side of the river, and the town itself had a strong garrison. The assault force consisted of three steamers, three schooner gunboats, three bomb brigs, and a landing force of 1,519 men with four pieces of artillery commanded by Capt. S. L. Breese of the *Albany*. As he had done at Vera Cruz, Perry sought broad participation and included officers and men from eleven different ships in the landing force.

On the morning of 18 April, Perry in the *Spitfire* led his forces over the bar and into the Tuxpan River. At 2:30 P.M., the boats sustained fire from the battery at La Peña. Comdr. Franklin Buchanan then landed his force and led a charge up the hill, throwing the defenders into disarray and retreat. Within minutes, the Stars and Stripes flew over La Peña. Continuing upstream, the flotilla received more gunfire, but within an hour the Americans had captured Tuxpan, where the landing force spent the night onshore. Although generally orderly, the Americans did discover and help themselves to a cache of champagne, wine, and cigars that the Mexican general had set aside for his own anticipated victory celebration. "Jack" had his "frolic that night," but with the "exception of breaking into General Cos's house, and drinking his health . . . we heard of no disorders," reported Lieutenant Semmes. Rather than occupy Tuxpan indefinitely, Perry rendered it militarily useless by destroying its guns and fortifications. A point of honor for Perry was the successful repossession of the guns the enemy had taken from the *Truxtun* in August 1846. Four days later, the American forces evacuated, leaving Captain Breese with two ships to guard the mouth of the river.[38]

Alas, for the glory-starved men of the squadron, the capture of Tuxpan occurred the very same day as the Battle of Cerro Gordo, a major victory for General Scott's army on its march to Mexico City. Once again, a naval achievement was overshadowed by an army victory that monopolized the news at home. The squadron had hoped that its exploits would be "heralded forth to the public in conspicuous editorials, and with *capitals*," lamented Semmes, "but we scarcely attained the dignity of the poet's corner, in village newspapers."[39]

Perry next targeted the town of Coatzacoalcos, 150 miles south of Vera Cruz, which the Americans occupied on 13 May without resistance but also without winning any military glory. Perry ordered the Coatzacoalcos River to be sounded and surveyed to Minatitlán, a distance of twenty-four miles. The surveying party returned with a map of the interior given to them by a British surveying party seeking an interocean canal route across the Isthmus of Tehuantepec. Perry, concerned by this foreign activity, immediately warned Secretary Mason of the "impolicy of permitting any European Power or interest to obtain a footing" here. Announcing that he had taken possession of the Coatzacoalcos River as far as he had ascended it, Perry recommended that any treaty of peace with Mexico include "the exclusive right of way across the Continent" for the United States.

The American force took possession of the coastal town of Carmen in Yucatán on 17 May, and Perry appointed Capt. James Magruder as its military governor. Perry's offensive operations had purposely avoided Tabasco up to this point because the Americans already occupied the mouth of the Grijalva River and had thus severed the city from the sea.[40] By early June, however, Perry had changed his mind, having learned that Tabasco was not so isolated as he had thought. Contraband trade continued to move through Tabasco to the Mexican forces inland. Perry preferred direct action against the town now to the more passive patrolling of the mouth of the Grijalva River, which offered no opportunities for combat gallantry. Moreover, Perry had left Tabasco in 1846 unsatisfied with his first expedition there. Although his orders then had not permitted him to occupy the town if any resistance developed, Perry still resented the treachery of General Traconis and his hollow claims of victory over the Americans. And he still lamented the death of Lt. Charles Morris, the son of Perry's fellow naval officer and longtime colleague Commo. Charles Morris.

Perry decided to launch a full-scale operation against Tabasco in June. He formed a landing force of 1,173 men and a flotilla of four small steamers, one schooner, one brig, three bomb brigs, and one merchant steamer. The previous October, Perry had surprised the Mexicans at Frontera and had ascended the entire seventy miles of river with little resistance. Now, Tabasco had a new commander and seemed well prepared to defend itself. Just above a treacherous part of the river named Devil's Bend the enemy had erected a breastwork, La Colmena, which extended from the river to a thick chaparral and commanded a place where submerged obstructions and pilings had been placed in the river. One mile farther upstream stood the Acachapan breastwork, and a mile and a half beyond that, the Independencia breastwork. One mile below the city stood newly built Fort Iturbide, armed with large- and small-caliber cannons. The new commander, Don Domingo Echagaray, had nine hundred troops to man the town and its river defenses. As Perry would discover, however, Echagaray was not a capable commander.

With a challenging mission ahead, Perry prepared meticulously "with more than his usual thoroughness." On the morning of 14 June, the flotilla crossed the bar and moved upstream. Perry was on the steamer *Scourge.* The steamers *Scorpion, Spitfire,* and *Vixen* followed, each towing other ships and boats carrying the landing force. The task force moved cautiously upstream that day and the morning of the next before meeting resistance. The American ships returned fire and continued through Devil's Bend. The next morning, 16 June, as the flotilla approached La Colmena and the underwater obstacles, Perry sent a boat to investigate. When the boat drew gunfire and had to turn back, Perry decided to land his ground force and take Tabasco by land. Comdr. Franklin Buchanan selected a site below the Colmena breastworks known as Seven Pines, and Perry was the first to land. Within ten minutes the entire eleven-hundred-man force was ashore, and within twenty-five minutes it was on the march along with seven fieldpieces.[41]

The column bypassed La Colmena and marched directly to Acachapan, where Colonel Hidalgo waited with three hundred infantry, three hundred cavalry, and two guns. Once the artillery barrage began, Perry organized his forces in a long line facing the breastwork. Perry, "heedless as usual about his personal safety, took an exposed position in front" to lead the charge. More of a headlong rush than a classic infantry charge, the American assault was marked by "great spirit but little organization." The panicked defenders fled the fortification and headed back to Tabasco. In the meantime, the river flotilla had dynamited the underwater obstacles to open a channel that permitted the American ships to pass. They reached Acachapan after the land forces had captured it and proceeded on to Tabasco. But Perry's reassembled land force had bogged down in the swamp and rough terrain on the route to Tabasco, and the oppressive heat took its toll on the men. It took several hours for the land force to reach the town, which in the meantime had surrendered to the river force and now flew the American flag. Under the command of Lt. David Dixon Porter, the river flotilla had bypassed Fort Iturbide and opened fire from its rear as Porter with a party of sixty-eight men took the fort. When the American ships reached the town, Captain Echagaray and his troops abandoned Tabasco and retreated upstream to regroup.[42]

The capture of Tabasco was Perry's major combat exploit in the Mexican War. It was well planned and executed even if Mexican resistance crumbled prematurely. The Americans suffered only five men wounded. Perry himself led and again displayed personal courage under fire; his conduct inspired his men. As he marched into Tabasco, "you would not have supposed from his appearance that he had been taking more than an ordinary walk," observed Commander Buchanan.

> He is at present certainly the man for the navy; in many respects he is an astonishing man, the most industrious, hard working, energetic, zealous, persevering, and enterprising officer of his rank in our navy. He does not spare himself or any one under him. This I like; his great powers of endurance astonish every one; all know he is by no means a brilliant man but his good common sense and judgment, his sociable manner to his officers, no humbuggery or mystery, make him respected and esteemed.

This was Perry's moment of pure satisfaction and glory. The robust leader, his endurance astonishing for a fifty-three-year-old man, and his forces had succeeded brilliantly through superb planning, fearless bravery, and aggressive initiative. "You have displayed skill, valor and energy, have disregarded personal privation and exposure, and done all your country" could expect, wrote Secretary Mason.[43]

Perry's men had good reason to admire their commander and savor their victory, but the moment passed quickly. Perry's good fortune, his health, and the high morale of his troops all proved transitory. Once Tabasco had been subdued, the squadron spent the next year again restricted largely to blockade and garrison duty. In addition, various developments tried the men's patience. Personally Perry was piqued by his lack of a suitable flagship. "I have previously disregarded comfort and the ordinary forms and ceremonies belonging to my station," he complained to Mason. But he needed a flagship with a "poop Cabin" to "keep myself aloof from the usual bustle of a large mess [so] as to be able to accomplish the great amount of writing devolving upon me." Perry was also annoyed when more marines were transferred from the squadron. The army was "already overflowing" with them, and his vessels "could never be efficient without Marines. . . . In a state of actual hostilities . . . [t]heir services are indispensable." He complained and asked the department for replacement marines to avoid "serious consequence, and some clamor."[44]

By early July, Perry yearned for the war to end. "God grant that we may soon have peace," he confided to his daughter Isabella, so that "this harrassing labour of mine will come to an end." When the war did not end quickly, Perry was forced to evacuate Tabasco. He had initially intended to garrison and occupy the town because of its strategic location on the contraband trade route from Yucatán to central Mexico, but disease and Mexican resistance had compelled him to change his mind. Enemy forces had adopted guerrilla tactics and constantly harassed the Americans. More serious was the coastal fever that hit the American garrison. The sick list included 120 men out of a total garrison of about 300. When Perry asked for a medical appraisal, Surgeon Lewis W. Minor and three medical assistants concluded that it would be "highly inexpedient" to remain because of the fever epidemic. Noting that there was "no guarding against the insidious approaches and dreadful ravages of pestilence," Perry evacuated Tabasco on 19 July 1847.[45]

By this time the fever was ravaging the entire Gulf Squadron. Although health precautions had been in force, they did not protect the crews because squadron duties required the men to operate in small ships close to shore and in small harbors and rivers along the coast. The fever epidemic of 1847 also contradicted traditional logic. Men who never left their ships and never went ashore seemed just as vulnerable as men on garrison duty onshore.

Although the fever did not prove fatal to many Americans, it weakened hundreds of men and seriously handicapped the squadron. Perry himself contracted the fever. On 2 August, Perry reported that the sick list at Salmadina hospital totaled 174. Two days later, it numbered 202. Perry would later report that 7 officers died and 70 others on the sick list returned to the United States between April and October 1847. The *Decatur, Saratoga,* and *Stromboli* all required reassignment. At one time, 100 of the 150 officers and men on the *Saratoga* and its commander were on the sick list.[46]

Perry was particularly exasperated by the condition of his flagship, the *Mississippi,* whose crew was so disabled that the medical officers urged him to send the ship home. Perry refused to do so, however, lacking "enough well firemen and coal heavers to manage" a voyage back to a northern port in the United States. Moreover, the *Mississippi* was the only oceangoing steamer in the Gulf Squadron. Perry questioned his medical officers on the causes of the epidemic and finally laid the blame on the *Mississippi,* whose hull had not been broken out and cleansed in six years. Perry also claimed that the disease had "doubtless proceeded from the extraordinary exposure and fatigue to which officers and men have been subjected." Nevertheless, Perry resisted losing the *Mississippi* because without it he would be unable to maintain communications with his squadron and garrisons, "especially after the Northers shall commence." Surgeon Minor insisted that Perry had no option but to send the *Mississippi* to a northern port as soon as possible. Perry finally agreed to send his flagship with its sick occupants to the United States, but only to Pensacola so that it could be cleansed, refitted, and returned as soon as possible.[47]

The situation worsened in early August. As the squadron lost ships and men to sickness, guerrilla activity increased at Frontera and Coatzacoalcos. Perry had sent six ships home in June. Now the department informed him that it could not provide replacements. On 16 August, Perry complained that the forces then at his disposal were inadequate to perform his mission. Of his nineteen remaining vessels, six were not available because they were under repair. In addition, manpower losses due to disease made it difficult to garrison, collect customs duties, and maintain trade regulations at various coastal ports. In response to the situation, the Navy Department advised Perry in early August not to attack or occupy "any other places than those now in your possession."[48]

Perry also learned of a minor but embarrassing setback. On 14 August, the British mail steamer *Treviot* had slipped through the blockade at Vera Cruz carrying Gen. Mariana Paredes y Arrillago, the former president of Mexico. Comdr. David Farragut was the officer in command of the *Saratoga* on the scene, but he had not boarded the *Treviot,* claiming that responsibility for inspecting incoming ships belonged to the army, not the navy. Chagrined by the incident, Perry blamed Farragut, thereby fueling the junior officer's long-standing hostility toward the Perry family. In his list of grievances, Farragut blamed Perry's brother-in-law George Washington Rodgers for his own failure to pass an officers' examination in the early 1820s. He also felt that Perry had misused him in the

Gulf campaign. When war erupted in 1846, Farragut had pressed for a combat role. He proposed and offered to participate in a naval assault on the Castle San Juan de Ulua, but the Navy Department had other priorities. Finally, on 9 March 1847, Farragut received orders to proceed to the Gulf in command of the *Saratoga*. To his great disappointment, the *Saratoga* reached Vera Cruz after the city and the castle had surrendered. When Perry assigned the *Saratoga* to blockade duty for the next several months, Farragut also missed the assaults on Tuxpan and Tabasco.

Thus deprived of the combat action he so desperately sought, Farragut resented his treatment and blamed his commander. In the summer of 1847, Farragut was stricken with yellow fever and almost died. In December, Farragut complained directly to Secretary Mason and asked to come home, claiming that when the commander of the squadron used his "trust with prejudice or partiality, there is no alternative to the subordinate but the one I seek, viz. to get from under his command."[49] Perry denied any prejudice whatsoever, defended his assignment of duties, and left it to the department to judge the "propriety of the language and tone of the letter of Commander Farragut." On 20 January 1848, the department recalled the *Saratoga* and Farragut. In his memoirs, Farragut remembered the cruise in the *Saratoga* as "the most mortifying" of his career. He wrote bitterly that he could never forgive the navy for the "great chance" it had missed at Castle San Juan de Ulua. "The Navy would stand on a different footing today if our ships had made the attack," claimed Farragut. Because Commodore Conner and the other old officers thought differently, "they all paid the penalty—not one of them will ever wear an Admiral's flag, which they might have done, if that castle had been taken by the Navy." These are the unmistakably self-aggrandizing sentiments of an officer more interested in his own personal glory than in the achievement of the main objective at Vera Cruz. Indeed, what might have been a costly assault on the castle was avoided when the castle was surrendered without the loss of a single American life.[50]

By the end of September, the fever was subsiding and the squadron was beginning to resume its normal activities. The sick list at Salmadina had declined to eighty men, but Perry remained mystified by the disease. While Vera Cruz was "comparatively healthy during the summer," the fever had prevailed "to an unusual extent" elsewhere on the coast, even among the natives. In the squadron, "the largest proportion of the deaths," noted Perry, were of "those who have not ascended the rivers, and with some who have scarcely left their respective vessels." The disease seems to have been combated successfully only on the *Vixen*, whose surgeon ordered the hatches and ports closed and steam from the boilers released into the enclosed compartments. The measure ruined the ship's woodwork but killed all the roaches and mosquitoes, thus ending the epidemic there.[51]

As the health of the squadron improved, so did Perry's own health and spirits. Residing onshore at Vera Cruz during October and November, he was delighted when the *Mississippi* returned on 22 October. Once again he had a large steamer to keep him in direct contact with the main ports along the coast. The reinvigorated Perry began to contemplate new initiatives for the squadron. He believed that the war should be escalated so that the Mexicans would "feel more sensibly the ordinary consequences of war." Confining himself to the operations of his squadron, Perry recommended a joint army and navy operation "across the Isthmus of Tehuantepec to the Pacific from the head waters of the Coatzacoalcos River" to establish "a military cordon." This offensive line would cut off the states of Tabasco and Chiapas from the rest of Mexico. Perry had learned from one of his commanders that both Tabasco and Chiapas were prepared, given a favorable moment, to separate from Mexico. After the invasion, American forces would thus control the Isthmus of Tehuantepec for present military purposes as well "as in reference to prospective measures" such as a railroad across the isthmus. A southern military cordon would also destroy the contraband trade route from the Gulf coast to the interior of Mexico and thus reduce pressure on the naval blockade.[52]

Had the war continued, this plan might have been considered in Washington, but Secretary Mason was more immediately concerned about Perry's poor health and irritated by his constant litany of complaints. On 18 October, Mason came close to reprimanding Perry for "the tone in which on more than one occasion you have commented on the orders of the Department." He relented slightly and added, "I have no reason to believe that they are intended to be disrespectful and have not regarded them in that light." Several weeks later, Mason thanked Perry for his plan but informed him that the military situation did not warrant a new operation. In fact, the fighting had ended in September

when Scott defeated Santa Anna and captured Mexico City. Shortly
thereafter, Santa Anna fled the country and was replaced as president by
General Pedro Maria Anaya, who informed the American peace commissioner, Nicholas Trist, that he wished to negotiate peace. Formal negotiations began on 2 January 1848 at Guadalupe Hidalgo, a suburb of Mexico City. There, Trist and Mexican officials signed the peace treaty on 2
February. Although Trist had not been authorized to conclude the agreement, and had, in fact, been recalled to Washington before the negotiations even began, Polk accepted the Treaty of Guadalupe Hidalgo. The
U.S. Senate ratified the agreement on 12 March and the Mexican Congress ratified it on 25 May. Formal ratifications were exchanged on
30 May 1848.[53]

Perry remained in the Gulf in command of the squadron until the
summer of 1848. Although the fighting had long since ended, Perry spent
the last eight months of the war dealing with another nettlesome issue.
From October 1847 to June 1848, the squadron had continued to impose
the blockade, collect duties, enforce customs regulations, and garrison
various ports, but its primary attention had shifted to Yucatán. This
province had begun the war as a neutral state, rejoined Mexico in
November 1846, and then one month later reasserted its neutrality and
asked the United States to recognize its independence. One political faction in the province sought union with Mexico while the other wanted
independence. Both factions were composed of whites who together
were outnumbered five to one by the indigenous Maya population.

Perry had occupied and then evacuated the coastal city of Carmen in
December 1846, then imposed a blockade that continued until May 1847,
when his forces reoccupied the town. Since Yucatán was unable to suppress illegal trade through its own territory, contraband goods flowed by
various routes through the province to Mexican military forces in the
interior. The situation became more sensitive in July 1847 when the neu-
tralist faction regained political control. The new rulers pressed the
United States to end its occupation of Carmen and lift its blockade. In
September 1847, Yucatán sent Justo Sierra O'Reilly to Washington to
appeal directly to the Polk administration.[54]

Perry believed that both the occupation of Carmen and the blockade
should be maintained. Although he realized that the occupation must
"be mortifying to its Government and injurious to its commerce and rev-
enues," it was a "necessary military expedience." If the United States left

Carmen, argued Perry, "a system of illicit commerce would be established . . . by which our enemy would be supplied with munitions of war in any quantities." With regard to Yucatán's pledge of nonintercourse with Mexico, Perry insisted that the province would not be able to enforce the agreement. En route to Washington, O'Reilly had two interviews with Perry at Vera Cruz but was unable to persuade Perry to change his position. Perry admitted that customs duties at Carmen might be modified, but he maintained that Yucatán should not be given "control of the Revenue Laws, as they would be insufficient, even if conscientiously administered, a result not to be expected, to prevent smuggling into the Enemy's Country."[55] In Washington, the administration agreed to Perry's maintaining both the occupation and the blockade until July 1848. Secretary of State Buchanan did, however, agree to abolish duties on Yucatán vessels passing between the peninsula and Carmen.[56]

Internal war in Yucatán complicated the political situation as indigenous forces attacked and threatened to overrun the white coastal settlements in early 1848. With no hope of securing assistance from the beleaguered Mexican government, Yucatán's rulers looked elsewhere. In 1847, an envoy had approached Secretary Buchanan about possible annexation by the United States, but the secretary abruptly dismissed the idea. Then, in 1848, with the Indians in Yucatán again on the offensive, O'Reilly asked Buchanan to permit Yucatán to import arms through the naval blockade for its defense. He also protested that the Treaty of Guadalupe Hidalgo did not include a pledge by Mexico not to punish Yucatán for its wartime neutrality. With the local war intensifying, O'Reilly also asked Buchanan for two thousand troops and $500,000. On 3 April, he pleaded with Buchanan to save the white population there from "utter extinction." Several weeks later, O'Reilly sent Buchanan a letter from Governor Santiago Mendez of Yucatán. Dated 25 March 1848, the letter offered "the dominion and sovereignty" of Yucatán to the United States in return for military assistance. Mendez had also sent identical letters to Great Britain and Spain.[57] Neither the United States, Great Britain, nor Spain accepted the offer. President Polk did, however, ask the Senate to approve such measures as were necessary to save the whites in Yucatán from extermination and from European colonization. The Senate discussed the matter but dropped it abruptly when the immediate crisis passed.

As these developments unfolded in early 1848, Perry prepared to return home. Although he had commanded the squadron for less than ten months, he requested in January to be relieved by 1 April. His previous illness and the "incessant toil" of his duties had impaired his health to the point that he would not "much longer be able to fulfill my duties with satisfaction to myself or the department." Under doctor's orders, he tried to hasten his recovery by riding every afternoon, but he complained that he was still "far from well" and that only his return to a "northern climate" would fully restore his health.[58] Perry also understood that the chance for further military action had passed, leaving only routine naval duties and the sensitive, messy situation in Yucatán. Perry expected his request to be granted and planned to depart on the *Mississippi* by 1 May, but Secretary Mason denied his request and explained that the president had deemed it of "great importance" that Perry remain until the peace treaty was ratified. The disappointed Perry complained that he was "becoming quite feeble" and had no appetite. With the return of the rainy season, his state of health dropped so low "as to render me almost incapable of keeping out of my bed."[59]

Compelled to deal with the ambiguous situation in Yucatán, Perry continued to occupy Carmen, impose the blockade, and avoid involvement in the civil war. He monitored the situation and reported regularly to Mason, but he refused to give credence to rumors suggesting that the British or the French were about to seize Yucatán. Praising his men for allowing the residents of Carmen to "enjoy a perfect quiet and protection," he refused to permit his men or ships to become further involved. He offered refuge to white women and children who were fleeing communities under attack, but the cowardly behavior of the male ruling class disgusted him. "Perhaps there has never been a more extraordinary example of disgraceful cowardice than has been exhibited by the people of Yucatán in this war with Indians," wrote Perry. "Men who will make no effort to defend their own fire sides, have no claim upon the friendly aid of others."[60] Perry reiterated this opinion to the department in May and reminded his commanders to "do no more than I have done, in aid of these unfortunate people."[61]

At the end of May, Perry received the news he had long awaited. Mexico had ratified the peace treaty, and he could finally go home. The news came none too soon, for he reported on 28 May that his strength had become "so much debilitated as scarcely to permit me to attend my duties." The fever had also returned to the squadron. On the *Cumberland,* all four lieutenants, most of the other officers, and one hundred men had been stricken with fever. As he prepared to leave, Perry returned the occupied towns and customhouses to Mexican officials and supervised the evacuation of eighteen thousand troops from Vera Cruz. He also secured various natural history items that he had collected in Mexico for friends back home. For William Redfield, he had collected and bottled in alcohol fish from the rivers and harbors of the Gulf coast. As a final gesture, Perry increased the garrison at Carmen to 250 men and four artillery pieces. By July, the immediate crisis in Yucatán had passed, although the "caste war" would continue until 1853.[62]

In spite of his eagerness to end his assignment, Perry did not reach New York until 19 July and did not relinquish command of the squadron until 20 November.[63] By that time the exhausted and weakened commodore could take at least some pleasure in his command performance. Under trying circumstances, his squadron had executed its support duties while prosecuting the war as aggressively as possible. Although Mexican resistance was generally light, the climate and geography alone rendered some of the landing objectives difficult. Securing each significant coastal town and establishing total control of the entire Mexican Gulf coast, Perry had demonstrated his maturity as commander of the squadron. He had also exercised excellent military and diplomatic judgment. Despite his own desire and the hunger of his men for combat, he was neither foolhardy nor impetuous in seeking combat opportunities. In the Mexican towns that he occupied, Perry had insisted that the customs regulations be administered honestly and that his forces respect the lives and property of Mexican civilians. He developed contempt for the Mexican people, but he tolerated no looting, pillaging, or attacks on civilians. Moreover, his forbearance and restraint in the last months of the war had helped to ensure that Yucatán did not become a major military or diplomatic problem for the United States. Occasionally Perry overreacted, as in the case of Lt. Charles Hunter at Alvarado, and his excessive complaints irritated his superiors in Washington, but these were minor shortcomings. As the navy's preeminent officer, the fifty-four-year-old Perry now welcomed shore duty and a respite from the rigors of war.

～7 ～

PLANNING THE NAVAL
EXPEDITION TO JAPAN

*The real object of the expedition should be concealed from public view,
under a general understanding, that its main purpose will be to examine the usual resorts of our whaling ships, with special reference to
their protection, and the opening to them of new ports of refuge and
refreshment.*

COMMO. MATTHEW PERRY TO
SECRETARY OF THE NAVY WILLIAM GRAHAM, 1851

On 7 November 1849, in the most fashionable wedding of the
year, August Belmont married Caroline Slidell Perry in New
York City. Rev. Francis Vinton performed the Episcopalian ceremony on a day on which "the atmosphere was as balmy as the bride was
beautiful." The bride's parents, Commodore and Mrs. Matthew C. Perry,
attended the service at the new Church of the Ascension, which stood
four blocks from Belmont's Fifth Avenue mansion. The marriage not
only created a personal union but also afforded important social advantages for Belmont and financial and social benefits for Caroline and her
family. The thirty-five-year-old Belmont, a German Jewish immigrant,
had married into a highly respected American naval family; twenty-year-
old Caroline had connected her family to one of the wealthiest and most
socially prominent men in New York City. Prior to the wedding, Belmont
gave his bride an entire city block in Manhattan.[1]

August Belmont was born in 1813 in the village of Alzey in the Grand
Duchy of Hesse-Darmstadt. As a young man he served as an apprentice

and confidential secretary to the Rothschilds in Frankfurt. In 1837, they sent Belmont to Cuba to monitor their interests there, but Belmont landed in New York during the early months of the Panic of 1837 and stayed on there as the company's agent. An ambitious and savvy man who understood international banking and enjoyed the credit of the Rothschilds to support him, Belmont quickly capitalized on the financial chaos and made handsome profits for his employer and for himself. By 1845, his worth was estimated to exceed $100,000; indeed, he was one of the wealthiest individuals in New York. Belmont was also a cultured man with European tastes in music, theater, and dress. He loved fashionable social events, kept expensive horses, reportedly employed the best chef in town, and entertained lavishly. His wealth, European sophistication, and personal style intrigued and attracted women, and he readily returned their attentions. Adding to his mystique was a slight limp, the result of a hip wound he had sustained in a duel fought in 1841 over the honor of a woman.[2]

Belmont met Caroline Perry through her in-laws, the Slidells and the Hones, in 1849. They courted that summer during the lavish social season at Saratoga Springs with its round of receptions, teas, picnics, and elaborate costume balls, then agreed to marry in the fall. Caroline was a delicate beauty known as "Tiny" to her family. Contemporaries described her as a lovely, soft, and small woman with large eyes and eyelids that drooped slightly, giving her the appearance of having just awakened from an afternoon nap. August spoke of her angelic face; others likened her to a fairy-tale princess.

For Commodore Perry and his wife, this marriage was not the conventional union they might have desired. Both Matthew and Jane held very traditional social views and were confirmed Episcopalians. Belmont was an older man and a German Jew with a rather racy past. There is no evidence, however, that either parent opposed the marriage. In fact, the commodore very much approved of Belmont's wealth, bright future, and social standing while Jane pointed to the great devotion August lavished on his new bride. The marriage started off so well that Jane felt the need to caution her daughter. She warned Caroline on her birthday in 1850 that she had "much to learn" before she appreciated fully "the great blessing of having a husband so devoted . . . whose chief aim seems to be your pleasure while surrounded by so much to make life easy and happy." Life, she warned, would certainly bring Caroline many changes and sorrows that could be borne only by seeing "the mysterious hand of God overruling all things for our own particular good. . . . It is the best and wisest plan to feel that the days cannot always be bright."[3] In fact, Caroline was destined to lead a long and privileged life. Her marriage produced five children and lasted forty-one years until August died in 1890. During their marriage, the Belmonts were leaders of New York society and pioneers of the post–Civil War social scene in Newport, Rhode Island.

Matthew Perry was almost twenty years older than his new son-in-law, but they developed a close friendship. While Perry lectured his children in a fatherly tone in his letters, he corresponded with August as a peer and enjoyed sharing political news and views with a fellow Democrat. Respecting Belmont's financial abilities, Perry asked his son-in-law's advice on monetary matters. And he turned to Belmont for assistance in handling his personal financial affairs during his extended absence on the expedition to Japan.

The Perry-Belmont wedding was the domestic centerpiece of Matthew Perry's four-year home stay following the Mexican War. With the marriage of Caroline, only fifteen-year-old Isabella remained at home. Sarah and Jane Oliver Hazard Perry had both been married since 1841. Of the boys, Matthew Calbraith Jr. continued to serve in the navy. After the Mexican War, William led an undistinguished civilian life. Oliver Hazard, who left the navy after the *Somers* affair, studied law in New Orleans, and in 1849 migrated to California to seek his fortune. After he had returned from Mexico, Matthew went home to Jane in New York and lived there as he attended to various shore duties. For Perry, these years provided a welcome contrast to the previous five years of mentally demanding and physically exhausting duty in Africa and the Gulf of Mexico. These commands had left Perry's normally robust constitution in such a weakened state that he was content to remain onshore for a time. Fifty-five years old in April 1849, Perry needed time in a moderate climate.

The Navy Department cooperated by appointing Perry to oversee a new federal program as general superintendent of ocean mail steamers. "I cannot imagine a more important duty in time of Peace," wrote Secretary Mason.[4] In 1845, Congress had authorized federal subsidies for a steamship line to carry mail across the Atlantic. Then, in 1847 legislation that funded four steam warships for the navy, Congress also authorized new mail subsidies for three companies: E. K. Collins, George Law, and the Sloo Line. For making twenty round trips between New York and Liverpool each year, the Collins Line was to receive $385,000 annually for ten years. With this federal subsidy, Collins was to build and operate mail steamers that could be converted into first-class steam warships. Each was to be at least two thousand gross tons, have one thousand horsepower or more, and carry passengers as well as mail across the Atlantic. The ships were designed by navy engineers but built by private contractors.[5]

Perry's charge was to inspect the new vessels as they were built "for the full and satisfactory performance of all stipulations of the several contracts," to suggest "such timely arrangements as will render them more readily available for vessels of war," and to communicate with the department "without reserve" with the assurance that it would adopt "any suggestions which will add to your efficiency or guard against any collision with the private interests of the contractors." Because the design and specifications had already been determined and construction was well under way before Perry began his duties, his actual role and precise authority were not clear. His instructions did not authorize him to order alterations or to correct defects during construction. Perry asked the department to clarify his duties, but his questions were never answered.[6]

Construction on some of the steamers proceeded on schedule; others lagged behind. The *Ohio,* built for A. G. Sloo, was finished in the summer of 1849; however, the Collins steamers did not come close to meeting their May 1849 completion deadline, requiring an act of Congress to extend the deadline. The first Collins steamer, the *Atlantic,* was finally completed in June 1850; the *Pacific, Arctic,* and *Baltic* all followed within four months. Perry complained that the steamers were too expensive, too extravagant, and too impractical. At the same time, when each was completed, Perry along with his fellow supervisors certified that the ships had been built "in conformity with the requirements of the Act of Congress . . . and to conform with the contract for carrying the mails." Moreover, the supervisors certified that "with the preparation and additions of suitable war appointments," each ship could "easily be converted into a War Steamer of the first class."[7]

The mail steamers were indeed both well built and expensive. Originally estimated to cost $400,000, each eventually cost $735,000, an 84 percent overrun. They needed to be stronger than ordinary domestic steamers so that heavy guns could be mounted in their conversion to warships, and the special construction requirements added to the cost. The use of high-priced private labor in New York shipyards already operating at nearly full capacity further increased the cost. In order to compete for passengers, the luxurious and extravagant mail steamers included private cabins, dining rooms, and a grand saloon built with fine wood wainscoting, rich gilding, and stained-glass windows and furnished with elegant sofas, comfortable armchairs, marble-topped tables, and handsome spittoons.[8]

Once launched, the new high-speed steamers created headlines. In October 1849, A. G. Sloo reported to Perry that the veteran naval officers onboard the *Ohio* for the ship's initial cruise "interpreted her performance to be the finest and fastest Steam Ship in the World." When the Collins liners began operation, they soon established records for the fastest transatlantic crossing between Liverpool and New York. In 1851, the *Pacific* made the westward passage in nine days and twenty hours. In 1852, the *Arctic* crossed in the opposite direction in nine days and thirteen hours. The times excited Americans because the vaunted rival British Cunard steamers could not equal them. Nonetheless, whether these publicly financed passenger liners could be converted into first-class steam warships remained an unanswered question, one that became a political and policy issue. In his annual report submitted in December 1849, skeptical Secretary of the Navy William B. Preston declared the mail steamer subsidies to be "fraught with incalculable mischief to the navy" because they involved "immense expenditures of public money." Congressional debate, inquiry, and criticism followed as one senator and then another denounced the cost and raised the conversion question.[9]

Perry was asked by Secretary Preston to answer questions about the new ships. Having certified in August 1849 that the *Ohio* could "easily be converted into a War Steamer of the first class," now, seven months later, Perry equivocated. The mail steamers, he wrote, were "excellent though somewhat different. The form and dimensions best adapted to a war steamer, would not be the most suitable for a commercial vessel." Speed, passenger comfort, and mail capacity were priorities in commercial vessels, and "little or no regard" was "paid in their construction to the protection of their engines and boilers from shot." Perry concluded that the

mail steamers could "easily be converted into war steamers for temporary service in cases of particular emergency," but he distinguished
between these auxiliary vessels and actual fighting ships. The mail
steamers could mount a few heavy-caliber guns and be used "in Convoy, in the transportation of Troops, carrying dispatches, conveying public functionaries, etc., etc., but this service could only be contingent
and . . . *temporary,*" advised Perry.

> The cost of converting them for war purposes would be large, and in
> no aspect would they be economical, or in any way equal to vessels
> built expressly for Government service; nor should they in my opinion
> interfere in the least with the organization and gradual increase of an
> efficient and permanent steam navy.[10]

Perry was attempting to find his way through a thorny political
thicket. On the one hand, he supported the building of the new mail
steamers that he had been ordered to oversee. He understood that the
mail steamer subsidies were strongly supported in New York financial
and commercial circles. In Congress, the key supporter of the subsidies
was Whig representative Thomas Butler King of Georgia, who had been
lavishly honored by the New York business community in March 1847.
On the other hand, Perry also knew that Secretary William Preston and
a group of politicians in Congress were critical of the program. And at
the same time, Perry felt thwarted by his own imprecise instructions and
lack of authority. Even when he objected, he had no control over excessive construction costs and could not order changes to remedy construction problems. His response was to steer an imperfect course by doing
his job and certifying that the new ships were built in accordance with
their contractual specifications as well as convertible into first-class war
steamers.[11]

Perry's contradictory position jeopardized his public credibility. In
1852, when an increasingly skeptical Congress debated the mail steamer
subsidies, various senators quoted Perry on both sides of the issue.
Finally, a critic of the program and the administration, Senator Solon
Borland of Arkansas, cited Perry's conflicting statements, observed that
Perry "has so far ridden on 'both sides of the sapling' at the same time,"
and suggested that "his testimony may well be dispensed with altogether." Since Perry had been selected to command the East India
Squadron by this time, Borland also proposed an "experiment" to get the

commodore's real opinion. Perry should be offered the mail steamers for the East India Squadron. Borland doubted that the veteran commodore would risk taking them. If he did, Perry should be regarded as a "fit companion for those famous 'three wise men of Gotham, who went to sea in a bowl.'" His expertise having been ridiculed, Perry was relieved that his views did not become a major point of contention in the Senate.[12]

During his shore duty after the Mexican War, Perry was not the assertive naval reformer he had been during the 1830s, but he did continue to express strong views about social reform and technological change in the navy. For years, humanitarian-minded reformers in the dynamic reform era of the 1840s had pressed to improve the lives and working conditions of navy sailors. Although some progress had been made, pay remained low, conditions harsh, and discipline severe. Without many incentives to offer recruits, the navy faced the same vexing problem Perry had faced in the 1820s. A naval apprentice system was instituted in the 1830s, but the *Somers* affair destroyed its credibility in 1842. As a result, U.S. naval vessels continued to be manned largely by foreigners or by Americans of inferior education or intelligence. Reformers now sought to improve the plight of the sailor by targeting two long-standing and apparently interrelated naval practices: the daily grog ration and flogging. They argued that the daily one-gill (eight-ounce) grog ration produced widespread drunkenness that undermined discipline and necessitated frequent flogging; and indeed, a given number of lashes was commonly imposed as punishment for drunkenness. While some reformers argued that elimination of the grog ration would significantly reduce flogging, others pressed for the abolition of flogging altogether. Numerous horror stories and gruesome descriptions of the brutal practice generated strong public and political support for reform. Reformers argued that since the navy would never eliminate flogging or the grog ration voluntarily, changes would have to be imposed externally. In December 1849, Senators Daniel Webster and William Henry Seward presented petitions requesting the end of the grog ration and flogging.[13]

Secretary Preston responded by surveying a cross section of eighty-four naval officers, including Perry. He asked what impact the abolition of flogging would have on the navy, whether restrictions short of abolition could be placed on the practice, and whether the spirit ration should be eliminated or replaced by a substitute. As in earlier proposed reforms, Perry focused on improving the efficiency of the navy, not the working conditions of its sailors. Both flogging and the grog ration were practical matters that should be modified only to enhance naval discipline and efficiency, not to improve the sailors' lot.

Perry in turn polled a number of veteran sailors at the Brooklyn Navy Yard and concluded that flogging could not "be entirely dispensed with consistent with the interests and efficiency of the Naval Service" unless an "immediate practical remedy" was found or the character of seamen improved. Alternatives such as "admonition," extra duty, imprisonment, restriction of privileges, or reduction of pay would certainly fail. Imprisonment or confinement on shipboard was the most obvious substitute, but this would endanger the "efficiency and safety of the ship" by forcing other men to perform the duties of the culprit. In that sense, confinement would be "rather a regard than a punishment." Flogging could be reduced, however, by making its infliction "more formal and consequently less frequent." Perry proposed the creation of a new navy bureau of garrison and courts-martial with elaborate regulations and procedures and an inferior court to hear the corporal punishment cases.[14]

With respect to the "spirit ration," which he had long sought ways to decrease, Perry suggested eliminating it and substituting a cash stipend or items such as extra tea, coffee, or sugar as alternatives. On long voyages when the daily diet was "barely sufficient" and fresh water was in short supply, fresh meat, fresh vegetables and fruits, or even wine could substitute for grog. Other officers generally agreed with Perry in supporting flogging, but most opposed elimination of the grog ration because they believed the practice did not threaten shipboard discipline and might well be replaced by the smuggling of liquor and even greater intoxication onboard. The prevailing views of the naval officers notwithstanding, Congress abolished flogging in both the navy and the merchant marine in September 1850. The daily spirit ration would endure for more than a decade until it too was eliminated in 1862.[15]

In July 1851, Secretary of the Navy William Graham requested Perry's views on coastal fortifications and the defense of the United States. The existing national defense policy had been formulated in two reports written in the 1820s and had remained unchanged since then. The army engineers who wrote the reports conceded the primary responsibility for protecting the coasts to the navy but urged construction and maintenance of a unified system of coastal fortifications that could be manned by a minimum number of army troops. The forts would not only discourage foreign attack or invasion but would also make a foreign blockade of the coast more difficult. Since the policy was never implemented, it remained more theory than practical reality, but now Graham was asking whether the policy should be modified.[16]

Perry used the secretary's request as an opportunity to lecture on the lessons of military history and the importance of modern technology for national defense. Additional forts were not needed, he argued, because technological and military developments had "gone far beyond the anticipation of the wildest visionary" in rendering the existing defense policy obsolete. Unless fully garrisoned, coastal forts were vulnerable to surprise attack and capture by enemy forces. Moreover, wrote Perry, "we have the experience of history to show that extensive military works are alike destructive of the prosperity and the liberties of the people saying nothing of the Enormous Cost of Construction." Fortifications such as those at Vera Cruz, Havana, Cartagena, and even Gibraltar, Perry claimed, "are in truth like chained monsters harmless beyond the reach of their manacles." Such was not the case with steam batteries; "*they* have the means of locomotion, and *their* power can be made effective at any point upon the coast." In Perry's view, foreign invasion was not a major danger. Of all the coasts of Europe, Great Britain was the least fortified and the least invaded because of its strong navy and the "warlike spirit" of its yeomanry. "And thus it should be with us, man to man, the Americans are equal to any other race, and they are fully capable of driving back to their ships, or capturing" any invading force.[17]

Furthermore, he continued, "no one can foretell or scarcely imagine the changes in the art of war that steam and other natural elements more recently brought into use are to produce." For example, steam warships could reintroduce old-fashioned tactics such as the naval ram. A wedge-shaped steamer with its screw propeller, crew, engine, and machinery below water level could travel at fourteen miles per hour. "Can any one imagine," asked Perry, "the overwhelming effect of a contact of this moving body with anything capable of floating upon the ocean? This is no *visionary* project, but one of simple demonstration and practical accomplishment." Since the United States was now a powerful nation with the potential to sustain a large navy, Perry urged Graham to rethink the basic national defense policy. With its "inexhaustible resources," its extensive and rapidly growing commerce, and its acknowledged superiority in building and managing sail and steam vessels, the

United States needed to think aggressively about its security. "Why should we barricade ourselves and wait within our defenses the coming of the Enemy?" Instead, why not plan to meet the enemy "beyond the threshold and thus preserve our waters and our soil inviolate? We possess the power, why not exercise it?" On the issue of national defense, Perry was ahead of his time, however, and his ideas were largely ignored.[18]

Perry continued officially as general superintendent of mail steamer construction until March 1852, but other interests now occupied his mind. More than a year earlier he had become interested in the idea of a naval expedition to Japan. Though Perry had never been to Asia, the East Indies, or even the Pacific Ocean, he developed an interest in Japan and the Pacific soon after he returned from the Mexican War. Several relatives and personal contacts provided firsthand information. His son-in-law John Hone was assistant collector of the Port of New York, a position that placed him in direct contact with the nine principal New York merchant houses involved in the China trade. His son Oliver Hazard Perry II, who had migrated to California in search of gold in 1849, provided his father with a firsthand account of the region's promise. His daughter Caroline's marriage to August Belmont gave Perry access to information emanating from New York financial circles. The most important contacts, however, resulted from his duties as supervisor of the construction of subsidized mail steamers. The companies involved were interested in a steamship route to the Pacific coast as well as mail runs to Europe. His own son Oliver had taken passage on the new mail steamer *California* to the Pacific coast. Through his supervisory duties, then, Perry became privy to the interests and plans of New York's leading shipbuilders and merchant houses for Asia.

His involvement with the construction of the new steamships made it obvious to Perry that future American commercial interests in the Pacific would depend on steamships and the establishment of a steamship line to Asia. As an experienced mariner, Perry realized that the great circle route offered the shortest distance between California and China. Directly along the route stood Japan, of more importance to the United States strategically as a place for steamships to stop and refuel on their way to China than as a potential market itself. Although other Americans such as Daniel Webster, A. H. Palmer, and the captains of whalers operating in the North Pacific all understood the importance of Japan in similar terms, most Americans at the time showed little interest in the small island nation. In that era of great expansionist dreams, their imaginations settled on places such as China and Cuba.[19]

By mid-century, the nation's most important maritime interest in the Pacific was its six-hundred-ship whaling fleet with an estimated two hundred ships operating in the waters of the North Pacific. But that was soon to change. The settlement of the Pacific coast, the creation of a transpacific steamship line, and the small but fast-growing trade between the United States and Asia promised a huge increase in the number of American merchant ships in Japanese waters—and, of course, a corresponding number of ships in distress and shipwrecked sailors. Reports that the Japanese mistreated shipwrecked whalers and foreign seamen troubled many Americans in 1850. Once they reached Japan, these hapless survivors were questioned, watched, forcibly confined, fed a meager diet of rice and fish, and transported from place to place in cages. For example, reports reached the United States that survivors of the whaling ship *Lawrence* received rough treatment in 1847 and that one man died before the rest were taken to Nagasaki.[20]

The Japanese viewed the situation quite differently. Since their presence on Japanese soil violated Japanese law, shipwrecked foreigners were naturally treated with suspicion, questioned, and confined. The Japanese also provided humane treatment by Japanese standards to these unfortunate seamen. The Americans received the normal daily Japanese diet of rice and fish. When transported, they were carried in a *norimon*, an enclosed palanquin about four feet long and three to four feet high. Considered to be a travel luxury rather than a hardship, the *norimon* was nevertheless uncomfortable for the taller and larger Americans.

Adding to the concerns of the Americans were allegations from the fifteen men from the whaler *Lagoda* who reached Japan in 1848. In reality, these men were troublesome deserters, not innocent survivors of a shipwreck. The Japanese had great difficulty controlling this unruly lot, who resisted supervision, attempted frequently to break away, and quarreled and fought among themselves. Although two of them died, one was strangled by one of his own mates. The Japanese confined the men, permitted them no exercise, and placed three of them in solitary confinement. Americans, however, ignored the behavior of the *Lagoda* deserters and focused on the cruel treatment they had received.[21]

In Washington, President Millard Fillmore was considering an official expedition to Japan, which had been isolated from the Western world for more than two centuries. The recent westward expansion of the United States had demonstrated the emerging importance of Japan. The acquisition of the Oregon Territory in 1846 and California in 1848 had given the United States an extensive Pacific coastline. Thousands of Americans were flocking to the new territories. With its recent victory in the Mexican War and its new Pacific frontage, the United States was confident and eager to embrace its commercial destiny in the Pacific. President Zachary Taylor had not viewed the Pacific as a priority, but his death in July of 1850 brought a new president and cabinet to power. Fillmore was a New York Whig who very much wanted to expand American influence and trade in the Pacific. And the new cabinet included Daniel Webster as secretary of state and William A. Graham as secretary of the navy. The sixty-nine-year-old Webster remained a towering political figure in 1851. He was experienced diplomatically and had served with distinction as secretary of state in 1841 and 1842. He also understood American interests in the Pacific and sought to advance them by protecting the sovereignty of the Sandwich Islands and establishing diplomatic relations with Japan.[22] The forty-five-year-old Graham was a North Carolina Whig who had served in the Senate and as governor. Although he had no diplomatic or naval experience, Graham understood that the United States had "arrived at a new era in our history, arising from our occupation and vast extension of our territories on the coast of the Pacific." He recommended expansion of the mail steamer subsidy program and establishment of a mail steamship line between San Francisco, Macao, and Shanghai.[23]

An expedition to establish diplomatic relations with Japan seemed a promising initiative for the new Fillmore administration. The idea was not a new one, but contact between the United States and Japan had been rare and sporadic for decades. In 1791, John Kendrick in the *Lady Washington* and another ship had attempted unsuccessfully to trade in Japan. Between 1797 and 1807, eight American ships chartered by the Dutch had entered the port of Nagasaki. In the United States, Commo. David Porter had been the first to propose an expedition to Japan, in 1815, but nothing came of his recommendation.[24]

Twenty years later, in 1847, Charles W. King organized an expedition. King was a partner in D. W. C. Olyphant and Company, an American merchant house in the China trade. The *Morrison* carried King and his wife, four Japanese castaways, and three missionaries on a peaceful mission intended to create friendship, initiate trade, and spread Christianity to Japan. The unarmed *Morrison* sailed to Uraga at the entrance to Edo Bay, where it was approached by Japanese boats. King permitted their crews to board unhindered and found the Japanese to be curious and friendly. But as soon as the visitors left, shore batteries opened fire, forcing the *Morrison* to move out of range. Having been totally rebuffed at Uraga, King sailed to Kagoshima, where his ship was again fired on. After that, recognizing the failure of his project, King sailed away from Japan with the four Japanese castaways, whom he had not been able to land.

Then in 1845, Capt. Mercator Cooper of the whaler *Manhattan* sailed into Japanese waters with fourteen shipwrecked Japanese sailors. Cooper landed several of the castaways onshore before he proceeded to Uraga so that they could apprise officials of his peaceful intentions. At Uraga, hundreds of Japanese guard boats appeared and surrounded the ship for five days, but they did not attack or make any threats. Japanese officials boarded the *Manhattan* and generously provided the Americans with food and gifts. They also presented Cooper with an official document that thanked him for returning the Japanese sailors but also stated that he was not to return to Japan. Cooper was impressed with his friendly reception and with the intelligence, politeness, and curiosity of the Japanese. His accounts reflected his positive impressions and his hope that closer relations would be established with Japan.

The following year, the United States sent a formal expedition to Japan to determine whether the Japanese would consider treaty negotiations. In July 1846, Commo. James Biddle entered Edo Bay near Uraga with the ship of the line *Columbus* and the sloop-of-war *Vincennes*. The Japanese made no effort to drive the ships away, and officials treated the Americans cordially. Providing fresh water and fresh foods, the Japanese boarded and toured the American warships, but no Americans were permitted onshore. One week after Biddle arrived, the Japanese delivered an edict that refused any negotiations and advised the Americans to depart immediately. A minor incident that later assumed significance occurred as Biddle was boarding a native junk to receive the Japanese reply. As he boarded, a Japanese seaman jostled Biddle and forced him back into his own boat. Biddle reacted by returning to the *Columbus* and insisting that the offender be punished. The Japanese apologized and assured Biddle that the man would be disciplined. Biddle sensibly accepted this response in good faith and let the matter rest. Reports that a lowly Japanese seaman had insulted an American naval commander with impunity rankled other American naval officers, however, and convinced them that a much tougher posture was needed.[25]

Comdr. James Glynn acted accordingly when he sailed to Nagasaki in the sloop-of-war *Preble* in 1849 to retrieve the fifteen American seamen from the *Lagoda* who reportedly were being held as Japanese prisoners. Although Japanese guard boats surrounded his ship and troops manned shore batteries, Glynn insisted that Japanese officials immediately release the American seamen. He also stated that if the Japanese did not satisfy his request, he would sail to Edo to demand satisfaction. When Japanese officials stalled, Glynn insisted on and received an immediate reply. The Japanese released the men, and Glynn departed.

In January 1851, Perry responded to the nation's growing interest in Japan by offering Secretary Graham a specific proposal for an expedition based on "all the best authorities in the Congressional Library . . . official reports, and . . . other reliable sources." Perry advised that the "real object" of a naval expedition "should be concealed from public view, under a general understanding that its main purpose" would be to open to American whaling ships "new ports of refuge and refreshment." Since the Dutch controlled Nagasaki, the only foreign port of entry in Japan, the squadron should select another port, where they should "suddenly appear and demand" the right of free access for American vessels to one or more ports "for refreshment and repair." The unexpected appearance of a formidable American naval force "would doubtless produce great surprise and confusion" among the "shrewd and cunning" Japanese, who tried every means— "cajolery— treachery—strategem—withholding of supplies, and force"— to get rid of foreigners. But by acting "with patience and forbearance, and judicious management . . . acting always on the defensive, though prompt at resenting insult," an American expedition could expect to succeed.[26]

Although Perry considered the Japanese inferior to Americans, he respected them and judged them superior to the Chinese. The Japanese might be "treacherous," but Perry labeled reports of their prejudice against foreigners "very much exaggerated." He mistakenly thought that geographic rivalries in Japan might be exploited and wrongly believed that the Japanese "masses would connive" with Americans to end the "absurd restrictions at present in force with respect to foreigners."[27]

Perry estimated that three first-class war steamers and one sloop-of-war would be required for the mission. Since very few Japanese had ever seen one, steamers were critical to the expedition's success. The Japanese would be astonished and perplexed "by the sudden, and to them mysterious, approach of these vessels . . . moving silently, and to all appearance stealthily along, without sails, and without regard to wind or tide." With "their guns of heavy caliber, their explosive shells, and rockets . . . and other productions of American ingenuity," American steamers would more effectively "command their fears, and secure their friendship" than all of the diplomatic missions of the previous one hundred years. Perry emphasized that the expedition should be "strictly naval, untrammeled by the interference of diplomatic agents," who were poor judges of employing a squadron in "remote and unfrequented seas." Once contact was established, "trade, and consequently diplomatic appointments would, of course, follow."[28] After proposing the expedition, Perry continued to collect information about U.S. interests in the Pacific. He corresponded with New Bedford whaling captain Joseph Delano, who furnished Perry with firsthand information on the needs of whalers and provided a letter from Capt. Mercator Cooper, the man who had sailed into Edo Bay in 1845.

In making his recommendation, Perry had joined a chorus of other men, such as Aaron H. Palmer and Comdr. James Glynn, who were pressing for an expedition to Japan. Palmer was a New York entrepreneur and lobbyist who was fascinated by Japan; for years he had collected information, published material, and pressed for U.S. contact with Japan. As director of the American and Foreign Agency of New York, Palmer had proposed an expedition to Secretary of State John Clayton in 1849. In 1851, Palmer renewed his efforts and met on several occasions with Secretary Webster. Glynn came to Washington in January 1851, fresh from his voyage to Japan, met with the president and submitted a proposal to him. Both Palmer and Glynn advocated the use of an imposing naval squadron to establish diplomatic relations and secure protection for shipwrecked American mariners. While Palmer was prepared to use force and establish a blockade of Japanese ports, Glynn advised a more restrained approach in order to establish the basis for a long-term amicable relationship with Japan.[29]

On 9 May 1851, Secretary Webster informed Secretary Graham that Capt. John H. Aulick, the new commander of the East India Squadron, would undertake the mission to Japan. Webster had accepted Aulick's proposal that seventeen shipwrecked Japanese sailors might be transported from San Francisco back to Japan and used to establish contact and formal relations with Japan. Aulick was to deliver a letter from President Fillmore to the emperor of Japan. The letter emphasized that Aulick was not a religious missionary and stated that the United States sought only to "promote friendship and commerce between the two countries." It asked the Japanese to permit American trade, to assist shipwrecked Americans on their coast, and to provide a place where steamers en route to China could purchase coal. "Our object is friendly commercial intercourse and nothing more."[30]

In his instructions to Aulick, Webster stressed that the primary objective of this mission was to secure Japanese coal; the protection of shipwrecked mariners and the right to trade were secondary goals. American ships had to be able to purchase coal from Japan in order to complete the last link in the route between the United States and China. Nor did the United States ask for something to which it had no right. Aulick was to tell the Japanese that the United States sought an agreement to purchase coal, "not the manufactures of his artizans or the results of the toil of his husbandmen,— but a gift of Providence, deposited, by the Creator of all things in the depths of the Japanese Islands, for the benefit of the human family." The Aulick mission did not embody Perry's recommendations, and it reflected naive optimism on the administration's part. Furthermore, the three ships assigned to the squadron were barely adequate for its duties in China, much less a special mission to Japan, and Aulick was supposed to undertake the Japanese initiative as part of his regular duties as commander of the East India Squadron.[31]

Once Aulick departed in 1851, Perry's thoughts turned to other matters. With August and Caroline Belmont planning an extended tour of Europe, Perry thought logically of the most prestigious command in the navy. In May, he wrote to his friend William Sinclair in the Navy Department that he was "particularly anxious to succeed Commo. Morgan on the Mediterranean Station." Perry thought his own "as good a claim as any other who might desire the command." His previous two commands had involved "special service of great responsibility and privation without any of the relaxation and agreeable duties usually belonging to a foreign command." And although Perry could bring "outside influence (personal as well as political) to bear," he considered such a course "improper" and instead asked Sinclair to speak to Secretary Graham about the matter.[32]

In October, with the Belmont family soon to depart, Perry wrote again to Sinclair about the command, but the department disappointed him with its reply. He was not to receive the Mediterranean command. Instead, on 18 November, Perry received a one-sentence letter from the secretary ordering him to proceed to Washington immediately. Graham had just relieved Aulick of the command of the East India Squadron, and Perry was to be his replacement. Aulick's mission had gone poorly from the start. Sailing in the new war steamer *Susquehanna*, Aulick had conveyed the U.S. and Brazilian ministers to Rio de Janeiro before proceeding to the Far East. On the first leg of the voyage, Aulick quarreled with the commander of the ship. Then Robert Schenck, the American envoy, charged Aulick with unethical conduct toward the Brazilian minister. Later, Aulick would also be charged with giving his son an illegal passage on the *Susquehanna*. A damaging rumor campaign having ensued, Aulick was removed shortly after he arrived in China and before he was able to visit Japan.[33]

In Washington, Graham informed Perry tersely that he was to replace Aulick. The secretary was so busy preparing his annual report to Congress that he had little time to spare for Perry, who returned to New York in poor spirits. Refused command of the Mediterranean Squadron, he could not welcome merely replacing Aulick, who was his junior in seniority. On 3 December, he wrote to Graham that it was a

> serious disappointment, and cause of personal inconvenience not to go to the Mediterranean, as I was led to believe from various reliable sources. . . . I hold that an officer is bound to go where his services are most required, yet I trust I may be pardoned for expressing a strong disinclination to go out as the mere relief or successor to Commodore Aulick without being charged with some more important service, and with a force competent to a possible successful issue. . . . [Since] rank and command is the greatest incentive to an officer, . . . I could only look to the Mediterranean for advance in that respect, as that station, in time of peace, has always been looked upon as the most desirable.

Perry considered relieving Aulick "a retrograde movement" for himself "unless indeed . . . the sphere of action of the East India Squadron . . . be so much enlarged as to hold out a well-grounded hope of its conferring distinction upon its commander."[34]

The Fillmore administration was not in a position to argue with Perry. With the presidential election less than a year away, Fillmore needed to claim credit for successful foreign policy initiatives, and the mission to Japan seemed ideal. As a result, Perry found the administration amenable to his request to enlarge the mission. In notes accompanying his letter to Graham, Perry predicted that the mission would generate support from the "commercial classes" with little cost to the government. In addition to the three ships already in Asia, only two more war steamers and one storeship would be required. At the very least, the expedition would perform "spiritual service" to U.S. whaling interests by securing "one or more Ports for purpose of refreshment & repair and a stopping place to the vessels bound to Shanghai." Estimating that two voyages to Japan would be required, Perry planned to discard the "established rule of diplomacy" and pursue "a course for which [the Japanese] would not be prepared." He would observe "kindness & forbearance towards them" but disregard "many of their absurd marine and municipal restrictions" while seizing on every opportunity "to make favorable impressions." Once the Japanese realized that Perry's ostensible object was to find shelter and supplies for U.S. ships, they would create ports for that purpose. "Having gained this much," Perry predicted, "time and diplomacy will accomplish the rest."[35]

Graham's response was favorable. By January 1852, Perry was planning the expedition. The history of embarrassments, failures, and missteps with Japan had convinced the administration to organize a major effort. Secretary Graham and later his successor, John Pendleton Kennedy, tried to accommodate as many of Perry's requests as possible. The steam frigate *Susquehanna* and the sloops-of-war *Plymouth* and *Saratoga* were already on station. In addition, Perry was to have the steamers *Mississippi, Alleghany,* and *Princeton;* the sloops *Macedonian* and *Vandalia;* the ship of the line *Vermont;* and three supply ships. Eventually, the expedition ended up with three steam frigates, four sloops-of-war, and three supply ships. For various reasons, the *Alleghany, Princeton,* and *Vermont* never joined the squadron; at the last moment, the department assigned the steamer *Powhatan* as a substitute. When assembled in East Indian waters, the formidable squadron represented the largest naval force ever sent overseas by the United States.[36]

From the outset, Perry referred to the expedition in intensely personal terms. In December 1851, in his frank letter to Graham, Perry had stated that he was interested in the assignment only if it was organized "to hold out a well-grounded hope of its conferring distinction upon its commander." As the months of preparations passed, Perry increasingly used the possessive "my" in referring to the expedition. He also selected commanders whom he personally respected and knew. Comdrs. Franklin Buchanan and Sidney Lee and Capt. Joel Abbot, all personal friends, commanded the *Susquehanna, Mississippi,* and *Macedonian,* respectively. Perry's chief of staff and captain of the fleet was Comdr. Henry Adams, who had served with Perry in the Mexican War, as had Flag Lt. Silas Bent. Comdrs. John Kelly and William S. Walker were already on station in command of the *Plymouth* and *Saratoga,* and Capt. W. J. McCluney commanded the *Powhatan.* Only one family member served with Perry in the expedition: his son Oliver Hazard II came along as his secretary.[37]

Particularly concerned about discipline because of the recent abolition of flogging, Perry advised his commanders to recruit landsmen and young men rather than tough, savvy, veteran seamen. In fact, his concern proved well founded; discipline eventually became a problem on some ships in the squadron. Indeed, before the *Powhatan* even reached the Far East, Surgeon Charles Wheelwright would complain that there "is no order or system. Officers are dissatisfied and crews disorderly." Two months later, he would report that the "crew is completely disorganized, almost mutinous, and the ship is generally in a nasty condition."[38]

Perry understood that ceremonial events, lively entertainment, wine and spirits, and good food played a part in naval diplomacy. Sumptuous meals with fine wine created an atmosphere that smoothed diplomatic discussions. Accordingly, he appointed a French chef and an Italian bandmaster to the expedition. Perry himself was no gourmet, but his ample frame attested to his penchant for good food. Perry also placed a premium on good band music, which helped to maintain shipboard morale and enhanced ceremonial occasions.[39]

Although the expedition was "altogether of a naval and diplomatic character," Perry planned "to subserve the objects of science" as well. A man of long-standing scientific interests, he had collected plant, animal, and shell specimens as well as historical artifacts on his previous cruises and sent them to various scientists, scientific societies, and the Naval Lyceum. In addition to charting coastal waters and collecting nautical and meteorological information on the expedition, he intended to compile an extensive record of natural history specimens, descriptions, and drawings. Beyond its inherent intellectual value, this information might prove instrumental in encouraging the development of trade with Japan. Beginning with the U.S. Exploring Expedition to the Pacific between 1838 and 1842, the U.S. Navy had organized a number of scientific expeditions for the specific purpose of collecting scientific, meteorological, and nautical information useful to American whalers, sea captains, and merchants around the globe. The head of the Naval Observatory in Washington, D.C., Lt. Matthew F. Maury, was the driving force behind these initiatives. His views reflected the prevailing attitude that in protecting American trade the navy should also actively assist American commerce overseas by collecting and publishing pertinent scientific and geographic information. Once the winds and currents of remote seas were cataloged, the remote coasts charted, and unexplored rivers examined, American ships and commerce would follow.[40]

Perry wanted his expedition to supply reliable information on the geography, people, and culture of Japan to replace the misconceptions that then abounded in the United States. He had hoped to have a special appropriation for this activity, but Congress did not approve any additional funds. Numerous "literary and scientific persons" asked to participate, but Perry generally declined because of the problems they might create. As civilians, they would chafe at naval discipline, the "narrow uncomfortable quarters," and various sanitary rules. They would be disappointed when they were not allowed to go wherever they wanted, and their inexperience might create problems with foreigners when they were permitted to go ashore. Instead, Perry used naval personnel whenever possible. Several naval surgeons had extensive knowledge of botany and geology. Chaplain George Jones, whom Perry had known and respected in the Mediterranean, put his extensive knowledge of astronomy and geology to use.[41]

Perry did recognize the need for a few civilian translators, writers, scientists, and artists. Since he did not have a special appropriation to hire civilians, Perry appointed them as acting master's mates at a salary of twenty-five dollars per month. This arrangement permitted Perry to include these individuals while retaining authority and disciplinary control over them. Perry clearly recalled the problems Lt. Comdr. Charles Wilkes had experienced in maintaining discipline and controlling some of the U.S. Exploring Expedition's civilian scientists. Among the civilians

Perry selected were artists William Heine and Eliphalet Brown Jr., whose sketches and paintings would create a pictorial record of the expedition. Also a professional photographer, Brown brought a daguerreotype and a supply of plates and eventually took several hundred still photos of scenery and individuals during the expedition. Dr. James Morrow was a physician with a background in tropical plants gained from his father's South Carolina plantation. Appointed by the State Department without Perry's consent, Morrow was an excellent scientist and collector but he did later become a problem for the commodore.[42]

Overlooking no detail, Perry believed that official gifts were a valuable way to create a favorable impression and advance American interests. He sought presents that would reflect the advanced civilization and culture of the United States, including manufacturing and mechanical specimens "illustrative of our extraordinary advancement in the useful arts" and items exhibiting the "proverbial ingenuity" of American artisans. Such gifts would "go far to convince" the Japanese to open relations with the outside world and eventually create a desire in Japan for American goods. When Secretary Graham agreed but specified that their collection was "to involve no expenditure of public money," Perry himself convinced individuals and businesses to donate gifts.[43] He traveled to Albany, Boston, New Bedford, and Providence to select the items personally, eventually assembling a vast assortment.[44]

The size of the squadron, the number of men onboard, and the distance involved combined to create an immense logistical challenge for Perry and his commanders. Fresh water, some supplies, and some fresh provisions could be acquired once the squadron reached China, but the majority needed to be transported to the East Indies along with the squadron. Coal for the steamers was a particular challenge. By later standards, steam machinery on the American ships was very inefficient. In fact, all of the steamers carried sails because they depleted their stores of coal so quickly. The *Mississippi*, for example, consumed twenty-six tons per day. In anticipation, Perry increased its coal storage capacity from 450 to 600 tons. Although he wanted to use steam power as frequently as possible to maximize the psychological effect of this technology on the Japanese, high-quality coal was not readily available in China. The European powers there transported their own coal and stored it near Hong Kong. The United States contracted with the firm of Howland and Aspinwall to do the same.[45]

Perry conducted diligent research on Japan prior to his departure. He continued to correspond with Joseph Delano and visited him at New Bedford in April 1852. Secretary of State Webster was successful in obtaining nautical charts from the Dutch. Perry combed the best material available, including government reports, naval documents, popular articles, and firsthand accounts. He obtained and studied *Nippon, Archiv zur Beschreibung von Japan,* by Phillipp Franz von Siebold, a German physician and naturalist who had resided at the small Dutch settlement on the island of Deshima in Nagasaki harbor in the 1820s and had traveled to the shogun's court at Edo. Perry read the popular *Manners and Customs of the Japanese,* published in 1852 and based on von Siebold's work, as well as an English translation of *The History of Japan,* a Dutch work by Engelbert Kaempfer. An abridged English version entitled *An Account of Japan* was published in 1853 and would later reach Perry before his second visit to Japan. Perry was particularly impressed by the writings of Sir Stamford Raffles, who had acquired Singapore for England three decades earlier. Various other accounts were available as well, including the three-volume *Recollections* by Russian naval captain Vasilii Golownin, who had been held captive in Japan for several years after being shipwrecked early in the nineteenth century.[46]

By the time the expedition departed, Perry's studies had given him a far more sophisticated view of Japan than the prevailing American perspective. Most mid-nineteenth-century Americans thought of Japan as a strange, isolated, and uncivilized country; backward technologically, it lacked the exotic charm and fascination of China. In fact, this picture of Japan was inaccurate, ethnocentric, and racially prejudiced. Americans and Europeans willingly acknowledged the intelligence of the Japanese and their firmness in dealing with foreigners. But rather than characterize the Japanese as tough, resourceful, and shrewd, Westerners constantly used pejorative terms such as *secretive, treacherous, cunning, deceitful,* and *duplicitous* to describe them. Perry held the predominant ethnocentric views of his time, but his reading compelled him to understand the Japanese as a highly civilized and cultured people with a tightly structured society. The Japanese people had "many redeeming traits." They were brave, generous, humane, intelligent, and inordinately curious; they loved pleasure and gave great importance to form and ceremony. Like other outsiders, Perry believed the Japanese to be treacherous in their dealings with foreigners. Contemptuous of weakness, they would readily capitalize on the kind of indecisive behavior shown by Commodore Biddle in 1846. At the same time, he rejected Dutch allegations that the Japanese were innately hostile to foreigners. Instead, Perry blamed their oppressive government for imposing capricious edicts that it enforced ruthlessly through an extensive espionage system in which one-half of the population spied on the other half.[47]

In spite of his respect for the Japanese, Perry shared with other Westerners a flawed and simplistic understanding of their political and social system. For example, he thought that Japan had two rulers, one religious and one secular. In fact, the shogun held and exercised civil and military authority while the revered but merely symbolic emperor was protected, isolated, and politically impotent. Centered in the imperial capital of Edo, the shogunate, or Bakufu, ruled through approximately 250 daimyo, or lords, and their ruling class of samurai. At one time the samurai had been warriors, but a long period of peace had enabled their gradual transformation into a class of government officials and bureaucrats.

In the mid-nineteenth century, Japan remained primarily a feudal society. The samurai administered and enforced an extensive and highly organized system that governed the great majority of peasants, artisans, and small merchants. By 1850 Japan had been ruled for more than two hundred years by the Tokugawa shogunate. Since the early nineteenth century, however, the regime had been under increasing pressure as the rise of commercial agriculture and a growing market economy sowed peasant discontent, impoverished the samurai, and created new social classes. Although Perry and other outsiders were not aware of these developments, they would work in his favor.[48]

Exclusion of all foreigners was a long-standing policy of the Tokugawa regime. For more than two centuries Japan had eliminated virtually all contact with the outside world in an effort to exclude European influence, particularly the introduction of Christianity, which the Japanese feared and despised. Japan expelled all foreigners who tried to enter, prohibited foreign commerce, and prevented virtually all communication with the outside world. The only exception was very limited contact and commerce with Korea, China, and the Dutch. On the tiny island of Deshima in the harbor of Nagasaki, the Japanese permitted a small Dutch settlement, Japan's only contact with the Western world. This policy of exclusion enabled an era of peace and stability. By the nineteenth century, however, the Russians had landed on the coast of Hokkaido and begun to settle the Kurile Islands and the British had a strong presence in China. As a result of the First Opium War, the British had imposed a trading system on the Chinese and had established a thriving settlement in Hong Kong, and they were expected by some to exert similar pressure on Japan. Across the Pacific, the United States had begun to expand its commercial presence to the west and was expected to create a steamship line from San Francisco to Shanghai and Hong Kong.

By 1850, then, the Japanese faced what the Chinese referred to as *naiyu-gaiken,* or "troubles at home, dangers from abroad." Economic and social tensions in Japan and the threat of foreign challenges bore down on the ill-prepared Bakufu, which the backward state of Japanese technology and science had helped to weaken further. Although Japan was a sophisticated and civilized society, its industrial and military technology was primitive. It had no railroads, no steam power, no effective navy, no modern ordnance, and no electric telegraph. Some Japanese officials worried that Japan would be unable to protect itself against a Western military force.

At the same time, Perry and other Westerners did not realize just how much Japanese rulers knew about Europe and the United States. Because the Japanese considered themselves a chosen people vastly superior to the Western barbarians, their interest in the outside world was born only of curiosity. They had no intention of emulating barbarian Western ways. Although their information came almost exclusively through the Dutch at Nagasaki and was subject to manipulation, a small number of Japanese had done their own research. A group of "Dutch scholars" translated Dutch sources to learn about the Europeans and the Americans. In an extraordinary series of interviews begun as early as 1809, the Dutch director at Nagasaki, Opperhoofd Hendrik Doerff, had explained to Japanese officials the American Revolution, the creation of the United States, and the role played by Gen. George Washington, who as the first "king" of the United States fascinated the Japanese. In addition, the Japanese required the Dutch to submit an annual report that summarized major events and developments in the outside world.[49] The Dutch reports to Japan from 1848 to 1852 included such American events as the war with Mexico, the discovery of gold in California, and the dispatch of a naval mission to Japan led "by a person named Perry."[50]

Accordingly, the Japanese were reasonably well informed about the United States. In February 1851, the Japanese received invaluable firsthand information from an unexpected source when a shipwrecked Japanese sailor returned to Japan. Manjiro Nakajma had originally been shipwrecked at age fourteen in 1841. He and four others survived six months on a Pacific island before they were rescued by Capt. William Whitfield of the whaler *John Howland.* Impressed by the intelligent and cheerful Manjiro, Whitfield offered to take him to the United States. Manjiro agreed and was taken to Fairhaven, Massachusetts, where he attended school for several years and apprenticed as a cooper. In 1846, Manjiro shipped on a whaler, joined the California gold rush, saved six hundred dollars, and sailed to Hawaii, where he and two of his friends arranged to be returned to Japan. The three eventually landed in the Ryukyu Islands, south of Japan, where they were arrested, questioned, tried, found innocent of violating Japanese law, and sent to Nagasaki for further interrogation. Manjiro provided specific information on America and subsequently wrote *Narratives of the Castaways.* Finally, in 1852, he was released and permitted to return temporarily to his home village to see his mother, who had long since given him up for dead.

Manjiro's personal experiences and the timing of his return made his account compelling to Japanese officials, who already knew about the planned American mission to Japan. Genuinely liking the United States, Manjiro presented a picture in sharp contrast to existing Japanese stereotypes. Assuredly Americans were different from the Japanese, but he had observed them to be warm, friendly, generous, hardworking, and law abiding. He spoke of American steamships, railroads, and telegraphs and described oceangoing whalers and powerful warships. Far from a barbaric place, Manjiro's America was a nation of civilized people, its government said to be the best in the world. "They are naturally gentle and sympathetic and prize integrity. Above all, they are industrious and trade with countries in all directions," he told his countrymen. "Upright and generous, [Americans] do no evil. Among them are neither homicides nor robberies as a rule."[51]

Unlike the Japanese, ordinary American men wore watches, removed their hats when visiting, and sat on chairs. American women had "quaint customs" such as making a hole in their ears and running a gold or silver ring through it as an ornament. Although Americans drank alcohol, Manjiro found them generally temperate; only "vulgar people," he said, "drink like the Japanese." Although "lewd" by nature, they were "otherwise well behaved." Husbands and wives were "very loving and families peaceful and affectionate." In their weddings, Manjiro continued, the husband and wife merely make "a proclamation to the gods, and become married, after which they usually go on a sightseeing trip to the mountains." Manjiro thought American homes cluttered with furniture. He observed that, unlike the Japanese, Americans used separate bathtubs and noted that toilets were "placed over holes in the ground. It is customary," he added, "to read books in them."[52]

This was clearly not a portrait of a threatening and uncivilized people. Nor did it delineate a nation determined to impose its laws, religion, and culture on Japan. The precise effect of Manjiro's report is not known, but it did help to dispel excessive fear and suspicion about Perry's expedition. Several years later, Capt. John Mercer Brooke, who led an American exploring expedition of the North Pacific, stated that he was "satisfied that [Manjiro] had more to do with the opening of Japan than any man living."[53]

When he had been appointed in January 1852, Perry had hoped to be under way by March. That hope was unrealistic; unanticipated complications and delays were inevitable in such a large military expedition. In this case, the delays dragged on for almost eleven months. Perry was fortunate that, in a presidential election year, his expedition did not become a political football. Although the details of the mission remained confidential, rumors abounded, and knowledgeable individuals in Washington knew that something important was afoot. In the Senate, Arkansas Democrat Solon Borland chided the Whig administration for using secret diplomacy and threatening a nation with whom the United States had no quarrel and, indeed, no relations. Senator John Hale of New Hampshire observed wryly that the expedition was simply a device "to use the bloated officer corps and unneeded ships." Direct criticism and snide ridicule notwithstanding, both Perry and the planned expedition escaped unscathed.[54]

Two developments that summer interrupted the preparations. In June, the Whig Party nominated Secretary Graham as the vice presidential running mate of nominee Winfield Scott. Soon thereafter, Graham resigned as secretary. Then, in July, Perry was dispatched in the *Mississippi* to Nova Scotia to help resolve a tense situation between American fishermen and local citizens.[55] The British had sent a naval squadron to police American fishermen in the coastal waters of Nova Scotia, an action that produced indignation and aroused anti-British sentiment in the United States. Perry sailed to Nova Scotia, met with British admiral George Seymour, and helped to calm the situation. The British admiral agreed to restrain his overzealous officers while Perry agreed to warn American fishermen to respect local restrictions and laws. A subsequent round of social events enhanced relations. At Halifax, Perry entertained and then was entertained in grand fashion. Admiral Seymour also gave Perry four books and a box of eighty charts relevant to the forthcoming expedition. Frustrated as he was by his delayed departure, Perry confided in writing to his wife, Jane, in August that he had gotten through "this delicate duty very much to my & to all satisfaction of the Government."[56]

By September, Perry was back in the United States. As the "vexatious" delays continued, he concentrated on the details of his formal mandate. The instructions from Secretary of the Navy John P. Kennedy were rather routine and reiterated the general instructions provided to Commodore Aulick in May 1851 when he assumed command of the East India Squadron. In addition to standard language regarding Perry's authority and various regulations, Kennedy stressed the importance of exploring the coasts of Japan and compiling social, political, and commercial information "especially of new objects of commercial pursuits." In addition, as positive "communication to the prints and newspapers" was of "great importance to the success of the expedition," Kennedy instructed Perry to "enjoin all under your command to abstain from writing to friends or others" and declared that the "journals and private notes of the officers and other persons in the expedition must be considered as belonging to the government." Perry pressed for full diplomatic as well as naval command and sought as much authority, as much discretion, and as broad a field of activity as possible. His clash with John Randolph in 1830, his experiences in the Mediterranean, and his service during the Mexican War had combined to teach Perry the importance of such authority. In the weeks before Secretary of State Daniel Webster died on 24 October, Perry took advantage of the sharp decline in the secretary's health to draft language that was incorporated into his instructions from the State Department. A healthy Webster probably would not have approved the great latitude and authority the instructions provided to Perry. In fact, Webster never reviewed them; but in early November they were reviewed and discussed by President Fillmore, his new secretary of state, Edward Everett, and the cabinet.[57]

In contrast to Kennedy's general instructions, those from the State Department were precise and detailed. Their language included specific details on the tactics Perry was to employ once he reached Japan. Noting the various indignities suffered by American sailors at Japanese hands and recent developments that had brought the two nations into much "closer proximity" and "greatly increased" intercourse, the State Department's charge to Perry outlined the mission's three objectives:

1. . . . [S]ome permanent arrangement for the protection of American seamen and property wrecked on these islands, or driven into their ports by stress of weather.

2. . . . [P]ermission to American vessels to enter one or more of their ports in order to obtain supplies of provisions, water, fuel, etc., or, in case of disasters, to refit. . . . It is very desirable to have permission to establish a depot for coal, if not on one of the principal islands, at least on some small uninhabited one. . . .

3. . . . [P]ermission to our vessels to enter one or more of their ports for the purpose of disposing of their cargoes by sale or barter.[58]

To achieve these objectives, Perry was to take his "whole force" to Japan, select a landing place on the coast, open communications with the government, and try to deliver personally the letter from the president to the emperor. Perry was to explain that the president entertained "the most friendly feeling towards Japan" but was grieved to learn that Americans who were shipwrecked there were treated "as if they were his worst enemies." Perry was also to assure the Japanese that the United States, which did not interfere with the religion of its own people, had no intention of interfering with the religion of Japan. Nor did the United States have any desire to conquer or invade as the Europeans had done in China. Instead, as an independent and "great country" with an expanding population and "rapidly increasing" commerce, the United States desired only "to live in peace and friendship with the emperor." Friendship could exist, however, only if Japan ceased to treat Americans as enemies.

If this friendly approach failed, the instructions ordered Perry to "change his tone, and inform [the Japanese] in the most unequivocal terms" that the United States would insist that all shipwrecked Americans "be treated with humanity" and that any acts of cruelty would be "severely chastised." The details of any agreement were to embodied in a treaty. Force was to be used only in self-defense. Perry was to be "courteous and conciliatory, but at the same time, firm and decided." He was to submit "with patience and forbearance to acts of discourtesy" and do nothing that would compromise "his own dignity, or that of the country." The Japanese must be impressed with "a just sense of the power and greatness" of the United States and convinced that "past forbearance" had been the result "not of timidity, but of a desire to be on friendly terms with them." Affirming that he had been granted "large discretionary powers," the instructions assured Perry that any errors of judgment he might commit would be viewed "with indulgence." Perry also received authority to extend commercial relations and secure ports of refuge with "any and all established and independent sovereignties in those regions."[59]

Along with the president's letter to his "Great and Good Friend" the emperor of Japan Perry carried an official letter of credence from President Fillmore certifying his diplomatic authority. It assured the emperor that Perry would not try to interfere in the religion or politics of Japan and had been charged "to abstain from every act which could possibly disturb the tranquility of your imperial majesty's dominions." Instead, as a friendly neighbor, the United States sought only "friendship, commerce, a supply of coal and provisions and protection for our shipwrecked people."[60]

Perry was pleased that his own language had not been modified and confided to his wife that recent interviews with both Secretary Kennedy and Secretary of State Edward Everett "were highly satisfactory & complimentary to me."

> No officer & perhaps no individual has before been entrusted with such extraordinary power, having not only the power to treat with the Emperor of Japan without limitation, but I have also power to treat with any other nations with whom the U. States are not already in diplomatic intercourse—these extraordinary powers only admonish me to exercise still greater prudence & discretion.[61]

The final hectic weeks before departure were for Perry a mixture of personal and professional obligations. The Perry family hosted a farewell gathering in Baltimore. Perry drafted a financial memorandum detailing his $1,697 in liabilities and his $30,400 in assets, which included a $20,000 "bond and mortgage" for his Tarrytown home, The Moorings, which he had recently sold so that Jane could return to New York City. Perry had to make a final, unexpected trip to Washington, where he impressed a distinguished group of government officials with his articulate statements and clear answers to questions about the expedition.[62] Making a personal visit to the *Mississippi*, President Fillmore and members of his cabinet wished Perry well.

Perry was anxious to get under way and distance himself from Washington politics, endless delays, and irritating press reports and comments. He was optimistic, but others remained skeptical. In Hong Kong, as he prepared to return to the United States, Commodore Aulick observed that "failure is looked upon as certain" because Perry's squadron was "not *large* enough for war, & *too large* for pacific purposes." The Japanese "will believe no friendly professions accompanied by so warlike a demonstration," he warned. Press reaction was mixed. The *National Intelligencer* praised the expedition, and the *Baltimore American* endorsed it as consistent "with the spirit of the age; . . . it belongs to a species of progress which [even] the most conservative may commend and support."[63] The *Public Ledger* of Philadelphia was dubious about the project, however, and the *Baltimore Sun* even urged "abandoning this humbug, for it has become a *matter of ridicule abroad and at home.*"[64] Finally, on 24 November 1852, the *Mississippi* departed. "I am about worn out with fatigue & vexation and shall be glad when I get to sea & free from the abominations of Washington," Perry wrote to Jane that day. Yet, Perry was also reflective and even a bit sentimental. He admitted that his authority and power "far exceed any that have hitherto been issued to any one—I only hope that I may be found equal to the trust they have confided to me." Expressing his great affection for Jane, his family, and his infant grandson Perry Belmont, the commodore chided his wife by saying that he hoped his children "will not acquire that repugnance to writing that seems to grow on you."[65]

As the *Mississippi* headed alone eastward across the Atlantic, Perry was in an uncharacteristic mood. For the moment, his letters captured the feelings of a sentimental and doting husband, father, and grandfather, not the thoughts of the resolute, demanding, veteran commander he was known to be. This mood soon passed as his mind returned to the daunting mission he had undertaken. Ahead lay thousands of miles of ocean to traverse. Sheer distance, however, was the least of the challenges that Perry would face in the next twenty-one months.

❦ 8 ❦

EAST ASIA AND JAPAN

The course which Perry has pursued in managing affairs connected with this expedition has astonished every officer in the Squadron; and every one who was opposed to him previous to sailing for Japan has now come over on the other side; and now says that he was the only officer in the Navy that could have accomplished what he has.

ENGINEER WILLIAM H. RUTHERFORD, 17 JULY 1853

A meteor appeared in the southwestern sky late the night after the American squadron anchored for the first time in Japanese waters. As "large in circumference as the crown of a man's hat," the brilliant body of the meteor was "molten iron" in color with a blue tail extending into an "emerald hue" and terminating in a smoky ball "resembling the flame of burning tar." The dramatic display lasted only about thirty seconds and was witnessed by only a few Americans, but amid their "exclamations of admiration and wonderment" they immediately pronounced the fireball to be an omen of good fortune. The commander of the watch on the *Mississippi*, Lt. John Duer, observed that the

> ancients would have construed this remarkable appearance of the heavens as an omen promising a favorable issue to an enterprise taken by them, and we may pray that our present attempt to bring a singular and half barbarous people into the family of civilized nations, may succeed without resort to bloodshed.[1]

Although it was dramatic and timely, the appearance of the meteor might just as easily have been a bad omen. In retrospect, it is apparent that Japan was militarily weak, politically divided, and less hostile to the United States than to European nations such as Russia and England. By the early 1850s, the opening of Japan and the establishment of diplomatic relations with the outside world were inevitable. There was, however, no certainty that it would be the Perry expedition that would achieve the breakthrough. Since the Bakufu remained opposed and could be expected to resist, the success of the American mission would depend to a large extent on the resourcefulness and will of its commander.

Perry's voyage to China went well. After a "boisterous passage of eighteen days," the *Mississippi* reached the Madeiras on 12 December to take on water, provisions, and 450 tons of coal. Here Perry also purchased eighty barrels of Madeira wine, some to be shipped back to the United States and some to be taken to Asia. Now that he was well under way, Perry felt confident that the expedition would succeed. "The honor of the nation calls for it, and the interest of commerce demands it." During this first leg of the voyage, Perry had also finalized his plans. Rather then proceed directly to Japan after he had gathered his squadron in China, Perry requested permission to go first to the Lew Chew Islands (Okinawa). As a "preliminary step, and one of easy accomplishment," Perry wanted to secure a port and depot there as a rendezvous point for the squadron. Although Okinawa was actually a dependency of Japan controlled by the prince of Satsuma, fear and intimidation rather than an actual Japanese occupation controlled the people, and the squadron would be unopposed. Perry intended to treat the Okinawans with "strict justice and gentle kindness" to win their "good will and friendship," an approach he had employed previously in Africa and Mexico. He would provide seeds and farm implements to the local people, establish rules for the purchase of labor and supplies, build a depot for coal and stores, and set up a printing press to counteract the falsehoods disseminated by the Dutch. Although Okinawa had not been mentioned in his official instructions, Perry argued that the "strictest rules of moral law" as well as the "laws of stern necessity" justified his plans. Perry also urged prompt measures to combat British influence in East Asia. Although Britain had colonial possessions in East India, Japan and many other islands in the Pacific remained "untouched by this unconscionable government." Since some of these Pacific islands would become crucial as the United States expanded its influence in the Pacific, it was essential to establish ports and supply depots there as soon as possible. Remaining silent on the question of acquiring ports of refuge, Secretary of State Edward Everett approved Perry's plan for Okinawa but warned him to pursue the "most friendly and conciliatory course." His men were not to plunder, and force was to be used only as a last resort for self-preservation.[2]

After sailing from Madeira, the *Mississippi* stopped for provisions and coal at St. Helena, the Cape of Good Hope, Mauritius, Ceylon, and Singapore before reaching Hong Kong on 7 April 1853—in all, a four-and-one-half-month passage. With his ship consuming coal at the rate of 26 tons per day, Perry took on 315 tons at St. Helena, 290 tons at Capetown, and 462 tons at Mauritius. At Ceylon, he found coal to be plentiful but unobtainable from the English Oriental Steam Navigation Company; only with difficulty did he secure 403 tons there. In Singapore, Perry faced similar obstacles but purchased 41 tons of wood and made arrangements to borrow 214 tons of coal until it could be returned at Hong Kong. By the time the *Mississippi* reached Hong Kong, it had traveled more than seventeen thousand miles and consumed 2,337 tons of coal. The voyage reinforced the importance of overseas coal sources to Perry. With a storage capacity of 600 tons, the *Mississippi* had a cruising range of only twenty to twenty-five days. And while coal was easy to obtain at some places, it was a dear commodity in others.[3] Without ample overseas coal sources and storage depots at key places, American private and naval steamers would be seriously handicapped.

At each port, Perry recorded the availability of water, provisions, and fresh foods; he also observed the chief nautical, geographic, and cultural features. He disliked St. Helena and thought Capetown "a dull and stupid place." The native residents of the Cape of Good Hope were "utterly disgusting"—"poor wretches" who had "but little opportunity of acquiring more civilized habits" because of the "cruel wantonness" of their European rulers. At the same time, Perry reflected that Americans had "no right to rail at other nations for wrongs they have inflicted upon the aborigines of countries seized by them. Though hardly equal to the English in . . . disgusting hypocrisy . . . [w]e are not far behind them in the frauds and cruelties committed upon our native tribes." The system of navigation aids and regulations at Mauritius impressed Perry. "How many useful lessons might the members of our Lighthouse Board learn," lamented Perry, "if they were to Look into these admirable regulations." Perry was most impressed by Singapore and England's achievements there. The island had become "a place of great resort for ships of all nations. . . . At anchor at the same time [were] Chinese, Siamese, Malay, Sumatra vessels bringing cargoes . . . and taking European and American goods." Because it was an open port Singapore had become the "entrepôt for the produce of the neighboring kingdoms of Sumatra, Borneo, Siam, Cambodia, and Cochin China."[4] In the next eighteen months Perry came to view Singapore and later Hong Kong as models for the United States to emulate. Although it welcomed the trade and ships of all nations, each was a British-owned free port that served as a British naval base and thriving center for British commerce.

When the *Mississippi* anchored at Hong Kong in early April, Perry was saluted by the *Plymouth* and *Saratoga* and officially welcomed by French and British officials. He was "surprised and disappointed" to learn, however, that his intended flagship, the *Susquehanna* under Comdr. Franklin Buchanan, had been sent to Shanghai by Comdr. John Kelly, the senior officer on station. This "extraordinary and injudicious exercise of a doubtful authority" would cause "serious delay," for Kelly had also authorized Buchanan to proceed two hundred miles up the Yangtze River to Nanking. To make matters worse, the U.S. commissioner to China, Humphrey Marshall, and his secretary of legation, Dr. Peter Parker, were both passengers on the *Susquehanna*. Perry had hoped to interview both men. Perry immediately dispatched Kelly to Shanghai in the *Plymouth* with orders for Buchanan to remain there until the *Mississippi* arrived.[5]

In April 1853, Perry celebrated his fifty-ninth birthday. Despite the ravages of previous overseas commands on his health, he remained an imposing figure. He looked younger than his years and retained a full head of brown hair. Although he was always dignified and reserved in manner, Perry's strong will and occasional bursts of anger were well known among men in the squadron. Some referred to him as "old Perry" or "old Matt" and others as "ursa major," but never when he might overhear. While he was respected for his energy and skill in "matters strictly military," some of his peers viewed him as "imperious . . . harsh, and too rigid." "The Comdre. is as close as an oyster," observed one critic. "He is as obstinate as a bull, has great energy and only wants head."[6] The Japan expedition, which he came to call "the great object of my life," had become a personal obsession, and Perry was a tougher, less patient, and more irritable commander than he had been with his squadrons in Africa and Mexico. He tolerated little discussion of his tactics and resisted anything he considered a threat to his mission. His demeanor surfaced most dramatically in his relations with his senior officers, who found him distant, aloof, and arrogant. A decade earlier Captain Abbot had written of the "harmony and good will" that existed among the officers and Commodore Perry. In those days, they had regularly played backgammon and chess with him and had enjoyed his personal friendship. Now they found themselves excluded from his thinking and his decisions but quickly targeted for their own shortcomings. It was soon clear to all that this expedition was an intensely personal mission rather than a cooperative team effort between a commander, his officers, and his crews.[7]

In China, Perry confronted a political situation that he had not anticipated and that threatened to further delay the expedition. Revolution and political uncertainty reigned. The Taiping Revolution, already several years old, had won considerable success. An agrarian, political, and religious uprising, the revolution was led by Hung Hsiu-chúan, who espoused Christian beliefs and sought to overthrow the Manchu dynasty. Although his views were generally Protestant, Hung did not subscribe to any particular Christian denomination.[8] Perry likened Hung's faith "to that of the Mormons in America" in that he claimed to be in "constant communication with God, and has been acknowledged as his Son."[9]

The political situation in China presented a distraction that Perry wanted to avoid altogether. Although he was the commander of the East India Squadron, Perry's instructions made only slight reference to China. Moreover, he had little interest in that nation and did not want his forces to become entangled there. A small but influential group of wealthy American merchants centered in Canton and Shanghai had grown uneasy about the situation, however, and expected Perry to use his naval forces to protect their lives and property. Further complicating Perry's attempts to remain uninvolved were the activities of Commissioner Humphrey Marshall. The forty-one-year-old Kentucky colonel, lawyer, and Whig politician was an energetic and able man, but he was also lacking in judgment, "autocratic, dictatorial, pitifully vain, and gifted with a singular capacity for controversy." In short, he was no diplomat. When he arrived in China in January 1853, he had asked that American warships be placed at his disposal. He received approval to be transported to Canton on the *Saratoga* to present his credentials, but, much to his embarrassment, the ship left him there. Unsuccessful in presenting his credentials in person, Marshall decided to travel to Shanghai and requested that the *Susquehanna* transport him. It was this request that Commander Kelly had approved prior to Perry's arrival.[10]

Although he was angry about Kelly's decision, Perry did not act precipitously. He spent April in south China visiting Hong Kong, Macao, and Canton. The latter disappointed him greatly. The route from Whampoa to Canton was "a muddy shallow stream" with banks "occupied by a wretched half-clad people." At Macao, D. N. Spooner of the firm Russell and Company improved Perry's spirits by offering him elegant accommodations. However, Perry found the American naval supply depot there to be inadequate. Since Macao had no harbor of its own, oceangoing ships anchored three miles away in an open roadstead; moving supplies between the warehouses onshore and the ships in the roadstead was expensive and time-consuming. In response, Perry moved the naval depot from Macao to Hong Kong, which had a magnificent harbor and where food, provisions, and limited amounts of coal were available.[11]

In China, Perry added several people to his entourage, including Bayard Taylor, a popular American writer who specialized in travel literature. Although Taylor stayed only for several months in 1853, his accounts helped publicize the expedition. Perry allowed Taylor considerable latitude and permitted him to submit reports back to his newspaper in the United States. The reports, which spoke highly of Perry and the expedition, appeared in the *New York Herald* in November 1853. Perry also persuaded Dr. Samuel Wells Williams to join the expedition as an interpreter. Born in Utica, New York, in 1812, Williams had come to China in 1833 to be the printer for the Canton press of the American Board of Commissioners for Foreign Missions. An unordained missionary and a scholar, Williams learned Chinese and wrote extensively about China for many years. Although he learned enough Japanese to translate the gospel of Matthew, Williams's command of the language was limited, as he readily admitted. Nevertheless, his extensive knowledge of botany and the Chinese language made him valuable to Perry as both a scientist and an interpreter. A devout Christian missionary, Williams believed the hand of God to be at work through the expedition, although he had little confidence in Perry. Williams viewed the ultimate purpose of the expedition to be religious, not diplomatic or commercial. Not surprisingly, he chafed at the strictures of navy life and complained frequently about naval disregard for the Sabbath and the crude behavior of the men. Nevertheless, his sharp eye for detail, close access to Perry, and considerable latitude of movement allowed Williams to compile an invaluable journal. As an assistant Williams brought a Chinese man, an opium addict who died at sea before the squadron even reached Japan. At Shanghai, Perry also added Anton Portman to serve as a Dutch interpreter.[12]

With little interest in China, Perry was not impressed by most of what he saw there. He viewed the Chinese as a "remarkable race of people; hardy, frugal, and industrious, and were it not for the viciousness of the government and laws they would become a formidable nation." Appalled, however, by the poverty and filth he observed, Perry also judged the Chinese to be "the most knavish" of all races. "From the highest mandarin to the lowest boatman, the art of deception and trickery is practiced with consummate skill and audacity." Not only were the Chinese prone "to cheat and rob those whom they call barbarians," they were also "equally prone to rob each other, both on land and water."[13]

When Perry arrived in Shanghai in early May, he faced a threatening political situation, a demanding American commissioner, and difficult navigation conditions. Shanghai, which was quickly becoming the center of American trade in China, was commonly viewed as the likely terminus of the proposed steamship line between China and California. It was also on the verge of falling to the Taiping rebels. American merchant houses were requesting U.S. naval protection and Chinese government officials were actively seeking European and American naval assistance to suppress the rebellion. In this atmosphere of unrest, Chinese officials had still not formally received Commissioner Marshall, who now wanted to be transported by a U.S. warship directly to Peking to present his credentials there. Perry's firsthand review of the situation confirmed his initial determination to avoid involvement. Navigation of the Chinese coast from Hong Kong to the Yangtze River was fraught with difficulty, and the mouth of the Yangtze, obstructed by shoals on both sides, was particularly dangerous. The entrance to the channel was not marked, and both the flood and ebb tides were extremely variable. The *Susquehanna, Plymouth,* and *Supply* had all grounded on the approach, and the *Mississippi* nearly met a similar fate. And, like Canton, Shanghai had little to commend itself to Perry, who was struck by the "filthiness of the city" and the "uncleanly habits" of the residents.

From Shanghai, Perry reported that the alarm created by the rebels had subsided. Judging the rebel leader to be "a very sagacious man," Perry thought that a "mighty revolution" and "the beginning of some great change in the conditions of the eastern nations" were under way there. The result would "prostrate the despotic power which is now in the ascendant, and rear up in its place forms of government more consonant to the spirit and intelligence of the age."[14] Given his view that these changes were "directed by an almighty hand, and . . . impelled by a divine power," Perry was not alarmed by the unrest. On his arrival in Shanghai Perry had paid a formal courtesy visit to the governor and the commander of the city. When the governor asked for American assistance, Perry declined and objected that Commissioner Marshall had not yet been officially accredited. While supporting Marshall's attempts to meet with Chinese officials, however, Perry rejected the commissioner's assessment of the political situation, refused his request for naval support, and prepared to depart for Okinawa. On 13 May, Marshall requested a warship to carry him to the mouth of the Peiho River en route to Peking and to remain there until he returned. Marshall intended to present his credentials directly to the imperial court and thereby become the first foreign diplomat to establish an official residence in Peking. Claiming that war with the United States might ensue if the emperor refused to see him, Marshall, who viewed the expedition to Japan as of secondary importance compared with what might be gained in China, wanted Perry to remain on hand until conditions in China were settled.[15] Marshall had badly misjudged the Chinese, but he had also irreparably damaged his relationship with Perry by disparaging the Japan expedition and underestimating both his own government's and Perry's commitment to it. Perry refused to assign the war steamers and informed Marshall that his proposed actions would likely injure relations between China and the United States.[16] Nevertheless, Perry did leave the *Plymouth* behind temporarily at Shanghai in response to an appeal that Marshall had received from five American merchant companies. On 16 May, the *Mississippi* moved downriver from Shanghai and was followed the next day by the *Susquehanna*. After waiting several days for a chartered steamship that did not arrive, the squadron, which now included the storeship *Supply*, departed for Okinawa.[17]

On 26 May, the squadron reached the harbor of Naha on the southwestern coast of Okinawa, known at the time as Great Lew Chew Island.

Coral reefs protected a narrow entrance to the sheltered anchorage. North of the harbor stood the town of Naha, where an estimated twenty thousand people lived. The town's streets were paved with coral blocks and the houses in the prosperous section protected by walls. The Americans thought the island an idyllic place. "It would be difficult for you to imagine the beauties of this island, with respect to the charming scenery and its marvelous perfection of cultivation," wrote Perry to his friend William Sinclair. Bayard Taylor thought he

> had never seen a more lovely landscape than the island presented. The bay was clasped by an amphitheatre of gently undulating hills, in some places terraced with waving rice-fields, in others covered with greenest turf, or dotted with picturesque groups of trees. Bowers of the feathery bamboo—almost concealed the dwellings which nestled together in the little dells opening into the bay, and which, with their stone enclosures and roofs of red tiles, hinted of a much higher civilization than we had expected. . . . [The scene] charmed us like a glimpse of Paradise, after the monotonous levees and polluted atmosphere of China.[18]

The *Mississippi* was first welcomed by local officials and then visited by Rev. Bernard Bettelheim. A Hungarian Jew with medical training, Bettelheim was a naturalized British citizen, Anglican convert, and missionary. At the time of Perry's arrival Bettelheim had lived with his English wife and three children at Naha in a shabby dwelling for seven years against the strong objections of local officials. During that time Bettelheim, lacking the temperament for his mission, had developed contempt for the Okinawans he was supposed to convert. Ostracized, isolated, and spied on constantly, he still persisted in spite of his miserable living conditions and his failure to win converts. Bettelheim was thrilled to see the American squadron. A friendly and obsequious man, he spent three hours with Perry, answering many questions and providing a firsthand description of Okinawa and its people. When Bettelheim confirmed that the people of Japan and its dependencies such as Okinawa were "unsurpassed in their chicanery and diplomatic treachery," Perry resolved to apply "a little Yankee diplomacy" as soon as an occasion permitted. Although he was an accomplished linguist whose knowledge of the local language was of great help to Perry, Bettelheim was also an erratic and eccentric man who often annoyed those around him. The interpreter

Williams grew to despise him. One officer later concluded: "Dr. B. seems to me about the worst kind of a person to have sent" to Okinawa. And Perry admitted that although Bettelheim's "manner and deportment" gave him "misgivings," he was determined to "make the best of our means" and use him as an interpreter.[19]

On 28 May, the regent of the kingdom, Shang Ta-mo, visited the *Susquehanna*. As the regent toured the ship, Perry remained out of sight in his cabin before emerging in dramatic fashion to greet his guest as the band played. In the interview, Perry indicated that he intended to return the visit in one week at the royal palace at Shuri, the seat of local government, and expected an appropriate reception. The regent, a feeble old man, protested vigorously, but to no avail.

Perry observed the people of Okinawa to be "industrious and inoffensive" but firmly under Japanese control and intimidated by an extensive system of spies and their constant surveillance. The local officials might try to be deceitful, but their clumsy tactics were transparent to Perry. In an effort to prevent his visit to Shuri, they lied repeatedly and attempted to trick him into changing his mind. First, they appealed for Perry to make his visit to Naha, not Shuri. Then the mayor of Naha planned a feast, which Perry suspected to be a trap. Since the regent would attend, Perry's presence might be interpreted as accepting the feast as a substitute for a formal return visit. Perry refused to attend. Okinawan officials also claimed that the queen was seriously ill and that Perry's visit to the palace would endanger her fragile health. Exercising forbearance, Perry refused to blame local officials, instead attributing "this pertinacious system of crooked diplomacy" to the Japanese overlords. "All the falsehood, tricking, and deception which they practice . . . is done to satisfy the spies," he believed, ". . . and to show that every means has been resorted to, to avert consequences which ultimately become inevitable, notwithstanding this duplicity."[20]

Since the Japanese would know everything that transpired on Okinawa, Perry planned to make his visit there a dress rehearsal and send a clear message to Japan. The Japanese must understand that although he commanded a formidable naval force, Perry's mission was one of peace and friendship, not an invasion or conquest. Unless compelled to act in self-defense, he would not use force. Because he was a high-ranking representative of the United States, he expected to be received and treated accordingly. He would not tolerate falsehoods, trickery, or deception; nor would he be deterred from his objectives. When he announced that he was going to do something, he intended to do it. His announced visit, then, to the palace at Shuri was a critical symbolic preview in which Perry would follow his script impeccably.[21]

In the days before the visit to Shuri, American naval officers and sailors made frequent visits to the island while surveying crews charted local waters. Perry sent a small party to explore the other islands, an activity that took several days and covered more than one hundred miles. Morrow, Taylor, Williams, and Heine collected geographic information, made sketches, and took notes while the officers and men enjoyed walking around the exotic island. Although irritated by the constant presence of spies, the Americans spoke well of the native residents, who were poor, shy, and fawning but also neat and industrious. They were virtual slaves to the taxes imposed on them, but the cleanliness of their villages contrasted sharply with the filth of China.

Perry had set Monday, 6 June, as the day for his visit to Shuri, a distance of four miles from Naha. In Shanghai, Perry had been taken to visit the mayor in an elaborate sedan chair as befitted an honored dignitary. The same pomp seeming requisite now, Perry had squadron carpenters construct a large sedan to carry him from the shore to Shuri. On the appointed day, the launches and cutters departed for shore at about 9:00 A.M. Onshore, dozens of seamen, marines, officers, musicians, and others assembled north of Naha at the tiny village of Tomari, two miles from Shuri. A cannon salute announced Perry's departure from the *Susquehanna* in a barge that included Commanders Adams, Buchanan, Lee, and Walker as well as Flag Lieutenant Contee.[22]

With interpreters Bettelheim and Williams walking in advance, two fieldpieces commanded by Lt. Silas Bent led the procession, followed by the band from the *Susquehanna* and a company of marines. Perry followed in his sedan chair, carried by four Chinese coolies with a relief contingent of four others. Two personal attendants and two marine bodyguards walked alongside. Following Perry were Captain of the Fleet Adams, Flag Lt. John Contee, and Perry's personal secretary and son, Oliver Hazard Perry II. Six Chinese coolies followed carrying gifts for the prince and queen dowager and guarded by a file of marines. The remaining naval officers walked behind them; then came their attendants, the band from the *Mississippi,* and a second company of marines, with Capt. William Slack at the end of the procession. Bayard Taylor estimated a procession of 215, including thirty-two officers, 122 marines and seamen, and thirty bandsmen.

The imposing procession moved without incident as astonished natives gathered to view the strange spectacle. "The beauty of the day, the brilliant green of the wooded hills throughout which our road lay, and the cheerful strains of the bands," wrote Taylor, "gave the occasion a most inspiring character." Creating very little alarm, the martial procession took on a "festive and friendly air" during the hour it took to reach Shuri. There local officials made one final attempt to deceive the Americans by directing them to the home of the regent, not the palace. Refusing to be diverted, the procession continued to the palace, where the gates were hurriedly opened for the commodore. The formal interview, held in the central court, lasted one hour. The regent and three of his associates conducted the interview, during which Perry invited the four officials to be his guests on the *Susquehanna*. After courtesies and formalities had been exchanged, the regent invited the American to his house for refreshments. Here a twelve-course meal was served, toasts were exchanged, and tension dissipated. With several hundred natives following, the Americans returned to their ships without incident, and the entire delegation was back onboard by mid-afternoon.[23]

The *Susquehanna* in company with the *Saratoga* left Naha three days later for the Bonin Islands, almost eight hundred miles north and east of Okinawa and more than five hundred miles south of Edo (Tokyo). First discovered in the sixteenth century, the islands were without clear sovereignty, having been uninhabited until the nineteenth century, when a small group of European and American settlers established a colony at Port Lloyd on Peel Island, or Chichi Jima. The colonists found abundant sea life, raised livestock, and cultivated vegetables and fruits, which they sold to passing whalers. Perry thought of the Bonin Islands in strategic terms as a possible coaling station for steamers on the proposed steamship route from San Francisco to Shanghai. And indeed, Port Lloyd was "admirably adapted for a coal depot and stopping place." Perry calculated that the entire route stretched 6,475 miles and could be traveled in thirty days, more than three weeks shorter than the fifty-two- to fifty-five-day English route from Liverpool to Shanghai. In effect, a letter dispatched from Shanghai would arrive about the same time in New York that a duplicate letter sent west from Shanghai would arrive at Liverpool. The creation of a transpacific line would redirect American mail, encourage American commercial expansion in the Pacific, and also facilitate the flow of Chinese immigrants to California. "These provident people are the most patient and enduring laborers and must, by their orderly habits," predicted Perry, "add greatly to the agricultural interests of California."[24]

During his four-day stay, Perry sent his men to explore Peel Island and survey its waters, collected pertinent geographic information, and made arrangements for an American coal depot. He acquired land in his own name at Port Lloyd; the private, handwritten agreement used neither military nor diplomatic title. Perry envisioned Port Lloyd as a small and thriving settlement that would prosper as a stopping place on the steamship route. To facilitate its development, Perry left bulls, cows, sheep, goats, and all types of garden seeds, and promised the residents that later he would provide farm implements and more animals. Although prepared to take possession of the islands, Perry did not do so because he recognized a problem with their sovereignty. He thought that Great Britain probably had the strongest claim, but other European nations, Japan, and the United States could also advance competing claims. Since no nation had attempted to settle, colonize, and rule the islands, Perry foresaw Port Lloyd as a free port for all nations, a status that would "prevent all future difficulties and mutually benefit the commerce" of both the United States and Great Britain.[25]

When Perry returned to Naha at the end of June, he found Commander Kelly and the *Plymouth*, which had left Shanghai on 2 June and reached Naha on 13 June. Although the political uncertainty continued, the situation at Shanghai had calmed. Even Marshall acknowledged that no immediate danger existed; nevertheless, he had wanted the *Plymouth* to remain. American merchants agreed, appealing to Kelly to delay his departure until they felt secure. Responding that no rebel threat on Shanghai was expected, Kelly had instead departed to join the expedition.[26]

Perry agreed and justified Kelly's decision immediately to the secretary of the navy. While naval commanders overseas wanted to extend as much protection as possible to the merchants, he explained, it was impossible to satisfy everyone. If he stationed vessels at Canton, Shanghai, and one or two other ports, he would have none left to carry out his mission to Japan. In Washington, the new secretary of navy, James Dobbin, agreed and approved the actions of Kelly.[27]

Back in Naha, Perry concentrated on final preparations for Japan but still kept his eyes on the local situation and his own agenda there. Perry wanted Americans to be able to move freely on the island without being followed by spies, he sought a residence onshore for some Americans to spend the night, he wanted to rent a shed to store coal, and he insisted on paying local residents for the goods they provided. But he did not press these issues or demand a formal treaty. Instead he appeased local officials and tried to convince them of America's goodwill. Learning that the regent with whom Perry had dealt on his first visit had been replaced, Perry acted as though his own actions and his insistence on making the trip to Shuri had played no part in the removal. He entertained local officials at an elaborate banquet with multiple courses of food, a selection of wine and liquor, and musical entertainment. The Americans also exhibited the daguerreotype and other technological items "to the utter astonishment of the people." In addition to befriending the Okinawans, Perry hoped that news of these modern wonders would be "duly recorded and transmitted to Japan."[28]

By this time Perry had come to pity the peasants of Okinawa. With the exception of the "miserable peons in Mexico," he concluded that "the apparent wretchedness these squalid slaves would seem to suffer" was unsurpassed in his own experience. The typical Okinawan peasant received only 20 percent of the crop he raised and supported a class system that placed him at the bottom. "With respect to Lew Chew, I can conceive of no greater act of humanity than to protect these miserable people against the oppression of their tyrannical rulers. Inhabiting an island beautiful beyond description, they are trodden to the earth." Perry concluded that it would be "politic and just to continue to these people the protection which I shall give them so long as I have the power and the countenance of American authority." Here at "the very door of the empire," the Japanese might be brought "to some sort of reason."[29]

Finally, after many delays, Perry and his four-ship squadron set course for Japan. Leaving the *Supply* at Naha, the squadron consisted of the *Saratoga* in the tow of the flagship *Susquehanna* and the *Plymouth* in tow of the *Mississippi*. As he sailed from Okinawa, Perry understood that the most formidable part of his mission was now at hand. He knew that Japanese officials were unresponsive to appeals of friendship, pleas for mercy, or arguments of mutual interest. They had treated the unarmed *Morrison* contemptuously in 1837 and exploited the vacillation of Commo.

James Biddle, with his two warships, in 1846. In contrast, the Japanese had responded with alacrity to the demands of Commo. James Glynn in 1849 when he threatened to use force at Nagasaki. Perry's challenge, then, was to pursue a strategy that employed his imposing armada without using actual force to establish formal relations and conclude a treaty of friendship. A treaty concluded at cannon point would, in fact, destroy any hope of establishing long-term, amicable diplomatic and commercial relations between the United States and Japan. Persistence and patience would be required. Tactical masters of delay and distraction, the Japanese would politely but persistently raise a litany of excuses to overturn every American request, and would take their own time in doing so. Since the American squadron had no base in the vicinity and carried only limited supplies of coal, water, and food, time was on the side of the Japanese. For this reason, Perry had decided long before that two visits to Japan would be necessary. He would deliver the president's letter, leave to give the Japanese ample time to consider their response, and then return the following year to receive the reply.

By 7 July the squadron was forty miles south of Cape Izu; on 8 July it steamed past Cape Sagami into the six-mile-wide Uraga Channel leading into Edo Bay. On each warship, the decks had been cleared for action: the guns shotted, small arms loaded, and "every precaution taken, in case we should meet with a hostile reception," reported Bayard Taylor. Near Cape Sagami, twelve to fifteen Japanese guard boats approached the squadron, but the American ships soon left them behind. The hazy day provided the Americans with a tantalizing first view of Japan. Taylor described the shores of Sagami as

> exceedingly picturesque and beautiful. They rise in abrupt bluffs, two hundred feet in height, gashed with narrow dells of the brightest verdure . . . while the country beyond rises in undulating hills, displaying a charming alternation of groves and cultivated fields. In the distance rose mountain ranges, receding behind each other until the vapor hid their farthest summits.

Finally, at about five o'clock, the squadron anchored in a line of battle outside the harbor of Uraga, less than thirty miles south of Edo.[30]

Two cannon shots from shore warned of the arrival of foreign ships. Almost immediately, Japanese guard boats approached. Each carried soldiers or officials and was sculled across the water by tall, athletic men.

As they had in the past, the guard boats surrounded and attempted to board the American ships, but they were repelled. The ropes of the Japanese boats were cut or cast overboard as their men tried to attach them, and boarders were repulsed with pikes and cutlasses. The Japanese protested to no avail. Finally, one guard boat approached the *Susquehanna* and displayed a scroll in French informing the Americans not to anchor and to depart immediately.[31]

Through an interpreter who spoke excellent Dutch, the Japanese in the boat informed the Americans that a high official was aboard and wished to be received. He was told to return to shore because the commander of the squadron represented the president of the United States and would receive only a government official of the highest rank. Finally, the Japanese official, representing himself as the vice governor of Uraga, was allowed onboard but was not permitted to see or speak to the commodore, only to Perry's flag lieutenant, John Contee. As it turned out, this man, named Nakajima Saburonsuke, was only an aide to the governor, not the vice governor. "The Japanese official, a fiery little fellow," observed Taylor, "was much exasperated at being kept in waiting, but soon moderated his tone." He asked many questions, which Contee did not answer. When asked why the governor of Uraga had not come, Nakajima replied that Japanese law forbade the governor from boarding a foreign ship.[32]

Contee informed Nakajima that Commodore Perry had come in peace to deliver a letter to the emperor from the president of the United States. When Nakajima replied that any communication must be delivered through the Dutch at Nagasaki, Contee, on behalf of Perry, told him that Perry would never go to Nagasaki. He had come to Uraga because it was close to Edo, where the emperor resided. In addition, the commodore wanted the Japanese guard boats to withdraw. If they did not do so at once, the commodore intended to "compel them to do so, and if they remained it would be at their own peril." In response, Nakajima issued an order that dispersed most of the guard boats. He also indicated that he would leave, consult with the governor, and return the next day. The Japanese had offered the Americans food, water, and fuel so that they would have no excuse for delaying their departure. Prepared for this gesture, the Americans refused the offer, and instead surprised the Japanese by offering to share American provisions with them.

Here the matter rested until the next day. Throughout the entire interview, Perry had remained in his cabin, invisible to the Japanese. He planned to remain invisible in the coming days, hidden behind the six-foot bulwarks of the *Susquehanna,* which allowed him to move freely on deck when Japanese visitors were not onboard without any fear of being seen. Perry well understood that "the more exclusive he should make himself . . . the more respect these people of forms and ceremonies would be disposed to award him."[33]

Perry had made a good start. In dealing with the Japanese, he had planned "to adopt an entirely contrary plan of proceedings from that of all others who had hitherto visited Japan on the same errand: to demand as a right and not to solicit as a favor those acts of courtesy which are due from one civilized nation to another." Seemingly insignificant details were crucial, and Perry had dealt with them adroitly, permitting "none of the petty annoyances" that the Japanese used "unsparingly" to disrespect "the dignity of the American flag." Perry had not allowed Japanese soldiers to board his ships or Japanese guard boats to surround the squadron; he had strictly limited conduct of official business to his flagship, where Japanese officials could deal only with designated American officers.

It was late in the evening of this unforgettable day that the spectacular fireball made its brief but dramatic appearance. Although some Americans interpreted it to be an omen of good fortune, Perry was not so sanguine; he made no written note of it at the time. The following day, 9 July, dawned bright and clear and revealed a stunning panorama. The view of Uraga "far surpassed my preconceived ideas of Japanese scenery," wrote Taylor. "The western shore is bold and steep, running here and there into lofty bluffs of light-gray rock," covered with bright fresh green turf and scattered groves of trees. From Uraga to the end of the promontory to the east stretched an "almost unbroken line of villages with houses of wood, with sharp roofs, some pointed in the Chinese style, some square and pyramidal." The bay was alive with small boats and junks. And dominating the entire scene, Mount Fujiyama rose to the west, looming "high above the hills" although it was sixty miles away. In the evening, its "solitary cone, of a pale violet hue, was defined with great distinctness against the rosy flush of sunset, but in the morning, when the light fell full upon it, we could see the scars of old eruptions, and the ravines of snow on its north side."[34]

That morning, a man claiming to be the governor of Uraga came aboard. In fact the man was Kayama Eizaemon, another of the governor's aides who was also the chief of police and who had previously dealt with Biddle and other foreigners. His presence, noted Perry, gave a lie to the claim of the previous day that the governor was not permitted to board a foreign ship. Since Kayama presumably ranked higher than Nakajima, he was permitted to speak to Commanders Buchanan and Adams. Kayama stated that Japanese laws forbade reception of the president's letter at Uraga. Instead the squadron must go to Nagasaki, where, through Dutch intermediaries, the Japanese government would receive the letter and provide a reply. Several times Kayama repeated this position, but Perry made it clear through his commanders that he would never consent to such an arrangement. Moreover, if the Japanese did not appoint a person of high rank to receive the letter, Perry indicated that he would land with a suitable force and deliver the letter directly to Edo. Perry had no intention of going to Nagasaki. He distrusted the Dutch and viewed Nagasaki as a symbol of fawning Dutch subservience where for decades the Dutch had prostituted their dignity and honor in return for a few niggling favors from Japan. He would not subject the American flag to the same humiliation.

In response to Perry's intransigence, Kayama announced that he would need to seek further instructions from his government in Edo, a process that would take at least eight days. Perry replied that he would wait only three days for a response before he began to move his ships. During the interview, the Americans showed Kayama the letter from the president and Perry's credentials, which were encased in "magnificent boxes . . . [t]he exquisite workmanship and costliness of which evidently surprised his excellency." Kayama asked why four warships were needed to deliver one letter, to which Perry replied that the size of his force was dictated by America's respect for the emperor.[35]

At daybreak that same morning, one surveying boat from each warship had begun to survey the harbor and bay of Uraga. Not knowing whether they would meet Japanese resistance, Perry ordered the men to remain within gun range of the ships. Although the Japanese sent their own boats to observe, they did not attempt to interfere with the Americans. During his interview later that day, Kayama asked about the activities of the American boats and was told that they were surveying the harbor. When Kayama responded that the Americans were violating Japanese laws, he was told that American laws required these surveys. At the conclusion of the interview, Kayama was informed that no further discussion would be necessary until the reply was received from Edo.

Perry's arrival and initial actions had caught the Tokugawa Bakufu off guard.[36] The Dutch had informed Japanese officials in 1852 of the planned American expedition to be led by a man named Perry, but when word reached Japan that the squadron had anchored at Okinawa, the Japanese, internally divided and lacking a unified foreign policy, did nothing. In fact, the Tokugawa regime recognized that it was weak politically and its defenses incapable of repelling an attack by American warships. Abe Masahiro, who had headed the regime since 1845 as senior councilor, was a thoughtful and able man, but he was not the kind of forceful individual to forge a consensus to meet the crisis. He personally favored opening some ports because he believed that war would probably result if the Japanese refused. He was supported by key officials such as the powerful Ii Naosuke of Hikone, the head of one of the great *fudai* houses. Although they opposed opening ports to foreigners, such officials accepted the idea as the only pragmatic approach for their militarily weak country. Opposing him, however, were influential lords such as Tokugawa Nariaki and Matsudaira Keiei, who objected strongly to making concessions to foreigners. Instead, they favored resistance and, if necessary, war to maintain the isolation of Japan. This division over foreign policy was exacerbated by the weakness of the government. By 1853, various economic forces had made the Bakufu vulnerable. Now, serious infighting threatened to open the way for the overthrow of the regime.[37]

When the American squadron sailed into Japanese waters on 8 July, thousands of Japanese had watched and word spread quickly around the country. The black steamships, belching smoke and moving steadily against the wind, astonished observers. Panic and alarm spread quickly. Edo was in an uproar. The Japanese mobilized 200,000 troops, but most officials realized that their military weakness precluded direct resistance to the American squadron. Nor did their leaders know what to expect from the Americans. Some thought that the Americans might invade and seize territory as Great Britain had in China. Others hoped that the visitors might be thwarted by unyielding diplomatic resistance. Having dealt successfully with Biddle in 1846, Abe hoped that the same tactics of intransigence, delay, and deception might also work with Perry. However, neither he nor his colleagues knew how to respond to Perry's direct and demanding manner and disregard for Japanese regulations.

The Americans quickly realized the weakness of the Japanese defenses and termed them "laughable." Along the shore the Japanese had installed false batteries of black canvas, which the Americans derisively labeled "dungaree" forts. Abe Masahiro decided that the only course open to him was to buy time. The government would receive the letters carried by Perry at Uraga to keep him as far from Edo as possible, and it would promise to provide a response the following spring. In the interim, Abe hoped to consult with various lords and agree on a strategy.[38]

As the Japanese deliberated, the Americans continued their surveys. Sunday, 10 July, was a day of worship and relaxation. A Japanese party approached the flagship but was refused permission to board because it had no official business to conduct. The surveying boats now moved away from Uraga and up the bay toward Edo. On the morning of 11 July, a tense confrontation occurred. As Lt. Silas Bent and his surveying boats passed Kannonsaki and entered Edo Bay proper, forty Japanese guard boats filled with soldiers approached from the opposite shore. A standoff ensued as Bent altered his course to avoid a collision and called for support from the *Mississippi*. When the steamship approached, the Japanese dispersed and Bent continued his work. Depicted in a painting by William Heine entitled *Crossing the Rubicon*, the Americans' movement unsettled officials in Edo because the foreigners had passed an imaginary line considered to be the entrance of Edo and a strategic line of defense for the imperial capital. The line ran between two fortified points, from Kannonsaki on the eastern side of Uraga Channel due north to a sandbar known as Futsusaki on the east side of Edo Bay.[39]

On the same day, Kayama boarded the *Mississippi*, reported that a decision from Edo was imminent, and inquired about the American boats surveying Edo Bay. He was informed that if the business that had brought the squadron to Japan were not finished during this visit, Perry would return the following spring with a larger force. And because Uraga did not provide a safe anchorage, the American squadron would need a better one closer to Edo. This was the first time that Perry had intimated to Japanese officials that he might return to Edo for a second visit.

On 12 July, Kayama returned to the *Susquehanna* to announce that a high official would receive the president's letter onshore. However, the Japanese reply would be delivered at Nagasaki through either Dutch or Chinese intermediaries. Perry responded that he would not go to Nagasaki; nor would he receive the reply through the Dutch or Chinese. If the "friendly letter" from the president to the emperor of Japan was not received and replied to by the Japanese themselves, Perry would consider it an insult to his country and could not be accountable for the consequences. Kayama left but later returned in the afternoon to assure Perry that he would be received by a very distinguished person with written credentials to validate his position. Kayama also informed the Americans that the reception was to take place at Kurihama, a small village about two miles from Uraga. For his part, Perry confirmed that he did not expect an immediate reply and would return in several months to receive it. Both sides also agreed that there would be no discussion or negotiation at the ceremony. The following day, Kayama returned to make final arrangements for the ceremony to be held on 14 July. Kayama also carried a letter with the imperial seal appointing "His Highness Toda, Prince of Izu, first councilor of the Empire" and Prince Ido of Iwami to receive Perry. The event was to be held in a specially constructed wooden building on a quiet section of beach that the Japanese had selected because it was away from Uraga, easily fortified, and near a place where thousands of Japanese troops could be held in reserve.[40]

According to travel writer Taylor, the Japanese response and their appointment of a "Chief Counsellor of the Empire" surprised and pleased the Americans: "This prompt and unlooked-for concession astonished us all. . . . We had obtained in four days, without subjecting ourselves to a single observance of Japanese law, what the Russian embassy . . . failed to accomplish in six months." Taylor attributed the success "to the decided stand the Commodore took during the early negotiations," which had been "admirably conducted." The American officers treated the Japanese "in such a polite and friendly manner as to win their good will, while not a single point to which we attached any importance was yielded. There was a mixture of firmness, dignity and fearlessness on our side, against which their artful and dissimilating policy was powerless."[41]

Soon after sunrise on 14 July, the morning fog cleared to reveal brilliant sunshine. At about eight o'clock the *Susquehanna* and *Mississippi* weighed anchor, moved a short distance toward Kurihama, and anchored near the beach where the American landing was to occur. The ships lay broadside to the shore, decks cleared, guns pointed, primed, and "ready for action, in case of treachery." Shortly thereafter, Perry received Kayama and Nakajima on the flagship and prepared to disembark. Perry and his senior officers had planned the landing with care and precision. On the shore, Japanese officials and an estimated five thousand soldiers waited. To accompany his delegation Perry brought along about 250 well-armed marines and sailors. He intended not just to deliver the letters but to impress the Japanese as well. Fifteen launches and cutters, followed by other boats and the commodore's barge, would convey the Americans, attired in their best uniforms. In addition to the marines and sailors, bands from the two steamers, a contingent of officers, and Perry's personal entourage comprised the American delegation.[42]

Commander Buchanan led the fifteen launches and cutters. Once he had reached shore and arranged the honor guard, the guns of the *Susquehanna* announced Perry's departure. For the Americans present, it was a thrilling and glorious moment.

> The gleam of arms, the picturesque mingling of blue and white in the uniforms, and the sparkling of the waves under the speedy strokes of the oarsmen, combined to form a splendid picture, set off as it was by the background of rich green hills, and the long lines of [Japanese] soldiery and banners on the beach.[43]

When Perry reached the shore, the Americans quickly formed their procession and marched a short distance down the beach as their bands played "Hail Columbia" and the national anthem. Although they remained impassive, the Japanese were impressed. "The adroit maneuvers of the guards in the van as well as in the rear, conducted just as if they had been marching into enemy territory," observed Japanese official Kayama Eizaemon, "truly left us in amazement." At the pavilion, the ceremony proceeded in an atmosphere of tense politeness. Received with stiff formality, Perry and his official delegation presented the letters and documents in their elaborate boxes. In return, the Japanese presented a scroll that acknowledged receipt of the documents and informed the Americans that they could now depart. A brief exchange ensued as Perry indicated that he would return in the spring. When asked whether he would be accompanied by all four ships, Perry replied that he would have these ships and additional warships as well. When the brief ceremony ended, the Americans marched back down the beach to their waiting boats as the two bands played a spirited rendition of "Hail Columbia" and "Yankee Doodle." Taylor noted that "few of those present, I venture to say, ever heard our national airs with more pride and pleasure." In less than twenty minutes, all the American boats were under way, and by noon both steamers had weighed anchor.[44]

Kayama and Nakajima returned to the *Susquehanna* with the landing party and remained onboard, their boats in tow, until the flagship reached Uraga. During their brief stay, the Japanese made a favorable impression on the American officers. They conducted themselves with "ease and propriety," and their faces "denoted a lively and active mind," wrote Taylor. "Notwithstanding that spirit of cunning and secrecy . . . their faces were agreeable and expressive . . . it was the unanimous opinion of all our officers that they were as perfect gentlemen as could be found in any part of the world."

By evening, all of the Japanese had departed, leaving the Americans alone to ponder the day. The visitors from the West were ecstatic. "Oh what a beautiful sight it was, I should have liked all of my Parents, and You my dear, to of seen us landing," wrote engineer William H. Rutherford to his sweetheart. Others noted the historical significance of the day. "This eventful day," wrote Samuel Wells Williams, "will be . . . noted in the history of Japan. [It is the day] on which the key was put into the lock and a beginning made to do away with the long reclusion of this nation." This day "will . . . mark the opening of Japan to the world," wrote clerk J. W. Spalding on the *Mississippi*. "America has said, 'Open sesame!'"[45]

Although he had been told to leave, Perry did just the opposite. He moved his squadron toward Edo and anchored at a place he called the American Anchorage, some ten miles closer to Edo than any foreign ship had ever been. During the next two days, the Americans' boats surveyed farther up the bay, to the alarm and consternation of the Japanese. Perry then shifted his pendant to the *Mississippi,* ignored Japanese warnings, and ascended to within five miles of Edo, intending to demonstrate to the Japanese "how little I regarded their order for me to depart." Surveying so close to Edo, he thought, would "produce a decided influence upon the pride and conceit of the government, and cause a more favorable consideration of the President's letter." Finally, on 16 July, Perry moved his squadron back toward Uraga. Kayama came aboard with predictions that the president's letter would be favorably received and with gifts for Perry, who informed Kayama that he would accept gifts only if Kayama accepted gifts in return. The usual exchange followed, with Perry refusing to accept Kayama's explanation that Japanese law forbade officials to accept gifts. American laws demanded reciprocity, Perry countered. Finally, an exchange of inexpensive gifts was arranged, and Kayama departed.[46]

Perry had long planned to make two visits to Japan, but he felt compelled to justify this decision to the Navy Department.[47] He explained in a letter to the secretary of the navy that since he lacked sufficient provisions or water to remain indefinitely, the Japanese could easily procrastinate and ultimately force him to leave, thus claiming victory over the Americans and seriously injuring his mission. Moreover, the unrest in China required an American naval presence there. Furthermore, he still awaited the arrival of additional warships, and many of the official gifts had not yet arrived. In fact, Perry was "glad to have a good excuse" to leave Japan. Before he departed, he sent a letter to the Japanese stating that he would return to Edo Bay the following spring to receive the emperor's reply.[48]

As he departed, the delighted Perry outlined in his personal journal the details of his success to date. He had dispersed the troublesome guard boats, surveyed the coastal waters leading to Edo, refused to confer with anyone "but a dignitary of the highest rank in the empire," and adhered strictly to the "simple rules of diplomatic courtesy." By insisting that the exchange of gifts be done on a "footing of equality," Perry believed that he had convinced the Japanese of the good intentions of the United States.[49]

The squadron sailed in high spirits for Naha. "Nothing could have been better managed," reported Bayard Taylor; "the final success . . . was owing to no fortunate combination of circumstances, but wholly to the prudent and sagacious plan pre-arranged by the Commodore." A navy veteran on the *Saratoga* remembered years later that "unquestionably [Perry's] insight into the oriental mind, his firmness and persistence, his stalwart physical presence, his portly bearing, his dignity, his poise, his stately courtesy, were prime factors in his success." Even those who disliked Perry or had doubted his success had "now come over on the other side," wrote engineer William Rutherford. Everyone agreed that "he was the only officer in the Navy that could of [sic] accomplished" the feat.[50]

The squadron reached Naha on 25 July without the *Saratoga*, which had been sent directly to China. Here Perry learned from the men of the *Supply*, which had been left at Naha, that the ever-present spies continued to harass Americans wherever they went onshore. Flushed with his success in Japan, Perry was not about to tolerate such indignities on Okinawa. That very day he sent Commander Adams and Reverend Williams to confer with local officials and transmit a letter to the regent. In it Perry demanded that the Okinawans rent to the Americans a home or shelter and erect onshore a coal-storage shed of six hundred tons' capacity for which the Okinawans would be paid an annual rent. The spies were to be discontinued. If they persisted in shadowing Americans onshore, "serious consequences" and "possible bloodshed" might result. The Americans must also be allowed to trade in the market and purchase goods from shops. Local officials should understand and accept the fact that American ships would rendezvous in the port of Naha for years to come.[51]

On 28 July, Regent Shang Hung-hsiu and Perry met formally onshore. Perry explained that he would leave in a few days for China but return the following year. Because his propositions were "reasonable and proper," Perry expected the Okinawans to accept them. Americans, he said, were persons of few words, but they always meant what they said. His mission to Japan had placed the United States and Japan on friendly terms; he hoped to establish similar relations with Okinawa. After a dinner of seven or eight courses had been served, the regent presented Okinawa's response to Perry. The interpreter Williams opened the envelope and read the letter aloud. Citing the poverty and small size of Okinawa, the letter respectfully explained why each of the American demands was either difficult or impossible to satisfy. Perry immediately pronounced the letter unsatisfactory and ordered it returned to the regent. In the conversation that followed, Perry reiterated that "all his demands were plain and simple and ought to be granted without hesitation." The Americans, said Perry, had no intention of injuring the people of Okinawa. When the regent reaffirmed his initial response, Perry rose and prepared to leave, declaring that unless he received a satisfactory answer by noon of the next day, he would land with two hundred men, march to Shuri, occupy the palace, and remain there until the matter was settled. Perry and his staff returned immediately to the *Susquehanna*. Within two days, the major of Naha informed the Americans that all of their demands had been accepted. In the face of Perry's intransigence and his undeniable naval power, clearly the rulers of Okinawa had no alternative to capitulating and making the best of a bad situation. "As a mouse in the talons of the eagle," observed clerk J. W. Spalding, "they promised everything."[52]

On 1 August, the *Susquehanna* and *Mississippi* sailed for China, leaving the *Plymouth* at Naha, where Commander Kelly was to remain until October before sailing to Port Lloyd to monitor the progress of the settlement there. En route to Hong Kong, Perry happily encountered the sloop-of-war *Vandalia,* one missing piece of his promised squadron. Perry had chosen the "safe and commodious" harbor of Cum Sing Moon, between Macao and Hong Kong, for the squadron's rendezvous. Within a month after Perry reached Hong Kong on 7 August, his squadron was nearly complete. The steamer *Powhatan* arrived on 25 August, the sloop-of-war *Macedonian* reached the Cum Sing Moon anchorage on 26 August, and the storeship *Southampton* arrived in September. Since the Navy Department had decided not to send the ship-of-the-line *Vermont,* the storeship *Lexington* was the only missing vessel. It was an important one, though, for it carried most of the official gifts, including a quarter-gauge railroad and a telegraph. Unfortunately, the *Lexington,* a notoriously slow sailer, would likely not reach China until late fall or early winter.

At Macao, which was conveniently located between Hong Kong, Canton, and Cum Sing Moon, Perry took a house for himself and established an office and a hospital for the squadron. Macao's daily mail service kept him in constant communication with his squadron. His workload was heavy and many of his duties tedious as he supervised the arrangement of the extensive scientific and geographic information that had already been collected and oversaw needed repairs to his ships. He reported that the *Susquehanna* was "not in good condition" but would have to answer for another season; both the *Powhatan* and *Mississippi* needed repairs. The humid climate of the region destroyed sails, cordage, and equipment, and the squadron needed equipment that was difficult to find and exorbitant in price.[53]

Perry complained of "wear and tear both of body and mind during the summer." "What with the heat of the climate, and the cares of command, the neglect of the Government in not sending me the promised additional ships, I have much to overcome and I find myself a little worse for it." His health did not improve during the fall. Although generally a "remarkably healthy place," Macao suffered a serious epidemic in 1853. Fortunately, Perry did not contract the fever, but his health declined and his rheumatism returned. Indeed, he was bedridden for a time.[54]

The political situation in China also distracted him. Conditions in south China had not improved when he returned in August. Although the insurgents had not directly threatened Canton, the weakness of the Manchu government permitted the entire area to swarm "with thieves and desperate fellows" who constantly endangered the lives and property of foreigners. To the north, Shanghai remained under great pressure

and, in fact, fell to an insurgent group on 7 September. The rebels secured the city with little bloodshed and established order before the foreign settlement was endangered seriously. As he had done the previous
spring, Perry refused to overreact. "Nothing of very important interest
has occurred in China," he reported to Washington. "Shanghai has
fallen into the hands of the insurgents, but neither the persons nor property of foreigners have been disturbed." When American merchants at
Canton petitioned for protection in August, Perry reassured them and
dispatched the armed storeship *Supply* to Canton.[55]

Perry now believed that the "Tartar dynasty" was likely to fall soon but
would not be replaced by a "solid government" for years because the
rebels were poorly organized. Accordingly, the United States should be
patient and should await the proper time to push aggressively for trade
rights and the right to establish a resident minister at Peking. To act prematurely by assisting one side might injure U.S. relations with the other
if it should prove victorious. For the present, argued Perry, the best policy would be to exercise "masterly inactivity" in China while concentrating on bringing the empire of Japan into the family of commercial or
trading nations.[56]

Perry's assessment of the situation in China was sound, and the navy's
immediate role there might not have become an issue at all but for the
continued presence of Commissioner Marshall, whose views, recommendations, and disposition contrasted sharply with Perry's. The result
was a sometimes distracting, sometimes humorous, but never productive
standoff between the two men during the last months of 1853. In spite of
Perry's support on the credentials issue, Marshall felt thwarted by the
commodore's refusal to provide him with the use of a warship. When the
American squadron had left Shanghai for Japan the previous May, Marshall complained that he had been "put ashore and abandoned by his
country's flag." He seethed a short time later when the last American
warship in China, the *Plymouth,* followed Perry to Okinawa.

After Chinese officials met with and accredited Marshall in July, he
softened his views and recommended that the United States join other
nations and actively assist the Manchu regime. "It is my opinion that the
highest interests of the United States are involved in sustaining China,"
argued Marshall; American interference "to . . . tranquilize China would
be a mission of humanity and charity." Marshall advised, however, that
China be required in return to accept certain conditions, including free-

dom of religion, trade, and movement to foreigners, along with the opening of the Yangtze River to steam navigation. Marshall denied that American intervention would violate a traditional U.S. policy of remaining
neutral in the internal disputes of other nations because these actions
would be only to protect the rights of American citizens.[57]

The merits of Marshall's views aside, his position clashed sharply with
Perry's recommendation of "masterly inactivity." If Marshall was to
increase American visibility in China, however, he would need the support of Perry's naval squadron. Given their disparate personalities, the
two proud and stubborn men were unlikely collaborators. Marshall was a
vain, demanding, and impetuous man whose behavior created more enemies than friends in China. Perry, although not impulsive or personally
vain, was determined to avoid any action that would diminish his chances
for success in Japan. He also resented having his judgments challenged
by an inexperienced diplomat who was almost twenty years his junior.
Their dispute was played out in letters to one another and to their respective supervisors in Washington, D.C. Marshall complained to both Perry
and Washington that the situation in China was more threatening than
Perry understood. In September, Marshall urged that warships be sent to
protect Amoy, Foochow, and Ningpo and directed the acting consul at
Canton to specify the naval force needed there. To the State Department,
Marshall charged that Perry had been "grossly discourteous" to him and
complained that his diplomatic power was "useless" as long as naval commanders could "with impunity" nullify his efforts by withdrawing the
naval force and even "denying him the means of locomotion."[58]

In response, Perry sent the *Plymouth* to Amoy, Foochow, and Ningpo
but reminded Marshall that there was no American property to be protected at any of those places. The only American residents there were
missionaries who had been treated kindly by the Chinese. Perry reaffirmed his desire to cooperate and to protect American lives, property,
and rights in China; however, so long as he remained in command, Perry
insisted that he would be the judge of the best interests of those who
sought his protection. Since he had come to China, he had not heard of
a single incident "wherein an American or any foreigner has been in the
least molested in person or property."[59]

Perry covered his political rear flank by justifying his position to Secretary of the Navy James Dobbin. In an era of intense partisanship, Perry
was potentially vulnerable because the Democrat Franklin Pierce was

now president. Perry had been appointed by the previous Whig administration, but then, so too had Marshall. Perry labeled Marshall's reports of danger to foreigners in China "greatly exaggerated." Even during the fall of Shanghai, Americans and other foreigners had walked through the streets without the least insult or hindrance. He also explained that since most American and foreign coastal trade violated the laws of China, naval officers had difficulty distinguishing between legal and illegal trade.[60]

On the critical issue of his authority, Perry argued that in "no navy in the world serving on foreign stations . . . has an ambassador, resident minister, or consul, the slightest right to interfere. If it were so, the commanders of such forces would find themselves entirely powerless to effect any object of usefulness." The naval commander was best qualified to judge the fitness of his ships for particular kinds of service; the obvious considerations of fuel and supplies, the condition of the steam engines, the nature of the navigation, and the health of the crew only the commander could assess. Meanwhile, Marshall pleaded his own case with Secretary of State William Marcy. Turning Perry's argument on its head, Marshall attacked the exclusive rights of naval commanders and asked the government to "establish some absolute regulation defining the 'prerogative' of the naval commanders." If the present situation continued, he said, there would be no role for "civil officers, except as assistants to the *naval diplomatists*."[61]

In December, Marshall made one final effort to secure Perry's support. After the fall of Shanghai, he had decided that the U.S. consul should continue to collect and pay customs duties to China even though Manchu officials had evacuated the city. Then, in December, Marshall decided to suspend payment of the duties in an effort to wring concessions from the Chinese government. When Marshall asked Perry for naval support to protect Americans in the event of trouble, Perry denied the request and reiterated that he alone would judge whether his naval force should intervene "in a civil war between a despotic government . . . and an organized revolutionary army gallantly fighting for a more liberal enlightened religious and political position." Furthermore, with Japan his priority, Perry would leave not one of his ships behind when he sailed because the success of that mission required the "most imposing force" he could muster.[62]

The dispute between the commodore and the commissioner ended in the early days of 1854. Word arrived that Marshall had been recalled, and he soon left for the United States. In the end, his preoccupation with Japan notwithstanding, Perry's assessment of the situation in China was more sensible and farsighted than Marshall's. Little lasting good would have come from American intervention in China in 1853. Despite its aspirations, the United States was then a minor diplomatic and military player there. It had neither the naval power, the diplomatic clout, nor the national will to sustain an interventionist policy. Regardless of Perry's reasons, the best policy for the United States was indeed "masterly inactivity" with a "studied regard to neutrality and non-interference."

His dispute with Marshall distracted Perry, but other developments worried him more. Rumors circulated that the French intended to dispatch a squadron to Japan and that the Russians wanted to join Perry's expedition and make it a joint mission. In late November, the French frigate *Constantine* suddenly put to sea from Macao under sealed orders. Although the ship was known to be going first to Shanghai, its subsequent destination was suspected to be Japan. And Russian Admiral E. V. Putiatin had just arrived from Nagasaki in the frigate *Pallas,* which lay anchored at Shanghai with three other Russian naval vessels. Perry suspected that Admiral Putiatin planned to sail to Edo Bay and "interfere very seriously" with U.S. operations there.[63]

Although winter weather and adverse seas waited in Japan, Perry decided to depart as soon as the *Lexington* arrived rather than wait for spring. As the fall passed, Perry's health improved gradually, but his appearance remained wan; in fact, one report that filtered back to Washington indicated that Perry had aged ten years since he joined the squadron. Very much alarmed, Jane Perry uncharacteristically wrote to her personal friend William Sinclair in the Navy Department that she was "very anxious" to join her husband in Macao. Her alarm apparently passed, for she remained in New York. Perry thought often of his family back in the United States. On 24 December, he assured Jane of his "undiminished affection" and wished his family a happy New Year. He had also been busy buying gifts for his family. He sent boxes of tea, china tea sets, paper lanterns, lacquer ware, and silks to family members. To Jane, he lamented that the temptation to buy was great but his means small, and he was thus unlikely to make any large purchases. Instead, the ever-practical commodore assured his wife that he would buy only "useful and ornamental" items and some articles of furniture for their home. Perry also referred frequently to retirement, or going "to Housekeeping," as he phrased it. "I do not expect to go to sea again unless we have War. This cruise will use me pretty well up for my duties are very trying to my health."[64]

Finally, the *Lexington* and its long-anticipated cargo appeared. As Perry hastened final preparations, he reported on 9 January 1854 with satisfaction that his were the only steamships operating in those seas. The French and Russian navies had exhausted their coal supplies, but he had loaned the English a limited amount because they could repay it. Perry set his departure date from Hong Kong for 14 January. By that time, the *Macedonian* and *Supply* were under way for Okinawa and the *Saratoga* and *Plymouth* were stationed elsewhere with orders to proceed to Okinawa. The flagship *Susquehanna* would sail in company with the *Powhatan* and *Mississippi* with the storeships *Lexington* and *Southampton* in tow. On the very hour that he was due to sail from Hong Kong, however, Perry received alarming new instructions from Secretary Dobbin dated 28 October 1853:

> Hoping that it may not interfere seriously with your plan of operations, you will, on receipt of this communication, immediately dispatch one of the war steamers of your squadron to Macao, to meet the Hon. R. M. McLane, our commissioner to China, to be subject to his control until other orders reach you.[65]

Perry was stunned. Preoccupied to the point of obsession, he had planned the return trip to Japan with meticulous care and great anticipation. Now his superiors in Washington were threatening to divert him "from this great object of my life." The angry Perry overreacted, protesting that the reassignment of one of his three steamers "would be seriously inconvenient and highly injurious to my plans, the execution of which has already commenced; indeed, it could not be done at this time without deranging the operations of the squadron." Only because it was his duty to obey, he agreed to detach one of the steamers for Macao—after the squadron had reached Edo Bay.[66]

In other words, Perry decided to disobey a direct order from the secretary of the navy. Sailing immediately with all three steamers, he reached Okinawa on 25 January. He explained to the secretary in a report mailed from there that he had adopted a course that would serve the department's considerations while obviating the "serious consequences of withdrawing a steamer so suddenly" from the expedition. Without the addition of the battleship *Vermont* and the steamer *Alleghany*, and with both the *Plymouth* and *Saratoga* scheduled for other duties, Perry complained that his force would be no larger than it had been the year before. He had chosen to deal with the problem by hastening his cruise to Japan and taking the *Susquehanna* along as scheduled. After the warship was "seen a few days by the Japanese," he would send it back to China to arrive by 20 or 25 March, possibly before Commissioner McLane even arrived there.

In fact, Perry had written a disingenuous explanation. He knew that his squadron was considerably larger than it had been the previous year. Perry expected to take to Japan a squadron of seven or eight ships, depending on the disposition of the *Susquehanna,* in contrast to the four ships he had taken in 1853. Perry also knew that since it had taken two and one-half months for the secretary's instructions to reach him, his response and the secretary's subsequent reply would most likely require another five months. At the least, then, Perry could be reasonably sure that he had five months to complete his mission. Just short of admitting his disobedience, he concluded his letter by appealing to the secretary's sympathy: "I will not permit myself to imagine for a moment, that a long life of forty-five years in service is to terminate in a manner to bring reproach upon my naval pride."[67]

At Naha, Perry found the *Macedonian, Vandalia,* and *Supply.* Conditions had improved on Okinawa, but the old problems persisted. The people were friendlier, the women no longer fled from the marketplaces when Americans appeared, and Americans could buy local goods and food. A seven-hundred-ton-capacity coal shed had been built and a building had been assigned onshore for the use of the Americans. However, local officials refused to accept payment for supplies they provided to the Americans and tried unsuccessfully to dissuade American parties from exploring the island. To "accustom the people of the capital to the visits of Americans to the palace," Perry notified officials that he intended another visit to the palace at Shuri to pay his respects to the regent. The Okinawans raised objections but Perry again made the trip in his sedan chair as part of a formal procession. During the visit Perry asked the regent to exchange local coins for American coins. Although the regent declared such an exchange impossible, Perry left $49.24 in American coins and showed his displeasure by refusing to receive poultry and other items from local officials. He determined to resolve the ongoing problems on Okinawa at a future date.

Perry also responded to a letter he had received from the governor general of the Dutch East Indies. Because the shogun had died recently, the Japanese government had asked the Dutch to request that Perry delay his return to Japan. Perry already knew of the emperor's death, but he was not about to change his plans or to use the Dutch to communicate with Japan. He thanked the governor general but informed him brusquely that the Japanese had already been apprised of his intentions.[68]

As his return to Japan neared, Perry contemplated the prospect of Japanese intransigence. It was possible that Japan would refuse to open one or more ports or to negotiate a formal treaty without being forced to do so, an alternative that would probably put the Americans "in the wrong." Instead, Perry proposed to the Navy Department that if the Japanese government refused to negotiate or to open a port for U.S. ships, he would take Lew Chew and hold it, on the "ground of reclamation for insults and injuries," until he received instructions from Washington. Claiming the Okinawans "would rejoice" in being independent of Japan, Perry "earnestly" requested instructions from the department on the matter. Although subsequent events rendered Perry's request moot, and the letter probably would not have arrived in time to make a difference, in his response Secretary Dobbin strongly admonished him against any hostilities and instructed Perry not to seize Okinawa.[69]

Finally, in early February, the squadron left Okinawa for Japan. The four sailing ships—the *Lexington, Vandalia, Macedonian,* and *Southampton*—left first, followed a week later by the three steamers. In anticipation of sending the *Susquehanna* back to China, Perry had its deck cabin removed and rebuilt on the *Powhatan,* which Perry intended to use as his flagship in Japan. When he left Japan six months earlier, Perry had been a pleased and confident man; his accomplishments on the first visit had exceeded his expectations. Now Perry was tense, anxious, and even pessimistic. His differences with Marshall, the rumors of French and Russian maneuvers, and recent correspondence from the Navy Department had unsettled his disposition. Although these matters were now behind him, other obstacles to a formal treaty loomed larger than they had the previous summer and magnified his doubts. A solemn and pensive Perry waited anxiously for Japan to reappear on the horizon.

~❧ 9 ❧~

A TREATY WITH JAPAN, SIGNED AND TESTED

*The United States of America, and the Empire of Japan, desiring to
establish firm, lasting and sincere friendship between the two Nations,
have resolved to fix in a manner clear and positive, by means of a
Treaty . . . the rules which shall in the future be mutually observed in
the intercourse of their respective Countries.*

TREATY OF KANAGAWA, 31 MARCH 1854

On the cold, blustery morning of 12 February 1854, Commodore Perry and his three war steamers sighted Mount
Fujiyama as they approached the entrance to Edo Bay. Now
"clothed in its winter garb of snow," the mountain and surrounding
countryside appeared much different from the scene the Americans had
viewed the previous summer. The lush, multihued landscape now looked
"withered, bleak, and sombre."[1]

Off the Sagami Peninsula the steamers discovered the *Macedonian*
and *Vandalia* close inshore; the *Macedonian* had run aground. Capt. Joel
Abbot had jettisoned coal, sand, and other heavy items and, with assistance from the *Vandalia*, successfully kedged free after almost twenty-
four hours of arduous effort. The mortified Abbot was immensely relieved that he had lost no lives and that his ship was unharmed. A
"merciful God and kind father" as well as "hard labor" had saved the
Macedonian, Abbot confided to a friend. The squadron now proceeded
up the Uraga Channel in a single line of six ships with the *Lexington*,

Vandalia, and *Macedonian* in tow of the *Susquehanna, Powhatan,* and *Mississippi.* At mid-afternoon on 13 February, they found the *Southampton* when they reached the American Anchorage in Edo Bay some twenty miles below Edo.[2]

Although optimism in the squadron was high, Perry himself was neither in good spirits nor in good health, and his behavior showed it. In an uncharacteristic outburst of anger over the grounding of the *Macedonian,* he blamed Abbot, a longtime friend in whom he had great confidence, for relying on an old map. In the coming days, his associates found him to be in "an unpleasant mood." Contributing to his dourness was a nagging attack of arthritis that keep Perry confined to his cabin for several days at a time.[3] The time of year and projected length of the second visit added to the challenge at hand. In returning earlier than he had originally planned, Perry had moved his squadron into Japanese waters during the winter months when inclement conditions prevailed.

Initially, the novelty and anticipation sustained morale as the crews drilled and entertained themselves. Perry had encouraged the men to produce theatrical or minstrel shows that had been performed in Hong Kong in December 1853 and would be performed later in 1854 in Japan. Although his small press printed only single sheets of approximately six by eight inches, Perry used it to convey information and to maintain spirits in the squadron. In addition to printing sailing directions for the harbors and coasts of Okinawa and Japan, the Japan Expedition Press produced playbills for theatrical performances and various documents to inform the men of the squadron's accomplishments. After most of the ships had been in Edo Bay for nearly two months with no shore leave for the crews, however, boredom and grumbling inevitably set in. To the ship-bound men, the negotiations seemed interminable as the weeks of February and March dragged on. Another irritant was the food. In anticipation of protracted negotiations, Perry had placed the squadron on a basic salt ration. In the midst of winter, fresh food was scarce, and Perry did not permit the men to hunt the abundant waterfowl in the coastal marshes.[4] Perry did not concern himself with the morale problem, expecting the commanders of his ships to do that. Instead he focused on negotiating a treaty with a reluctant government. His task the previous year had been relatively easy by contrast. Then he had only to establish respect for the American flag, place his government on an equal footing with that of Japan, and deliver letters from the president to the emperor.

Now Perry must convince the Japanese to end more than two centuries of isolation and sign a treaty with a nation they considered uncivilized.

In July 1853, the very real threat that Perry's four warships would proceed to Edo had forced the ill-prepared Japanese to receive the letter at Uraga. Since then the Japanese had had seven months to prepare, while Perry was returning with little additional leverage. His squadron had increased by six ships, but only one, the *Powhatan,* was steam-powered. He also questioned how long he could keep his force together. Already the *Susquehanna* had been ordered back to Hong Kong; additional orders from Washington might further reduce his force. Even with his squadron at full strength, however, the use of force was not an option. The administration back in Washington opposed it except as a last resort in self-defense. And Perry himself understood that any use of force would poison relations with Japan. Throughout his career Perry had refrained from using force in peacetime assignments. Always willing to intimidate and make a show of force, he had invariably refrained from initiating hostilities. The one exception had occurred at Little Berebee in Africa, where Perry retaliated and exacted retribution when the local king attacked him.

As he faced this challenge, Perry's determination and sense of purpose were invaluable assets. He intended the expedition to be the crowning achievement of his career. Despite moments of doubt, frustration, and anxiety, Perry was confident of his ability to deal effectively with the Japanese. His meticulously prepared plan called for him to direct another imposing naval demonstration, express his nation's desire for friendship, make requests that were entirely reasonable, and then adhere to his position without wavering. He would establish a "character of unreasonable obstinacy" rather than one "of a yielding disposition." On "the impression thus formed by" the Japanese, he realized, "would in a measure hinge the tenor of our future relations." His dealings with other foreigners had convinced him that it was "necessary either to set all ceremony aside, or to out-Herod Herod in assumed personal consequence and ostentation." Thus, he adopted pomp when it was proper and avoided pomp when it was not. He determined to meet the highest-ranking Japanese only on terms of "perfect equality" even while Japanese of "comparative distinction . . . were cringing and kneeling." Perry was also determined to avoid contact with subordinates and to deal directly only with "the princes of the empire."[5]

Although Perry was unaware of it, the continued weakness and dis-unity of the Japanese government was working in his favor. After Perry had sailed from Japan in July 1853, Abe circulated copies of the Ameri-can letters and asked Bakufu officials, representatives of the Tokugawa family, and daimyo throughout Japan to submit their views on the best way for the imperial government to respond to Perry in the spring. This unprecedented move revealed the political weakness of the Bakufu, and the disparate responses prevented a consensus. One minority group urged that Japan's defenses be strengthened immediately so that the demands of the Americans could be safely rejected. Believing trade was either necessary or desirable, another advised concessions to avoid war and a certain Japanese defeat. Between these two extreme positions stood a third group who opposed concessions but understood that con-tinued expulsion of foreigners was not possible. These lords advised Abe that the Bakufu could avoid war by adopting a conciliatory tone while making no concessions.[6]

Eventually Abe settled on an uncomfortable middle ground. He would avoid war by making limited concessions but also minimize domestic political criticism by refusing to trade with the United States. The de-mands of better treatment for shipwrecked sailors and ships in distress would be granted, but the demands to open ports and begin trade would be denied. The government hoped that it would not be forced to decide between the alternatives of additional concessions and war. If forced to choose, however, the Bakufu would have little choice but to grant addi-tional concessions. The Japanese commissioners, then, were left with the distasteful task of employing every tactic possible to both minimize their concessions and avoid war. Under no circumstances was Perry to be permitted to land at Edo and negotiate there. As part of their strategy, the Japanese continued to be exceedingly polite, courteous, and even friendly to the Americans. They offered them water and fresh foods, and found and returned a hogshead of coal jettisoned by the grounded *Mace-donian,* a gesture of courtesy that required a twenty-mile trip.[7]

Japanese officials approached and were permitted to board the *Powhatan* soon after it anchored on 13 February. Perry again remained in his cabin while Captain Adams and Dr. Williams received the Japanese. Led by Kurokawa Kahei, the Japanese delegation welcomed the Ameri-cans and informed them that the Japanese government had appointed commissioners of "high distinction" to confer with Perry. Kurokawa informed Adams that Kamakura, a site some twenty miles beyond Uraga and farther away from Edo, had been designated as the meeting place. Since the *Macedonian* had grounded here, Perry was familiar with the site and objected through Adams. The Japanese then indicated that they had no objection to using Uraga, where a pavilion had already been built for that purpose. Perry objected to Uraga as well because of "the inconvenience and actual unsafety of the anchorage at this boisterous season." Instead Perry felt bound to go farther up the bay to Edo or as close by as possible to find a better site and smoother anchorage. To this the Japanese replied that Uraga was the only place where conferences could be held according to an edict from the emperor. Perry still refused to accept Uraga but did agree to meet the commissioners "anywhere between the American Anchorage and Edo." Here the discussions stalled in spite of many "mutual compliments and acts of courtesy," the serving of refreshments, and Japanese offers of provisions, which the Americans refused. The Japanese remained friendly and cheerfully imbibed their favorite American drink, a sweet concoction of whiskey and coarse brown sugar.[8]

For the next ten days neither camp budged on the issue of a site. On 18 February, Perry transferred his pendant from the *Susquehanna*, where it was difficult for him to remain invisible, to the *Powhatan*, where his deck cabin had been relocated. The Japanese visited the flagship almost daily, and on 21 February Adams led an American delegation to Uraga on the *Vandalia*. Undeterred by a fierce wind, the Americans went ashore and met with Japanese officials the following day. Although the meetings were generally cordial, they had tense moments. On one occasion, Izawa Mimasaka no kami, who headed the Japanese delegation, started the meeting by folding his fan "with a sharp report." The gunshot-like sound startled the Americans; their expressions tensed, and their hands went to their pistols. As Mimasaka slowly put on his spectacles and began to examine the formal identification cards, the Americans realized their false alarm and relaxed.[9]

Perry had a formal letter read to the Japanese delegation and later had Captain Adams deliver another letter at Uraga. Reiterating that Uraga was unacceptable, Perry asked for the meeting to be held in "a more commodious harbor higher up the bay." He intended to move as close as possible to Edo, where he could communicate with Japanese officials, present gifts to the emperor, and receive distinguished guests of the imperial court. To reinforce his demand, Perry moved the squadron closer to Edo. "So near indeed," wrote Perry, "that from the masthead we could distinctly hear the striking of the city bells during the night." Perry also dispatched boats to survey the upper bay, which he pronounced to be a "magnificent sheet of water."[10]

As the discussions proceeded, the Japanese commissioners traveled twice to Edo to confer among themselves. The Bakufu did not want to yield but still intended at all costs to prevent Perry from coming to Edo. Finally Abe authorized the commissioners to compromise on a meeting place somewhere between Uraga and Edo. On 24 February, the Japanese sent a letter to Perry reiterating their insistence on Uraga. Shortly thereafter, Kayama Eizaemon, the "governor" of Uraga, appeared on the *Powhatan* to make a personal appeal. When Perry remained "immovable," Kayama suddenly changed his position and proposed an alternative site close to the nearby fishing village of Yokohama, which offered "a very convenient spot, directly opposite the ships." Perry accepted the Japanese proposal after sending Adams to examine the spot. Perry had the good sense not to press further. He had carried his point, and Yokohama was close enough to Edo. He believed the compromise had vindicated his own unyielding behavior and underscored the "deceitful conduct of those people." After ten days of presenting every objection possible, the Japanese had suddenly reversed position and agreed to Perry's demand. Having agreed to this site, Perry also agreed to defer his visit to Edo until after the negotiations had been completed. He announced, however, that he would anchor near the city at a future time "to do honor to his Imperial Majesty by salutes, etc." After surveying the area, Perry moored his squadron in line within one mile of Yokohama and prepared for the formal negotiations.[11]

In retrospect, Perry's insistence on a site between Uraga and Edo may seem arrogant and unreasonable. It mattered little whether the actual negotiations were at Uraga or a few miles closer to Edo. Perry was sensitive to this argument but believed that his position was both tactically and substantively correct. "It struck me that it was better to have no treaty than one that would in the least compromise the dignity of the American character," explained Perry, by yielding in the "remotest degree" to the kind of demeaning restrictions the Dutch had long accepted. And in fact, the anchorage at Uraga was unsafe and exposed. Perry realized that his persistence would provoke charges of arrogance and noted that he had been opposed by all about him, but he "was simply adhering to a course of policy determined upon after mature reflection, and which had hitherto worked so well."[12]

The Japanese quickly built a spacious reception hall at Yokohama and set 8 March as the date for the first meeting. In Edo, Abe prepared final instructions for the commissioners. They were to resist the opening of trade; if pressed, they were to offer to begin trade in five years. If that failed, they were to offer to begin trade in three years. The commissioners were also authorized to open Shimoda as a port of refuge; to provide coal at Nagasaki; and to supply wood, water, and food to American ships. Through conversations with other Americans, Kayama tried to discern Perry's intentions. Tension mounted among the Japanese in the days before the negotiations began. There was a report that Perry had threatened to wage war if his proposals were rejected. In that event, the Japanese anticipated the worst: "he would have 50 ships in nearby waters and 50 more in California, and . . . if he sent word he could summon a command of one hundred warships within twenty days."[13]

On 8 March 1854, the "Commodore's usual good fortune attended him . . . in a fine, clear day, not overmuch cold either," observed Dr. Williams. The landing area was only a short distance from the new pavilion. From each side of the building and extending down to the water the Japanese had stretched curtains enclosing the area and restricting it from general view. Although these curtains were intended "entirely for show, and to do honor to the occasion," Perry thought them ominous and ordered them removed. "Perry wants honor to be given in his own style or not at all," sneered Williams. The American landing was similar to that of the previous July. Comdr. Franklin Buchanan again led the American contingent of approximately five hundred marines, sailors, officers, and musicians. Once assembled onshore, the Americans once again presented an impressive and colorful sight—the marines in full dress; the sailors in blue jackets and trousers; and the officers in their frock coats, caps, epaulettes, and swords. Their muskets, pistols, cutlasses, and musical instruments glistened in the midday sun. A seventeen-gun salute announced Perry's departure from the flagship. Once he was ashore, the bands played the "Star-Spangled Banner" and twenty-one-gun and seventeen-gun salutes followed.[14] Although J. W. Spalding, a veteran of the first landing, claimed there was "very little of the excitement or interest" that had accompanied the previous landing, the spectacle thrilled others. "It was an imposing sight," wrote cabin boy William Allen,

> to see the bluff, burly commodore marching up between the bristling ranks, bareheaded and surrounded by his staff,—the marines on his left in full uniform, their arms and accoutriments [sic] bright and glittering—the sailors on his right in their neat and tidy dresses,—the officers saluting—the bands . . . playing the national airs—the boats fireing [sic] and last tho' not least the strange dresses, arms, and looks of the natives who came from all parts of the empire to view this strange, and to them wonderful sight.[15]

Waiting to receive Perry was an official Japanese delegation of five commissioners headed by Hayashi, Daigaku no kami, the lord rector of the university at Edo. Perry noted that "being myself alone, the odds were as one to five," but in fact, only Hayashi negotiated for Japan in the opening session. After greetings and preliminaries in the pavilion, three hours of substantive discussion followed. The negotiations were conducted in a small room only twelve feet square with a door at one end and a window at the other. Seated on divans, the Japanese commissioners directly faced Perry, Adams, Oliver Hazard II, and interpreters Williams and Portman. Between Hayashi and Perry knelt Japanese interpreter Moryama Einosuke. Actual communication was laborious. When Perry spoke, Portman translated Perry's English into Dutch for Moryama, who translated the Dutch into Japanese for Hayashi. The replies reversed the process from Japanese to Dutch to English. Perry's written communications were transmitted in English, Dutch, and Chinese versions while the written Japanese documents were transmitted in Japanese, Dutch, and Chinese.

The Japanese presented an official written response to the president's letter while Perry presented a draft treaty and other documents. Although the Japanese response cited the immutable "laws of our imperial ancestors" and the recent death of the shogun as reasons why the laws could not be altered, it acknowledged "the spirit of the age" and the "imperative necessity" of a positive response. Accordingly, Japan would accept ships and mariners in distress and provide them with wood, water, and provisions. The Japanese would also provide a harbor, which was to be approved by the Americans, and would be prepared to open it in five years. Meanwhile, coal would be provided at Nagasaki beginning in February 1855 at a price to be fixed by Japanese officials. What, the Japanese asked, did the Americans mean by "provisions," and how much coal would be required? They also offered to provide supplies to the squadron at prices to be fixed by Moryama and Kurokawa Kahei. Once these points had been settled, the Japanese were prepared to conclude and sign the treaty at the next interview.[16]

Although he did not record his initial reaction, Perry must have been surprised by the Japanese offer. It had taken two weeks of negotiation merely to agree to a meeting place. Now, in one session and without argument, the Japanese had agreed to sign a treaty and had conceded most of what President Fillmore sought. Still not satisfied, Perry replied that the United States sought a treaty similar to the 1844 Treaty of Wanghia with China, which had opened several ports to trade. He pressed the Japanese to establish commerce with the United States, indicating that he did not dare return from his mission without a trade agreement. Lord Rector Hayashi confirmed that the Japanese were prepared to provide wood, water, and provisions for ships in distress, to furnish coal, and to guarantee proper treatment for shipwrecked sailors, but they would not agree to requests for trade.

In the midst of the interview, Perry unexpectedly raised another issue. A burial place was needed for marine Robert Williams, who had died two days earlier. Taken aback, the Japanese commissioners withdrew for discussion and finally proposed a temple at Nagasaki reserved for the burial of foreigners. The body would first be taken to Uraga and then transported by the Japanese to Nagasaki for burial. Instead, Perry proposed Natsushima Island, a small, uninhabited island nearby called Webster's Island by the Americans. In his journal, Perry referred to an "ulterior motive" in making this suggestion. Although he never elaborated, Perry possibly envisioned this island as a tiny American foothold in Japanese waters. In any event, the Japanese finally agreed to an alternate burial site in a temple yard near Yokohama, for which Perry expressed his profound gratitude. One Japanese observer believed that the American commodore had actually been moved to tears.[17]

The most heated exchange involved Japan's treatment of shipwrecked American sailors. Perry alleged that the Japanese treated these men as though they were slaves. Indeed, he said, the Japanese government's small regard for human life could be seen in the cruel treatment of its own citizens. The number of Americans ships in Japanese waters would soon increase, he continued, as would the number of vessels and sailors in distress. As a great nation, the United States expected humane treatment of its mariners and was prepared to wage war if necessary to ensure it. The Japanese were also prepared, responded Hayashi, "if forced by circumstances," to go to war. He denied that shipwrecked sailors were treated harshly, claiming that Perry had been misled. The Japanese had great respect for human life, as demonstrated by their two centuries of peace and internal stability. In accordance with Japanese law, shipwrecked sailors were treated humanely, sent to Nagasaki, and then returned to their homeland. The men of the *Lagoda*, however, had been justified exceptions. They were unruly deserters whom Hayashi labeled "not of good character." They had refused to obey Japanese laws, and accordingly had been forcibly detained until they could be taken to Nagasaki.[18]

After the exchange on shipwrecked sailors, the conversation returned to commerce as Perry again pressed for the opening of trade. Commerce, he reasoned, allowed a country to acquire goods it lacked in exchange for commodities it produced to generate wealth and profit. Hayashi answered that Japan already produced everything it needed. In obtaining an agreement to protect shipwrecked sailors, Hayashi continued, "you have attained your purpose. Now, commerce has to do with profits, but has it anything to do with human life?" Perry had no ready answer and, according to one Japanese account, agreed with Hayashi: "You are right. As you say, I came because I valued human life, and the important thing is that you will give our vessels help. Commerce brings profit to a country, but it does not concern human life. I shall not insist upon it." Nevertheless, he did provide and ask Hayashi to read a copy of the Treaty of Wanghia.[19]

In effect, this exchange marked the boundaries of the negotiations that followed. Hayashi had adeptly managed to force Perry to distinguish between human life and commerce; that is, between a treaty of amity and friendship and a treaty of amity, friendship, and commerce. Perry did not record this interchange in his journal or in the official narrative; nor did he ever explain his response. Clearly, the Japanese had set limits to the negotiation to exclude commercial relations and Perry had reluctantly accepted them. It may be that Hayashi simply outsmarted Perry, who was under great personal pressure and in poor health. In fact, by planning his tactics single-handedly and carrying the load himself, Perry had victimized himself. Unlike his experience a decade earlier as commander of the African Squadron, when he had held frequent councils with his senior officers to plan tactics, Perry had proceeded in Japan without extensive consultation. The exchanges, involving two interpreters, were tedious, and the session lasted more than three tiring hours. Perry was not verbally facile or quick on his feet. As a senior naval officer, he was accustomed to preparing written responses or dictating to subordinates who followed orders. Nor was Perry an experienced diplomat or negotiator, especially in dealings with adversaries who were his equal. His previous diplomatic experience had involved conferring with tribal leaders in Africa and dictating terms to defeated officials during the Mexican War. He had never negotiated a peacetime agreement with another nation on relatively equal terms.

Be that as it may, Perry, who arrived extremely well prepared and knowledgeable on the issues, should have easily been able to argue the manifest benefits of commerce to human life. In a long naval career associated with overseas commerce, Perry had personally observed that commerce produced not only profit but improved civilization and human happiness as well. More likely, then, Perry made a calculated judgment that the Japanese were not prepared to open trade and that his own instructions did not demand it. Perry did not know, of course, that Hayashi's instructions authorized him, if pressed, to open trade in five, or even three, years.

Perry's foremost objective had been a formal treaty, and the Japanese had agreed to most of his demands. But Perry was not yet satisfied: "Entertaining the opinion that something still more advantageous might be gained, I thought it good policy to hold out for a specific treaty." In the next three weeks, Perry would press hard, in fact, for additional concessions, but with the exception of demanding the establishment of an American consulate in Japan, none of his demands involved the opening of Western-style trade. Clearly he believed that shaping a trade agreement would be the work of future diplomats.[20]

At the end of the negotiations on 8 March, Perry invited the commissioners to visit his flagship once the weather improved. Hayashi then left the room first, to indicate that his rank was higher than Perry's, while the other four commissioners remained to eat with the American delegation. During the session the bands had played outside the treaty house, and some Americans mingled with the Japanese crowd. American artists

William Heine and Eliphalet Brown drew the scene while Japanese artists rendered the Americans. According to J. W. Spalding, the Japanese artists always began their portraits of Americans by drawing a large nose and then sketching in the rest of the features around it.[21]

The next day, the funeral for marine Robert Williams was held at a small temple near Yokohama. To the sound of a muffled drumbeat, the solemn procession carried the body to the temple as an estimated two thousand Japanese watched. There a chaplain read the burial services from the Episcopal Book of Common Prayer as Williams was interred, and a marine guard fired a salute. Then a saffron-robed Buddhist monk rang a gong, burned incense, chanted prayers, and deposited into the grave a viaticum containing rice, candles, money, and other items for Williams's journey to the heavenly kingdom. This gesture impressed the Americans and helped to convince them of the goodwill of the Japanese.[22]

As negotiations proceeded in later days, the Japanese agreed to receive gifts from the United States prior to the actual signing of the treaty. On 13 March, a miserable rainy day, Capt. Joel Abbot supervised the landing, unpacking, and arranging of the gifts in reception sheds on the beach. Carefully selected by Perry to demonstrate the technological superiority and advanced civilization of the United States, the gifts were intended for the emperor and empress, the commissioners, and the senior councilors of the Bakufu. The gifts for the emperor included a miniature steam engine, tender, and car to run on a quarter-size track; a fully operable electric telegraph with wire, insulators, and batteries; a copper surfboat and a copper lifeboat; a collection of farm implements; a series of coastal survey charts; a weights and measures series; a telescope; a stove; a perfume assortment; and various rifles, pistols, muskets, and swords. To serve mind and spirit, an assortment of whiskey, Madeira wine, champagne, and cordials was also included along with various reading materials—John James Audubon's nine-volume *Birds,* a sixteen-volume natural history of New York, George Bancroft's four-volume *History of the United States,* a farmer's guide, and various government journals and documents. Each of the commissioners and the councilors received a smaller but similar assortment. Abe Masahiro received two illustrated histories of the recent Mexican War.[23]

On 24 March, the Japanese presented their gifts to the United States. Perry received them with a landing party of about two hundred Americans. The reception pavilion was decorated with pots of japonica in full flower and overflowed with carefully arranged and wrapped gifts. The items included writing tables, lacquered and gold paper boxes, fine porcelain, elegant silks, flowered crepe, brooms, fans, umbrellas, writing paper, and sundry other items. For the squadron, the emperor provided three hundred chickens and two hundred bales of rice, each weighing 135 pounds. In his journal, Perry complained that most of the personal gifts had little "intrinsic value," but even those would be retained by the U.S. government rather than permitting American officers to keep them as mementos.

After the presentation of gifts, the Japanese provided an exhibition of sumo wrestling. The huge sumo wrestlers amazed and intrigued the Americans, although they had little appreciation for the sport. They were more impressed when the sumo wrestlers later carried the bags of rice on their shoulders, in their hands at arm's length, or even by their teeth from the shed to the American boats. Their immense strength was underscored when the Americans themselves struggled with the heavy, unwieldy bags. For entertainment, Perry ordered the marines to perform a close-order drill, an exercise the Japanese had not seen. The commissioners also attempted to use the telegraph and observed the small train in operation. "It was a curious, barbaric spectacle, reminding one of the old gladiators," confided Williams to his journal.

> Indeed, there was a curious melange today here, a function of east and west, railroads and telegraph, boxers and educated athletes, epaulettes and uniforms, shaved pates and night-gowns, soldiers with muskets and drilling in close array, soldiers with petticoats, sandals, two swords, and all in disorder, like a crowd—all these things, and many others, exhibiting the difference between our civilization and usages and those of this secluded, pagan people.

According to Williams, the American gifts showed a "higher civilization" and "the success of science and enterprise," while the Japanese sumo exhibition was a "disgusting display" of "brutal animal force" and their gifts a meager assortment.[24]

On 27 March, Perry entertained the Japanese on the *Powhatan*, the five commissioners dining with Perry in his cabin while the rest of the Japanese entourage joined their American hosts at long tables on deck. Perry spared "no pains in providing most bountifully" for the occasion to impress his guests with "some idea of American hospitality in comparison with their portions of fish soup." His Paris chef labored night and day for a week to prepare a feast that "would have done credit to Delmonico of New York." A bullock, sheep, and different kinds of poultry had been prepared along with hams, tongues, preserved fish, vegetables, and fruits. Wine, champagne, whiskey, cordials, and punch provided the liquid refreshment. In the cabin, the chief commissioner drank and ate carefully, but one of his colleagues got "gloriously drunk, and the other three quite mellow."[25]

On deck, the Japanese guests relished the occasion. They ate and drank freely, carried away what they did not finish eating, and were greatly amused by the American custom of toasting the emperor, the president, the commodore, the commissioners, and even the ladies of Japan. When the band began to play, several Japanese began to shuffle and dance and were joined, observed Lt. George Preble, by a number of "our greyest and gravest officers. A funny sight to behold—these bald-pated bundles of clothes—and Doctors, Pursers, Lieutenants and Captains all jumping up and down to the music." After dinner, Perry brought the commissioners on deck where they watched with apparent delight a presentation of the "Japanese minstrels by the Ethiopian Band" of the *Powhatan*. Perry remained serious throughout the festivities. "No one appreciates a joke less than he does," observed Midn. John G. Sproston. Later, as the Japanese prepared to leave, Hayashi's secretary, who had freely consumed the various spirits, suddenly threw his arms around Perry's shoulders and neck and repeated several times: "Nippon and America, all the same heart." To this unexpected gesture, Perry remarked, "Oh, if he will only sign the treaty he may kiss me."[26]

By this time the Americans had been largely confined to their ships for more than a month. As the negotiations continued, some officers and men were permitted to walk onshore. But a crisis quickly developed when Chaplain E. C. Bittinger of the *Susquehanna* determined to walk directly to Edo. When Japanese officials tried to stop him, he waved them off with his sword and continued. Alarm spread and word of Bittinger's sojourn reached Perry, who became very angry and ordered four cannon shots, the signal to return. A messenger finally reached Bittinger at the Rokugo River, and he turned back. According to the Japanese, Bittinger became "very pale and seemed to be in great terror" when he realized the enormity of his error. With tears in his eyes he asked to be taken to Captain Buchanan's ship, not to Perry's vessel, where he would have to face the wrath of the commodore. In fact, Perry had good reason to be furious; this thoughtless excursion came at a sensitive moment in the negotiations and threatened the limited shore privileges enjoyed by the officers.[27]

Confinement, inclement weather, and food of poor quality combined to undermine the squadron's morale. Fresh provisions were limited and salt rations continued to be the fare of the day. Those who worked in the surveying boats, such as Lieutenant Preble, found the work cold, difficult, and monotonous. For those back onboard, conditions seemed worse. "Diplomacy may have been all very well for those engaged in it, and getting a munch of something fresh while on shore, but the enchantment lent to those confined on board and compelled to take exercise on a hurricane deck, was very slight indeed," wrote clerk Spalding on the *Mississippi*. "We were undergoing all the annoyances of a state of siege, without any of its excitement." The food brought from China was gone, and fresh vegetables were scarce. The few chickens provided by the Japanese were incredibly tough. Spalding claimed that neither "molars nor incisors" could make an impression on them; Preble and his friends speculated that the chickens must have been alive at the time the Portuguese were expelled from Japan.[28]

After the initial conference on 8 March, Perry met formally with the Japanese officials on several occasions, various Japanese officials visited the *Powhatan* almost daily, and the commissioners came to the flagship for formal negotiations on one occasion. Despite the quick and positive initial response from the Japanese, deliberations took the entire month of March because the translation of various documents took time and differences on specific points needed to be resolved. The ports to be opened needed to be identified and agreed on; the issue of American reimbursement for Japanese supplies needed to be addressed; and the exact nature of commercial contact needed to be defined. After the first meeting Perry decided to change his initial demand and insist that five or six ports, not one or two, be opened. This inconsistency disgusted interpreter Williams, who noted that while the Japanese had granted what President Fillmore had asked for, Perry now "says it is by no means all *he* wants, nor all the President intended." He continued: "Perry cares no more for the right, for consistency, for his country, than will advance his own aggrandizement and fame." Yet Williams, always the Christian evangelist, recognized that whatever the means, "great good" might result to the Japanese from opening several ports even though Perry's new demand had lowered his opinion of its author.[29]

The Japanese initially offered Nagasaki as one of the ports, with a second port to be opened some years later. Perry flatly rejected Nagasaki and after a heated exchange agreed tentatively to Shimoda provided it was deemed acceptable after examination by his ships. The issue of additional ports remained unresolved until the Japanese offered and Perry accepted Hakodate as the northern port, subject again to his examination. Although an issue of negotiation, the port at Naha on Lew Chew Island was not part of the final treaty. Perry did not insist on it, believing that he could secure the island separately as an open port and had in effect already done so.

The issues of trade and reimbursement for Japanese supplies presented other sticking points. Because the Japanese refused to budge on foreign commerce, a trade agreement similar to that between the United States and China was totally unacceptable. Having previously agreed not to press on trade, Perry searched for a way to reopen the issue. The subject of reimbursements for supplies offered a slight opening because the Japanese refused to accept payment for the "gifts" of provisions and fuel they provided to American ships. Perry insisted that the Japanese must be reimbursed for these commodities. Finally, Hayashi and Perry found a compromise. Perry suggested and Hayashi agreed that the Americans might provide "gifts" in return for the "gifts" of provisions they received. Moreover, since the acceptance of American goods as gifts resembled trade, Hayashi agreed that the Americans might reimburse the Japanese in gold or silver. The Japanese also agreed that American ships entering the harbors of Shimoda and Hakodate would be permitted to exchange American gold and silver coins and "goods" for other "articles of goods" under regulations established by the Japanese government. Although these terms did not approximate a trade agreement, they did define a very restricted kind of trade and created a precedent that could later be expanded.[30]

As the negotiations continued, the tension eased and the atmosphere improved. In late March, Perry finally dispatched the *Susquehanna* to China, and on one occasion the American delegation came unarmed to a session onshore. The two parties resolved their outstanding differences, but last-minute obstacles arose with respect to the dating of the document because the words "in the year of our Lord Jesus Christ" were unacceptable to the Japanese. They also refused to sign the English version of the treaty. These issues were at last resolved, however, and the treaty was finally signed on 31 March. "Eureka! It is finished! The great agony is over! In vulgar parlance the egg has hatched its chicken today," proclaimed Lieutenant Preble on the *Macedonian*. "Even Old Bruin would smile if he only knew how to smile." At the dinner afterward, the Japanese were warm hosts and Perry graciously apologized for any difficulties he might have caused by not appreciating the strictness of traditional Japanese laws. He expressed friendship for Japan and offered U.S. guns and warships if the Japanese ever had to fight a war.[31]

The Treaty of Kanagawa was an agreement of peace and friendship between the United States and Japan. Under its terms, Shimoda was opened immediately to American ships for supplies, and Hakodate would be opened one year later. Except in cases of severe distress, American ships were to enter no other ports. The Japanese would assist American ships, and shipwrecked sailors were not to be confined but would be taken to one of the open ports for repatriation. An American consul was to be permitted to reside at Shimoda after a period of eighteen months. Finally, the treaty contained a most-favored-nation clause; any privilege or concession extended by the Japanese to any other nation in the future would automatically be extended to the United States. Perry considered this clause to be "a most important article, so there can be little doubt that . . . the English, French, and Russians will follow our example."[32]

After signing the treaty, Perry busied himself in preparing documents and letters to be transported to the United States on the *Saratoga*, which sailed for Honolulu on 4 April. Its departure created an emotional scene in the squadron. As some men cheered and others wept, the bands played "Home Sweet Home." At Honolulu, Captain Adams left the *Saratoga* and proceeded via Panama to Washington, reaching his destination in mid-June. The *Saratoga*, which had to round Cape Horn, finally reached Boston in September.[33]

After the treaty had been signed, relations between the Americans and Japanese warmed. On 6 April, Perry took a long walk in the countryside and paid his respects to the mayor of Kanagawa. At his house, where refreshments were served by the mayor's admiring wife and sister, Perry handed a piece of candy to the "unwashed baby" of the mayor's wife and toasted the health of the household. American officers wandering about the Yokohama area were greeted with "great civility" and courtesy. The weather had also improved. Spring had come and, with it, a softening of the Americans' attitudes toward the Japanese. Williams had been disgusted in February by the way Perry and many of the other officers referred to the Japanese, "calling them savages, liars, a pack of fools, poor devils; cursing them and denying practically all of it by supposing them worth making a treaty with. Truly," he exclaimed, "what sort of instruments does God work with!"[34] In April, however, Perry and his officers spoke positively of the Japanese, who were now friendly, civilized, and polite. They impressed the Americans as being healthy and hardy people. They also seemed intelligent, quick to learn, and "remarkable for their curiosity," wrote Perry. They followed Americans around, seized every occasion to "examine every part of their garments," and always tried to obtain a button or two. The Japanese allowed onboard the ships "were equally inquisitive, peering into every nook and corner accessible to them, measuring this and that, and taking sketches." The formality of the Japanese, their extraordinary courtesy, and their devotion to elaborate shows of ceremony favorably impressed Perry. He was also moved by their respectful thoughtfulness on occasions such as the burial of Robert Williams at Yokohama.[35]

Perry did find other aspects of Japanese culture less pleasing. Japanese food, for instance, was nothing special. Nor did Perry ever come to appreciate sumo wrestling. The assembled naked wrestlers moved Perry to remark that he had never seen "so many brawny men giving a better idea of an equal number of stall-fed bulls than human beings." Each of the professional wrestlers had a frame covered "with a mass of flesh which to our idea of athletic qualities would seem to incapacitate him from any violent exercise." Perry was asked to poke, press, and feel the girth, arms, and neck of one wrestler, who responded with a "self-satisfied grunt."[36]

Perry and his officers were also embarrassed by what they considered to be the lewdness of the Japanese people. In February, a Japanese woman onshore had gone "so far as to raise her drapery and expose her person" to a nearby surveying boat. At one point, the Japanese presented Perry with a "box of obscene paintings of naked men and women"; on another occasion, a Japanese official visiting the *Macedonian* during a wet and dreary March day remarked that it was "a fine day for lieing [sic] with the ladies." Straitlaced Americans like Perry, Preble, and Williams just could not understand the lack of modesty in the dress of Japanese women and in the communal bathhouses. William Heine observed that the traditional Japanese kimono provided a "seemly cover to the body" when the wearer was still, but a moving woman often gave observers glimpses of her breasts and legs.[37] Williams was less tolerant. "Modesty," he wrote, "might be said to be unknown, for the women make no attempt to hide the bosom, and every step shows the leg above the knee." After stepping into a bathhouse, Lieutenant Preble

> stepped out again almost as quickly. It is anything but agreeable for me at least to see a dozen or twenty of both sexes, and of all ages in a state of entire nudity, grouped indiscriminately in a small apartment not fifteen feet square scrubbing away as for dear life. . . . Such a scene is I think calculated to cure the most sensual person of all lascivious emotions.

A "single bathhouse serves all comers" wrote an amazed Heine. "Old and young, men and women, boys and girls; they scramble about together in a remarkable medley as naked as frogs. Yet they stay calm even when foreigners appear." Preble was appalled when a pretty woman disappeared with a man behind a screen while her female companions demonstrated to the Americans "by the most indecent signs . . . what they had gone for."[38]

Perry had mixed opinions about the few Japanese women he saw. At Kanagawa, he judged them to be "tolerably good looking." He thought the younger girls to be "well formed and rather pretty," but he was disgusted by married women's practice of blackening their teeth. Admitting his own national partiality, Perry concluded that "the women of the United States deserve the palm." Other Americans as well were put off by the toilette of married Japanese women. The beauty of Japanese women "is not much under the best circumstances," wrote Spalding, "but when it is remembered that on marrying they shave off their eyebrows, and blacken their teeth with some iron rust and acid, as a badge of the marital state, their appearance becomes most repulsive."[39]

One trait that Perry especially criticized in the Japanese was their cunning. *Deceitful, treacherous,* and *lying* were all terms used frequently by the Americans to describe the behavior of the Japanese. Perry attributed the deceitfulness he observed to the rigid structure of the society, the oppressive autocracy of the government, and the pervasive presence of spies. As time passed, Perry realized that far from considering it a fault, the Japanese considered deceit a virtue. On several occasions, when he challenged someone expressing an obvious lie, the speaker took it as a compliment, not as an insult, as a Westerner would have done. The Japanese seemed to think it their "duty" to lie.[40]

The cordial relations between the Americans and the Japanese were dangerously jeopardized after the treaty was signed when Perry committed an obstinate and egocentric act. Near the conclusion of the negotiations, Perry had informed the Japanese that he intended to take the squadron to Edo. As always, the Japanese commissioners objected strongly. Hayashi pleaded personally with Perry to desist because such a visit would embarrass Hayashi before his government. Perry responded that he would be embarrassed if he did not go because his president expected it—a false statement. On 10 April, Moryama and a group of officials came aboard as the *Powhatan* and the squadron moved toward Edo. Begging Perry to turn back, one official even threatened to place himself in front of one of the cannons if Perry tried to fire a salute. One of the interpreters became physically ill while another official threatened seppuku. Handing his cloak and long sword to an American, the official kept only the short dagger to disembowel himself. Finally, after being assured that a landmark visible from the ship was actually in Edo and that the masts ahead were those of ships in the harbor, Perry turned the squadron around and headed back down the bay.[41]

A tense and potentially harmful moment passed and an unnecessary crisis was averted. Escaping the possible consequences of his ill-advised action, Perry explained that he had relented "in consideration of the very kind and friendly manner" in which he had been treated. Since the commissioners might be held "personally accountable for any catastrophe" that occurred, he thought it better not to proceed and possibly "endanger the very friendly position which we already held with these people. It would have been a source of never-ending regret for which I could not have forgiven myself if, to gratify a profitless curiosity, misfortune should have been brought upon our good friends the commissioners." In fact, Perry's stubborn determination to follow through on any stated intention during his mission to Japan was a serious mistake. His approach to Edo served no purpose other than to satisfy his own ego and to confirm that the city could "be destroyed by a few steamers of very light draft" carrying heavy-caliber guns. Having creating the dangerous situation, however, Perry recognized and reversed his decision before it was too late.[42]

Although with the signing of the treaty Perry had achieved the great object of his mission, he did not return directly to Hong Kong because important, if anticlimactic, work still remained to be done in Japan and at Okinawa. He needed to inspect Shimoda and Hakodate firsthand and confer with officials there about various details. Regulations on the purchase of water and supplies and the movements of Americans onshore needed to be defined, as did a system of currency exchange to permit American purchases onshore. The two visits would allow him to collect geographic and scientific information, to survey the harbors and their approaches, and to arrange for the purchase of coal at Shimoda. Finally, Perry wanted to use the American naval presence to test Japanese goodwill and specific provisions of the treaty.

On 18 April, the *Powhatan* and *Mississippi* made the short trip from the American Anchorage to Shimoda. Earlier Perry had dispatched the *Vandalia* and the storeships *Southampton*, *Supply*, and *Lexington* there. In proposing Shimoda as one of the ports, the Japanese had chosen a beautiful site for a port of refuge, but its geographic isolation presented significant limitations for the Americans. Either Osaka or Nagoya would have been preferable from an American perspective, but Perry had no way of knowing that at the time. Located near the end of the Izu Peninsula, Shimoda was separated from the interior by foothills and the Agami Mountains. "The scenery is the most picturesque we have seen," wrote an engineer on the *Mississippi*. The early spring foliage on the trees covering the shore was "in beautiful verdure, brown and rich green delightfully mixed, a pleasant spot for the eye to linger on." High protective bluffs surrounded the narrow entrance to the secure harbor. Near the center of the entrance channel, the *Southampton* discovered a large and dangerous rock, which had to be marked by a buoy. The town of Shimoda and the small fishing village of Kakisaki lay near the head of the fan-shaped harbor, which was approximately one mile long and one-half mile wide. Two small, extensively cultivated valleys stretched away from the town. Wooded headlands and high hills surrounded the area. The Americans thought the setting bore a "resemblance very great to the scenery in the Potomac, at Harper's Ferry." The town contained numerous temples and approximately 120 houses positioned on neat streets with gates at either end. The houses were "ornamentally stuccoed in light blue and white diamond shapes." Although this picturesque harbor would serve the letter of the treaty as a port of refuge, remote Shimoda was not a trading center; both coal and provisions would be difficult to obtain there.[43]

As surveying of the harbor proceeded, Perry tested Japanese willingness to honor the new treaty. He sent a request for supplies to local officials and permitted his officers to go ashore. Because the movements of Americans had been very limited in Yokohama, Perry used the greater freedom provided by the treaty in Shimoda to collect geographic information and specimens. Accordingly, Drs. James Morrow and Williams explored the countryside and gathered plant samples. Perry also requested rest houses onshore for himself and his officers and permission for his officers to purchase souvenirs and other items from shopkeepers.

Although most of the supplies he requested were unavailable in Shimoda, Japanese officials assigned the guest quarters of a temple to Perry for his use and provided a burial site in the village of Kakisaki after a young American seaman died. The Japanese also arranged for Americans to make individual purchases, albeit under a cumbersome exchange system. Americans first identified items they wished to purchase, and then Japanese officials supervised the exchange of money and the delivery of the items. Further discouraging trade was the local exchange rate, which discounted the American currency by 200 to 300 percent. The intense surveillance of Americans onshore also infuriated Perry. Although the American officers roamed freely around Shimoda and its environs, armed officers followed them everywhere, forced onlookers away, and warned shopkeepers to close. Objecting strongly to the ever-present guards, Perry threatened at one point to take his own armed guard ashore, capture anyone who followed him, and then sail with his prisoners directly to Edo. Eventually the Japanese eased their surveillance, but only temporarily.

As he tried to press officials to honor the terms of the treaty, Perry also endeavored to be faithful to them. One test of his resolve occurred shortly after the Americans arrived, when two young Japanese men approached clerk J. W. Spalding unexpectedly near Shimoda and asked to be taken to America. Later, the men stole a boat, rowed to the *Mississippi* at 3:00 A.M., boarded, and repeated their request. Yoshida Shoin and Kaneko Shigenosuke, students of a Dutch scholar, wanted to broaden their knowledge by leaving Japan. Although their demeanor impressed Perry, he knew that he could not agree to their request without violating the spirit, if not the letter, of the treaty. Perry did agree, however, to say nothing and to put the two men ashore. Unfortunately, Japanese authorities found their boat. Shortly thereafter, the two surrendered and were confined, sent to Edo, and imprisoned. Although Japanese officials made repeated inquiries, the Americans insisted that they knew nothing about the men or the incident.[44]

At the same time, Perry used an incident onshore to insist that American rights be protected. After spending a day rambling and hunting birds in the countryside, three American officers decided to spend the night in one of the Buddhist temples near town. They informed one of the Japanese translators, who initially offered no objection but later returned with a group of armed men who ordered the Americans to return to their ships. The Americans refused. While the Japanese interpreter proceeded to the flagship to demand that Perry recall his men, the Japanese at the temple became belligerent and pulled on the feet of the Americans to get them to rise. In response, the Americans kicked over the lanterns and pulled their pistols. Fortunately, the Japanese left and violence was averted. The next day Perry insisted on an apology from the Japanese. If he did not get one, he threatened to land his marines and arrest the Japanese guards. Finally, after a long exchange, the Japanese conceded their wrong and apologized.

These incidents notwithstanding, the Americans liked Shimoda. Although the rigid system for purchasing items allowed them to acquire few souvenirs, the Americans found the local people to be warm, open, and friendly. Of particular interest were the women. Unlike Perry, Williams, and Preble, most of the officers and men enjoyed the communal bathhouses where Japanese men and women bathed together and the scanty attire worn by people going to and from the bathhouses. The Americans also realized quickly that Shimoda housed a number of brothels, which were off limits to the Americans. Having been cooped up on their ships and denied the company or even the sight of women for several months, the men were undaunted by the restrictions. Some used their ingenuity and their monetary resources to enjoy the full pleasures of a few Shimoda women.[45]

Most of the sailors and marines, however, left their ships only as boat crews or for monotonous work details. Even the improved spring weather did not lift their morale. The food continued to be the chief source of complaint. Shimoda was able to supply only limited amounts of fresh food for the hundreds of men in the squadron. Most of the fresh fish, chicken, and sweet potatoes were assigned to the officers while the men ate turnip greens and radish tops along with their beans, rice, and salted meat. On the *Vandalia*, a food strike erupted when the cooks refused to prepare the greens. The men claimed that they were being deprived of their proper rations. When the cooks finally gave in and prepared the greens, the men refused to eat them. The stalemate was finally resolved when the *Macedonian* returned from the Bonin Islands with an ample supply of fresh fish and turtles. The men still refused to eat the greens, but the issue ended when they were discovered to be rotten and had to be discarded. Nevertheless, by early May 1854, the grumbling and complaining had grown more audible as the squadron prepared for the next leg of its journey.[46]

In early May, Perry dispatched the *Macedonian, Vandalia,* and *Southampton* to Hakodate and then followed with the *Powhatan* and *Mississippi.* The steamers reached Hakodate on 17 May to find the three other American ships already there. While Shimoda had been a flawed choice as one of the two Japanese ports of refuge, Hakodate was a superb site. Located on the Tsugaru Strait, which separates the large islands of Hokkaido and Honshu, Hakodate was positioned on a major passage between the North Pacific and the Sea of Japan. Hundreds of foreign vessels passed through the strait each year without being permitted to land, while Japanese junks carried on a thriving trade between Honshu and Hokkaido. For a Pacific steamship line using the great circle route, Hakodate would be an ideal stopping place. Perry was pleased: "This is one of the safest and most convenient harbors I have ever seen for vessels of all classes, and it is sufficiently capacious to hold half the navies of the world."[47]

The town itself was a fishing and trading port of six thousand residents. The harbor was dominated by a bold, high promontory connected to the mainland by a low isthmus. "The Bay of Hakodate reminds me of Gibraltar Bay," wrote Lieutenant Preble. "Its shores are hilly and mountainous and there is the same rocky mew separated by a low vertical ground." The town's "wooden houses, shingled roofs, board fences, stone wharves, wooden warehouses and sea and yellow hills" reminded Preble of a "New England town, wanting however the pointed spires and pepper box bellfries of our New England temples of worship." Hakodate was part of the domain of Matsumae Izu, a daimyo who resided in the castle town of Matsumae on Hokkaido. Located in a remote part of the empire, Matsumae was one of the most autonomous of the Japanese lords because he was exempt from much of Edo's tight control. On Hokkaido, the Matsumae family traded freely with the Ainus, the white aborigines of Hokkaido, and through the Ainus with the Russians.[48]

Hakodate's officials and residents were not prepared for the Americans because Japanese government officials had not yet arrived with instructions, but news of the treaty had preceded the squadron. The town was in state of high anxiety, and most of the women and children had been evacuated. Although local officials refused to meet officially with Captain Abbot when the *Macedonian* arrived, they readily agreed to arrangements for the purchase of supplies, the use of some buildings onshore by the Americans, and the allowance of some trade. However, they absolutely refused Perry's request to visit the daimyo's castle at Matsumae, and they insisted on referring to Edo the issue of American movements onshore.

Ultimately, the Americans were allowed to move freely in Hakodate but were permitted little contact with its residents. To purchase the limited local goods, the Americans were sent to a bazaar where Perry received first pick and the officers had to make do with what was left. The officers were not happy with the arrangement. After Perry "monopolized the Bazaar," they complained, "little was left from his selection for outsiders," and that for exorbitant prices. On one occasion, they embarrassed themselves in an unruly scramble for the remaining items. Local officials complained to Perry about the rowdy conduct of his officers. They gambled in the temples, climbed walls to enter private houses, took goods without paying for them, and stole swords. Informed of these charges, Perry confined his officers for one day, conducted a search, and returned the stolen goods and swords he uncovered.[49]

On 27 May, Perry dispatched Williams to town to complain that the emissaries from Edo had still not arrived and that the continued absence of women and children from Hakodate was a symbol of hostility. If the emissaries did not appear within six days, Williams was told to say, Perry intended to return to Shimoda. Four days later, he sent the *Macedonian* to Shimoda to underline his threat. Perry soon received word that the emissaries would meet with him, but when he sent Flag Lieutenant Bent to bring them to the flagship, they ignored the lieutenant. Only when

Perry prepared to send a detachment of marines with two fieldpieces did the emissaries suddenly appear at the flagship. The subsequent discussions proved cordial but ineffectual. The Japanese explained that the women of Hakodate were very shy, fearing not only the foreigners but Japanese officials from Honshu as well. The Japanese continued to insist on deferring to the commissioners the issue of how far the Americans could walk onshore. Perry was, however, able to arrange a burial site for two more Americans who had died recently. Outside the town in "a small, neglected burial ground" located at an "exceedingly picturesque" spot, the two received an American funeral and Buddhist prayers. When thick fog prevented a planned reception and military parade in town, Perry decided to depart without going ashore himself. Instead, he sent his presents and regards ashore and sailed for Shimoda on 3 June.[50]

The *Powhatan* and *Mississippi* reached Shimoda four days later, and Perry and the commissioners were able to agree on the details regarding the designation of Shimoda and Hakodate as ports of refuge. By this time, Perry had been in Japanese waters for almost four months and was anxious to finish his business, but the Japanese insisted on debating each point in detail. With neither side inclined to compromise, the talks lasted for two tedious and sometimes tense weeks. As both sides postured, good feelings dissipated. At one point, both Perry and his counterpart, Hayashi, boycotted an elaborate banquet onshore. On several occasions, the unruly and drunken conduct of Americans onshore complicated the discussions. Another distraction was the presence of Sam Patch (Sentaro), a Japanese sailor on the *Powhatan* who had wished to return to his homeland. The Japanese demanded his return, but Perry called for a guarantee of Patch's safety and insisted that the decision to stay or leave was entirely up to Patch. Eventually, he decided to stay with the Americans.[51]

Finally, on 17 June 1854, more than five months after Perry had sailed from Hong Kong, Perry and the commissioners signed the additional regulations at Shimoda. The agreement specified that Americans could travel seven ri (one ri = 2.43 miles) from Shimoda and five ri from Hakodate. Americans who exceeded those limits would be arrested and returned to their ships. A temple in Shimoda and another in Kakisaki were designated as resting places for Americans, who could enter shops and visit temples but not private houses or military posts. The Japanese agreed to provide a harbor master and "three skillful pilots" at Shimoda.

Americans were forbidden to shoot "birds and animals" on Japanese soil. The trade system that forced Americans to use Japanese officials as middlemen was reaffirmed, and Perry also agreed to an exchange rate of sixteen hundred copper cash to one dollar, a rate most Americans viewed as unfair. The agreement also specified that coal was to be furnished at Hakodate but said nothing about coal at Shimoda. This omission resulted from the fact that coal at Shimoda was hard to get, inferior in quality, and cost an exorbitant $30 per ton. Perry agreed to explain the situation to his government so that the Japanese would be relieved from this obligation at Shimoda. To seek another source, Perry dispatched the *Macedonian* to Formosa, where Abbot found an ample supply of high-quality coal available at $1.50 per ton.[52]

Once the agreement had been signed, Perry lingered only long enough for the final banquets and exchange of gifts. On the *Powhatan* a minstrel show played to an estimated three hundred Japanese. In town the squadron's bands presented a public concert, a final bazaar was held, and officials took their final walks around Shimoda. Then, on 23 June, Perry transferred his broad pendant to the *Mississippi*, settled accounts, and conducted a final interview. Bad weather delayed his departure, and Perry left Shimoda and Japan for the last time on 28 June. Three days later, the two steam warships reached Naha for Perry's fifth and final visit there.

The subject of Naha as the third port of refuge had not been included in the Treaty of Kanagawa because the commissioners claimed that they lacked jurisdiction. Perry now intended to address the issue by signing a formal treaty with local officials. But first he had to deal with other unrelated matters. On his arrival Perry had received the unexpected news that an American sailor from the *Lexington* had recently been murdered and that several minor acts of hostility had been committed against other Americans. Perry immediately insisted that the Okinawans explain the death and produce the culprit. If they did not, Perry threatened to seize the forts in the harbor and prevent any junks from sailing. The subsequent investigation revealed that the American victim had been the aggressor. In an inebriated condition, he had entered a private house and attempted to rape a young girl. When she screamed, neighbors responded. The American fled but was pursued and stoned. He managed to reach the harbor but fell into the water and drowned. When local officials did not produce the man responsible for the murder, Perry detached twenty marines to occupy the forts. One day later, officials produced a man they claimed to be the chief culprit. Refusing to take jurisdiction, Perry insisted on local punishment and was pleased to learn that the culprit would be banished to a remote island for life and that his five associates would also be punished along with the four officials who had initially filed a false report.[53]

Perry now turned to the issue of a treaty. The defenseless Okinawans, continually intimidated by Perry, could not resist his demands. They were most concerned about the reference to them in the draft treaty as an independent nation. Since they maintained a tributary relationship with China and had been subjugated by the Shimazu clan of Japan, they insisted that the document say nothing about their political status. The eventual agreement was a direct and basic document that guaranteed privileges the Americans had already extracted. It specified that Americans were to receive courteous treatment on Okinawa. They had the right to purchase supplies and provisions and to move unhindered onshore. The American graveyard was to be maintained, and harbor pilots were to be appointed. Spalding characterized the agreement cynically as a horse-and-chicken agreement: the chicken agreed not to tread on the toes of the horse if the horse would not tread on him. The treaty was signed on 11 July, and six days later the *Mississippi* and *Powhatan* sailed for China, leaving no American warships in the Naha harbor for the first time in more than a year. As Perry left, he carried several building blocks of stone from Okinawa and Japan as well as a temple bell from Okinawa. The *Powhatan* headed for Ningpo with departing missionary Bernard Bettelheim and his family onboard. On the *Mississippi*, Perry sailed directly to Hong Kong, which he reached in late July.[54]

When Perry left Hong Kong six and one-half months earlier he had been tense about his prospects for success. Although he now returned relieved, proud, and successful, he had paid a high physical price for his efforts. He was "worn down by long-continued anxiety of mind, ill health of body . . . and an increasing debility." Previously Perry had asked to be relieved of his command once he completed his expedition to Japan. He had little interest in China and was too mentally and physically exhausted to command the East India Squadron. Fortunately, his orders from the Navy Department awaited him. A letter from Secretary Dobbin dated 25 February 1854 authorized Perry to leave Abbot in command and return to the United States on either the *Mississippi* or by the overland route.[55]

The political situation in China had not improved since January. The insurgents were no longer in the ascendancy, but they still held Shanghai, controlled large areas of the interior, and threatened Canton. Their internal divisions widening, the rebels had, however, lost momentum. Their victory no longer seemed the inevitable outcome it had the previous year. Nevertheless, foreigners in China remained unsettled. Ironically, although the political situation had deteriorated, Perry found himself in a better position than before. The new commissioner, Robert McLane, was a much more capable and sensible diplomat than Humphrey Marshall had been. The question of authority over the squadron had not been resolved by the Pierce administration and continued to rankle McLane, but the issue was temporarily moot. After the *Susquehanna* had returned to Hong Kong, McLane set up his embassy onboard, used the steamer to convey him from place to place, and worked cooperatively with Comdr. Franklin Buchanan. The two were even in the process of planning a joint trip to Peking. In Perry's absence, Commander Kelly in the *Plymouth* had also resolved an insult to the American flag and joined British forces to dislodge imperial forces from a threatening position in Shanghai.

The improved naval-diplomatic cooperation effectively relieved the pressure from Perry and allowed him to recuperate physically, accept various plaudits, and prepare for his return to the United States. Although he had not yet received an official response from Washington on the treaty with Japan, there was a letter from Dobbin cautioning him about some of his previously stated aggressive intentions. The letter praised his recommendations regarding the "coal depot at Port Lloyd" but disapproved of his suggestion that Okinawa be occupied because the president was "disinclined without the authority of Congress to stake and retain possession of an island in that distant country."[56]

On 4 September, the American merchant community in China formally praised Perry and expressed its appreciation in a letter signed by the representatives of twenty-three American merchant houses. In profuse and exaggerated language, the letter proclaimed that Perry's achievements had elevated him to "a proud position in the eyes of the world." The Perry name, which had long adorned the naval profession, would now

be enrolled with the highest in diplomacy. Columbus, De Gama, Cook, La Perouse, Magellan—these inscribed their names in history by striving with the obstacles of nature. You have conquered the obstinate will of man, and by overturning the cherished policy of an empire, have brought an estranged but cultivated people into the family of nations.[57]

But even as Perry was being praised and fêted he came under private criticism from some of his officers. His conduct and the demands of the expedition had taken a toll on his reputation within the squadron. Although he continued to be on amicable terms with Perry, Capt. Joel Abbot confided to his son that Perry had "not been a warm attachment to him in the squadron" and had "had difficulties with a number of his commanders." Some junior officers thought Perry pompous and arrogant; he insulted them at the slightest provocation. On the *Mississippi*, the engineering officers resented what they believed was a capricious decision in forbidding them from going ashore at Shimoda. In his journal, clerk J. W. Spalding on the *Mississippi* referred to Perry in July 1854 as the "American Opperhevelhebber," a derisive term derived from the title of the Dutch director at Nagasaki. Spalding also faulted Perry for taking his pendant ashore on Okinawa to march to Shuri and for an incident on the *Mississippi* in which Perry was compared to Jesus in a Sunday sermon. Perry, he said, "sat . . . listening to all this without evincing, so far as any one could perceive, the slightest displeasure."[58]

Perry's falling out with Commander Buchanan over events on Buchanan's ship poisoned their previously close relationship and mutual respect dating back to the Mexican War. Perry had chosen to mitigate two disciplinary sentences that Buchanan imposed on the *Susquehanna*. In the first, a crewman had been sentenced to double irons and bread and water, and Perry decided to have the man examined periodically by the ship's surgeon to ensure that his health was not injured seriously. In the second case, a seaman who had resisted and threatened an officer with a gun was court-martialed and sentenced to death for his offense. After consulting with Commissioner McLane, Perry concluded that the court had not deliberated sufficiently and thus commuted the sentence to life imprisonment. A headstrong officer with a strong sense of right and wrong, the outraged Buchanan appealed Perry's decision unsuccessfully to the Navy Department. Although Buchanan permanently lost respect for his superior, Perry's decision was a sound one. He had experienced firsthand the uproar attending the executions on the *Somers* in

1842 as well as the serious harm the execution of Samuel Jackson did to morale in the Gulf Squadron in 1846. Perry had every right to assume that an execution might have a similar impact on his expedition.[59]

The saddest case was Perry's ruptured relationship with Joel Abbot. Having served with distinction and praise from Perry in the African Squadron and the Mexican War, Abbot had been personally selected by Perry for the expedition to Japan. Abbot had genuine affection for Perry and considered him a close personal friend. But their relationship began to sour in Japan. Perry blamed Abbot personally for grounding the *Macedonian* in Japanese waters in February 1854 and thereafter remained aloof from him. Although Perry assigned Abbot independent responsibilities, praised his cruise to Taiwan, and recommended him as the new commander of the East India Squadron, he angered Abbot by refusing to allow him to fly a commodore's pendant when Perry departed for the United States. Furthermore, Abbot believed that Perry did not adequately recognize and share credit for his success in Japan with his senior commanders. "He is a rather hard & unpleasant horse to be associated with," confided Abbot to Commo. Joseph Smith,

> being very selfish & exacting & feeling but little disposition to benefit others any further than it has a direct bearing upon his own fame & interest. . . . He therefore does not make many real warm hearted friends. And I fear he would disparage & pull down any one for a small amount of imaginary buncombe & consideration for himself or family connections.[60]

At the same time, Perry earned high marks and the gratitude of senior officers such as Capt. H. A. Adams, who had commanded the *Saratoga*. The men of the *Mississippi* also expressed their "high sense of respect and esteem" for Perry "both as our commander and real friend," wished him "future welfare and happiness," and concluded that "we shall never feel greater confidence, or stronger pride, than while under your command."[61]

Before Perry could depart, he had to address one last problem. The North Pacific Expedition, an American naval exploring mission under the command of Comdr. Cadwallader Ringgold, had arrived in Hong Kong in June 1854 and had been sidetracked by the political situation in China. That summer, Ringgold contracted a fever, experienced delirium, and began to act in a bizarre manner. Rumors spread about malaria, alcohol, and even drugs. Perry convened a court of medical inquiry,

removed Ringgold from command, and sent him home. As his replacement, Perry appointed Lt. John Rodgers, the son of Perry's former commander and mentor. Perry had taken the right action, but the outcome
guaranteed nasty allegations about the machinations of the Perry-
Rodgers-Slidell clan.[62]

Finally, on 11 September, Perry boarded the steamer *Hindostan* with
Flag Lt. Silas Bent. Perry stood with tears in his eyes as the *Mississippi*
and *Macedonian,* their decks lined with crewmen, fired thirteen-gun
salutes. After almost two years away, the sixty-year-old commodore was
going home. Forty-five years after joining the navy, Perry had relinquished command of a warship for the last time.

⁓ 10 ⁓

HOME AT LAST

*It may therefore be assumed, that a few small [American] settlements,
scattered through the Pacific Ocean and subject to their own local
laws, will sooner or later be established as measures of necessary expediency and convenience to our growing commerce. . . . They would be
offshoots from us rather than, strictly speaking, colonies.*

COMMO. MATTHEW PERRY, 1856

*M*atthew Perry's final voyage was an atypically cir-
cuitous and leisurely one. Once he left Hong Kong in
September on the Pacific and Orient steamer *Hin-
dostan*, Perry's journey carried him via the Isthmus of Suez to Trieste,
Vienna, Dresden, Berlin, and finally Holland. After a ten-week trip, he
reached The Hague, where his son-in-law August Belmont was serving
as U.S. minister to the Court of King William III, to visit Belmont, Caroline, and their three small children. In addition to the Belmonts, Perry
was greeted by his wife, Jane, and youngest daughter, Isabella. Graciously
received by the king and queen of the Netherlands, he spent a pleasant
time there with the family but declined to remain for Christmas. He
departed without Jane for England to inspect new English steam warships before sailing for New York, which he reached on 11 January 1855
on the Collins line steamer *Baltic*, one of the mail ships whose construction he had supervised.

Even before he reached Europe, Perry had been aware that the Treaty of Kanagawa, signed by President Franklin Pierce on 7 August, had generated little public notice, and he expected little acclaim when he returned to the United States. Writing from The Hague to his friend James Watson Webb, Perry reported that he had been received with "marked attention from the very highest classes" in Europe but complained that he could "expect nothing from my fellow citizens at home especially the mercantile community for whose interests I have devoted a whole life."[1]

On this point, however, the commodore was mistaken. Laudatory letters arrived from former president Millard Fillmore, former secretary of the navy John P. Kennedy, former secretary of state Edward Everett, and Washington Irving. "I congratulate you and the country upon the brilliant success of your mission," wrote Fillmore. "The result has indeed exceeded my most sanguine expectations." Everett assured Perry that "not merely our own country, but the civilized world is under obligations to you for the judicious, skillful, & decided course pursued by you." Irving commended Perry for achieving "a lasting name . . . without shedding a drop of blood or inflicting injury on a human being. What naval commander ever won laurels at such a rate!"[2] Perry was also overwhelmed with events in his honor. The New York Chamber of Commerce convened a special meeting on 15 January at which Perry was praised lavishly, and eventually presented him with a 381-piece silver service estimated to be worth more than six thousand dollars. At his mansion, Mayor Fernando Wood held a dinner in honor of Perry attended by such dignitaries as Winfield Scott, Martin Van Buren, Washington Irving, and George Bancroft. The merchants of Boston struck a gold medal with Perry's profile on one side and an inscription of appreciation on the other. They also provided silver replicas of the medal to his officers and bronze versions to his men. At Newport, Rhode Island, in June 1855, the legislature and governor honored Perry with a reception and a large silver salver inscribed with gracious words of appreciation to their famous native son.[3]

Even official Washington recognized him generously. Secretary of the Navy James Dobbin had already commended him for the success of his "novel and interesting mission." Now he met personally with President Pierce. Congress voted its thanks and took the unusual step of providing twenty thousand dollars to reimburse him for the diplomatic duties he had performed. It also appropriated funds to finance publication of thirty-four thousand copies of the official account of the expedition and authorized Perry to keep one thousand copies for his own use. Perry was "a lucky fellow to secure both fame & money," observed fellow officer Joseph Smith; "your gallant Commodore . . . has been the Lion of the times, been feasted & toasted and better than that, he has rec'd $20,000 besides pay and rations for his extraordinary services." The fulsome attention erased Perry's earlier bitterness.[4]

Despite these personal honors from high officials, public praise for the Treaty of Kanagawa and for Perry himself was lukewarm. Few newspapers or magazines extolled his achievements, and the nation generally did not salute Perry as a great national hero. Most Americans, in fact, viewed Perry's accomplishments as modest. True, the mission had avoided bloodshed or armed hostilities. And with the exception of fifteen men from the *Plymouth* who were lost in a boat during a typhoon off the Bonin Islands in October 1853, the loss of life was not excessive for a naval expedition of this magnitude. Moreover, the expedition had established diplomatic contact and concluded a treaty of friendship with a nation that had been closed to the outside world for more than two hundred years. Yet Japan remained a distant land of secondary importance to the United States; it was much smaller, seemed less fascinating, and offered more modest economic potential than China. Moreover, critics pointed out that Perry had come up short in not opening actual trade with Japan. James Gordon Bennett in the *New York Herald* even labeled the expedition an expensive failure.

In 1855, before the official account of the expedition appeared, two books critical of the expedition were published. In *Japan as It Was and Is,* Richard Hildreth faulted Perry for not obtaining a commercial agreement. J. W. Spalding, a clerk on the *Mississippi* for the entire voyage, gave the mission mixed reviews. In violation of Perry's general order, Spalding had kept an extensive account of the expedition which he did not relinquish to Perry but instead published in 1855 as *The Japan Expedition: Japan and around the World.* Although it presents a favorable account of the expedition, the book ridicules Perry's personal arrogance and condemns the American merchant community in China for claiming that Perry had opened "the '*commerce*' of Japan, 'not only to us, but to the world.' What nonsense." Although such harsh criticism was rare, most Americans understood that the treaty with Japan would not have an immediate and far-reaching impact on the United States. While a few

American ships might stop at Shimoda or Hakodate, actual trade with Japan would not begin for several years and then only on a small scale. In short, the expedition and the treaty had not captured the imagination of the American people.[5]

Those Americans involved commercially in Asia saw far greater potential in China than in Japan, as did American expansionists. Commercial magazines such as *DeBow's Review* and *Hunt's Merchant Magazine* devoted far more attention to China than to Japan. Moreover, during the 1850s, the focal points of American expansionism were Latin America, the Caribbean, and particularly Cuba. The political atmosphere in the United States had also changed significantly since Perry's departure in November 1852. A Democratic administration was now in power, and sectional politics increasingly dominated the national political stage. In May 1854, Congress passed the Kansas-Nebraska Bill, which reopened the issue of slavery in the federal territories by allowing the residents of those territories to decide whether or not they would permit slavery. The results were a running guerrilla war in Kansas and a national political uproar that created the Republican Party. In this atmosphere, few Americans dwelled on the accomplishments of a sixty-year-old naval officer and a minor diplomatic agreement with a tiny, distant country.

To avoid the potential discomfort of a winter passage, Jane did not return to New York with Isabella until June 1855. Then the Perrys set up housekeeping in a new house at 38 West Thirty-second Street in New York City. They were now prominent citizens moving in the best circles. Isabella made her debut into society, and on occasion her parents escorted her to leading balls. For the first time in thirty-five years, Perry voted in a presidential election. Although he felt that he ought to vote for Millard Fillmore in 1856, Perry voted instead for Democrat James Buchanan because Fillmore had "no chance" and Perry strongly opposed Republican candidate John C. Frémont. Perry also took special care to ensure the preservation of the expensive silver service gift. He asked August and Caroline Belmont, who agreed, to take responsibility for preserving the gift "in posterity in the family."[6]

The commodore had plunged into various activities on his return. He was upset at the loss of one of the steamers whose construction he had supervised. On a westbound voyage in September 1854, the *Arctic* had collided with a French steamer in a heavy fog off Cape Race and then sunk. Only 88 of the 457 passengers and crew survived, including not one of the women or children onboard. In response, Perry wrote a letter that appeared in *DeBow's Review* in March 1855 recommending ways to improve the safety of steamers at sea.[7] Perry did not seek another sea command, but he remained on active duty and served as a member of the so-called Navy Retiring Board in 1855, a post he soon regretted.

In February 1855, Congress had passed legislation to improve the efficiency of the navy by reviewing all naval officers to determine which ones were incapable of fulfilling the shore and sea duties required of them. Since the navy had no way to compel senior officers to retire, many remained years beyond their useful service and prevented younger, more capable officers from being promoted. By the mid-1850s, a few senior officers were in their seventies while the navy had some thirty-year-old midshipmen and forty-five-year-old lieutenants. By eliminating the deadwood, the navy could promote its most capable officers. Consisting of five captains, five commanders, and five lieutenants, the fifteen-member board met in Washington virtually every weekday from 20 June to 26 July, when it submitted its recommendations to Secretary of the Navy Dobbin. Known as the "plucking board," the group reviewed more than 700 officers and recommended that 201 of them be either discharged or placed on leave pay or furlough pay. The board's deliberations were secret and were based largely on the collective knowledge of the board members rather than on formal testimony or evidence submitted by the officers being reviewed. Secretary Dobbin and President Pierce accepted the recommendations, and the officers on the list received official notification in September. Because the list included such prominent and politically influential names as seventy-seven-year-old War of 1812 hero Commo. Charles Stewart and Lt. Matthew Fontaine Maury, an uproar ensued in the press and in the Senate.[8]

Perry had objected to the board but believed that it was his unpleasant duty to serve on it. Nevertheless, he thought the board's procedures were illegal and complained to the president and secretary of the navy. When the procedures and actions of the board came under attack, Perry found himself a target of public criticism. Perry personally blamed the "villainy" of his old friend and fellow board member Samuel Du Pont for the board's drastic recommendations. Although the board had kept no records of its deliberations, it was known that Du Pont and Franklin Buchanan had taken a hard line in eliminating as many questionable officers as possible. They criticized Perry for taking a soft stand on some officers while voting privately against others whom he publicly claimed to have supported. Particularly galling to Perry was the fact that his son and namesake, Matthew Calbraith Perry Jr., was one of the officers placed on the inactive list. After extensive controversy, Congress passed legislation in February 1857 permitting any officer affected to request a hearing before a naval court of inquiry. Eventually more than one hundred officers appealed, and sixty-eight of them were restored to active duty. Matthew C. Perry Jr. was among the officers reinstated, but Matthew Sr. remained bitter about the whole experience.[9]

Even during the period of frequent retirement board meetings, however, Perry focused most of his attention on preparing the official narrative of his expedition. He was determined to provide a comprehensive account that would include the mission's diplomatic activities, scientific findings, and observations of Asian people and places. He endeavored to avoid the mistakes that Comdr. Charles Wilkes had made with his narrative of the U.S. Exploring Expedition more than a decade earlier. Wilkes had personally written the five-volume account, but it was so poorly executed that few read it. With the task at hand daunting and his own writing ability modest, Perry decided to select and recruit an established author to write the manuscript. Before he did that, however, he needed to assemble and organize the voluminous material he had collected. In addition to his own official correspondence and journals, Perry had access to the journals of his senior officers; the sequestered accounts of various other participants; reports written by officers dispatched on special details; other official documents; various charts and maps; and an array of drawings, sketches, paintings, and daguerreotypes.

Congress appropriated $400,000 to underwrite the publication of thirty-four thousand copies, but the money materialized unevenly, complicating the publication process. Perry wanted Nathaniel Hawthorne to author the report and had visited the writer in England before returning to the United States; but Hawthorne declined. Eventually Perry retained Rev. Francis L. Hawks, rector of Calvary Church, New York City. Hawks was a popular preacher, the author of historical and biographical works, and an experienced traveler. Dr. Robert Tomes, a physician and writer, served as an assistant and later edited an abridged version of the narrative. Housed in two rooms of the building occupied by the American Bible Society in New York City, the project commenced in the late spring of 1855.

The work went surprisingly fast. The prefatory note was signed on New Year's Day 1856, and the first of three volumes appeared that spring. *Narrative of the Expedition of an American Squadron to the China Seas and Japan* is generally considered to be a classic of American exploration literature. It was well received although not widely reviewed. Volume 1 is a detailed chronological account of the expedition complete with extensive sections on Japan, Okinawa, and the Bonin Islands. Although Perry's thoughts, actions, and intentions are the focal point of the account, it acknowledges the contributions made by other expedition officers. Written in the fulsome literary style of the mid-nineteenth century, the text reads well nevertheless and is easy to follow. To serious readers at the time, the *Narrative* provided a fascinating story of adventure as well as a travel account rich in the history, geography, and customs of the places visited by the expedition.[10]

Appearing in 1857, volumes 2 and 3 contain official documents, nautical and scientific material, and various special reports. Volume 2 includes four dozen separate documents, reports, and articles. Perry wrote several pieces himself and included reports on such topics as the exploration of Okinawa and the Bonin Islands, the coal regions of Formosa, the agriculture of China, and the North Pacific gulf stream (or Kuro-Siwo). In addition, Perry convinced several eminent scientists to study the expedition's notes and write chapters on such subjects as cyclones and the birds, fish, and shells of Japan. Volume 3 consists of a report by Chaplain George Jones on zodiacal lights.[11]

The *Narrative* was expensively and handsomely printed. Its more than one thousand pages of text include numerous sketches, prints, maps, and paintings, some of which are full-color plates. As Congress had dictated, Perry personally received one thousand copies of the *Narrative*, half of which he used to compensate Hawks and the contributors. Perry also arranged to have a trade edition of volume 1 published by Appleton of New York in 1856.

As Perry worked on the *Narrative*, he pondered the future of the United States in Asia. Although he had spent less than two years of his long naval career in the Pacific, he believed that his country was destined to play a major role there. He expressed his thoughts on the subject in two personal articles in volume 2 of the *Narrative* and in a paper that Reverend Hawks read in Perry's presence to the American Geographical and Statistical Society in New York on 6 March 1856.[12]

Not a traditional diplomat or politician, Perry did not view the world in systematic geopolitical terms. Nor did he mirror any prevailing school of expansionist thought. Unlike commercial expansionists centered in Boston and New York, he was not preoccupied by trade with China. Although he recognized the importance of China, Perry emphasized the great potential of Japan, Cochin China, Formosa, Sumatra, and Borneo as well. Nor was Perry a territorial expansionist. Since he had never been a farmer and had always lived along the eastern seaboard, Perry did not associate expansion into the Pacific with the acquisition of new territory. He did not advocate or foresee the acquisition of Alaska, Hawaii, or the Philippines.

Instead, Perry's expansionism was shaped largely by his personal naval experiences. Long a proponent of a steam-powered navy, he understood the operating requirements of steam warships. His experience had taught him that the navy should be used as both a commercial and a diplomatic agent. Its long reach offered the best means of protecting and promoting American commerce overseas while safeguarding American interests against the competing interests of the European powers. Perry also understood what he considered to be the "prejudices" of his government. With its long tradition of maintaining a naval force much smaller than its overseas interests justified, the United States was unlikely to establish and maintain overseas colonies as European nations did.

Perry's cruise from the United States to China from November 1852 to April 1853 had done much to shape his views and concerns, which centered on naval logistics. With its 600-ton capacity, the *Mississippi* usually burned 25 to 30 tons of coal per day, thus requiring seven coaling stops en route. One engineer calculated that the *Mississippi* had burned 2,337 tons of coal on the 17,076-mile cruise to China. Although supply ships waited at two places and coal was readily available at others, the farther the *Mississippi* traveled, the more scarce coal became. Perry secured only 230 tons at Singapore, 174 tons at Hong Kong, and 236 at Macao. By the time he reached China, Perry realized that coal was critical to naval operations there. Care needed to be taken to ensure a ready supply not only for his expedition but also for the East India station in the future.[13]

The places Perry visited en route to China also informed his thinking on American interests in East Asia. He was particularly impressed with Singapore and Hong Kong. Although they were British possessions, he viewed them as commercial entrepôts rather than typical European colonies. Small but exceptionally well located, both settlements were thriving international trade centers that provided strategic naval bases to the British while attracting goods and commodities from many places. Perry was also disturbed by the extensive European presence he found in East Asia. The Dutch, French, Russians, and, particularly, the British seemed to be aggressively establishing outposts throughout the region. Alarmed by this, Perry urged the United States to expand its own presence in Asia as quickly and aggressively as possible.

In his writings in 1856, Perry outlined a course of action, but not a comprehensive policy, for the United States. Perry urged the United States to maintain a strong naval presence in East Asia and to work actively with European powers to bring about a successful civil and military revolution in China. In 1853, Perry had counseled "masterly inactivity" in China, but now he urged foreign intervention to "Europeanize" China and open it to Western commerce and social institutions. The United States also needed to continue to open "new avenues of trade" by signing treaties with Cambodia, Cochin China, Borneo, Sumatra, and other major islands. In addition, Perry thought the United States should establish a Pacific steamship line connecting the United States, Japan, and China. A Pacific steamship route would increase contact and stimulate commerce between Asia and the United States. The proposed line would also provide American merchants on the eastern seaboard with critical "priority of information" because mail and news could travel from Shanghai to New York eleven to fourteen days faster by the Pacific route than it could travel from Shanghai to London. Moreover, Perry estimated that once the United States had built a transcontinental railroad, the advantage would increase so significantly that all news from China to London would travel via the Pacific route, across the United States, and then across the Atlantic to England.[14]

Perry also understood that for American commerce in East India to thrive, Americans needed to emigrate and settle the unoccupied or sparsely settled islands of the western Pacific. In his mind, Formosa and the Bonin Islands were the two most obvious sites—Formosa because of its rich coal deposits, and the Bonin Islands because of their location on the proposed Pacific steamship route. Although the U.S. government had long opposed overseas colonies, Perry argued confidently that the American people themselves would choose to settle in places such as

Formosa and the Bonin Islands, where they would establish thriving communities, their own political institutions, and open markets. "It may therefore be assumed, that a few small settlements, scattered through the Pacific Ocean and subject to their own local laws, will sooner or later be established as measures of necessary expediency to our growing commerce." These autonomous settlements would be established for "purposes of trade or some religious or moral object" and need "not be considered strictly as colonies." They would not be subject to the rule of any external power because they would be "minor places" of insignificant importance in international disputes between major powers.[15]

Using Singapore and Hong Kong as models, Perry also proposed that the United States secure a number of additional ports of refuge in the region and establish commercial settlements in the Pacific. Both were "vitally necessary" to American commerce there. Specifically, the United States should create an entrepôt on Formosa at Keelung. "Unshackled by the restrictions of duties upon foreign or domestic commerce," it would attract trading vessels from all nations, and would soon rival Hong Kong and Singapore.[16]

Perry's recommendations on U.S. Pacific policy were neither systematic nor comprehensive. He was vague on some points and made no specific suggestions beyond suggesting Formosa and the Bonin Islands as possible American outposts. But for all of their omissions and ambiguities, his recommendations clearly envisioned the development of an American commercial and maritime empire in East Asia even if Perry did not use the term *empire of the seas,* as later politicians would. Moreover, he looked to the westward march by the American people as proof that Americans would eventually settle many islands in the Pacific just as they were settling the North American continent. "The people will emigrate and settle in remote places," wrote Perry, "and in this way we shall have foreign settlements, even if they are not established by positive enactment." Instead of a formal network of colonies established and governed by the United States, these settlements would be independent entities, populated and governed by Americans—"offshoots from us rather than, strictly speaking, colonies," predicted Perry. In this way, Perry envisioned that American commerce, dominion, and power would spread until it embraced the Pacific and "placed the Saxon race upon the eastern shores of Asia." In the conclusion of his paper to the American Geographical and Statistical Society, Perry predicted that eventually the

"Saxon and the Cossack" would meet in Asia in a "fierce and final encounter" between "freedom and absolutism."[17]

Although Perry retained his full head of brown hair and his appearance belied his years, the years of service in harsh climates overseas had irreparably damaged his body. By 1857 Perry had become weaker and spent more and more time confined to bed. "Your father is still very far from being well," wrote Jane to daughter Caroline on Christmas Day 1857. "He has been confined to the house for more than a fortnight for having sprained his ankle." In February 1858, he caught a severe cold, and his rheumatism returned. Confined to bed for several weeks, he did not respond to medical treatment and continued to decline. Perry died unexpectedly on 4 March 1858.[18]

In New York, flags flew at half-mast on public buildings and on ships in the harbor for three days. The funeral was held on 6 March. Although it was a blustery, cold Saturday, large crowds lined the procession route from Perry's home on West Thirty-second Street to St. Mark's Church. Leading the procession were a band and five hundred members of the 7th Regiment of the New York National Guard and two hundred members of the New York Militia. The pallbearers, dignitaries, naval officers who had served with Perry, and two hundred U.S. marines escorted the body, along with a contingent of seamen from the Japan expedition as well as members of the Common Council and Chamber of Commerce. Friends and family members in carriages brought up the rear of the procession. As the large crowd watched in silence, the solemn procession moved along its route to the sound of bells tolling from nearby churches. In the harbor and at the navy yard in Brooklyn, ships fired their minute guns. At the church, Reverend Hawks and three other clergymen presided over a solemn, dignified, and traditional Episcopalian burial service. Afterward, the pallbearers carried Perry into the churchyard where his body was placed in the Slidell family vault. A particularly moving tribute of "respect and affection" was the presence of dozens of "weather-beaten tars" of the Japan expedition, who had gathered at "great personal inconvenience" to pay this last tribute "to one whom they had once loved to obey." Dozens of family members, friends, and other mourners lingered before departing. Finally, however, the "great Commander" was left to his long repose.[19]

In the days after the funeral, the family received many condolences, and Perry a number of public tributes. But his death did not elicit a national outpouring of grief. In a time of economic depression brought on by the Panic of 1857 and of growing sectional tension fueled by the ongoing controversy over slavery, Perry seemed to be a figure from the past, a military hero without a single stirring combat victory. The expansionist confidence and exuberant nationalism of the early 1850s having dissipated, the treaty with Japan seemed more an interesting curiosity than a historical turning point. The country now had more pressing business, and other issues crowded the daily newspapers. The strongest and the most apt tribute to Perry appeared in the *Morning Courier and New York Enquirer*, edited by his friend James Watson Webb. The commodore, Webb wrote, "was a model of a Naval Officer, scrupulously exact in his discipline, and thoroughly American in all his views. . . . He had the valor of a hero and the capacity of a statesman, but both were outshone by a magnanimous heart which beat only to the measures of generosity and justice."[20]

Matthew C. Perry was, indeed, a model naval officer. As the preeminent naval officer of his antebellum generation, a progressive naval reformer, and a resourceful naval diplomat, he set a standard for other officers to emulate throughout the nineteenth century. He lived almost sixty-four years and spent forty-five of those years in the navy, his service spanning virtually the entire period from the War of 1812 to the Civil War. Although he never commanded a ship or a squadron in a formal naval battle, Perry forged a distinguished career nonetheless. Taking his naval oath as seriously as he took his marital vows, Perry responded to a long succession of duty calls with energy and dedication. On occasion, this dedication to orders would earn him the criticism of posterity. Historians have accused Perry of not aggressively policing American involvement in the slave trade while he was the commander of the African Squadron in the 1840s. In fact, although he might have employed his small force in a different manner, Perry was doing precisely what his superiors had ordered by protecting American commerce in West Africa. Given the horror of the slave trade, it is tempting to fault Perry, but that would place him in a historically inaccurate context. By doing his duty, Perry won the approbation of his government at a time when most Americans paid little attention to the slave trade in Africa.

Like other officers able to do so, Perry used his family and political connections to advance his career and to secure particular assignments. Sometimes he failed; sometimes he succeeded; and in the case of Japan he received the coveted command only after failing to secure it on his first try. But never did he avoid demanding assignments on difficult stations. Denied the prestigious Mediterranean Squadron, he served on four cruises to West Africa and remained dutifully, if unhappily, with the Gulf Squadron for months after any hope for military glory had passed in the Mexican War.

Perry was first, foremost, and always a naval officer of high professional standards. But his expectations that his officers and men would execute their responsibilities to the same rigorous standards that he set for himself did not win him popularity. At times overzealous in the performance of his duties, Perry was an exacting ship and squadron commander without a winning personality. And as he grew older, he became more difficult to deal with personally. His obsession with the Japan expedition as the great personal undertaking of his life alienated such longtime friends as Joel Abbot and Franklin Buchanan. At least his practices were even-handed, a quality that awarded him respect, if not affection. His men knew that important things happened on his cruises. They also thought him "bluff, positive and stern on duty, and a terror to the ignorant and lazy," but those who performed their duties well held "Old Matt" in esteem. Years later, an old salt who had served with Perry in Japan remembered that "if a man walked straight on that crack [line] he'd get good square treatment, but it he got off of it, th' Lord ha' mercy on him!"[21]

Perry certainly made his share of mistakes. Like many naval officers of his generation, he was very sensitive to matters affecting his reputation and authority. He took ready umbrage at rumors or allegations that minimized the achievements of his men or demeaned him personally. Over more than three decades, he grew accustomed to command and relished its accouterments. Once he had achieved the status of commodore, he loved the broad blue pendant that symbolized his authority. On two occasions, in Africa in 1845 and China in 1854, his reluctance to give up his commodore's pendant caused needless misunderstandings with the men who replaced him.

Although he was remarkably restrained in most tense situations throughout his long career, Perry overreacted on occasion. Sometimes these actions seemed almost humorous and had little effect on the task at hand. Such was the case with Lt. Charles Hunter, whom Perry precipitously discharged after Hunter's well-intentioned, if vainglorious, actions at Alvarado in 1847. At other times, the consequences were serious. In the aftermath of the melee at Little Berebee in December 1843, Perry ordered his forces to destroy several African villages in an unjustified retribution. With few exceptions, however, Perry was generally restrained in his dealings with the native peoples he encountered in Africa, Mexico, China, Okinawa, and Japan. Although he held ethnocentric views typical for Americans and Europeans of his time and had little respect for the tribal Africans along the coast of West Africa or the Mexicans along the Gulf coast, Perry still treated them in a civil and fair manner. In his palavers as commander of the African Squadron, Perry met with tribal leaders, listened to their version of events, and often accepted their explanations for attacks on American trading ships. He also reported to Washington that the Africans were more often sinned against than sinners themselves. In Mexico, he grew contemptuous of Mexicans in the towns he occupied, but he insisted that his men respect Mexican civilians and their property.[22] In Okinawa, he quickly came to pity the native residents, whom he considered to be defenseless pawns of their Japanese overlords. In addition to demanding that his men not injure the Okinawans or their property, he took the somewhat unusual step of insisting that local authorities, not American officials, assume responsibility for punishing the killers of the American seaman who had attempted to rape a local girl.

As an exemplary antebellum naval officer, Perry embodied the confidence of his country and its strong sense of national mission. He believed that his work in the navy advanced not only his nation's specific political and economic interests but also the causes of commerce, civilization, and democracy. He also embodied the best attributes of the antebellum navy in his efforts to shape its future. Against considerable resistance he labored to transform a traditional force of wooden sailing ships into a modern, steam-powered navy. For this work he is rightfully considered to be the father of the American steam navy. And he championed an array of other technological improvements: the adoption of propellers, the use of iron armament, the use of explosive-shell guns, and the building of modern lighthouses to improve naval and civilian navigation. He also pressed for various reforms to improve the recruitment and training of naval officers and men. The first to propose an apprentice system, Perry created the naval steam officer corps and advocated the creation of a naval academy seventeen years before it was ultimately established. Perry was not a social or humanitarian reformer. His goal was to improve the efficiency of the navy, not to improve the lot of the common sailor or to better society at large. Accordingly, he opposed the abolition of flogging in the navy and sought to modify, but not necessarily eliminate, the daily grog ration. On slavery, the great public issue of his day, Perry remained an advocate of colonization who refused to condemn slavery on moral or political grounds. Perry achieved only limited success in his reform attempts, but his persistent efforts facilitated the growth of a modern navy in an era when many naval officers resisted it and most political leaders opposed it.

As a squadron commander overseas, Perry enhanced his reputation. In Africa, he assisted the new American settlements, protected American commerce, and dealt skillfully with the British. Although Perry was ineffective in combating American participation in the slave trade, his naval successors in Africa accomplished little more than he did. Moreover, his performance in Africa earned Perry the approbation of his superiors and helped earn him command of the Gulf Squadron in the Mexican War, a difficult assignment in which he excelled.

No other officer of Perry's generation approached his stature or his record, but it was the expedition to Japan that in large part raised him above his fellow officers by establishing his reputation as an outstanding diplomat as well as an exemplary naval officer. Although the idea of a naval expedition to Japan did not originate with Perry, he was the one who planned, organized, and executed the enterprise. Even before he received the command, Perry did extensive research and thoughtfully outlined the strategy and requirements for the expedition. He fully appreciated the challenge of establishing diplomatic relations with a nation that had isolated itself from the outside world for more than two centuries. Better than other proponents of a mission to Japan, Perry realized that success depended not only on a formidable naval force but also on the commander's persistence, resourcefulness, and patience. Once appointed to head the expedition, Perry insisted that it be a scientific and cultural mission as well as a naval and diplomatic one. In the eleven months preceding his departure, Perry labored indefatigably to ensure that as many of the military, diplomatic, and scientific requirements as possible could be met. Perry also prepared himself to play the role of his life, knowing that effective cultural theater would be essential to diplomatic success. Only a dignified, resolute, and elevated persona would impress and make headway with the Japanese. In his own words, he needed "to out-Herod Herod in assumed personal consequence and ostentation." As some American observers looked askance, Perry succeeded by playing his role flawlessly.[23]

It can be tempting in retrospect to minimize Perry's achievement in Japan, for the opening of diplomatic relations between Japan and the West was inevitable. If Perry had not succeeded, a naval officer or diplomat from another nation would have. Moreover, his treaty with Japan did not establish commercial relations; it merely opened the way for a subsequent commercial agreement to be negotiated. While these statements are true, they unfairly underestimate Perry's accomplishments. Perry's preparation, resourcefulness, and "mastery of cultural theater" allowed him to succeed where others had failed. Although Japanese society was in a state of flux, Japan's rulers remained firmly opposed to a treaty with any foreign power. It was Perry who finally forced Japan to conclude an agreement in 1854. And despite its limited concessions, the Treaty of Kanagawa was much more than a simple treaty of "amity and friendship." It was a breakthrough that ended more than two centuries of Japanese diplomatic isolation. The treaty had far-reaching consequences for both the United States and Japan by redefining their relations and helping initiate the transformation of Japan. Indeed, Perry's conduct even won the respect of his Japanese adversaries, who erected a monument in his honor at Uraga in 1901.

When he was entombed in the Slidell family vault at St. Mark's Church in New York City in March 1858, Perry had not yet reached his final resting-place. He had wished to be buried in Newport, his birthplace, but weather conditions at the time of the funeral made that impossible. His body rested for eight years in the Slidell vault before it was finally moved in 1866 to the Island Cemetery in Newport, Rhode Island. There, by the sea, his long journey finally ended very close to where it had begun almost seventy-two years earlier and where he would be joined fifteen years later by his beloved Jane.[24]

Notes

ABBREVIATIONS USED IN THE NOTES

AL   Alderman Library, University of Virginia
ASP   American State Papers
BL   Beinecke Rare Book and Manuscript Library, Yale University
HSP   Historical Society of Pennsylvania
HU   Houghton Library, Harvard University
LC   Library of Congress
MCP   Matthew Calbraith Perry
NA   National Archives
NAM   U.S. Naval Academy Museum
NASP   New American State Papers
ND   Navy Department
NHF   Naval Historical Foundation Collection (housed in the Library of
        Congress)
NL   Nimitz Library, U.S. Naval Academy
R   Microfilm reel or roll number
SED   Senate Executive Document
SL   Sterling Library, Yale University

CHAPTER 1. A RHODE ISLAND NAVAL HERITAGE

1. Bayard Taylor, *A Visit to India, China, and Japan in the Year 1853*, 418, 419.

2. For Perry's account, see Matthew C. Perry, *The Japan Expedition, 1852–1854: The Personal Journal of Commodore Matthew C. Perry*, ed. Roger Pineau, 98–100; Francis L. Hawks, *Narrative of the Expedition of an American Squadron to the China Seas and Japan*, 1:313–24.

3. The best accounts of the landing in 1853 are Peter Booth Wiley, *Yankees in the Land of the Gods: Commodore Perry and the Opening of Japan*, 314–21; Samuel Eliot Morison, *"Old Bruin": Commodore Matthew C. Perry, 1794–1858*, 331–35; and Arthur Walworth, *Black Ships off Japan: The Story of Commodore Perry's Expedition*, 90–103.

4. John S. Sewall, *The Logbook of the Captain's Clerk: Adventures in the China Seas*, 157. Detailed contemporary accounts of the landing include B. Taylor,

Visit to India, China, and Japan; S. Wells Williams, "A Journal of the Perry Expedition to Japan, 1853–1854"; and J. W. Spalding, *The Japan Expedition: Japan and around the World, an Account of Three Visits to the Japanese Empire*. Taylor's firsthand account was published in the *New York Tribune*, 5 November 1853.

5. Calbraith B. Perry, *The Perrys of Rhode Island and Tales of Silver Creek*, 7–11, 43–47; also *The Perry Family*.

6. C. B. Perry, *The Perrys of Rhode Island*, 53–56. For accounts of the Perry family, see Morison, *"Old Bruin,"* 3–12; and William E. Griffis, *Matthew Calbraith Perry: A Typical American Naval Officer*, 6–14.

7. Griffis, *Perry*, 6–8, 11–14; C. B. Perry, *Perrys of Rhode Island*, 53–58.

8. Griffis, *Perry*, 430–31; C. B. Perry, *Perrys of Rhode Island*, 65; George C. Channing, *Early Recollections of Newport*, 32, 33. Also George C. Mason, *Reminiscences of Newport*; and George C. Mason, *Newport Illustrated in a Series of Pen and Pencil Sketches*; George Howe, *Mount Hope: A New England Chronicle*.

9. Remarks of Perry to Governor of Rhode Island at Newport [June 1855], Perry Papers, HU.

10. Alexander Slidell Mackenzie, *The Life of Commodore Oliver Hazard Perry*, 35–37.

11. Lynne Withey, *Urban Growth in Colonial Rhode Island: Newport and Providence in the Eighteenth Century*, 109; also Morris A. Gutstein, *The Story of the Jews of Newport; Two and a Half Centuries of Judaism, 1658–1908*, 214–21; "The Newport Jews," in Mason, *Reminiscences of Newport*, 53–69.

12. The population statistics are from *A Century of Population Growth from the First Census of the United States to the Twelfth, 1790–1900*, 47, 57.

13. Ibid., 82, 133, 135, 222. Joanne Melish, *Discovering Slavery: Gradual Emancipation and "Race" in New England, 1780–1860*, 66–75, 93–94, 101–3. On African American merchant seamen, see W. Jeffrey Bolster, *Black Jacks: African American Seamen in the Age of Sail*; also Martha S. Putney, "Black Merchant Seamen of Newport, 1803–1865: A Case Study in Foreign Commerce," 156–68.

14. Channing, *Recollections of Newport*, 59–61.

15. Peter J. Coleman, *The Transformation of Rhode Island, 1790–1860*, 22.

16. Ibid., 51; Jay Coughtry, *The Notorious Triangle: Rhode Island and the African Slave Trade, 1700–1807*, 25.

17. Coleman, *Transformation of Rhode Island*; Elizabeth Donnan, "The New England Slave Trade after the Revolution," 255–56.

18. Rayford Logan, *The Diplomatic Relations of the United States and Haiti, 1776–1891*, 101, 104–5; Thomas Ott, *The Haitian Revolution, 1789–1804*, 114.

19. Letter of Jonathan Almy, Council Clerk, 20 August 1800, as quoted in Edward Field, ed., *State of Rhode Island and Providence Plantations at the End of the Century*, 2:32–34.

20. James E. Valle, *Rocks and Shoals: Order and Discipline in the Old Navy, 1800–1861*, 256–57.
21. Ibid., 257; also Morison, *"Old Bruin,"* 21, 23–24.
22. Christopher McKee, *A Gentlemanly and Honorable Profession: The Creation of the U.S. Naval Officer Corps, 1794–1815*, 417–18.
23. Ibid., 91; Douglass Adair, "Fame and the Founding Fathers," 3–26.
24. Charles O. Paullin, *Commodore John Rodgers: Captain, Commodore, and Senior Officer of the American Navy, 1773–1838*, 163.
25. McKee, *Gentlemanly and Honorable Profession*, 122, 131–33.
26. Morison, *"Old Bruin,"* 29.
27. Paullin, *Rodgers*, 223–28; Alfred T. Mahan, *Sea Power in Its Relations to the War of 1812*, 1:256–59.
28. Journal of the *President*, 24 June 1812, Rodgers Family Papers, LC.
29. Paullin, *Rodgers*, 250–56. The classic naval history of the war is Mahan, *Sea Power in Its Relations to the War of 1812*. General histories of the war include Reginald Horsman, *The War of 1812*; and John K. Mahon, *The War of 1812*.
30. Louis M. Sears, *John Slidell*, 5–15.
31. Jane Perry Tiffany to Ambassador C. MacVeagh, 19 October 1927, Presentation of the Relics of Commodore Matthew Calbraith Perry . . . , copy in the Perry Papers, HU; C. B. Perry, *Perrys of Rhode Island*, 67–68; also MCP to S. Southard, 28 April 1828, Commanders' Letters, NA, M147.
32. See, e.g., McKee, *Gentlemanly and Honorable Profession*, 303–5, also 87, 352.
33. C. B. Perry, *Perrys of Rhode Island*, 66, 78–79.
34. Mackenzie, *Oliver Hazard Perry*, 2:96–98.
35. McKee, *Gentlemanly and Honorable Profession*, 159; MCP to B. W. Crowninshield, 20 December 1815, 30 July 1816, Officers' Letters, NA, M148.

Chapter 2. Lieutenant in West African and Caribbean Waters

1. K. Jack Bauer, "Naval Shipbuilding Programs, 1794–1860," 34; also Craig L. Symonds, *Navalists and Antinavalists: The Naval Policy Debate in the United States, 1785–1827*, 213–31; Harold Sprout and Margaret Sprout, *The Rise of American Naval Power, 1776–1918*, 96–101.
2. John H. Schroeder, *Shaping a Maritime Empire: The Commercial and Diplomatic Role of the American Navy, 1829–1861*, 3–18.
3. Vincent Ponko Jr., *Ships, Seas, and Scientists: U.S. Naval Exploration and Discovery in the Nineteenth Century*; also Geoffrey Smith, "The Navy before Darwinism: Science, Exploration, and Diplomacy in Antebellum America," 41–55.
4. Valle, *Rocks and Shoals*, 88.
5. See P. J. Staudenraus, *The African Colonization Movement, 1816–1865*; also Judd Scott Harmon, "Marriage of Convenience: The United States Navy in Africa, 1820–1843," 264–76.

6. MCP to J. S. Mill, 14 April 1820, in Charles H. Huberich, *The Political and Legislative History of Liberia*, 1:216, 127–28.

7. Edgar Stanton Maclay, *Reminiscences of the Old Navy*, 7–24; also George M. Brooke Jr., "The Role of the United States Navy in the Suppression of the African Slave Trade," 28–41; Alan R. Booth, "United States African Squadron," 77–117.

8. Journal of the *Cyane*, 14 April 1820, NAM; Staudenraus, *African Colonization Movement*, 64–67.

9. Journal of the *Cyane*, 14 April 1820.

10. Ibid., 19, 10 March 1820.

11. Letters describing the local situation are printed in Huberich, *Political and Legislative History of Liberia*, 1:118–32. For local tensions, see Amos Sawyer, *The Emergence of Autocracy in Liberia: Tragedy and Challenge*, 77–81; Tom Shick, *Behold the Promised Land: A History of Afro-American Settler Society in Nineteenth-Century Liberia*, 20–31.

12. Journal of the *Cyane*, 13, 20 March 1820. For background on disease in West Africa, see Philip D. Curtin, *Disease and Empire: The Health of European Troops in the Conquest of Africa*, 1–28.

13. Journal of the *Cyane*, 20 March 1820.

14. Huberich, *Political and Legislative History of Liberia*, 1:144; Maclay, *Reminiscences*, 24. An excellent study of mortality is Antonio McDaniel, *Swing Low, Sweet Chariot: The Mortality Cost of Colonizing Liberia in the Nineteenth Century*, esp. 41–106.

15. MCP to S. Thompson, 31 March, 9 May 1821, Officers' Letters, NA, M148, R26.

16. Valle, *Rocks and Shoals*, 45.

17. W. R. Lynch, *Naval Life, or, Observations Afloat and on Shore. The Midshipman*, 148–49.

18. Ibid., 141–42. Also Christopher Lloyd, ed., *The Health of Seamen: Selections from the Works of Dr. James Lind, Sir Gilbert Blane and Dr. Thomas Totter*.

19. Lynch, *Naval Life*, 145.

20. Ibid.

21. MCP to S. Thompson, 19 January 1822, Officers' Letters, NA, M148, R28; Hugh Thomas, *The Slave Trade: The History of the Atlantic Slave Trade, 1440–1870*, 617.

22. MCP to Secretary of the Navy, 17 January 1822, Officers' Letters, NA, M148, R28.

23. Ibid.

24. Lynch, *Naval Life*, 153–54.

25. Gardner W. Allen, *Our Navy and the West Indian Pirates*, 243; also Francis B. C. Bradlee, *The Suppression of Piracy in the West Indies, 1820–1832*; Raymond L. Shoemaker, "Diplomacy from the Quarterdeck," 169–79.

26. David F. Long, *Nothing Too Daring: A Biography of Commodore David Porter, 1780–1843*, 204; David Dixon Porter, *Memoir of Commodore David Porter of the United States Navy*, 271.

27. An excellent picture of piracy and the activities of the U.S. Navy in the Caribbean at this time is presented in the correspondence printed in *American State Papers, Class VI: Naval Affairs*, 1:132–440.

28. Porter, *Memoir*, 271.

29. S. Thompson to MCP 7 February 1822; MCP to J. Moorhead, 28 March 1822, both in Perry Letter Book, NA.

30. MCP to S. Thompson, 28 March 1822, Perry Letter Book, NA; Long, *Nothing Too Daring*, 215.

31. MCP to Biddle, 29 June 1822, Perry Letter Book, NA.

32. Ibid.; also MCP to Biddle, n.d., Perry Letter Book, HSP. For prizes taken by the U.S. Navy in 1822–23 in the Caribbean, see George F. Emmons, *The Navy of the United States from the Commencement, 1775 to 1853*, 76–77.

33. MCP to S. Thompson, 12 December 1822, Officers' Letters, M148 R29, NA; see also MCP to ———, 12 December 1822, *ASP, VI: Naval Affairs*, 1:1099.

34. MCP to E. Caldwell, 18 November 1822, Perry Letter Book, NA; MCP to S. Thompson, 12 December 1822, Officers' Letters, NA, M148, R29; also MCP to———, 12 December 1822, *ASP, VI: Naval Affairs*, 1:1099.

35. See, e.g., Thomas, *The Slave Trade*, 615–16, 727; James T. de Kay, *Chronicles of the Frigate "Macedonian,"* 220–21, 224–25; Daniel Mannix, *Black Cargoes: A History of the Atlantic Slave Trade*, 229; W. E. B. Du Bois, *The Suppression of the African Slave Trade to the United States of America, 1638–1870*, 161.

36. C. B. Perry, *Perrys of Rhode Island*, 79; Booth, "United States African Squadron," 89–100.

37. John Quincy Adams, *Memoirs of John Quincy Adams, Comprising Portions of the Diary from 1795 to 1848*, 29 June 1822, 6:36. This issue is discussed in detail in Samuel Flagg Bemis, *John Quincy Adams and the Foundations of American Foreign Policy*, 409–35.

38. MCP to S. Thompson, 12 December 1822, Officers' Letters, NA, M148, R29; MCP to Wiley, December 1822, Perry Letter Book, NA.

39. MCP to D. Porter, 26 April 1823, Perry Letter Book, NA; MCP to S. Thompson, 9 July 1823, Officers' Letters, NA, M148, R31; also "Correspondence of David Porter and Officers," *ASP, VI: Naval Affairs*, 1103–21.

Chapter 3. First Lieutenant and Commander in the Mediterranean

1. Alexander Slidell Mackenzie, *A Year in Spain*, 2:263–65.

2. MCP to J. F. Cooper, 24 July 1824, Cooper Papers, BL.

3. Paullin, *Rodgers*, 327, 330–31.

4. Paul J. Zingg, "To the Shores of Barbary: The Ideology and Pursuit of American Commercial Expansion, 1816–1906," 408–24, 413; also James A. Field Jr., *America and the Mediterranean World, 1776–1882*, 133–34.

5. S. Southard to Rodgers, 29 December 1825, Rodgers Family Papers, NHF, LC; Paullin, *Rodgers*, 328–29; William McNally, *Evils and Abuses in the Naval and Merchant Service Exposed; with Proposals for Their Remedy and Redress*, 23–24.

6. J. A. Field, *America and the Mediterranean World*, 106–12; Walter Colton, *Ship and Shore, in Madeira, Lisbon, and the Mediterranean*, 197; Roland F. Gould, *The Life of Gould, an Ex–Man-of-War's Man with Incidents on Sea and Shore*, 63. See also Francis Schroeder, *Shores of the Mediterranean with Sketches of Travel*, 21–37; Harry Gringo [H. A. Wise], *Scampavias from Gibel Tarek to Stamboul*.

7. Colton, *Ship and Shore*, 203.

8. Paullin, *Rodgers*, 350; J. A. Field, *America and the Mediterranean World*, 135.

9. Harold D. Langley, *A History of Medicine in the Early U.S. Navy*, 274.

10. MCP to W. C. Nicholson, 3 October 1836, Perry Letter Book, HSP.

11. Ibid.

12. Ibid.

13. James M. Merrill, *Du Pont: The Making of an Admiral: A Biography of Samuel Francis Du Pont*, 30, 28; also James M. Merrill, "Midshipman Du Pont and the Cruise of the *North Carolina*, 1825–1827," 211–25.

14. James Holly Garrison, *Behold Me Once More: The Confessions of James Holly Garrison*.

15. Ibid., 85.

16. Ibid., 83, 82.

17. Henry Mayer, *All on Fire: William Lloyd Garrison and the Abolition of Slavery*, 270; Valle, *Rocks and Shoals*, 45.

18. Paullin, *Rodgers*, 335–36.

19. Ibid., 336; Morison, *"Old Bruin,"* 97.

20. MCP to My Dear Father, J. Slidell, 25 February 1827, Perry Papers, LC; Paullin, *Rodgers*, 349, 351.

21. MCP to J. Slidell, 25 February 1827, Perry Papers, LC.

22. MCP to S. Southard, 19 October 1827, Commanders' Letters, NA, M147, R13.

23. Quotation of Rear Admiral Almy as cited in Griffis, *Perry*, 98; C. B. Perry, *Perrys of Rhode Island*, 67.

24. MCP to J. Rodgers, 22 November 1827, 8 January, 6 February 1828; MCP to Secretary of the Navy, 11 February 1828; G. M. Rodgers to MCP, 22 November 1827, all in Rodgers Family Papers, NHF, LC.

25. Perry Letter Book, HSP; Griffis, *Perry*, 441–42.

26. Symonds, *Navalists and Antinavalists*, 231; Paullin, *Rodgers*, 324. On Perry's authorship, see Harold D. Langley, *Social Reform in the United States Navy, 1798–1862*, 100–101, n. 10.

27. *National Gazette* (Philadelphia), 15 December 1827. The articles appeared in the newspaper's editions of 15, 24 December 1827, 7, 15, 26 January, and 5, 12 February 1828.

28. MCP to Rodgers, 6 February 1828, Rodgers Family Papers, NHF, LC.

29. *National Gazette* (Philadelphia), 7 January 1828.

30. Ibid., 12 February 1828.

31. MCP to J. Branch, 6 April 1830, Commanders' Letters, NA, M147, R15.

32. J. Branch to MCP, 1 June 1830, Perry Papers, HU.

33. John M. Belohlavek, *"Let the Eagle Soar": The Foreign Policy of Andrew Jackson,* 30.

34. MCP to J. Branch, 14 June 1830, Perry Letter Book, HSP; William Cabell Bruce, *John Randolph of Roanoke, 1773–1833,* 1:636.

35. J. Randolph to A. Jackson, 28 June 1830, in *Correspondence of Andrew Jackson,* ed. John Spencer Bassett, 4:158; MCP to J. Branch, 24 June 1830, Perry Letter Book, HSP.

36. MCP to J. Branch, 20 July 1830, Commanders' Letters, NA, M147, R15.

37. J. Randolph to MCP, 24 July 1830; J. Randolph to J. D. Williamson, 20 July 1830, both in Commanders' Letters, NA, M147, R15; also J. Randolph to MCP, 27 July 1830, Perry Papers, HU; MCP to J. Randolph 20 July 1830, Perry Letter Book, HSP.

38. Belohlavek, *"Let the Eagle Soar,"* 83–84.

39. See MCP to J. Branch, 1 August 1830, Commanders' Letters, NA, M147. Included as attachments to the letter is the correspondence between Perry and Randolph as well as accounts of the episode from Perry's officers. Copies of these letters are also in the Perry Letter Books, Historical Society of Pennsylvania. Also MCP to J. Branch, 17 August and 9 September 1830, Commanders' Letters, NA, M147.

40. MCP to J. Branch, 1 August 1830, Commanders' Letters, NA, M147, R15; MCP to J. Rodgers, 28 July 1830, HSP, as cited in Morison, *"Old Bruin,"* 111–12.

41. J. Randolph to M. Van Buren, 3 August 1830, Martin Van Buren Papers, Microfilm edition, LC; J. Randolph to MCP, 1 August 1830, Perry Papers, HU; MCP to Branch, 1 August 1830, Commanders' Letters, NA, M147, R15.

42. J. Randolph to A. Jackson, 24 October 1831, in *Correspondence of Andrew Jackson,* 4:363–64.

43. MCP to L. Woodbury, 16 February 1832, Commanders' Letters, NA, M147 R17.

44. Langley, *Social Reform in the United States Navy,* 139–41.

45. MCP to W. Nicholson, 3 October 1836, Perry Letter Book, HSP.

46. MCP to David Porter, 1832; MCP to J. Glidden [U.S. consul at Alexandria], 3 April 1832; MCP to J. Biddle, 6 April 1832; MCP to D. Offley, 14 May 1832, all in Perry Letter Book, HSP.

47. MCP to H. S. Dearborn, 22 April 1831, 21 February 1832, 11 March 1832, all in Perry Letter Book, HSP.

48. MCP to C. Morris, 28 November 1830, Perry Letter Book, HSP.

49. Belohlovek, *"Let the Eagle Soar,"* 140–49; Howard R. Marraro, *Diplomatic Relations between the United States and the Kingdom of the Two Sicilies,* 1:286–87; J. A. Field, *America and the Mediterranean World,* 208.

50. David F. Long, *Gold Braid and Foreign Relations: Diplomatic Activities of U.S. Naval Officers, 1798–1883,* 179; Morison, *"Old Bruin,"* 179.

51. Patterson to MCP, 1 October 1832, Commanders' Letters, NA, M147 R17; Belohlavek, *"Let the Eagle Soar,"* 147; Long, *Gold Braid,* 179.

52. J. A. Field, *America and the Mediterranean World,* 208.

53. MCP to Woodbury, 21 December 1832, Commanders' Letters, NA, M147, R17; Act of Congress, 3 March 1835; Morison, *"Old Bruin,"* 123; Griffis, *Perry,* 98.

CHAPTER 4. CAPTAIN AND NAVAL REFORMER

1. MCP to L. Woodbury, 22 December 1832, Commanders' Letters, NA, M147, R17.

2. Mackenzie, *Oliver Hazard Perry,* 2:140–41.

3. Carl Bode, *The American Lyceum: Town Meeting of the Mind.*

4. Lt. Comdr. S. De Christofaro, "The Naval Lyceum," 869; "The Naval Lyceum" and "Constitution and By Laws," *Naval Magazine* 1 (January 1836): 5–18, 31–42.

5. *Naval Magazine* 1:39–42; also Sir J. Franklin to MCP, 21 August 1834, Perry Papers, HU.

6. "Report of the Naval Lyceum," 391.

7. Ibid., 392.

8. "Thoughts on the Navy," 9–10. Alexander Slidell Mackenzie and Perry were co-authors. See also [A. S. Mackenzie], *Popular Essays on Naval Subjects.*

9. "Thoughts on the Navy," 13.

10. Ibid., 33.

11. "On Steamers of War," 355.

12. McNally, *Evils and Abuses in the Naval and Merchant Service Exposed,* 18–20. The best discussion of the issue is Langley, *Social Reform,* 75–96.

13. Langley, *Social Reform,* 71; Fred Fitzgerald De Roos, *Personal Narrative of Travels in the United States and Canada,* 65–67; Nathaniel Ames, *A Mariner's Sketches,* 199.

14. MCP to S. Thompson, 21, 29 July 1821, Officers' Letters, NA, M148, R26; MCP to J. Rodgers, 25 July 1824, Rodgers Family Papers, HSP.

15. MCP to S. Southard, 5 January 1824, printed in *Army and Navy Chronicle* 10 (April 1840): 217.

16. Ibid.; *Historical Statistics of the United States from Colonial Times to 1970,* series Y, 457–65:1115.

17. Langley, *Social Reform,* 100–101; Michael J. Birker, *Samuel L. Southard: Jeffersonian Whig,* 90–113; also Edwin M. Hall, "Samuel Lewis Southard," in *American Secretaries of the Navy,* ed. Paolo Colletta, 1:131–40.

18. MCP to Secretary of the Navy, 20 October 1834, Perry Letter Book, HSP.

19. MCP to M. Dickerson, 10 January 1835, Commanders' Letters, NA, M147, R20.

20. Langley, *Social Reform,* 106.

21. *Naval Magazine* 2 (May 1837): 58; MCP to M. Dickerson, 10 March 1837, Perry Papers, HU; MCP to M. Dickerson, 20 March 1837, Commanders' Letters, NA, M147, R21.

22. MCP to Hudson, 30 June 1836, Perry Letter Book, HSP; also MCP to J. Rodgers, 2 December 1836, Rodgers Family Papers, NHF, LC; Matthew C. Perry et al., "The Exploring Expedition to the South Seas," *Naval Magazine* 2 (January 1837): 64–76.

23. MCP to J. Bayly, 4 December 1837; MCP to Hudson, 30 June 1836, both in Perry Letter Book, HSP; William Stanton, *The Great United States Exploring Expedition of 1838–1842,* 59–60.

24. Frank M. Bennett, *The Steam Navy of the United States,* 1:17; Bernard Brodie, *Sea Power in the Machine Age.*

25. M. Dickerson, "Report on a System of Defense by Armed Steamer," 26 June 1838, in *NASP, Naval Affairs,* ed. K. Jack Bauer, 1:133–34; J. K. Paulding, "Report on Building a Steam Warship," 16 January 1839, in *NASP, Naval Affairs,* 1:137–39.

26. Brodie, *Sea Power,* 36; Bauer, "Naval Shipbuilding Programs," 37–38; Sprout and Sprout, *Rise of American Naval Power,* 125–26.

27. J. K. Paulding to G. Kemble, 8, 16 June 1839, in *The Letters of James Kirke Paulding,* ed. Ralph M. Aderman, 258.

28. Bennett, *Steam Navy,* 20–21; MCP to Goldsborough, 28 October 1839, Perry Letter Book, NA.

29. MCP to Board of Navy Commissioners, 28 December 1837, in *NASP, Naval Affairs,* 10:211–12; Bauer, "Naval Shipbuilding Programs," 36.

30. Griffis, *Perry,* 120–25; Letter of MCP as quoted in Griffis, *Perry,* 122–25.

31. I. Chauncy, Board of Navy Commissioners, to M. Dickerson, 15 September 1837, in *NASP, Naval Affairs,* 10:210–11.

32. Morison, *"Old Bruin,"* 128–29; MCP to J. K. Paulding, 2 March 1839, Perry Letter Book, NA.

33. MCP to J. K. Paulding, 8 July 1839; MCP to J. K. Paulding, 26 December 1839, 21 April 1840; MCP to J. Renshaw, 20 April 1840, all in Perry Letter Book, NA.

34. M. Dickerson to MCP, 9 June 1838, Perry Letter Book, NA.

35. MCP to J. K. Paulding, 8, 28 July 1838, Perry Letter Book, NA; also MCP to W. Redfield, 23 September 1838, William Redfield Papers, BL. (Paulding began as secretary of the navy on 1 July 1838.)

36. MCP to J. Davis, 28 August 1838; MCP to C. Morris, 24 August 1838, both in Perry Letter Book, NA; also MCP to W. Redfield, 23 September 1838, Redfield Papers, BL.

37. Arnold B. Johnson, *The Modern Light-House Service,* 15; George Weiss, *The Lighthouse Service: Its History, Activities and Organization,* 1–12; George R.

Putnam, *Lighthouses and Lightships of the United States;* SED 428, 25th Cong., 2d sess.

38. Putnam, *Lighthouses and Lightships,* 31–44; Johnson, *Modern Light-House Service,* 13–24; Weiss, *Lighthouse Service,* 1–12.

39. MCP to M. Dickerson, 10 April 1837, Commanders' Letters, NA, M147, R21; MCP to Secretary of the Navy, 28 July 1838, Perry Letter Book, NA; also MCP to C. Morris, 26 August 1838; MCP to J. Davis, 25 August 1838, both in Perry Letter Book, NA. This letter book includes a section from July 1838 to May 1839 devoted exclusively to correspondence on the lighthouse issue.

40. MCP to E. Vail, 15 June 1839, Perry Papers, LC; also MCP to E. Vail, 11 August 1839, Perry Papers, HU.

41. MCP to E. Vail, 2 January 1841, Perry Papers, HU; also MCP notes on lighthouses in the Andrew Stevenson Papers, LC. Perry's report on lighthouses is in SED 619, 26th Cong., 1st sess. (25 July 1840).

42. MCP to C. Stewart, 5 April 1839, in *NASP, Naval Affairs,* 10:213–14.

43. MCP to J. K. Paulding, 2 March 1839, 2 January 1841, both in Perry Letter Book, NA; also MCP to T. Stephens, 4 April 1839, Perry Papers, Naval Historical Center Library, Washington, D.C.

44. See, e.g., MCP to Board of Navy Commissioners, 19 October 1840, 27 February 1841, 24, 26 October 1841; MCP to J. K. Paulding, 25 January 1840, all in Perry Letter Book, NA.

45. MCP to Goldsborough, 28 October 1839, Perry Letter Book, NA.

46. Diary of Philip Hone as quoted in Morison, *"Old Bruin,"* 126.

47. MCP to D. Conner, 24 November 1841.

48. MCP to E. Vail, 2 January 1841, Perry Papers, LC.

49. For an excellent account, see Edwin H. Hall, *Abel Parker Upshur: Conservative Virginian, 1790–1844,* 120–93.

50. MCP to Badger, 15 March 1841, Perry Letter Book, NA.

51. W. Redfield to MCP, 20 March, 13 May, 5 July 1841; also MCP to Redfield, 15 July 1841, all Redfield Papers, BL.

52. W. Redfield to MCP, 14 June, 29 July 1841, Redfield Papers, BL.

53. Hall, *Upshur,* 124–25; A. Upshur to MCP, 20, 22 November 1841, Letters to Officers of Ships, NA, M149 R32. Also Leonard D. White, *The Jacksonians: A Study in Administrative History, 1829–1861,* 220; *Congressional Globe,* 27th Cong., 2d sess., app., 922–23.

54. Howard I. Chapelle, *The History of the American Sailing Navy: The Ships and Their Development,* 430–33.

55. The best account is Morison, *"Old Bruin,"* 144–62. Also *Proceedings of the Naval Court Martial in the Case of Alexander Slidell Mackenzie . . . to Which Is Annexed an Elaborate Review by James Fenimore Cooper;* Frederic F. Van de Water, *The Captain Called It Mutiny;* Harrison Hayford, ed., *The "Somers" Mutiny.*

56. See, e.g., C. McIlvaine to A. S. Mackenzie, 14 January 1843; C. Sumner to A. S. Mackenzie, 17 August 1843, both in Perry Papers, HU.

Chapter 5. Commodore of the African Squadron

1. MCP to B. Kennon, 23 March 1843, Perry Letter Book, HSP.
2. MCP to I. Mayo, 10 March 1843; MCP to W. Shubrick, 17 March 1843, both in Perry Letter Book, NA, M206. The microfilm copy of M206 is contained on one roll.
3. MCP to Goldsborough, 20 March 1842, 10 April 1843, both in Perry Letter Book, NA, M206; also MCP to Goldsborough, 10, 11 March 1843, both in Perry Letter Book, NA, M206.
4. MCP to B. Kennon, 7 April 1843; MCP to Goldsborough, 10 April 1843; MCP to A. Upshur, 16 May 1843, 13 April 1843, all in Perry Letter Book, NA, M206.
5. J. Abbot to J. Picliens, December 1843, Joel Abbot Papers, Microfilm copy, NL.
6. Howard Jones, *To the Webster-Ashburton Treaty: A Study in Anglo-American Relations, 1783–1843*; David Hunter Miller, ed., *Treaties and Other International Acts of the United States of America, 1776–1863*, 4:363–70.
7. A. Upshur to MCP, 30 March 1843, Miscellaneous Letters, Department of State, March–May 1843, NA.
8. Ibid.
9. Ibid.
10. Ibid.
11. Philip D. Curtin, *The Atlantic Slave Trade: A Census*, 73–75, 234.
12. Adams, *Memoirs of John Quincy Adams*, 31 May 1843, 11:380; also 7, 11 August 1843, 11:406–7. See also Jones, *Webster-Ashburton Treaty*, 69–86; Howard Jones, "The Peculiar Institution and National Honor: The Case of the Creole Slave Revolt," 28–50.
13. MCP to J. K. Paulding, 6 October 1839, Perry Letter Book, NA; MCP to J. Tattnall, 21 June 1843; also MCP to A. Lewes, 17 April 1843, both in Perry Letter Book, NA, M206.
14. Horatio Bridge, *Journal of an African Cruiser . . .* , ed. Nathaniel Hawthorne, 12–13.
15. Sawyer, *Emergence of Autocracy in Liberia*, 43–44; also Shick, *Behold the Promised Land*, 24–28.
16. Huberich, *Political and Legislative History of Liberia*, 1:767–69. Also Staudenraus, *African Colonization Movement*; Penelope Campbell, *Maryland in Africa: The Maryland State Colonization Society, 1831–1857*.
17. Sawyer, *Emergence of Autocracy in Liberia*, 47–48, 66–69, 71–95.
18. MCP to Rev. I. Clark (Edina, Liberia), 1 November 1844; also MCP to Rev. Payne, 11 November 1844, both in Perry Letter Book, NA, M206.
19. MCP, "American Settlement on the Coast of Africa, 1843–1844," Perry Letter Book, HSP.

20. MCP to A. Upshur, 4 August 1843, Perry Letter Book, NA.

21. Ibid.; MCP to A. Lewes, 17 April 1843, Perry Letter Book, NA, M206.

22. MCP to J. Russwurm, 12 August 1843; MCP to H. S. Stellwagen, 12 August 1843; both in Perry Letter Book, NA; MCP to A. Upshur, 5 September 1843, Perry Letter Book, NA, M206.

23. Bridge, *African Cruiser,* 61.

24. Ibid., 64.

25. Ibid.

26. Ibid., 71.

27. Notes, Council of December 9 & 10, 1843, Perry Letter Book, HSP.

28. Bridge, *African Cruiser,* 75–77.

29. Accounts of the incident include MCP, Notes of a Palaver, Perry Letter Book, HSP; MCP to D. Henshaw, 21 December 1843; MCP to Brown, 28 December 1843, both in Perry Letter Book, NA; also Journal of J. Abbot, 13 December 1843, Abbot Papers, Microfilm copy, NL. Secondary accounts include Donald Wright, "Matthew Perry and the African Squadron," 80–90; de Kay, *Chronicles of the Frigate "Macedonian,"* 212–25.

30. Bridge, *African Cruiser,* 82–83.

31. MCP, Notes of a Palaver, Perry Letter Book, HSP.

32. MCP to D. Henshaw, 21 December 1843; MCP to Brown, 28 December 1843, both in Perry Letter Book, NA, M206.

33. Bridge, *African Cruiser,* 84–85.

34. MCP to D. Henshaw, 21, 26 December 1843, Perry Letter Book, NA, M206.

35. MCP to I. Mayo, 30 November 1843, Perry Letter Book, NA, M206; Bridge, *African Cruiser,* 66, 68–69; "Notes of Perry Interview with Russwurm," 7 December 1843, *NASP, Explorations,* ed. Thomas C. Cochran, 9:29–30.

36. MCP to Goldsborough, 15 January 1844, Perry Letter Book, NA.

37. Roberts to MCP, 3 January 1844; Russwurm to MCP, 23 December 1843; Kelly to MCP, Hazelhurst to MCP, all in *NASP, Explorations,* 9:49–51; Abbot to Picliens, December 1843, Abbot Papers, Microfilm copy, NM.

38. MCP to Goldsborough, 5 September 1843, Perry Letter Book, NA, M206.

39. MCP to W. Irving, 26 April 1844, Perry Letter Book, HSP.

40. MCP to A. Upshur, 21 July 1843; also MCP to Goldsborough, 27 June 1843; MCP to D. Henshaw, 22 November 1843; MCP to Goldsborough, 21 November 1843; MCP to Russwurm, 6 December 1843, all in Perry Letter Book, NA, M206.

41. MCP to Shubrick, 16, 17 May 1844; MCP to Secretary of the Navy, 17 May 1844, all in Perry Letter Book, NA, M206.

42. MCP to A. Upshur, 3 August 1843, *NASP, Explorations,* 9:12; Russwurm to MCP, 10 July 1843, ibid., 9:37; MCP to Henshaw, 26 December 1843, ibid., 9:16.

43. MCP to Tattnall, 12 February 1844; MCP to Henshaw, 26 December 1843, both in Perry Letter Book, NA, M206.

44. On the operation of the trade, see H. Thomas, *The Slave Trade;* George E. Brooks Jr., *Yankee Traders, Old Coasters and African Middlemen: A History of*

American Legitimate Trade with West Africa in the Nineteenth Century, 105–24; Peter Duignan and Clarence Clendenen, *The United States and the African Slave Trade, 1619–1862*.

45. MCP to A. Upshur, 7 April 1843; MCP to W. Hunter, 18 March 1843; MCP to Goldsborough, 7 April 1843, all in Perry Letter Book, NA, M206; also MCP to Secretary of the Navy, 21 March 1844, *NASP, Explorations*, 9:134–35.

46. Upshur to Perry, 30 March 1843, Miscellaneous Letters, Department of State, March–May 1843. On Perry's performance, see H. Thomas, *The Slave Trade*, 615–16, 627; Mannix, *Black Cargoes*, 220; de Kay, *Chronicles of the Frigate "Macedonian,"* 220–21, 224–25; Du Bois, *Suppression of the African Slave Trade*, 160–61. Booth, "United States African Squadron," 89–91.

47. MCP to Henshaw, 29 January 1844, *NASP, Explorations*, 9:153–56; also Bridge, *African Cruiser*, 53.

48. General Order 5, 21 July 1843, MCP to Foote, July 1843, both in Perry Letter Book, NA, M206.

49. MCP to Commanding Officers of Vessels . . . , 1 August 1843, Perry Letter Book, NA, M206.

50. MCP to J. Slidell, 23 March 1844, Perry Letter Book, HSP; J. Mason to MCP, 11 June 1844, 5 December 1844, 11 January 1845, Confidential Letters, I, NA.

51. MCP to Foote, 18 May 1844; MCP to Henshaw, 21 May 1844; MCP to T. Craven, 11 June 1844, all in Perry Letter Book, NA, M206.

52. The correspondence between Perry and Foote in March 1844 is in *NASP, Explorations*, 9:121–33. The quotation is from p. 133.

53. MCP to J. Mason, 25 November 1844, *NASP, Explorations*, 9:191.

54. MCP to Henshaw, 26 December 1843; DuBarry to MCP, 21 December 1843, both in *NASP, Explorations*, 9:103, 104; MCP to Henshaw, 2 March 1844, Perry Letter Book, NA, M206.

55. MCP to Secretary of the Navy, 4 July 1844, Perry Letter Book, NA, M206.

56. MCP to I. Mayo, 21 August, 30 September 1844; MCP to Glasson, 28 November 1844; MCP to J. Mason, 20 January 1845; MCP to Mason, 10 February 1845, all in Perry Letter Book, NA, M206.

57. DuBarry to MCP, 21 December 1843; Glentworth to DuBarry, 9 December 1843, both in *NASP, Explorations*, 9:104; Bridge, *African Cruiser*, 116, 155.

58. MCP to [Attorney General] J. Nelson, 2 December 1844; MCP to Mason, 23 January 1845; MCP to Roberts, 27 January 1845; also MCP to T. Freelon, 8 January 1845, all in Perry Letter Book, NA, M206.

59. MCP to Mason, 18 February 1845, Perry Letter Book, NA, M206.

60. Mason to MCP, Confidential Letters, I, NA; MCP to Skinner, 17 February 1845; MCP to Mason, 21 February 1845, both in Perry Letter Book, NA, M206.

Chapter 6. Commodore of the Gulf Squadron

1. *Congressional Globe*, 29th Cong., 1st sess. (1846), 792.

2. Russel B. Nye, *George Bancroft: Brahmin Rebel*, 144; G. Bancroft to Board

of Examiners, 13 June 1845, as printed in James Russell Soley, *Historical Sketch of the U.S. Naval Academy*, 43; also Charles Todorich, *The Spirited Years: A History of the Antebellum Naval Academy*, 14–18.

3. Report of Board to Bancroft, 25 June 1845, as printed in Soley, *Historical Sketch*, 44–49; also Report of the Secretary of Navy, *Congressional Globe*, 29th Cong., 1st sess. (December 1845), app., 17; Nye, *Bancroft*, 143–46; Craig L. Symonds, *Confederate Admiral: The Life and Wars of Franklin Buchanan*, 67–82; Charles Lee Lewis, *Admiral Franklin Buchanan: Fearless Man of Action*, 92–113.

4. MCP to Bancroft, 9 January 1846, Perry Letter Book, HSP.

5. Spencer Tucker, *Arming the Fleet: U.S. Navy Ordnance in the Muzzle-Loading Era*, 170–76, 196; Emmons, *The Navy of the United States*, 206.

6. MCP to W. Sinclair, 15 June 1851; also F. Buchanan to MCP, 9 February 1849, both in William Sinclair Papers, NAM.

7. Philip S. P. Conner, *The Home Squadron under Commodore Conner in the War with Mexico . . . 1846–1847*, 6; Conner to MCP, 12 November 1845; Bancroft to MCP, 10 December 1845, both in Perry Papers, HU.

8. J. Mason to MCP, 20 August 1846, Confidential Letters, I, NA.

9. The definitive account of the U.S. Navy in the Mexican War is K. Jack Bauer, *Surfboats and Horse Marines: U.S. Naval Operations in the Mexican War, 1846–1848*; also see K. Jack Bauer, *The Mexican War, 1846–1848*.

10. Raphael Semmes, *Service Afloat and Ashore during the Mexican War*, 107.

11. Ibid., 79; Letter of Semmes, [1846], as quoted in John M. Ellicott, *Life of John Ancrum Winslow, Rear Admiral, United States Navy*, 34.

12. Fitch W. Taylor, *The Broad Pennant; or, A Cruise in the United States Flag Ship of the Gulf Squadron*, 250; Letter of Winslow, 10 August 1846, as quoted in Ellicott, *Winslow*, 37.

13. F. W. Taylor, *Broad Pennant*, 256–62.

14. James D. Bruell, *Sea Memories, or Personal Experiences in the U.S. Navy in Peace and War*, 42; Letter of Winslow, 20 September 1846, as quoted in Ellicott, *Winslow*, 39; also F. W. Taylor, *Broad Pennant*, 283.

15. MCP to J. Hone, 6 October 1846, Perry Papers, HU.

16. Bauer, *Surfboats and Horse Marines*, 47; Semmes, *Service*, 88–89.

17. MCP to Conner, "With a Detailed Account . . . ," 3 November 1846, Squadron Letters, NA, M89, R85.

18. Semmes, *Service*, 90; Letter of Winslow, 4 November 1846, Ellicott, *Winslow*, 43.

19. Nelson Reed, *The Caste War of Yucatan*.

20. MCP to Conner, 17 December 1846, Squadron Letters, NA, M89, R85.

21. Memo of MCP, [January 1847], Squadron Letters, NA, M89, R86.

22. Ibid.

23. J. Slidell to JB/JKP, 6 January 1847, as printed in George Tichnor Curtis, *Life of James Buchanan, Fifteenth President of the United States*, 1:603–4. Also see William Harwar Parker, *Recollections of a Naval Officer, 1841–1865*, 67.

24. Semmes, *Service,* 480; Conner, *Home Squadron,* 11–12; James K. Polk, *The Diary of James K. Polk, 1845–1849,* ed. Milo M. Quaife, 2:392; J. Polk to J. Mason, 26 February 1847, Perry Papers, HU.

25. Mason to MCP, 25 February, 17 March 1847, Confidential Letters, I, NA; also MCP to J. Hone, 6 March 1847, Perry Papers, HU.

26. Winfield Scott, *Memoirs of Lieut.-General Scott,* 2:423–24.

27. Semmes, *Service,* 105–6.

28. Conner to Wife, 2 March 1847, as quoted in Morison, *"Old Bruin,"* 213; Semmes, *Service,* 128.

29. An excellent account of the landing is Bauer, *Surfboats and Horse Marines,* 242–47; also Semmes, *Service,* 126–27.

30. Mason to Conner, 3 March 1847, Confidential Letters, I, NA; Griffis, *Perry,* 222; also Semmes, *Service,* 133.

31. J. Upshur as quoted in Griffis, *Perry,* 222–23.

32. Bauer, *The Mexican War,* 251–52.

33. MCP to Mason, 29 March 1847, Squadron Letters, NA, M89, R86; Bauer, *Surfboats and Horse Marines,* 97; Mason to MCP, 15 April 1847, Confidential Letters, I, NA.

34. F. Buchanan to MCP, 9 February 1849, Sinclair Papers, NAM; Semmes, *Service.*

35. Bauer, *Surfboats and Horse Marines,* 100–102; Robert E. May, *John A. Quitman: Old South Crusader,* 175–76.

36. Mason to MCP, 4, 17 March, 3 April 1847, Confidential Letters, I, NA.

37. MCP to J. Hone, 30 April 1847, Perry Papers, HU; also MCP to Mason, 11 May 1847, Squadron Letters, NA, M89, R86.

38. Bauer, *Surfboats and Horse Marines,* 103–5; Morison, *"Old Bruin,"* 225–27; Symonds, *Confederate Admiral,* 86–87.

39. Mason to MCP, 17 May 1847, Confidential Letters, I, NA; Semmes, *Service,* 157–58.

40. MCP to Mason, 24 May 1847, Squadron Letters, NA, M89, R86; MCP to Mason, 13 May 1847, Perry Letter Book, HSP.

41. MCP to Mason, 24, 25 June 1847, Squadron Letters, NA, M89, R86.

42. C. L. Lewis, *Buchanan,* 120–21.

43. Ibid., 122; Mason to MCP, 23 July 1847, Confidential Letters, I, NA.

44. MCP to Mason, 1 May 1847; MCP to Henderson, 28 June 1847; MCP to Mason, 28 June, 4 July 1847, all in Perry Letter Book, HSP.

45. MCP to I. Perry, 8 July 1847, Perry Papers, Navy Historical Center Library, Washington, D.C.; also Dr. Lewis Minor to M. Blackford, 1 February 1848, William Lewis Minor Papers, AL.

46. MCP to Mason, 3, 4 August, 30 September 1847, all in Squadron Letters, NA, M89, R87; Loyall Farragut, *The Life of David Glasgow Farragut, First Admiral of the United States Navy,* 164.

47. MCP to Mason, 4 August, 28 July 1847; L. Minor to MCP, 5 August 1847, all in Squadron Letters, NA, M89, R87.

48. MCP to Mason, 16 August 1847, Squadron Letters, NA, M89, R87; Mason to MCP, 4 August 1847, Confidential Letters, I, NA.

49. Charles Lee Lewis, *David Glasgow Farragut: Admiral in the Making*, 140–41, 248–49; Farragut, *Farragut*, 156–57.

50. MCP to Mason, 17 December 1847, Squadron Letters, NA, M89, R87; Farragut, *Farragut*, 158.

51. MCP to Mason, 27 August, 30 September 1847, Squadron Letters, NA, M89, R87; Bauer, *Surfboats and Horse Marines*, 125.

52. Van Brunt to MCP, 13 August 1847; MCP to Mason, 17, 19, 14 October 1847, all in Squadron Letters, NA, M89, R87; also NASP, *Naval Affairs*, 5:183–86.

53. Mason to MCP, 9, 18 October 1847, 12 November 1847, Confidential Letters, I, NA.

54. Mary W. Williams, "Secessionist Diplomacy in Yucatan," 132–42; also N. Reed, *Caste War of Yucatan*, 53–97.

55. MCP to Mason, 25 September 1847, Squadron Letters, NA, M89, R87.

56. Louis De Armond, "Justo Sierra O'Reilly and Yucatan–United States Relations," 420–36.

57. M. Williams, "Secessionist Diplomacy in Yucatan," 139.

58. MCP to Mason, 10 January 1848, Squadron Letters, NA, M89, R88; MCP to J. Perry, 15, 16, 29 February 1848, Perry Papers, HU.

59. Mason to MCP, 24 February 1848; also Mason to MCP, 17 March 1848, both in Confidential Letters, I, NA; MCP to J. Hone, 28 March 1848, Perry Papers, HU; MCP to Mason, 7 June 1848, Squadron Letters, NA, M89, R89.

60. MCP to Mason, 13, 25 March, 25 April 1848, Perry Letter Book, HSP.

61. MCP to Bigelow, 16 May 1848; also MCP to Bigelow, 5 May, 30 June 1848; MCP to Mendez, 10 June 1848, all in Squadron Letters, NA, M89, R89.

62. W. Redfield to MCP, 29 December 1847, 25 January, 6 March 1848; MCP to Redfield, 4 August 1848, all in Redfield Papers, BL.

63. MCP to Mason, 21 November 1848, Squadron Letters, NA, M89, R89.

CHAPTER 7. PLANNING THE NAVAL EXPEDITION TO JAPAN

1. *New York Herald*, 9 November 1849.

2. Diary of Philip Hone, 3 September 184, in Samuel Eliot Morrison Papers, LC. For Belmont, see David Black, *King of Fifth Avenue: The Fortunes of August Belmont*; and Irving Katz, *August Belmont: A Political Biography*.

3. Jane Perry to Caroline Perry, 19 August 1850, Perry Papers, HU.

4. Mason to MCP, 14 November 1848, Rodgers Family Papers, NHF, LC.

5. John G. B. Hutchins, *The American Maritime Industries and Public Policy, 1789–1914*, 353–54. Also David B. Tyler, *Steam Conquers the Atlantic*.

6. MCP to Preston, 14 June 1849, Captains' Letters, NA, M125, R345; also Harold D. Langley, "William Ballard Preston," in *American Secretaries of the Navy*, ed. Paolo Colletta, 1:243–56, 246.

7. David B. Tyler, *Steam Conquers the Atlantic*, 200; MCP to Preston, 14 June 1849; MCP et al. to Preston, 31 August 1849, Captains' Letters, NA, M125, R346.

8. Hutchins, *American Maritime Industries*, 355–56; Morison, *"Old Bruin,"* 259.

9. Sloo to MCP, 15 October 1849, Perry Letter Book, SL; Tyler, *Steam Conquers the Atlantic*, 183; Morison, *"Old Bruin,"* 258; also Charles B. Stuart, *The Naval and Mail Steamers of the United States.*

10. MCP to Preston, 9 April 1850, Captains' Letters, NA, M125, R347.

11. MCP to Graham, 22 September 1851; also MCP to Graham, 30 July, 28 August 1851, all in Perry Letter Book, SL.

12. *Congressional Globe*, 32d Cong., 1st sess., app., 609 (17 May 1852); also Tyler, *Steam Conquers the Atlantic*, 205. After a collision in the Atlantic, the *Arctic* sank off Newfoundland in September 1854.

13. Langley, *Social Reform*, 237–38. For a contemporary fictional description of flogging, see Herman Melville, *White Jacket, or, The World in a Man of War*, 135–53.

14. MCP to Preston, 4 February 1850, Perry Letter Book, SL.

15. Langley, "Preston," in Colletta, ed., *American Secretaries*, 1:249.

16. Russell Weigley, *The American Way of War: A History of United States Military Strategy and Policy*, 60; ASP, *Military Affairs*, 2:304–13, 3:245–60.

17. MCP to Graham, 25 July 1851, Perry Letter Book, SL.

18. Ibid.; also MCP to Graham, 2 letters dated 2 November 1850, Captains' Letters, NA, M125, R347; Sprout and Sprout, *Rise of American Naval Power*, 137–40.

19. Tyler Dennett, *Americans in Eastern Asia: A Critical Study of the Policy of the United States with Reference to China, Japan and Korea in the Nineteenth Century*; John K. Fairbank, *Trade and Diplomacy on the China Coast: The Opening of the Treaty Ports, 1842–1854*; Eldon Griffin, *Clippers and Consuls: American Consular and Commercial Relations with Eastern Asia, 1845–1860*; Foster Rhea Dulles, *The Old China Trade.*

20. Schroeder, *Shaping a Maritime Empire*, 143; also Elmo P. Hohman, *The American Whalemen: A History of Life and Labor in the Whaling Industry*; Alexander Starbuck, *History of the American Whale Fishery from Its Earliest Inception to the Year 1876*; Walter S. Tower, *A History of the American Whale Fishery.*

21. Foster Rhea Dulles, *Yankees and Samurai: America's Role in the Emergence of Modern Japan, 1791–1900*, 23–26, 30–32; "Cruise of the U.S. Sloop-of-War *Preble*, Commander James Glynn, to Napa and Nangasacki [*sic*]," SED 59, 32d Cong., 1st sess., in *NASP, Naval Affairs*, 3:246–61.

22. See, e.g., "Daniel Webster and the Pacific and East Asia," in *The Papers of Daniel Webster: Diplomatic Papers,* ed. Kenneth E. Shewmaker and Kenneth R. Stevens, 2:245–59; also Elbert B. Smith, *The Presidencies of Zachary Taylor and Millard Fillmore,* 223–25; Robert Remini, *Daniel Webster: The Man and His Time,* 710–13.

23. *Congressional Globe,* 31st Cong., 2d sess., app., 12. For Graham as secretary of the navy, see Max R. Williams, "Secretary William A. Graham, Naval Administrator, 1850–1852," 53–72; Harold D. Langley, "William Alexander Graham," both in *American Secretaries of the Navy,* ed. Paolo Colletta, 1:257–67.

24. Long, *Nothing Too Daring,* 173–74; Allan B. Cole, "Captain David Porter's Proposed Expedition to the Pacific and Japan, 1815," 61–65; Dulles, *Yankees and Samurai,* 1–39; Dennett, *Americans in Eastern Asia;* Shunzo Sakamaki, "Japan and the United States, 1790–1853," 175–90.

25. David F. Long, *Sailor-Diplomat: A Biography of Commodore James Biddle,* 209–20; "Report of a Visit to Japan," SED 59, 32d Cong., 1st sess., in *NASP, Naval Affairs,* 3:241–43.

26. MCP to Graham, 27 January 1851, in William A. Graham, *The Papers of William Alexander Graham,* ed. J. G. de Roulhac Hamilton, 4:16–22, 22, 18, 17.

27. Ibid., 18.

28. Ibid., 20–21.

29. "Daniel Webster and the Pacific and East Asia," 2:253–55.

30. Webster to Graham, 9 May 1851; Fillmore to Emperor of Japan, 10 May 1851, both quoted in "Daniel Webster and the Pacific and East Asia," 253, 289.

31. Webster to Aulick, 10 June 1851, in "Daniel Webster and the Pacific and East Asia," 290; Graham to Aulick, 31 May 1851, *NASP, Naval Affairs,* 3:268–75.

32. MCP to Sinclair, 26 May 1851; also 6, 15 June 1851, all in Sinclair Papers, NAM.

33. Graham to MCP, 18 November 1851, *Graham Papers,* 4:216.

34. MCP to Graham, 3 December 1851, *Graham Papers,* 4:221–22.

35. Notes Accompanying Letter, 2 December 1851, Perry Letter Book, SL.

36. Accounts of preparations, in Wiley, *Yankees in the Land of the Gods,* 104–20; Morison, *"Old Bruin,"* 270–89; Walworth, *Black Ships off Japan,* 19–31.

37. MCP to Graham, 3 December 1851, *Graham Papers,* 4:222.

38. Letters of Dr. Charles Wheelwright, 16 May, 28 July 1853, in Charles H. Wheelwright, *Correspondence of Dr. Charles H. Wheelwright, Surgeon of the United States Navy,* ed. Hildegarde B. Forbes, 187, 193.

39. Graham to MCP, 27 March 1852, Confidential Letters, II, NA; Samuel Eliot Morison, "Commodore Perry's Japan Expedition Press and Shipboard Theatre," 36–37.

40. Hawks, ed., *Narrative,* 1:78; also Ponko, *Ships, Seas, and Scientists;* G. Smith, "The Navy before Darwinism," 41–55.

41. MCP, *Personal Journal*, 8, 6. The most detailed firsthand account of the preparations for the expedition is Hawks, *Narrative*, 1:75–80.

42. Stanton, *Great United States Exploring Expedition*, 116, 119, 120–21, 137–38. For Perry's relations with Dr. James Morrow, see A. Hunter Dupree, "Science vs. the Military: Dr. James Morrow and the Perry Expedition," 29–37; also James Morrow, *A Scientist with Perry in Japan: The Journal of Dr. James Morrow*.

43. MCP to Graham, 27 March 1852, Rodgers Family Papers, NHF, LC; Graham to MCP, 31 March 1852, Confidential Letters, II, NA.

44. A list of the gifts is included in MCP, *Personal Journal*, app. D, 233–34.

45. Wiley, *Yankees in the Land of the Gods*, 114–15.

46. Morison, "*Old Bruin*," 276.

47. MCP to Graham, 27 January 1851, *Graham Papers*, 4:17, 18.

48. For background on Japan, see W. G. Beasley, *The Meiji Restoration*; Conrad Totman, *Politics in the Tokugawa Bakufu, 1600–1843*; Richard T. Chang, *From Prejudice to Tolerance: A Study of the Japanese Image of the West, 1826–1864*; *The Nineteenth Century*, vol. 5 of *The Cambridge History of Japan*, ed. Marius B. Jansen, 259–366; J. Victor Koschmann, *The Mito Ideology: Discourse, Reform and Insurrection in Late Tokugawa Japan, 1790–1864*; George B. Sansom, *A History of Japan, 1615–1867*.

49. Beasley, *The Meiji Restoration*, 41; an excellent summary is Peter Duus, *The Japanese Discovery of America: A Brief History with Documents*.

50. Sakamaki, "Japan and the United States," 127.

51. Hisakazu Kaneko, *Manjiro: The Man Who Discovered America*; Emily V. Warinner, *Voyager to Destiny*; Katherine Plummer, *The Shogun's Reluctant Ambassadors*.

52. Dulles, *Yankees and Samurai*, 49.

53. Ibid., 50; George M. Brooke Jr., *John M. Brooke: Naval Scientist and Educator*, 201.

54. *Congressional Globe*, 32d Cong., 1st sess., 943–44; also Wiley, *Yankees in the Land of the Gods*, 112–13.

55. J. P. Kennedy to MCP, 25 July 1852, Confidential Letters, II, NA.

56. MCP to Secretary of the Navy, 13 December 1852; also MCP to Seymour, 13 1852, SED 34, 33d Congress, 2d sess., 11, 12; MCP to J. Perry, 18 August 1852, Perry Papers, HU.

57. Kennedy to MCP, 13 November 1852, SED 34:2–3.

58. Conrad to Kennedy, 5 November 1852, SED 34:5–6.

59. Ibid., 7, 8, 9.

60. Official Proclamation of President Millard Fillmore, 11 November 1852; Fillmore to Emperor of Japan, n.d., SED 34:9–11.

61. MCP to J. Perry, 17 November 1852, Perry Papers, HU.

62. "Memorandum of Property and Liabilities of M. C. Perry, 1 November 1852," Perry Papers, HU.

63. *Baltimore American* as printed in *National Intelligencer,* 9 November 1852; see also ibid., 18 November, 7 December 1852.

64. *Baltimore Sun,* 25 November 1852, as quoted in Inazo Nitobe, *The Intercourse between the United States and Japan,* 43.

65. MCP to J. Perry, 24 November 1852, Perry Papers, HU.

Chapter 8. East Asia and Japan

1. Spalding, *The Japan Expedition,* 130–31; MCP, *Personal Journal,* 91; also Sewall, *Logbook of the Captain's Clerk,* 352.

2. MCP to Kennedy, 14 December 1852; Everett to MCP, 15 February 1853, both in SED 34:12–15.

3. Robert Danby, "Journal of a Cruise in the United States Steam Frigate *Mississippi* [1852–1855]", Misc. Manuscripts, LC; also MCP, *Personal Journal,* 19. For an estimate of coal consumption, see entry for 7 April 1853 in Danby, "Journal."

4. MCP, *Personal Journal,* 22, 24, 46–47.

5. Ibid., 53–54; MCP to Secretary of the Navy, 9 April 1853, SED 34:17.

6. Edward Robie, Pocket Diary, 1853, Edward Dunning Robie Papers, NAM; F. Mallory to Graham, 5 November 1850, *Graham Papers,* 3:476; Wheelwright to My Dear Mary, 28 July 1853, *Wheelwright Correspondence,* 193; also Sewall, *Logbook of the Captain's Clerk,* 157–58; Robie, Pocket Diary, 1854.

7. J. Abbot to Mrs. Abbot, 22 April 1844, Abbot Papers, Microfilm copy, NL.

8. Curtis T. Henson Jr., *Commissioners and Commodores: The East India Squadron and American Diplomacy in China;* Robert Erwin Johnson, *Far China Station: The U.S. Navy in Asian Waters, 1800–1898;* Fairbank, *Trade and Diplomacy on the China Coast;* Te-kong Tong, *United States Diplomacy in China, 1844–1860;* Griffin, *Clippers and Consuls.*

9. MCP, *Personal Journal,* 57.

10. Dennett, *Americans in Eastern Asia,* 206; Chester A. Bain, "Commodore Matthew Perry, Humphrey Marshall and the Taiping Rebellion," 258–70, 259–60.

11. MCP, *Personal Journal,* 54; MCP to Secretary of the Navy, 3 May 1853, Squadron Letters, NA, M89, R7; R. E. Johnson, *Far China Station,* 60.

12. Journal of S. W. Williams, 4 July 1853, in *The Life and Letters of Samuel Wells Williams,* 192–93; also S. W. Williams, "Journal of the Perry Expedition," 89, 142; and, on crudeness of officers, 114.

13. MCP, *Personal Journal,* 55.

14. MCP to Secretary of the Navy, 6 May 1853, SED 34:19; MCP, *Personal Journal,* 57–58.

15. MCP to Secretary of the Navy, 7 May 1853; Marshall to MCP, 13 May 1853, both in SED 34:19–20, 23–26.

16. See Henson, *Commissioners and Commodores,* 92–95; Bain, "Perry and Marshall"; R. E. Johnson, *Far China Station,* 62; Dennett, *Americans in Eastern Asia,* 206.

17. MCP to Marshall, 16 May 1853; Kelly to MCP, 15 May 1853; Merchants to Marshall, 7 May 1853; Marshall to MCP, 7 May 1853; MCP to Marshall, 12 May 1853, all in SED 34:22–23, 27–28.

18. William Heine, *With Perry in Japan. A Memoir by William Heine*, ed. Frederic Trautman; MCP to Sinclair, as quoted in Morison, *"Old Bruin,"* 303; B. Taylor, *Visit to India, China, and Japan*, 366, 367; also Spalding, *The Japan Expedition*, 103–5.

19. S. W. Williams, "Journal of the Perry Expedition," 11, 17, 20, 41, 42, 46, 80–88, 248; Danby, "Journal," 22–23; George Henery Preble, *The Opening of Japan: A Diary of Discovery in the Far East, 1853–1856*, ed. Boleslaw Szczesniak, 107; MCP, *Personal Journal*, 61. For Bettelheim's account, see William L. Schwartz, ed., "Commodore Perry at Okinawa, from the Unpublished Diary of a British Missionary," 262–76.

20. MCP, *Personal Journal*, 65.

21. Hawks, *Narrative*, 1:193.

22. Firsthand descriptions include S. W. Williams, "Journal of the Perry Expedition," 20–23; Spalding, *The Japan Expedition*, 120–24; Heine, *With Perry in Japan*, 44–48; and B. Taylor, *Visit to India, China, and Japan*, 377–88.

23. B. Taylor, *Visit to India, China, and Japan*, 373, 374, 388.

24. MCP to Secretary of the Navy, 25 June 1853, SED 34:31, 29.

25. The handwritten agreement is in the Perry Papers, HU; MCP, *Personal Journal*, 74, 79; MCP to Secretary of the Navy, 25 June 1853, SED 34:31–32.

26. J. Kelly to MCP, 26 June 1853; Russell & Company et al. to J. Kelly, 23 May 1853, both in SED 34:40–41, 42.

27. MCP to Secretary of the Navy, 28 June 1853; J. Dobbin to MCP, 18 October 1853, both in SED 34:40, 43.

28. MCP to Secretary of the Navy, 25 June 1853, SED 34:32.

29. MCP, *Personal Journal*, 85, 86.

30. B. Taylor, *Visit to India, China, and Japan*, 412, 413.

31. Ibid., 413, 415.

32. MCP, *Personal Journal*, 90–91.

33. Ibid., 91; Hawks, *Narrative*, 1:235.

34. MCP, *Personal Journal*, 92; B. Taylor, *Visit to India, China, and Japan*, 418, 419.

35. MCP, *Personal Journal*, 94; Buchanan was the chief American negotiator. In his negotiations he used the title "Admiral" because the Japanese were not familiar with "Commodore." See F. Buchanan to J. Dobbin, 3 March 1855; and Buchanan's "Notes on Interviews, 9, 11, 12, 13 July 1853," Commanders' Letters, NA, M147.

36. Beasley, *The Meiji Restoration*, 87–90; Conrad Totman, "The Struggle for Control of the Shogunate (1853–1858)"; Conrad Totman, "Political Reconciliation

in the Tokugawa Bakufu: Abe Masahiro and Tokugawa Nariaki," Harold Bolitho, "Abe Masahiro and the New Japan," 173–88.

37. W. G. Beasley, trans. and ed., *Select Documents on Japanese Foreign Policy, 1853–1868,* 20–22.

38. B. Taylor, *Visit to India, China, and Japan,* 420, 419; Beasley, *Select Documents,* 23.

39. Hawks, *Narrative,* 1:241; Wiley, *Yankees in the Land of the Gods,* 304, 308.

40. Hawks, *Narrative,* 1:240–41; MCP, *Personal Journal,* 96.

41. B. Taylor, *Visit to India, China, and Japan,* 417–18.

42. Ibid., 426.

43. Ibid., 427; also Heine, *With Perry in Japan,* 70–74; Spalding, *The Japan Expedition,* 152–65; S. W. Williams, "Journal of the Perry Expedition," 65.

44. Morison, *"Old Bruin,"* 332. Among the items presented to the Japanese were a white flag and a letter from Perry. The letter attempted to intimidate Japanese officials by explaining that in the event the Japanese elected war rather than negotiation, they could use the white flag to sue for peace since victory would naturally belong to the Americans. See "Perry's Letter in Connection with the Delivery of a White Flag, [July 14], 1853," trans. Masatoshi Knishi, in *Meiji Japan through Contemporary Sources,* 2:15–16; Miwa Kimitada, "Perry's 'White Flags': From Their Deletion in His Own Records to Their Reemergence in Historical Writings." Perry did not mention the white flag or the letter in his *Personal Journal,* the *Narrative,* or his correspondence with the Navy Department.

45. B. Taylor, *Visit to India, China, and Japan,* 434; William Rutherford to Sarah L. Baldwin, 17 July 1853, William H. Rutherford Papers, LC; S. W. Williams, "Journal of the Perry Expedition," 65; Spalding, *The Japan Expedition,* 165.

46. MCP, *Personal Journal,* 100–102.

47. Notes Accompanying MCP Letter to Graham, 2 December 1851, Perry Letter Book, SL; also MCP to J. Perry, 25 April, 31 May 1853, Perry Papers, HU.

48. Hawks, *Narrative,* 1:273; MCP, *Personal Journal,* 103; Letter of MCP, 14 July 1853, *Personal Journal,* 103; MCP to Secretary of the Navy, 3 August 1853, Squadron Letters, NA, M89, R7.

49. MCP, *Personal Journal,* 100, 103–4.

50. W. Rutherford to S. Baldwin, 17 July 1853, Rutherford Papers, LC; B. Taylor, *Visit to India, China, and Japan,* 440.

51. MCP, *Personal Journal,* 109.

52. Ibid., 110–11; Spalding, *The Japan Expedition,* 134.

53. MCP, *Personal Journal,* 120; MCP to Secretary of the Navy, 2, 26 September 1853, both in SED 34:64, 69.

54. MCP to J. Perry, 19 August 1853, Perry Papers, HU.

55. American Merchants to MCP, 18 August 1853; MCP to American Merchants, 24 August 1853; MCP to Secretary of the Navy, 26 September 1853, all in SED 34:61–63, 69.

56. MCP to Secretary of the Navy, 31 August 1853, SED 34:59–60.

57. Marshall to W. Marcy, 6 July 1853, in *American Diplomatic and Public Papers: The United States and China. Series 1: The Treaty System and the Taiping Rebellion, 1842–1860*, ed. Jules Davids, 4:68–74.

58. Marshall to MCP, 22 September 1853, SED 34:72; Marshal to Marcy, 21 September 1853, in Davids, *American Diplomatic and Public Papers*, 4:230, 198–205.

59. MCP to Marshall, 29 September 1853, SED 34:73, 74.

60. MCP to Secretary of the Navy, 2 September, 9 October 1853, both in SED 34:64–65, 70.

61. Marshall to Marcy, 30 October 1853, in Davids, *American Diplomatic and Public Papers*, 4:234–42, 235.

62. MCP to Marshall, 29 December, 2 September 1853, both in SED 34:64–65.

63. MCP, *Personal Journal*, 136; MCP to Secretary of the Navy, 20 November 1853, SED 34:78.

64. J. Perry to W. Sinclair, 17 November 1853, Sinclair Papers, NAM; MCP to J. Perry, 24 December, 25 November 1853, both in Perry Papers, HU.

65. MCP to Secretary of the Navy, 9 January 1854, SED 34:101–2; Dobbin to MCP, 28 October 1853, Confidential Letters, III, NA.

66. MCP to Secretary of the Navy, 2 September 1853, 14 January 1854, both in SED 34:65, 105–6.

67. MCP to Secretary of the Navy, 25 January 1854, SED 34:108–11.

68. D. Van Twist to MCP, 23 December 1853; MCP to Van Twist, 23 January 1854, both in SED 34:111–12.

69. Dobbin to MCP, 14 November 1853, 30 May 1854, Confidential Letters, III, NA.

CHAPTER 9. A TREATY WITH JAPAN, SIGNED AND TESTED

1. Hawks, *Narrative*, 1:336; for the weather, see Preble, *Diary of Discovery*, 116, 117; S. W. Williams, "Journal of the Perry Expedition," 99–100; Henry R. Graff, ed., *Bluejackets with Perry in Japan. A Day-by-Day Account Kept by Master's Mate John R. C. Lewis and Cabin Boy William B. Allen*, 162–63; Wheelwright to T. B. Pope, 22 March 1854, *Wheelwright Correspondence*, 202.

2. Journal of J. Abbot, 11, 12 February 1854; Abbot to J. Smith, 23 March 1854, Abbot Papers, Microfilm copy, NL.

3. MCP, *Personal Journal*, 156; Journal of J. Abbot, 28 February 1854, Abbot Papers, Microfilm copy, NL; also Edward Robie, Pocket Diary, March 1854, Robie Papers, NAM; S. W. Williams, "Journal of the Perry Expedition," 107; William Speiden, Journal, LC.

4. Morison, "Commodore Perry's Japan Expedition Press," 36–43; Spalding, *The Japan Expedition*, 175; Preble, *Diary of Discovery*, 156.

5. MCP, *Personal Journal*, 159.

6. Beasley, *Select Documents*, 97; Beasley, *The Meiji Restoration*, 89–97; Wiley, *Yankees in the Land of the Gods*, 327–46.

7. Beasley, *Select Documents*, 24–25.
8. "Diary of an Official of the Bakufu," ed. D. Hayashi, 98–119, 98, 99–101; MCP, *Personal Journal*, 158.
9. "Diary of an Official of the Bakufu," 99.
10. Letter of MCP, 20 February 1854, as printed in MCP, *Personal Journal*, 160–61; also Letter of MCP, 18 February 1854, MCP, *Personal Journal*, 160. The description of Edo Bay is from ibid., 162; also J. Goldsborough to A. D. Bache, 15 May 1854, in Julia MacLeod, "Three Letters Relating to the Perry Expedition to Japan," 228–37, 236.
11. MCP, *Personal Journal*, 163; MCP to Hayashi, 1 March 1854, ibid., 163–64.
12. Ibid., 164.
13. "Diary of an Official of the Bakufu," 101.
14. S. W. Williams, "Journal of the Perry Expedition," 123; Spalding, *The Japan Expedition*, 224–25.
15. Graff, *Bluejackets with Perry*, 165; other descriptions include S. W. Williams, "Journal of the Perry Expedition," 123–27; Spalding, *The Japan Expedition*, 224–25; John Glendy Sproston, *A Private Journal of John Glendy Sproston*, ed. Shio Sakanishi, 8–10.
16. MCP, *Personal Journal*, 184, 185; Response of Japan to Letter of President Fillmore, printed in ibid., app. E, 222; "Diary of Official of the Bakufu," 102–6; S. W. Williams, "Journal of the Perry Expedition," 124–27.
17. "Diary of an Official of the Bakufu," 103; MCP, *Personal Journal*, 165–66. Also Wiley, *Yankees in the Land of the Gods*, 401.
18. "Diary of an Official of the Bakufu," 104, 105.
19. Ibid., 106. An excellent discussion of this incident is Wiley, *Yankees in the Land of the Gods*, 405.
20. MCP, *Personal Journal*, 166; MCP to Graham, 27 January 1851, *Graham Papers*, 4:20–21; Notes Accompanying Letter from MCP to Graham, 2 December 1851, Perry Letter Book, SL.
21. "Diary of an Official of the Bakufu," 106; Spalding, *The Japan Expedition*, 232.
22. Graff, *Bluejackets with Perry*, 130; S. W. Williams, "Journal of the Perry Expedition," 128; Spalding, *The Japan Expedition*, 235–40 (the account in Spalding is of the chaplain of the *Mississippi*); Speiden, Journal, 165–79, Speiden Papers, LC; Hawks, *Narrative*, 1:353–55.
23. The list of gifts is printed in MCP, *Personal Journal*, app. D, 233–34; Sproston, *Private Journal*, 10; Spalding, *The Japan Expedition*, 241–43.
24. S. W. Williams, "Journal of the Perry Expedition," 147–48; Spalding, *The Japan Expedition*, 247–48; Sproston, *Private Journal*, 13–14; "Diary of an Official of the Bakufu," 111–12. An excellent secondary account is Wiley, *Yankees in the Land of the Gods*, 418.
25. MCP, *Personal Journal*, 188.

26. Preble, *Diary of Discovery,* 153; also S. W. Williams, "Journal of the Perry Expedition," 249–51.

27. "Diary of an Official of the Bakufu," 110–11; Spalding, *The Japan Expedition,* 244–46; S. W. Williams, "Journal of the Perry Expedition," 136–37; Wheelwright to T. B. Pope, 22 March 1854, *Wheelwright Correspondence,* 204. Secondary accounts are Wiley, *Yankees in the Land of the Gods,* 410; and Morison, *"Old Bruin,"* 372–73.

28. On the miserable weather, see Preble, *Diary of Discovery,* 124, 137, 142, 154, 160. On the food, ibid., 156; Spalding, *The Japan Expedition,* 243–44.

29. S. W. Williams, "Journal of the Perry Expedition," 129; "Diary of an Official of the Bakufu," 108–10, 114–15.

30. Wiley, *Yankees in the Land of the Gods,* 410–12; "Diary of an Official of the Bakufu," 112; MCP to Secretary of the Navy, 1 April 1854, SED 34:145–46; MCP, *Personal Journal,* 174.

31. Preble, *Diary of Discovery,* 155; "Diary of an Official of the Bakufu," 115.

32. "Notes explanatory of the several articles of the treaty with Japan, [April, 1854]," SED 34:148–50, 149. The Treaty of Kanagawa and related material is printed in Miller, *Treaties and Other International Acts of the United States,* 6:439–666.

33. S. W. Williams, "Journal of the Perry Expedition," 158; Spalding, *The Japan Expedition,* 256; Graff, *Bluejackets with Perry,* 178.

34. MCP, *Personal Journal,* 180–81; S. W. Williams, "Journal of the Perry Expedition," 158–59, 114.

35. Wheelwright to Pope, 22 March 1854, Wheelwright to E. Wheelwright, 3 May 1854, *Wheelwright Correspondence,* 203, 204, 205, 207–8; Spalding, *The Japan Expedition,* 266; MCP, *Personal Journal,* 177, 186.

36. MCP, *Personal Journal,* 186, 188, 190.

37. Hawks, *Narrative,* 1:405; Preble, *Diary of Discovery,* 123, 126, 137; Heine, *With Perry in Japan,* 136.

38. S. W. Williams, "Journal of the Perry Expedition," 183–84; Preble, *Diary of Discovery,* 204–5; Heine, *With Perry in Japan,* 133–34.

39. MCP, *Personal Journal,* 181; Spalding, *The Japan Expedition,* 272–73.

40. MCP, *Personal Journal,* 180; Hawks, *Narrative,* 1:17, 395.

41. "Diary of an Official of the Bakufu," 117, 119; Preble, *Diary of Discovery,* 161; Spalding, *The Japan Expedition,* 258–60; Also MCP, *Personal Journal,* 198–200; and Hawks, *Narrative,* 1:398–99.

42. MCP, *Personal Journal,* 200, 198.

43. Danby, "Journal"; Spalding, *The Japan Expedition,* 264–65; also S. W. Williams, "Journal of the Perry Expedition," 203–4; Sproston, *Private Journal,* 36–42, 56–58; Preble, *Diary of Discovery,* 203–5.

44. Wiley, *Yankees in the Land of the Gods,* 428; Spalding, *The Japan Expedition,* 276, 281–85.

45. Oliver Statler, *The Black Ship Scroll: An Account of the Perry Expedition at Shimoda in 1854 and the Lively Beginnings of People-to-People Relations between Japan and America*, 60–61, 75–76.

46. Wiley, *Yankees in the Land of the Gods*, 433; Graff, *Bluejackets with Perry*, 228–30, 233.

47. MCP to Secretary of the Navy, 30 May 1854, SED 34:151; description from Preble, *Diary of Discovery*, 186–88; Sproston, *Private Journal*, 43–48.

48. Sproston, *Private Journal*, 43; Preble, *Diary of Discovery*, 186, 188.

49. Preble, *Diary of Discovery*, 196; S. W. Williams, "Journal of the Perry Expedition," 191; Wiley, *Yankees in the Land of the Gods*, 436; also Sproston, *Private Journal*, 50.

50. Hawks, *Narrative*, 1:473–75.

51. S. W. Williams, "Journal of the Perry Expedition," 122–23.

52. Wiley, *Yankees in the Land of the Gods*, app. 2, 504–5.

53. S. W. Williams, "Journal of the Perry Expedition," 228–42; also Spalding, *The Japan Expedition*, 336; Hawks, *Narrative*, 1:493–95; Wiley, *Yankees in the Land of the Gods*, 447, 537, n. 38.

54. Spalding, *The Japan Expedition*, 339; Wiley, *Yankees in the Land of the Gods*, 447. The treaty and related material is printed in Miller, *Treaties and Other International Acts of the United States*, 6:743–86.

55. Dobbin to MCP, 25 February 1854, SED 34:116.

56. Dobbin to MCP, 30 May 1854, SED 34:112–13.

57. American Merchants to MCP, 4 September 1854, SED 34:186–87.

58. 18 September 1854 Abbot to Son John; also Abbot to J. Pope, 18 September 1854, both in Abbot Papers, Microfilm copy, NL; Edward Robie, Pocket Diary, 1854, Robie Papers, NAM; Spalding, *The Japan Expedition*, 336, also 337, 339, 351.

59. Symonds, *Confederate Admiral*, 112–14.

60. Abbot to J. Smith, 9 September 1854, Abbot Papers, Microfilm copy, NL.

61. Letter to Perry, 31 July 1854, SED 34:185.

62. R. E. Johnson, *Far China Station*, 72–73.

CHAPTER 10. HOME AT LAST

1. MCP to Webb, 12 December 1854, as quoted in Wiley, *Yankees in the Land of the Gods*, 456–57.

2. Fillmore to MCP, 21 January 1855; Everett to MCP, 6 January 1855; Irving to MCP, 5 January 1855; also Kennedy to MCP, 25 January 1855, all in Perry Papers, HU.

3. Remarks of MCP to Governor of Rhode Island at Newport, [June 1855], Perry Papers, HU.

4. J. Smith to Abbot, 15 March 1855, Abbot Papers, Microfilm copy, NL.

5. Richard Hildreth, *Japan, as It Was and Is*, 537–38; Spalding, *The Japan Expe-*

dition, 351–53. For a pessimistic note on future trade prospects, see S. W. Williams, "Products of Japan—Probable Effect of Opening of Japan to Foreign Trade"; Hildreth, *Japan, as It Was and Is,* 558–69.

6. MCP to C. Perry, 29 December 1856; MCP to Belmont, 7 November 1856, 26 May, 23 July 1856, all in Perry Papers, HU.

7. "Safety of Steamers at Sea," *DeBow's Review* 18 (1855): 369–73.

8. Frances L. Williams, *Matthew Fontaine Maury, Scientist of the Sea,* 269–93; Symonds, *Confederate Admiral,* 115–27.

9. MCP to Belmont, 18 August 1857; J. Perry to C. Perry, 12 November 1855; also J. Perry to C. Perry, 17 September 1856; MCP to Belmont, 14 March 1856, all in Perry Papers, HU. For Buchanan's attitude, see Symonds, *Confederate Admiral,* 117–19, 125.

10. Hawks, *Narrative.* For reviews, see *North American Review* 82 (1856): 559–62; *Harper's Weekly,* 13 March 1858, 172–74; and *Leslie's Illustrated,* 13 March 1858, 119.

11. Hawks, *Narrative.*

12. "Remarks of Commodore Perry upon the Expediency of Extending Further Encouragement to American Commerce in the East"; "Remarks of Commodore Perry upon the Probable Future Commercial Relations with Japan and Lew Chew," both in Hawks, *Narrative,* 2:173–84, 185–90; MCP, *A Paper by Commodore M. C. Perry, U.S.N., Read before the American Geographical and Statistical Society . . . March 6th, 1856.*

13. Danby, "Journal."

14. MCP, *Paper before the American Geographical and Statistical Society,* 10.

15. Ibid., 28; MCP, "Remarks upon American Commerce in the East," in Hawks, *Narrative,* 181–82.

16. Ibid., 180.

17. MCP, *Paper before the American Geographical and Statistical Society,* 28, 29.

18. J. Perry to C. Perry, Christmas Day 1857, Perry Papers, HU.

19. *Morning Courier and New York Enquirer,* 8 March 1858; also *New York Herald,* 7 March 1858.

20. *Morning Courier and New York Enquirer,* 5 March 1858.

21. C. B. Perry, *Perrys of Rhode Island,* 67.

22. Semmes, *Service,* 149.

23. MCP, *Personal Journal,* 159.

24. Certificate, Department of Health, New York City, 11 May 1866, Perry Papers, HU. A copy of Perry's will is also in the Perry Papers, HU.

⁓ᴈ *Bibliography* ᴂ⁓

PRIMARY SOURCES

UNPUBLISHED OFFICIAL RECORDS AND MANUSCRIPTS

Joel Abbot Papers (Microfilm), Nimitz Library, U.S. Naval Academy, Annapolis, Maryland.

John Aulick Papers, Nimitz Library, U.S. Naval Academy, Annapolis, Maryland.

Robert Danby Journal, Manuscript Division, Library of Congress.

Frank Marx Etting Papers, Historical Society of Pennsylvania.

Simon Gratz Papers, Historical Society of Pennsylvania.

Journal of the *Cyane,* 1820, Naval Academy Museum.

Journal of the *President,* 1812, Rodgers Family Papers, Historical Society of Pennsylvania.

Logbook of the *Concord,* 1830–32, National Archives.

Logbook of the *Concord,* 1832, Historical Society of Pennsylvania.

Logbook of the *Cyane,* 1820, National Archives.

Logbook of the *Shark,* 1822–23, National Archives.

William Lewis Minor Papers, Alderman Library, University of Virginia.

Samuel Eliot Morison Papers, Manuscript Division, Library of Congress.

Hamilton Patterson Journal, Historical Society of Pennsylvania.

Matthew Calbraith Perry Papers, Historical Society of Pennsylvania.

Matthew Calbraith Perry Papers, Houghton Library, Harvard University.

Matthew Calbraith Perry Papers, Manuscript Division, Library of Congress.

Matthew Calbraith Perry Papers, National Archives.

Matthew Calbraith Perry Papers, Naval Academy Museum.

Matthew Calbraith Perry Papers, Naval Historical Center Library.

Matthew Calbraith Perry Papers, Sterling Library, Yale University.

Matthew Perry Letter Books, Historical Society of Pennsylvania.

Matthew Perry Letter Books, National Archives.

Matthew Perry Letter Book, Sterling Library, Yale University.

William Redfield Papers, Beinecke Library, Yale University.

Edward Dunham Robie Papers, Naval Academy Museum.

Rodgers Family Papers, Historical Society of Pennsylvania.

Rodgers Family Papers, Manuscript Division, Library of Congress.

Rodgers Family Papers, Naval Historical Foundation, Manuscript Division, Library of Congress.

William H. Rutherford Papers, Manuscript Division, Library of Congress.

William Sinclair Papers, Naval Academy Museum.

William Speiden Jr. Papers, Manuscript Division, Library of Congress.

Stevenson Family Papers, Manuscript Division, Library of Congress.

U.S. Department of the Navy Records, National Archives

Confidential Letters Sent by the Secretary of the Navy to Officers, 1842–1861, 4 vols. RG45.

Letters Received by the Secretary of the Navy from Captains ("Captains' Letters"), 1807–1861, 370 vols. RG45, M125.

Letters Received by the Secretary of the Navy from Commanders ("Commanders' Letters"), 1804–1886, 124 vols. RG45, M147.

Letters Received by the Secretary of the Navy from Commanding Officers of Squadrons ("Squadron Letters"), 1841–1886, 300 vols. RG45, M89.

Letters Received by the Secretary of the Navy from Officers below the Rank of Commander ("Officers' Letters"), 1802–1886, 518 vols. RG45, M148.

Letters Sent by the Secretary of the Navy to Officers ("Letters to Officers of Ships"), 1798–1868, 86 vols. RG45, M149.

Martin Van Buren Papers (microfilm), Manuscript Division, Library of Congress.

BOOKS AND ARTICLES

Adams, John Quincy. *Memoirs of John Quincy Adams, Comprising Portions of the Diary from 1795 to 1848.* Ed. Charles Francis Adams. 12 vols. Philadelphia: J. B. Lippincott, 1875.

Aderman, Ralph M., ed. *The Letters of James Kirke Paulding.* Madison: University of Wisconsin Press, 1962.

Adler, James B., ed. *CIS US Serial Set Index.* 12 parts. Washington, D.C.: Congressional Information Service, 1975.

Ames, Nathaniel. *A Mariner's Sketches.* Rev., corr., and enl. ed. Providence: Cory, Marshall and Hammond, 1830.

Bassett, John Spencer, ed. *Correspondence of Andrew Jackson.* 7 vols. Washington, D.C.: Carnegie Institution, 1929.

Bauer, K. Jack, ed. *The New American State Papers, 1798–1966, Naval Affairs.* 10 vols. Wilmington, Del.: Scholarly Resources, 1981.

Beasley, W. G., trans. and ed. *Select Documents on Japanese Foreign Policy, 1853–1868.* Tokyo: Centre for East Asian Cultural Studies, 1970.

Belmont, Perry. *The American Democrat: The Recollections of Perry Belmont.* New York: Columbia University Press, 1941.

Bridge, Horatio. *Journal of an African Cruiser . . .* Ed. Nathaniel Hawthorne. New York: George P. Putnam, 1853.

Bruell, James D. *Sea Memories, or Personal Experiences in the U.S. Navy in Peace and War.* Biddleford Pool, [Maine]: published by the author, 1886.

Channing, George H. *Early Recollections of Newport.* Newport: A. J. Ward and C. E. Hammett Jr., 1868.

Cochran, Thomas C., ed. *The New American State Papers, 1789–1860, Explorations and Surveys.* 15 vols. Wilmington, Del.: Scholarly Resources, 1972.

Colton, Walter. *Ship and Shore, in Madeira, Lisbon, and the Mediterranean.* New York: Leavitt, Lord and Company, 1835.

———. *A Visit to Constantinople and Athens.* New York: Leavitt, Lord and Company, 1836.

Cooper, James Fenimore. *Proceedings of the Naval Court Martial in the Case of Alexander Slidell Mackenzie. . . . To Which Is Annexed an Elaborate Review.* New York: H. G. Langley, 1844.

Davids, Jules, ed. *American Diplomatic and Public Papers: The United States and China.* Series 1: *The Treaty System and the Taiping Rebellion, 1842–1860.* 21 vols. Wilmington, Del.: Scholarly Resources, 1973.

De Roos, Fred Fitzgerald. *Personal Narrative of Travels in the United States and Canada in 1826 . . . with Remarks on the Present State of the American Navy.* London: William Harrison Ainsworth, 1827.

Emmons, George F. *The Navy of the United States from the Commencement, 1775 to 1853.* Washington, D.C.: Gideon and Company, 1853.

Gould, Roland F. *The Life of Gould, an Ex–Man-of-War's Man with Incidents on Sea and Shore.* Claremont, N.H.: Claremont Manufacturing Company, 1867.

Graff, Henry F., ed. *Bluejackets with Perry in Japan: A Day-by-Day Account Kept by Master's Mate John R. C. Lewis and Cabin Boy William B. Allen.* New York: New York Public Library, 1952.

Graham, William A. *The Papers of William A Graham.* Ed. J. G. de Roulhac Hamilton. 6 vols. Raleigh: North Carolina Department of Archives and History, 1867.

Griffis, William E. *Matthew Calbraith Perry: A Typical American Naval Officer.* Boston: Cupples and Hurd, 1887.

Hawks, Francis L., ed. *Narrative of the Expedition of an American Squadron to the China Seas and Japan, Performed in the Years 1852, 1853, and 1854, under the Command of Commodore M. C. Perry, United States Navy.* 3 vols. Washington, D.C.: Beverley Tucker, Senate Printer, 1856–57.

Hayashi, D., ed. "Diary of an Official of the Bakufu." *Transactions of the Asiatic Society of Japan,* ser. 2, 7 (1930): 98–119.

Heine, William. *With Perry in Japan. A Memoir by William Heine.* Ed. Frederic Trautman. Honolulu: University of Hawaii Press, 1990.

Kimitada, Miwa. "Perry's 'White Flags': From Their Deletion in His Own Records to Their Re-emergence in Historical Writings."

King, Charles. *The Claims of Japan and Malaysia upon Christendom.* New York: E. French, 1839.

Kojima, Matajiro. *Commodore Perry's Expedition to Hakodate, May, 1854: A Private Account with Illustrations.* 2 vols. Hakodate, Japan: Hakodate Kyodo Bunkakai, 1953.

Lynch, W. R. *Naval Life, or, Observations Afloat and on Shore. The Midshipman.* New York: Charles Scribner, 1851.

Mackenzie, Alexander Slidell. *Popular Essays on Naval Subjects.* New York: G. Dearborn, 1833.

———. *Spain Revisited.* 2 vols. New York: Harper and Brothers, 1836.

———. *A Year in Spain.* 2 vols. 5th ed. 1831. New York: Harper and Brothers, 1847.

Maclay, Edgar Stanton. *Reminiscences of the Old Navy; from the Journal and Private Papers of Captain Edward Trenchard.* New York: G. P. Putnam's Sons, 1898.

MacLeod, Julia H. "Three Letters Relating to the Perry Expedition." *Huntington Library Quarterly* 6 (1943): 228–31.

Marraro, Howard R. *Diplomatic Relations between the United States and the Kingdom of the Two Sicilies; Instructions and Despatches, 1816–1861.* 2 vols. New York: S. F. Vanni, 1951–52.

Mattice, Harold A. "Perry and Japan: An Account of the Empire and an Unpublished Record of the Perry Expedition." *Bulletin of the New York Public Library* 46 (1942): 167–84.

Mason, George C. *Newport Illustrated in a Series of Pen and Pencil Sketches.* Newport: C. E. Hammet, 1854.

———. *Reminiscences of Newport.* Newport: C. E. Hammet, 1884.

McCauley, Edward Yorke. *With Perry in Japan: The Diary of Edward Yorke McCauley.* Ed. Thomas C. Cochran. Princeton: Princeton University Press, 1942.

McDaniel, Antonio. *Swing Low, Sweet Chariot: The Mortality Cost of Colonizing Liberia in the Nineteenth Century.* Chicago: Chicago University Press, 1995.

McLane, Robert M. *Reminiscences, 1827–1897, Governor Robert M. McLane.* Wilmington, Del.: Scholarly Resources, 1972.

McNally, William. *Evils and Abuses in the Naval and Merchant Service Exposed; with Proposals for Their Remedy and Redress.* Boston: Cassady and March, 1839.

Meiji Japan through Contemporary Sources. 3 vols. Tokyo: Center for East Asian Cultural Studies, 1969–72.

Merrill, Walter I., ed. *Behold Me Once More: The Confessions of James Holley Garrison.* Cambridge: Riverside Press Cambridge, 1954.

Miller, David Hunter, ed. *Treaties and Other International Acts of the United States, 1776–1863.* 8 vols. Washington, D.C.: Government Printing Office, 1931–48.

Morris, Charles. *The Autobiography of Commodore Charles Morris.* Boston: A. Williams and Company, 1880.

Morrow, James. *A Scientist with Perry in Japan: The Journal of Dr. James Morrow.* Ed. Allen B. Cole. Chapel Hill: University of North Carolina Press, 1847.

Nordhoff, Charles. *Man-of-War Life, a Boy's Experience in the United States Navy, during a Voyage around the World in a Ship of the Line.* Philadelphia: J. B. Lippincott, 1856.

Palmer, Aaron Haight. *Documents and Facts Illustrating the Origin of the Mission to Japan.* Washington, D.C.: Henry Polkhorn, 1857.

Parker, William Harwar. *Recollections of a Naval Officer, 1841–1865.* New York: Charles Scribner's Sons, 1883.

Perry, Matthew C. *The Japan Expedition, 1852–1854. The Personal Journal of Commodore Matthew C. Perry.* Ed. Roger Pineau. Washington, D.C.: Smithsonian Institution Press, 1968.

———. *A Paper by Commodore M. C. Perry, U.S.N., Read before the American Geographical and Statistical Society . . . March 6th, 1856.* New York: D. Appleton, 1856.

Polk, James K. *The Diary of James K. Polk: 1845–1849.* Ed. Milo M. Quaife. 4 vols. Chicago: A. C. McClurg, 1910.

Ponko, Vincent Jr. *Ships, Seas, and Scientists: U.S. Naval Exploration and Discovery in the Nineteenth Century.* Annapolis: Naval Institute Press, 1974.

Porter, David Dixon. *Memoir of Commodore David Porter of the United States Navy.* Albany, N.Y.: J. Munsell, 1875.

Preble, George Henry. *The Opening of Japan. A Diary of Discovery in the Far East, 1853–1856.* Ed. Boleslaw Szczesniak. Norman: University of Oklahoma Press, 1962.

Schroeder, Francis. *Shores of the Mediterranean with Sketches of Travel.* New York: Harper and Brothers, 1846.

Schwartz, William L., ed. "Commodore Perry at Okinawa, from the Unpublished Diary of a British Missionary [Bernard Bettelheim]." *American Historical Review* 51 (1946): 262–76.

Scott, Winfield. *Memoirs of Lieut.-General Scott.* 2 vols. New York: Sheldon and Company, 1864.

Semmes, Raphael. *Service Afloat and Ashore during the Mexican War.* Cincinnati: Wm. H. Moore, 1851.

Sewall, John S. *The Logbook of the Captain's Clerk: Adventures in the China Seas.* Ed. Arthur Power Dudder. Bangor: Chas. H. Glass, 1905.

———. "With Perry in Japan." *Century Magazine* 70 (1905): 349–60.

Shewmaker, Kenneth E., and Kenneth R. Stevens, eds. *The Papers of Daniel Webster: Diplomatic Papers.* 2 vols. Hanover: Dartmouth University Press, 1987.

Shick, Tom. *Behold the Promised Land: A History of Afro-American Settler Society in Nineteenth-Century Liberia.* Baltimore: Johns Hopkins University Press, 1977.

Spalding, J. W. *The Japan Expedition: Japan and around the World, an Account of Three Visits to the Japanese Empire.* New York: Redfield, 1855.

Sproston, John Glendy. *A Private Journal of John Glendy Sproston.* Ed. Shio Sakanishi. Tokyo: Sophia University, 1940.

Statler, Oliver. *The Black Ship Scroll: An Account of the Perry Expedition at Shimoda in 1854 and the Lively Beginnings of People-to-People Relations between Japan and America.* Trans. Richard Lane. New York: Japan Societies of San Francisco and New York, 1963.

Taylor, Bayard. *A Visit to India, China, and Japan in the Year 1853.* New York: G. P. Putnam's Sons, 1891.

Taylor, Fitch W. *The Broad Pennant; or, A Cruise in the United States Flag Ship of the Gulf Squadron, during the Mexican Difficulties . . .* New York: D. Appleton, 1848.

United States Bureau of Census. *A Century of Population Growth from the First Census of the United States to the Twelfth, 1790–1900.* Washington, D.C.: Government Printing Office, 1909.

United States Congress. *American State Papers, Class VI: Naval Affairs.* 2 vols. Washington, D.C.: Gales and Seaton, 1834, 1860.

———. *Congressional Globe: 23rd Congress to the 42nd Congress, 2 December 1833–3 March 1873.* 46 vols. Washington, D.C.: Gales and Seaton, 1834–73.

Wermuth, Paul C., ed. *Selected Letters of Bayard Taylor.* Lewisburg, Pa.: Bucknell University Press, 1997.

Wheelwright, Charles H. *Correspondence of Dr. Charles H. Wheelwright, Surgeon of the United States Navy.* Ed. Hildegarde B. Forbes. Boston: Thomas Todd, 1958.

Williams, S. Wells. "A Journal of the Perry Expedition to Japan, 1853–1854." *Transactions of the Asiatic Society of Japan* 37, pt. 2 (1910): 1–259.

Winslow, Arthur. *Francis Winslow: His Forbears and Life Based upon Family Records and Correspondence during Thirty Years.* Norwood, Mass.: Plimpton Press, 1935.

[Wise, H. A.] Gringo, Harry. *Scampavias from Gibel Tarek to Stamboul.* New York: Charles Scribner, 1857.

SECONDARY SOURCES

Adair, Douglass. "Fame and the Founding Fathers." In *Fame and the Founding Fathers: Essays by Douglass Adair.* Ed. Trevor Colbourn, 3–26. New York, W. W. Norton, 1974.

Allen, Gardner W. *Our Navy and the West Indian Pirates.* Salem, Mass.: Essex Institute, 1929.

Armond, Louis De. "Justo Sierra O'Reilly and Yucatan–United States Relations, 1847–1848." *Hispanic American Historical Review* 31 (1951): 420–36.

Arnold, Samuel Greene. *History of the State of Rhode Island and Providence Plantations.* New York: D. Appleton, 1860.

Bain, Chester A. "Commodore Matthew Perry, Humphrey Marshall and the Taiping Rebellion." *Far Eastern Quarterly* 10 (1951): 258–70.

Barr, Pat. *The Coming of the Barbarians: The Opening of Japan to the West, 1853–1870.* New York: E. P. Dutton, 1967.

Barrows, Edward M. *The Great Commodore. The Exploits of Matthew C. Perry.* Indianapolis: Bobbs-Merrill, 1935.

Bauer, K. Jack. *The Mexican War, 1846–1848.* New York: Macmillan, 1974.

———. "Naval Shipbuilding Programs, 1794–1860." *Military Affairs* 29 (1965): 29–40.

———. *Surfboats and Horse Marines: U.S. Naval Operations in the Mexican War, 1846–1848.* Annapolis: Naval Institute Press, 1969.

Baxter, James Phinney. *The Introduction of the Ironclad Warship.* Cambridge: Harvard University Press, 1933.

Beasley, W. G. *Great Britain and the Opening of Japan, 1834–1856.* London: Luzac, 1951.

———. *The Meiji Restoration.* Stanford: Stanford University Press, 1972.

Beatly, Richmond C. *Bayard Taylor, Laureate of the Gilded Age.* Norman: University of Oklahoma Press, 1936.

Belohlavek, John M. *"Let the Eagle Soar": The Foreign Policy of Andrew Jackson.* Lincoln: University of Nebraska Press, 1985.

Bemis, Samuel Flagg. *John Quincy Adams and the Foundations of American Foreign Policy.* 1949. Reprint. New York: W. W. Norton, 1973.

Bennett, Frank M. *The Steam Navy of the United States.* 2 vols. 2d ed. Pittsburgh: Warren and Company, 1897.

Bicknell, Thomas W. *The History of the State of Rhode Island and Providence Plantations.* 5 vols. New York: American Historical Society, 1920.

Binder, Frederick M. *James Buchanan and the American Empire.* Selinsgrove, Pa.: Susquehanna University Press, 1994.

Birker, Michael J. *Samuel L. Southard: Jeffersonian Whig.* Rutherford, N.J.: Fairleigh Dickinson University Press, 1984.

Bix, Herbert P. *Peasant Protest in Japan, 1590–1884.* New Haven: Yale University Press, 1986.

Black, David. *King of Fifth Avenue: The Fortunes of August Belmont.* New York: Dial Press, 1981.

Bode, Carl. *The American Lyceum: Town Meeting of the Mind.* New York: Oxford University Press, 1956.

Bohnen, Charles H. *John Pendleton Kennedy.* Baltimore: Johns Hopkins University Press, 1961.

Bolitho, Harold. "Abe Masahiro and the New Japan." In *The Bakufu in Japanese History,* ed. Jeffrey P. Mass and William B. Hauser, 173–88. Stanford: Stanford University Press, 1985.

Bolster, W. Jeffrey. *Black Jacks: African American Seamen in the Age of Sail.* Cambridge: Harvard University Press, 1997.

Borton, Hugh. "Peasant Uprisings in Japan of the Tokugawa Period." *Transactions of the Asiatic Society of Japan,* ser. 2, 16 (1938).

Bradford, James C., ed. *Captains of the Old Steam Navy: Makers of the American Naval Tradition: 1840–1880.* Annapolis: Naval Institute Press, 1986.

————. *Command under Sail: Makers of the American Naval Tradition, 1775–1850.* Annapolis: Naval Institute Press, 1985.

Bradlee, Francis B. C. *The Suppression of Piracy in the West Indies, 1820–1832.* Salem, Mass.: Essex Institute, 1922.

Brock, R. A. "New England and the Slave Trade." *New England Quarterly,* ser. 2, 3 (1894): 176–78.

Brodie, Bernard. *Sea Power in the Machine Age: Major Naval Inventions and Their Consequences on International Politics, 1814–1940.* Princeton: Princeton University Press, 1941.

Brooke, George M. Jr. *John M. Brooke: Naval Scientist and Educator.* Charlottesville: University Press of Virginia, 1980.

————. "The Role of the United States Navy in the Suppression of the African Slave Trade." *American Neptune* 21 (1961): 28–41.

Brooks, George E. Jr. *Yankee Traders, Old Coasters and African Middlemen: A History of American Legitimate Trade with West Africa in the Nineteenth Century.* Boston: Boston University Press, 1970.

Bruce, William Cabell. *John Randolph of Roanoke, 1773–1833. A Biography Based Largely on New Material.* 2 vols. New York: G. P. Putnam's Sons, 1922.

Burns, Richard Dean, ed. *Guide to American Foreign Relations since 1700.* Santa Barbara: ABC-CLIO, 1983.

Campbell, Penelope. *Maryland in Africa: The Maryland State Colonization Society, 1831–1857.* Urbana: University of Illinois Press, 1971.

Chang, Richard T. *From Prejudice to Tolerance: A Study of the Japanese Image of the West, 1826–1864.* Tokyo: Sophia University, 1970.

Chapelle, Howard I. *The History of the American Sailing Navy: The Ships and Their Development.* New York: Bonanza Books, 1969.

Cole, Allan B. "Captain David Porter's Proposed Expedition to the Pacific and Japan, 1815." *Pacific Historical Review* 9 (1940): 61–65.

Coleman, Peter J. *The Transformation of Rhode Island, 1790–1860.* Providence: Brown University Press, 1963.

Colletta, Paolo, ed. *American Secretaries of the Navy.* 2 vols. Annapolis: Naval Institute Press, 1980.

Conner, Philip S. P. *The Home Squadron under Commodore Conner in the War with Mexico . . . 1846–1847.* Philadelphia: n.p., 1896.

Coughtry, Jay. *The Notorious Triangle: Rhode Island and the African Slave Trade, 1700–1807.* Philadelphia: Temple University Press, 1981.

Curtin, Philip D. *The Atlantic Slave Trade: A Census.* Madison: University of Wisconsin Press, 1969.

————. *Death by Migration: Europe's Encounter with the Tropical World in the Nineteenth Century.* Cambridge: Cambridge University Press, 1989.

————. *Disease and Empire: The Health of European Troops in the Conquest of Africa.* Cambridge: Cambridge University Press, 1998.

Curtis, George Ticknor. *Life of James Buchanan, Fifteenth President of the United States.* 2 vols. New York: Harper, 1883.

Danby, Robert. "Journal of a Cruise in the United States Steam Frigate *Mississippi* [1852–1855]." Manuscript Division, Library of Congress.

De Christofaro, S. "The Naval Lyceum." *U.S. Naval Institute Proceedings* 76 (1951): 869–73.

de Kay, James T. *Chronicles of the Frigate "Macedonian."* New York: W. W. Norton, 1995.

Dennett, Tyler. *Americans in Eastern Asia: A Critical Study of the Policy of the United States with Reference to China, Japan and Korea in the Nineteenth Century.* New York: Macmillan, 1922.

Donnan, Elizabeth. "The New England Slave Trade after the Revolution." *New England Quarterly* 3 (1930): 251–78.

Du Bois, W. E. B. *The Suppression of the African Slave Trade to the United States of America, 1638–1870.* 1896. Reprint. Millwood, N.Y.: Kraus-Thomson, 1973.

Dulles, Foster Rhea. *The Old China Trade.* New York: Houghton Mifflin, 1930.

———. *Yankees and Samurai: America's Role in the Emergence of Modern Japan, 1791–1900.* New York: Harper and Row, 1965.

Dupree, A. Hunter. "Science vs. the Military: Dr. James Morrow and the Perry Expedition." *Pacific Historical Review* 22 (1953): 29–37.

Duus, Peter. *The Japanese Discovery of America: A Brief History with Documents.* New York: Bedford Books, 1997.

Ellicott, John M. *Life of John Ancrum Winslow, Rear Admiral, United States Navy.* New York: G. P. Putnam's Sons, 1902.

Fairbank, John K. *Trade and Diplomacy on the China Coast: The Opening of the Treaty Ports, 1842–1854.* Stanford: Stanford University Press, 1969.

Farragut, Loyall. *The Life of David Glasgow Farragut, First Admiral of the United States Navy.* New York: D. Appleton, 1879.

Feipel, Louis N. "The United States Navy in Mexico, 1821–1914." *U.S. Naval Institute Proceedings* 41 (1915) 33–52.

Field, Edward, ed. *State of Rhode Island and Providence Plantations at the End of the Century. A History.* 3 vols. Boston: Mason Publishing Company, 1902.

Field, James A. Jr. *America and the Mediterranean World, 1776–1882.* Princeton: Princeton University Press, 1969.

Fowler, William M. *William Ellery: A Rhode Island Politico and Lord of the Admiralty.* Metuchen, N.J.: Scarecrow Press, 1973.

Fox, Early Lee. *The American Colonization Society, 1817–1840.* Baltimore: Johns Hopkins University Press, 1919.

Fox, Grace. *Britain and Japan, 1858–1883.* Oxford: Clarendon Press, 1969.

Gibson, Arrell Morgan, and John S. Whitehead. *Yankees in Paradise: The Pacific Basin Frontier.* Albuquerque: University of New Mexico Press, 1993.

Glenn, Myra. "The Naval Reform Campaign against Flogging: A Case Study in Changing Attitudes toward Capital Punishment, 1830–1850." *American Quarterly* 35 (1983): 408–25.

Griffin, Eldon. *Clippers and Consuls: American Consular and Commercial Relations with Eastern Asia, 1845–1860.* Ann Arbor: Edwards, 1938.

Gulliver, L. J. "The Navy and the U.S. Ocean Mail Ships." *U.S. Naval Institute Proceedings* 65 (1939): 1264–69.

Gutstein, Morris A. *The Story of the Jews of Newport: Two and a Half Centuries of Judaism, 1658–1908.* New York: Bloch, 1936.

Hagan, Kenneth J., ed. *In War and Peace: Interpretations of American Naval History, 1775–1978.* Westport, Conn.: Greenwood Press, 1978.

Hall, Edwin H. *Abel Parker Upshur: Conservative Virginian, 1790–1844.* Madison: University of Wisconsin Press, 1964.

Hall, John Whitney. *Japan from Prehistory to Modern Times.* New York: Dell, 1970.

Harmon, Judd Scott. "Marriage of Convenience: The United States Navy in Africa, 1820–1843." *American Neptune* 32 (1972): 264–76.

Hayford, Harrison, ed. *The "Somers" Mutiny.* Englewood Cliffs, N.J.: Prentice-Hall, 1959.

Hearn, Chester G. *Admiral David Dixon Porter.* Annapolis: Naval Institute Press, 1996.

Henson, Curtis T. Jr. *Commissioners and Commodores: The East India Squadron and American Diplomacy in China.* Tuscaloosa: University of Alabama Press, 1982.

Hildreth, Richard. *Japan, as It Was and Is.* Boston: Phillips, Sampson, 1855.

Hohman, Elmo P. *The American Whalemen: A History of Life and Labor in the Whaling Industry.* New York: Longman, Green, 1928.

Horan, Leo F. S. "Flogging in the United States Navy: Unfamiliar Facts Regarding Its Origin and Abolition." *U.S. Naval Academy Proceedings* 76 (1950): 969–75.

Horsman, Reginald. *The War of 1812.* New York: Alfred A. Knopf, 1960.

Horton, James O., and Lois E. Horton. *In Hope of Liberty: Culture, Community, and Protest among Northern Free Blacks, 1700–1860.* New York: Oxford University Press, 1997.

Houchins, Chang-su. "Artifacts of Diplomacy: Smithsonian Collections from Commodore Matthew Perry's Japan Expedition (1853–1854)." *Smithsonian Contributions to Anthropology* 37 (1995): 1–155.

Howe, George. *Mount Hope: A New England Chronicle.* New York: Viking Press, 1959.

Huber, Thomas. *The Revolutionary Origins of Modern Japan.* Stanford: Stanford University Press, 1981.

Huberich, Charles H. *The Political and Legislative History of Liberia.* 3 vols. New York: Central Book Company, 1947.

Hutchins, John G. B. *The American Maritime Industries and Public Policy, 1789–1914.* Cambridge: Harvard University Press, 1941.

Jansen, Marius B., ed. *The Nineteenth Century.* Volume 5 of *The Cambridge History of Japan.* 6 vols. Cambridge: Cambridge University Press, 1988.

Johnson, Arnold B. *The Modern Light-House Service.* Washington, D.C.: Government Printing Office, 1889.

Johnson, Lucius W. "Yellow Jack, Master of Strategy." *U.S. Naval Institute Proceedings* 76 (1950): 1075–83.

Johnson, Robert Erwin. *Far China Station: The U.S. Navy in Asian Waters, 1800–1898.* Annapolis: Naval Institute Press, 1979.

Jones, Howard. "The Peculiar Institution and National Honor: The Case of the Creole Slave Revolt." *Civil War History* 21 (1975): 28–50.

———. *To the Webster-Ashburton Treaty: A Study in Anglo-American Relations, 1783–1843.* Chapel Hill: University of North Carolina Press, 1977.

Kaneko, Hisakazu. *Manjiro: The Man Who Discovered America.* Boston: Houghton Mifflin, 1956.

Katz, Irving. *August Belmont: A Political Biography.* New York: Columbia University Press, 1968.

Kemble, John H. *The Panama Route, 1848–1869.* Berkeley: University of California Press, 1943.

Kerr, George H. *Okinawa: The History of an Island People.* Rutland, Vt.: Charles E. Tuttle, 1958.

Koschmann, J. Victor. *The Mito Ideology: Discourse, Reform and Insurrection in Late Tokugawa Japan, 1790–1864.* Berkeley: University of California Press, 1987.

Langley, Harold D. *A History of Medicine in the Early U.S. Navy.* Baltimore: Johns Hopkins University Press, 1995.

———. "The Negro in the Navy and Merchant Service, 1798–1860." *Journal of Negro History* 52 (1968): 273–86.

———. "Robert Y. Hayne and the Navy." *South Carolina Historical Magazine* 82 (1981): 311–30.

———. *Social Reform in the United States Navy, 1798–1862.* Urbana: University of Illinois Press, 1967.

Lensen, George Alexander. *The Russian Push toward Japan: Russo-Japanese Relations, 1697–1875.* Princeton: Princeton University Press, 1959.

———. *Russia's Japan Expedition of 1852 to 1855.* Gainesville: University of Florida Press, 1955.

Lewis, Charles Lee. *Admiral Franklin Buchanan: Fearless Man of Action.* Baltimore: Norman Remington, 1929.

———. *David Glasgow Farragut: Admiral in the Making.* 2 vols. Annapolis: Naval Institute Press, 1941.

Lewis, William S., and Murakami Naojiro, eds. *Ranald MacDonald: The Narrative of His Early Life.* Spokane: Eastern Washington State Historical Society, 1923.

Livermore, Seward. "American Naval-Base Policy in the Far East, 1850–1914." *Pacific Historical Review* 13 (1944): 113–35.

Lloyd, Christopher, ed. *The Health of Seamen: Selections from the Works of Dr. James Lind, Sir Gilbert Blane and Dr. Thomas Totter.* London: Navy Records Society, 1965.

Logan, Rayford. *The Diplomatic Relations of the United States and Haiti, 1776–1891.* Chapel Hill: University of North Carolina Press, 1941.

Long, David F. *Gold Braid and Foreign Relations: Diplomatic Activities of U.S. Naval Officers, 1798–1883.* Annapolis: Naval Institute Press, 1988.

———. *Nothing Too Daring: A Biography of Commodore David Porter, 1780–1843.* Annapolis: Naval Institute Press, 1970.

———. *Sailor-Diplomat: A Biography of Commodore James Biddle, 1783–1848.* Boston: Northeastern University Press, 1983.

Lovett, Robert W. "The Japan Expedition Press." *Harvard Library Bulletin* 12 (1958): 242–52.

Mackenzie, Alexander Slidell. *The Life of Commodore Oliver Hazard Perry.* 2 vols. 1840. Reprint. New York: Werner, 1910.

Mahan, Alfred T. *Sea Power in Its Relations to the War of 1812.* 2 vols. Boston: Little, Brown, 1919.

Mahon, John K. *The War of 1812.* Gainesville: University of Florida Press, 1872.

Mannix, Daniel P. *Black Cargoes: A History of the Atlantic Slave Trade.* New York: Viking Press, 1965.

May, Robert E. *John A. Quitman: Old South Crusader.* Baton Rouge: Louisiana State University Press, 1985.

Mayer, Henry. *All on Fire: William Lloyd Garrison and the Abolition of Slavery.* New York: St. Martin's Press, 1998.

McKee, Christopher. *A Gentlemanly and Honorable Profession: The Creation of the U.S. Naval Officer Corps, 1794–1815.* Annapolis: Naval Institute Press, 1991.

Melish, Joanne. *Discovering Slavery: Gradual Emancipation and "Race" in New England, 1780–1860.* Ithaca: Cornell University Press, 1998.

Melville, Herman. *White-Jacket, or, The World in a Man of War.* 1850. Reprint. New York: New American Library, 1979.

Merrill, James M. *Du Pont: The Making of an Admiral: A Biography of Samuel Francis Du Pont.* New York: Dodd, Mead, 1986.

———. "Midshipman Du Pont and the Cruise of the *North Carolina*, 1825–1827." *American Neptune* 40 (1980): 211–25.

Merrill, Walter M. *Against Wind and Tide: A Biography of William Lloyd Garrison.* Cambridge: Harvard University Press, 1963.

Mooney, James L., ed. *The Dictionary of American Naval Fighting Ships.* 8 vols. Washington, D.C.: Naval Historical Center, 1959–81.

Morison, Samuel Eliot. "Commodore Perry's Japan Expedition Press and Shipboard Theatre." *Proceedings of the American Antiquarian Society* 77, pt. 1 (1967): 36–43.

Murdock, James. *A History of Japan*. New York: Frederick Ungar, 1964.

Nitobe, Inazo. *The Intercourse between the United States and Japan*. Baltimore: Johns Hopkins University Press, 1891.

Nye, Russel B. *George Bancroft: Brahmin Rebel*. New York: Alfred A. Knopf, 1945.

Ott, Thomas. *The Haitian Revolution, 1789–1804*. Knoxville: University of Tennessee Press, 1973.

Paullin, Charles O. *Commodore John Rodgers: Captain, Commodore, and Senior Officer of the American Navy, 1773–1838. A Biography*. Cleveland: Arthur H. Clark, 1910.

———. *Diplomatic Negotiations of American Naval Officers, 1778–1883*. Baltimore: Johns Hopkins University Press, 1913.

———. *Paullin's History of Naval Administration, 1775–1911: A Collection of Articles from the U.S. Naval Institute Proceedings*. Annapolis: Naval Institute Press, 1968.

Perry, Calbraith B. *The Perrys of Rhode Island and Tales of Silver Creek, the Bosworth-Bourn-Perry Homestead*. New York: Tobias A. Wright, 1913.

The Perry Family. Arlington, Va.: American Genealogical Research Institute, 1973.

Plummer, Katherine. *The Shogun's Reluctant Ambassadors*. Tokyo: Lotus Press, 1984.

Putnam, George R. *Lighthouses and Lightships of the United States*. Boston: Houghton Mifflin, 1917.

Putney, Martha S. "Black Merchant Seamen of Newport, 1803–1865: A Case Study in Foreign Commerce." *Journal of Negro History* 57 (1972): 156–68.

Reed, Harry. *Platform for Change: The Foundation of the Northern Free Black Community*. East Lansing: Michigan State University Press, 1994.

Reed, Nelson. *The Caste War of Yucatan*. Stanford: Stanford University Press, 1964.

Ridgely-Nevith, Cedric. *American Steamships on the Atlantic*. Newark: University of Delaware Press, 1981.

Sakai, Robert K. "Shinazu Nariakira and the Emergence of National Leadership." In *Personality in Japanese History*, ed. Albert M. Craig and Donald H. Shively, 209–33. Stanford: Stanford University Press, 1970.

Sakamaki, Shunzo. "Japan and the United States, 1790–1853." *Transactions of the Asiatic Society of Japan*, ser. 2, 18 (1933).

Sansom, George. *A History of Japan, 1615–1867*. Stanford: Stanford University Press, 1963.

———. *The Western World and Japan: A Study in the Interaction of European and Asiatic Cultures*. Rutland, Vt.: Charles C. Tuttle, 1950.

Sawyer, Amos. *The Emergence of Autocracy in Liberia: Tragedy and Challenge*. San Francisco: Institute for Contemporary Studies, 1992.

Schroeder, John H. "Matthew Calbraith Perry: Antebellum Precursor of the Steam Navy." In *Captains of the Old Steam Navy: Makers of the American Naval Tradition, 1840–1880*, ed. James C. Bradford, 3–25. Annapolis: Naval Institute Press, 1986.

———. *Shaping a Maritime Empire: The Commercial and Diplomatic Role of the American Navy, 1829–1861.* Westport, Conn.: Greenwood Press, 1985.

Scudder, Horace, and Marie Hansen-Taylor. *Life and Letters of Bayard Taylor.* 2 vols. Boston: Houghton Mifflin, 1884.

Sears, Louis M. *John Slidell.* Durham: Duke University Press, 1925.

Shoemaker, Raymond L. "Diplomacy from the Quarterdeck: The U.S. Navy in the Caribbean, 1815–1830." In *Changing Interpretations and New Sources in Naval History,* ed. Robert W. Love, 169–79. New York: Garland, 1980.

Skaggs, David C., and Gerard T. Altoff. *A Signal Victory: The Lake Erie Campaign 1812–1813.* Annapolis: Naval Institute Press, 1997.

Smith, Elbert B. *The Presidencies of Zachary Taylor and Millard Fillmore.* Lawrence: University of Kansas Press, 1988.

Smith, Geoffrey. "The Navy before Darwinism: Science, Exploration, and Diplomacy in Antebellum America." *American Quarterly* 18 (1976): 41–55.

Soley, James Russell. *Historical Sketch of the U.S. Naval Academy.* Washington, D.C.: Government Printing Office, 1876.

Somerville, Col. Duncan S. *The Aspinwall Empire.* Mystic, Conn.: Mystic Seaport Museum, 1983.

Soulsby, Hugh G. *The Right of Search and the Slave Trade in Anglo-American Relations, 1814–1862.* Baltimore: Johns Hopkins University Press, 1933.

Spears, John R. *David G. Farragut.* Philadelphia: George W. Jacobs, 1905.

Spencer, Warren F. *Raphael Semmes: The Philosophical Mariner.* Tuscaloosa: University of Alabama Press, 1997.

Sprout, Harold, and Margaret Sprout. *The Rise of American Naval Power, 1776–1918.* 1939. Reprint. Princeton: Princeton University Press, 1967.

Stanton, William. *The Great United States Exploring Expedition of 1838–1842.* Berkeley: University of California Press, 1975.

Starbuck, Alexander. *History of the American Whale Fishery from Its Earliest Inception to the Year 1876.* 2 vols. 1878. Reprint. Secaucus, N.J.: Castle, 1989.

Staudenraus, P. J. *The African Colonization Movement, 1816–1865.* New York: Columbia University Press, 1961.

Stuart, Charles B. *The Naval and Mail Steamers of the United States.* New York: C. B. Norton, 1853.

Swisher, Earl. "Commodore Perry's Imperialism in Relation to America's Present Day Position in the Pacific." *Pacific Historical Review* 16 (1947): 30–40.

Symonds, Craig. *Confederate Admiral: The Life and Wars of Franklin Buchanan.* Annapolis: Naval Institute Press, 1999.

———. *Navalists and Antinavalists: The Naval Policy Debate in the United States, 1785–1827.* Annapolis: Naval Institute Press, 1980.

Te-kong Tong. *United States Diplomacy in China, 1844–1860.* Seattle: University of Washington Press, 1864.

Thomas, Hugh. *The Slave Trade: The History of the Atlantic Slave Trade, 1440–1870.* London: Picador, 1997.

Thomas, James C. Jr., et al. *Sentimental Imperialists: The American Experience in East Asia.* New York: Harper and Row, 1981.

Thomas, R. P., and R. N. Bean. "The Fishers of Men: The Profits of the Slave Trade." *Journal of Economic History* 34 (1974): 885–914.

Thompson, Mack. *Moses Brown: Reluctant Reformer.* Chapel Hill: University of North Carolina Press, 1962.

Todorich, Charles. *The Spirited Years: A History of the Antebellum Naval Academy.* Annapolis: Naval Institute Press, 1984.

Totman, Conrad. "Political Reconciliation in the Tokugawa Bakufu: Abe Masahiro and Tokugawa Nariaki, 1844–1852." In *Personality in Japanese History,* ed. Albert M. Craig and Donald H. Shively, 180–208. Berkeley: University of California Press, 1970.

———. *Politics in the Tokugawa Bakufu, 1600–1843.* Cambridge: Harvard University Press, 1967.

———. "The Struggle for Control of the Shogunate (1853–1858)." In *Papers on Japan.* Cambridge, Mass.: East Asian Research Center, 1961.

Tower, Walter S. *A History of the American Whale Fishery.* Philadelphia: University of Pennsylvania, 1907.

Tucker, Spencer. *Arming the Fleet: U.S. Navy Ordnance in the Muzzle-Loading Era.* Annapolis: Naval Institute Press, 1989.

Tyler, David B. *Steam Conquers the Atlantic.* New York: D. Appleton-Century, 1939.

Valle, James E. *Rocks and Shoals: Order and Discipline in the Old Navy, 1800–1861.* Annapolis: Naval Institute Press, 1980.

Van de Water, Frederic F. *The Captain Called It Mutiny.* New York: Washburn, 1954.

Van Sant, John E. *Pacific Pioneers: Japanese Journeys to America and Hawaii, 1850–1880.* Urbana: University of Illinois Press, 2000.

Vernon, Manfred C. "The Dutch and the Opening of Japan by the United States." *Pacific Historical Review* 28 (1959): 39–48.

Wakabayashi, Bob Tadashi. *Anti-foreignism and Western Learning in Early Modern Japan: The New Theses of 1825.* Cambridge: Harvard University Press, 1986.

Walworth, Arthur. *Black Ships off Japan: The Story of Commodore Perry's Expedition.* New York: Alfred A. Knopf, 1946.

Warinner, Emily V. *Voyager to Destiny.* Indianapolis: Bobbs-Merrill, 1956.

Warren, Howard. *American Slavers and the Federal Law, 1837–1862.* Berkeley: University of California Press, 1963.

Watanabe, Shujiro. *Abe Masahiro jiseki.* 2 vols. 1910. Reprint. Tokyo: Tokyo University Press, 1978.

Weigley, Russell. *The American Way of War: A History of United States Military Strategy and Policy.* New York: Macmillan, 1973.

Weiss, George. *The Lighthouse Service: Its History, Activities and Organization.* 1926. Reprint. New York: AMS Press, 1974.

White, Leonard D. *The Jacksonians: A Study in Administrative History, 1829–1861.* New York: Macmillan, 1954.

Wiley, Peter Booth. *Yankees in the Land of the Gods: Commodore Perry and the Opening of Japan.* New York: Viking Press, 1990.

Williams, Frances L. *Matthew Fontaine Maury, Scientist of the Sea.* New Brunswick: Rutgers University Press, 1963.

Williams, Frederick Wells. *The Life and Letters of Samuel Wells Williams.* New York: Putnam, 1889.

Williams, Mary W. "Secessionist Diplomacy in Yucatan." *Hispanic American Historical Review* 9 (1929): 132–43.

Williams, Max R. "Secretary William A. Graham, Naval Administrator, 1850–1852." *North Carolina Historical Review* 48 (1971): 53–72.

Withey, Lynne. *Urban Growth in Colonial Rhode Island: Newport and Providence in the Eighteenth Century.* Albany: State University of New York Press, 1984.

Wright, Donald. "Matthew Perry and the African Squadron." In *America Spreads Her Sails: U.S. Seapower in the Nineteenth Century,* ed. Clayton J. Barrow Jr., 212–25. Annapolis: Naval Institute Press, 1973.

Zilversmit, Arthur. *First Emancipation: The Abolition of Slavery in the North.* Chicago: University of Chicago Press, 1967.

Zingg, Paul J. "To the Shores of Barbary: The Ideology and Pursuit of American Commercial Expansion, 1816–1906." *South Atlantic Quarterly* 79 (1980): 408–24.

⤳ *Further Reading* ⤶

Although there are numerous books on Perry and his career, there have been only two scholarly biographies in the last century and a half. William E. Griffis's *Matthew Calbraith Perry: A Typical American Naval Officer* is still useful because the author interviewed a number of Perry's contemporaries and excerpts from those interviews appear in the book. Samuel Eliot Morison's *"Old Bruin": Commodore Matthew C. Perry, 1794–1858* is a laudatory and uncritical biography by a renowned naval historian. The nautical and geographic descriptions are classic Morison, but the book is now somewhat outdated. Since it was published in 1967, excellent scholarly studies have appeared on topics that relate to virtually every aspect of Perry's life and naval career. This scholarship includes general histories, monographs, and articles on naval biography and military history, social and political history, and studies of U.S. diplomacy and relations with West Africa, the Caribbean, Japan, and China. In fact, most of the secondary sources cited in this essay have appeared since 1967.

The relative lack of scholarly attention to Perry is surprising because of the extensive manuscript material available on his life and career. Most important are his personal letter books. Several volumes are available at the National Archives. Several volumes of letter books are also available along with correspondence, miscellaneous manuscript items, and the log of the *Concord* in the Rodgers Family Papers at the Historical Society of Pennsylvania. The Perry Papers at Houghton Library of Harvard University are a valuable collection of personal and family manuscripts. In the Manuscript Division of the Library of Congress there are two large collections of Rodgers family papers, each of which contains important Perry manuscripts, as well as a small collection of Perry papers. Also located at the Library of Congress are the Samuel Eliot Morison Papers, which contain the research notes for Morison's biography of Perry. Although scattered Perry manuscript items can be found in numerous libraries, there are small but useful collections of Perry papers at the Sterling Library of Yale University, the Naval Academy Museum, and the Library of the Naval Historical Center. The microfilm edition of the Joel Abbot Papers housed at the Nimitz Library of the U.S. Naval Academy was also particularly useful. The Smithsonian Institution has the largest collection of artifacts from the expedition to Japan. A number of maps and charts from the expedition are in the American Geographical Society at the University of Wisconsin–Milwaukee.

The official records of the Department of the Navy (Record Group 45) in the National Archives provide a basic archival source for Perry's naval career as well as for the U.S. Navy prior to the Civil War. The correspondence of the secretary of the navy (listed in the bibliography) is an especially valuable contemporary source. The "Squadron Letters" contain Perry's official correspondence as commander of the African Squadron from 1843 to 1845, the Home Squadron in 1847 and 1848, and the East India Squadron from 1852 to 1855. Record Group 45 also contains other useful items, including the logs and journals of various ships on which Perry served.

Printed document collections are another basic primary source of information on Perry's career. *The American State Papers, Class VI: Naval Affairs* is especially useful for the period prior to 1830; and K. Jack Bauer, ed., *The New American State Papers, 1798–1860, Naval Affairs*, covers the entire antebellum period. Documents on antebellum naval exploring expeditions, including the Perry expedition, are included in Thomas C. Cochran, ed., *The New American State Papers, 1789–1860, Explorations and Surveys*. For early relations with China, an excellent collection of official records is Jules Davids, ed., *American Diplomatic and Public Papers: The United States and China*. Series 1: *The Treaty System and the Taiping Rebellion, 1842–1860*. The annual messages of the president of the United States and the annual reports of the secretary of the navy are printed conveniently in *The Congressional Globe*. Various diplomatic and naval reports, documents, and correspondence are printed in the Serial Set of the U.S. Congress. An invaluable index to this valuable resource is James B. Adler, ed., *CIS US Serial Set Index*. The various treaties negotiated by Perry along with supporting documentation are printed in

David Hunter Miller, ed., *Treaties and Other International Acts of the United States.*

Useful references on the navy and naval diplomacy include Paolo Colletta, ed., *American Secretaries of the Navy*; Richard Dean Burns, ed., *Guide to American Foreign Relations since 1700*; David F. Long, *Gold Braid and Foreign Relations: Diplomatic Activities of U.S. Naval Officers, 1798–1883*; and essays by David F. Long and Geoffrey S. Smith on the antebellum navy in Kenneth J. Hagan, ed., *In War and Peace: Interpretations of American Naval History, 1775–1978*. For an excellent collection of biographical essays on officers in the Old Navy, see two volumes edited by James C. Bradford: *Command under Sail: Makers of the American Naval Tradition, 1775–1850* and *Captains of the Old Steam Navy: Makers of the American Naval Tradition, 1840–1880*. An excellent history of American military policy is Russell Weigley, *The American Way of War: A History of United States Military Strategy and Policy*. A basic reference on individual ships is the *Dictionary of American Naval Fighting Ships*, edited by James L. Mooney.

On the Perry family, see Calbraith B. Perry, *The Perrys of Rhode Island and Tales of Silver Creek*. Alexander Slidell Mackenzie's *The Life of Commodore Oliver Hazard Perry* contains useful information on Matthew's childhood and family. For reminiscences of Newport at the beginning of the nineteenth century, see George C. Channing, *Early Recollections of Newport*. Excellent studies of Rhode Island include Peter J. Coleman, *The Transformation of Rhode Island, 1790–1860*; and Lynne Withey, *Urban Growth in Colonial Rhode Island: Newport and Providence in the Eighteenth Century*. On the slave trade, see Jay Coughtry, *The Notorious Triangle: Rhode Island and the African Slave Trade, 1700–1807*. On race, see Joanne Melish, *Discovering Slavery: Gradual Emancipation and "Race" in New England, 1780–1860*; and Martha S. Putney, "Black Merchant Seamen of Newport, 1803–1865: A Case Study in Foreign Commerce." An excellent study of African American sailors is W. Jeffrey Bolster's *Black Jacks: African American Seamen in the Age of Sail*.

A detailed and insightful study of the officer corps Perry joined in 1809 is Christopher McKee, *A Gentlemanly and Honorable Profession: The Creation of the U.S. Naval Officer Corps, 1794–1815*. Charles O. Paullin's biography of John Rodgers, *Commodore John Rodgers: Captain, Commodore, and Senior Officer of the American Navy, 1773–1838*, is old but still useful. The classic naval history of the War of 1812 is Alfred T.

Mahan's *Sea Power in Its Relations to the War of 1812*. Modern histories of the war are Reginald Horsman, *The War of 1812*; and John K. Mahon, *The War of 1812*.

Two works that are particularly good on government naval policy are Harold Sprout and Margaret Sprout, *The Rise of American Naval Power, 1776–1918*; and Craig L. Symonds, *Navalists and Antinavalists: The Naval Policy Debate in the United States, 1785–1827*. On the peacetime role of the navy, see John H. Schroeder, *Shaping a Maritime Empire: The Commercial and Diplomatic Role of the American Navy, 1829–1861*. On the navy's scientific role, see Geoffrey Smith, "The Navy before Darwinism: Science, Exploration, and Diplomacy in Antebellum America"; and Vincent Ponko Jr., *Ships Seas, and Scientists: U.S. Naval Exploration and Discovery in the Nineteenth Century*.

On colonization, see P. J. Staudenraus, *The African Colonization Movement, 1816–1865*. For the African American settlements, see Charles H. Huberich, *The Political and Legislative History of Liberia*; Amos Sawyer, *The Emergence of Autocracy in Liberia: Tragedy and Challenge*; Tom Shick, *Behold the Promised Land: A History of Afro-American Settler Society in Nineteenth-Century Liberia*; and Penelope Campbell, *Maryland in Africa: The Maryland State Colonization Society, 1831–1857*.

For background on disease in West Africa, see Philip D. Curtin, *Death by Migration: Europe's Encounter with the Tropical World in the Nineteenth Century*; and Curtin, *Disease and Empire: The Health of European Troops in the Conquest of Africa*. A detailed study of mortality in Liberia is Antonio McDaniel, *Swing Low, Sweet Chariot: The Mortality Cost of Colonizing Liberia in the Nineteenth Century*. Also see Harold D. Langley, *A History of Medicine in the Early U.S. Navy*.

Two brief accounts of the navy in Africa are Judd Scott Harmon, "Marriage of Convenience: The United States Navy in Africa, 1820–1843"; and George M. Brooke, "The Role of the United States Navy in the Suppression of the African Slave Trade." For firsthand contemporary accounts, see Edgar Stanton Maclay, *Reminiscences of the Old Navy*; and W. R. Lynch, *Naval Life, or, Observations Afloat and on Shore. The Midshipman*.

On piracy in the Caribbean, see Raymond L. Shoemaker, "Diplomacy from the Quarterdeck: The U.S. Navy in the Caribbean, 1815–1830"; and David F. Long, *Nothing Too Daring: A Biography of Commodore David Porter, 1780–1843*. The two traditional studies are Gardner W. Allen, *Our*

Navy and the West Indian Pirates; and Francis B. C. Bradlee, *The Suppression of Piracy in the West Indies, 1820–1832.*

A superb study of American relations in the Mediterranean is James A. Field Jr., *America and the Mediterranean World, 1776–1882.* On American diplomatic relations, see John M. Belohlavek, *"Let the Eagle Soar": The Foreign Policy of Andrew Jackson.* Contemporary accounts of travel and naval service in the Mediterranean are Alexander Slidell Mackenzie, *A Year in Spain;* Walter Colton, *Ship and Shore, in Madeira, Lisbon, and the Mediterranean;* Roland F. Gould, *The Life of Gould, an Ex–Man-of-War's Man with Incidents on Sea and Shore;* Francis Schroeder, *Shores of the Mediterranean with Sketches of Travel;* and Harry Gringo [H. A. Wise], *Scampavias from Gibel Tarek to Stamboul.*

An excellent study of discipline is James E. Valle, *Rocks and Shoals: Order and Discipline in the Old Navy, 1800–1861.* For discipline on the *North Carolina,* see James M. Merrill, "Midshipman Du Pont and the Cruise of the *North Carolina,* 1825–1827"; and James Holly Garrison, *Behold Me Once More: The Confessions of James Holly Garrison.*

The subject of naval reform has received uneven treatment. Recruiting practices, flogging, and temperance are well treated in Harold D. Langley, *Social Reform in United States Navy, 1798–1862.* For steam technology, see Bernard Brodie, *Steam Power in the Machine Age: Major Naval Inventions and Their Consequences on International Politics, 1814–1940.* An excellent study of naval ordnance is Spencer Tucker, *Arming the Fleet: U.S. Navy Ordnance in the Muzzle-Loading Era.* There is no scholarly study of the lighthouse issue. Two excellent biographies of naval reformers are Edwin H. Hall, *Abel Parker Upshur: Conservative Virginian, 1790–1844;* and Frances L. Williams, *Matthew Fontaine Maury, Scientist of the Sea.* On the U.S. Naval Academy, see Charles Todorich, *The Spirited Years: A History of the Antebellum Naval Academy.*

For the diplomatic background on the creation of the African Squadron, see Howard Jones, *To the Webster-Ashburton Treaty: A Study in Anglo-American Relations, 1783–1843.* On the slave trade, see Hugh Thomas, *The Slave Trade: The History of the Atlantic Slave Trade, 1440–1870;* Philip D. Curtin, *The Atlantic Slave Trade: A Census;* George E. Brooks, *Yankee Traders, Old Coasters and African Middlemen: A History of American Legitimate Trade with West Africa in the Nineteenth Century;* and Daniel Mannix, *Black Cargoes: A History of the Atlantic Slave Trade.* An excellent contemporary account is Horatio Bridge, *Jour-*

nal of an African Cruiser . . . , edited by Nathaniel Hawthorne. Critics of Perry's performance in Africa include Thomas, *The Slave Trade*; Mannix, *Black Cargoes*; James T. de Kay, *Chronicles of the Frigate "Macedonian"*; and W. E. B. Du Bois, *The Suppression of the African Slave Trade to the United States of America, 1638–1870.*

The definitive account of the U.S. Navy in the Mexican War is K. Jack Bauer, *Surfboats and Horse Marines: U.S. Naval Operations in the Mexican War, 1846–1848.* A general history of the war is Bauer, *The Mexican War, 1846–1848.* Firsthand accounts of naval operations in the Gulf of Mexico include James D. Bruell, *Sea Memories, or Personal Experiences in the U.S. Navy in Peace and War*; William Harwar Parker, *Recollections of a Naval Officer, 1841–1865*; Raphael Semmes, *Service Afloat and Ashore during the Mexican War*; and Fitch W. Taylor, *The Broad Pennant; or, A Cruise in the United States Flag Ship of the Gulf Squadron.* On the Yucatán, see Nelson Reed, *The Caste War of Yucatan*; Louis De Armond, "Justo Sierra O'Reilly and Yucatan–United States Relations, 1847–1848"; and Mary W. Williams, "Secessionist Diplomacy of Yucatan."

On the mail steamers, see John G. B. Hutchins, *The American Maritime Industries and Public Policy*; and David B. Tyler, *Steam Conquers the Atlantic*; also Charles B. Stuart, *The Naval and Mail Steamers of the United States.*

Nineteenth-century American relations with Asia have been treated in a number of detailed studies, including Tyler Dennett, *Americans in Eastern Asia: A Critical Study of the Policy of the United States with Reference to China, Japan and Korea in the Nineteenth Century*; Arrell Morgan Gibson and John S. Whitehead, *Yankees in Paradise: The Pacific Basin Frontier*; Eldon Griffin, *Clippers and Consuls: American Consular and Commercial Relations with Eastern Asia, 1845–1860*; and Foster Rhea Dulles, *The Old China Trade.* On the policy of the Fillmore administration, see "Daniel Webster and the Pacific and East Asia," in *The Papers of Daniel Webster*; *Diplomatic Papers*; also Elbert B. Smith, *The Presidencies of Zachary Taylor and Millard Fillmore.*

For early contact between the United States and Japan, see Foster Rhea Dulles, *Yankees and Samurai: America's Role in the Emergence of Modern Japan, 1791–1900*; Shunzo Sakamaki, "Japan and the United States, 1790–1953"; Inazo Nitobe, *The Intercourse between the United States and Japan*; and David F. Long, *Sailor-Diplomat: A Biography of Commodore James Biddle.*

For background on Japan, see W. G. Beasley, *The Meiji Restoration;* Conrad Totman, *Politics in the Tokugawa Bakufu, 1600–1843;* Richard T. Chang, *From Prejudice to Tolerance: A Study of the Japanese Image of the West, 1826–1864; The Nineteenth Century,* vol. 5 of *The Cambridge History of Japan* edited by Marius B. Jansen; J. Victor Koschmann, *The Mito Ideology: Discourse, Reform and Insurrection in Late Tokugawa Japan, 1790–1864;* and George Sansom, *A History of Japan, 1615–1867.* An excellent summary is Peter Duus, *The Japanese Discovery of America: A Brief History with Documents.* See also John E. Van Sant, *Pacific Pioneers: Japanese Journeys to America and Hawaii, 1850–1880.* On Japanese politics, see Shujiro Watanabe, *Abe Masahiro jiseki;* Conrad Totman, "The Struggle for Control of the Shogunate (1853–1858)"; Totman, "Political Reconciliation in the Tokugawa Bakufu: Abe Masahiro and Tokugawa Nariaki"; and Harold Bolitho, "Abe Masahiro and the New Japan."

For American relations with China, see John K. Fairbank, *Trade and Diplomacy on the China Coast: The Opening of the Treaty Ports, 1842–1854;* and Te-kong Tong, *United States Diplomacy in China, 1844–1860.* On the navy, see Curtis T. Henson Jr., *Commissioners and Commodores: The East India Squadron and American Diplomacy in China;* Robert E. Johnson, *Far China Station: The U.S. Navy in Asian Waters, 1800–1898;* and Chester A. Bain, "Commodore Matthew Perry, Humphrey Marshall and the Taiping Rebellion."

For the expedition to Japan, Perry's accounts are to be found in volume 1 of Francis L. Hawks, ed., *Narrative of the Expedition of an American Squadron to the China Seas and Japan . . . ;* and Matthew C. Perry, *The Japan Expedition, 1852–1854. The Personal Journal of Commodore Matthew C. Perry.* The *Narrative* still makes fascinating reading and is handsomely illustrated with dozens of lithographs and woodcuts. Correspondence on the expedition is printed in Senate Executive Document no. 34, 33d Congress, 2d session (1854–1855). For the Japanese artifacts and gifts collected by the expedition, see Chang-su Houchins, "Artifacts of Diplomacy: Smithsonian Collections from Commodore Perry's Japan Expedition (1853–1854)."

Peter Booth Wiley's *Yankees in the Land of the Gods: Commodore Perry and the Opening of Japan* is an excellent account critical of Perry. With the assistance of Korogi Ichiro, Wiley drew on Japanese as well as American sources. Other detailed accounts are Morison, *"Old Bruin";* and Arthur Walworth, *Black Ships off Japan: The Story of Commodore*

Perry's Expedition. An excellent recent biography is Craig L. Symonds, *Confederate Admiral: The Life and Wars of Franklin Buchanan.* The author argues that Buchanan exercised considerable personal autonomy in conducting the negotiations for Perry with Japanese officials in July 1853.

Numerous firsthand contemporary accounts of aspects of the expedition can be found in diaries, memoirs, and personal letters. Among the most interesting and useful are S. Wells Williams, "A Journal of the Perry Expedition to Japan 1853–1854"; and Bayard Taylor, *A Visit to India, China, and Japan in the Year 1853.* Both men served directly under Perry; Williams on both voyages to Japan, and Taylor on the first voyage in 1853.

Other accounts include J. W. Spalding, *The Japan Expedition: Japan and around the World;* John S. Sewall, *The Logbook of the Captain's Clerk;* George Henry Preble, *The Opening of Japan. A Diary of Discovery in the Far East.* John Glendy Sproston, *A Private Journal of John Glendy Sproston;* Henry F. Graff, ed., *Bluejackets with Perry in Japan: A Day-by-Day Account Kept by Master's Mate John R. C. Lewis and Cabin Boy William B. Allen;* Edward Yorke McCauley, *With Perry in Japan: The Diary of Edward Yorke McCauley;* James Morrow, *A Scientist with Perry in Japan: The Journal of Dr. James Morrow;* Charles H. Wheelwright, *Correspondence of Dr. Charles H. Wheelwright, Surgeon of the United States Navy;* William Heine, *With Perry in Japan. A Memoir by William Heine.* For Rev. Bernard Bettelheim's impressions, see William L. Schwartz, ed., "Commodore Perry at Okinawa from the Unpublished Diary of a British Missionary."

Japanese accounts include "Diary of an Official of the Bakufu," edited by D. Hayashi. Various Japanese documents are printed in W. G. Beasley, trans. and ed., *Select Documents on Japanese Foreign Policy, 1853–1868;* and Masatoshi Knishi, trans., *Meiji Japan through Contemporary Sources.* See also Oliver Statler, *The Black Ship Scroll: An Account of the Perry Expedition at Shimoda in 1854 . . .* ; and Matajiro Kojima, *Commodore Perry's Expedition to Hakodate, May 1854: A Private Account with Illustrations.*

~➛ Index ➤~

About the Author

John H. Schroeder is a professor of history at the University of Wisconsin–Milwaukee. A recipient of two university awards for distinguished teaching, Dr. Schroeder is a specialist on nineteenth-century American history and the author of numerous articles and reviews as well as two books: *Shaping a Maritime Empire: The Commercial and Diplomatic Role of the American Navy, 1829–1861* and *Mr. Polk's War: American Opposition and Dissent, 1846–1848*.

Dr. Schroeder earned his B.A. degree in history from Lewis and Clark College in Portland, Oregon, and completed his graduate work at the University of Virginia, earning his Ph.D. in 1971. In addition to his academic responsibilities, he has held several administration positions at the University of Wisconsin, including serving as university chancellor from 1990 to 1998. He and his wife, Sandra, reside in Milwaukee.

The Naval Institute Press is the book-publishing arm of the U.S. Naval Institute, a private, nonprofit, membership society for sea service professionals and others who share an interest in naval and maritime affairs. Established in 1873 at the U.S. Naval Academy in Annapolis, Maryland, where its offices remain today, the Naval Institute has members worldwide.

Members of the Naval Institute support the education programs of the society and receive the influential monthly magazine *Proceedings* and discounts on fine nautical prints and on ship and aircraft photos. They also have access to the transcripts of the Institute's Oral History Program and get discounted admission to any of the Institute-sponsored seminars offered around the country.

The Naval Institute also publishes *Naval History* magazine. This colorful bimonthly is filled with entertaining and thought-provoking articles, first-person reminiscences, and dramatic art and photography. Members receive a discount on *Naval History* subscriptions.

The Naval Institute's book-publishing program, begun in 1898 with basic guides to naval practices, has broadened its scope years to include books of more general interest. Now the Naval Institute Press publishes about one hundred titles each year, ranging from how-to books on boating and navigation to battle histories, biographies, ship and aircraft guides, and novels. Institute members receive significant discounts on the Press's more than eight hundred books in print.

Full-time students are eligible for special half-price membership rates. Life memberships are also available.

For a free catalog describing Naval Institute Press books currently available, and for further information about subscribing to *Naval History* magazine or about joining the U.S. Naval Institute, please write to:

Membership Department

U.S. Naval Institute

291 Wood Road

Annapolis, MD 21402-5034

Telephone: (800) 233-8764

Fax: (410) 269-7940

Web address: www.usni.org